Don't Call It Love

For information on Patrick J. Carnes's lecture
and workshop schedule, please send a stamped
self-addressed envelope to:

Patrick J. Carnes, Ph.D.
Institute for Behavioral Medicine
4101 Golden Valley Road
Golden Valley, Minnesota 55422

For information on Patrick J. Carnes's audio and video
cassette tapes, write:

The Gentle Press
P.O. Box 11185
Minneapolis, Minnesota 55411
or call 1-800-828-8001

Don't Call It Love

RECOVERY FROM
SEXUAL ADDICTION

Patrick J. Carnes, Ph.D.

BANTAM BOOKS

NEW YORK · TORONTO · LONDON · SYDNEY · AUCKLAND

DON'T CALL IT LOVE

A Bantam Book / March 1991

Grateful acknowledgment is made for the permission to reprint the following:

"Whoever's in New England" (Kendal Franceschi, Quentin Powers) copyright © 1985 WBM MUSIC CORP. (SESAC) & SILVER MUSIC, INC. (BMI) All Rights on behalf of SILVERLINE MUSIC, INC. Administered by WARNER-TAMARLANE PUBLISHING CORP. (BMI) All Rights Reserved. Used by Permission.
Excerpts from the article "Hot for Teacher" reprinted with permission from *SASSY* magazine. Copyright © 1988 by Matilda Publications.
"I Hate Myself for Loving You" by Desmond Child and Joan Jett copyright © 1988 EMI APRIL MUSIC INC./DESMOBILE MUSIC CO., INC./LAGUNATIC MUSIC Rights for DESMOBILE MUSIC CO., INC. Controlled and Administered by EMI APRIL MUSIC INC. All Rights Reserved. International Copyright Secured. Used by Permission.
Excerpts from THE BONFIRE OF THE VANITIES by Tom Wolfe. Copyright © 1987 by Tom Wolfe. Reprinted by permission of Farrar, Straus and Giroux, Inc.

Library of Congress Cataloging-in-Publication Data

Carnes, Patrick, 1944–
    Don't call it love : recovering from sexual addiction / by Patrick Carnes.
        p.   cm.
    ISBN 0-553-07236-6
    1. Sex addiction.   2. Sex addicts—Rehabilitation.   I. Title.
RC560.S43C37   1990
616.85'83—dc20   90-1255
                                                                                    CIP

Published simultaneously in the United States and Canada

Bantam Books are published by Bantam Books, a division of Bantam
Doubleday Dell Publishing Group, Inc. Its trademark, consisting of the
words "Bantam Books" and the portrayal of a rooster, is Registered in
U.S. Patent and Trademark Office and in other countries. Marca
Registrada, Bantam Books, 666 Fifth Avenue, New York, New York 10103.

PRINTED IN THE UNITED STATES OF AMERICA

RRH   0 9 8 7 6 5 4 3 2 1

C O N T E N T S

INTRODUCTION

Nearly one thousand sex addicts helped us write this book by sharing their stories with us in surveys and interviews. Although the details of their lives vary, their struggles are the same. Common to all is self-destructive sexual behavior that they are unable to stop. Family breakups, financial disaster, loss of jobs, and risk to life are familiar themes in their stories. Many are professionals—ministers, physicians, therapists, politicians, executives; others come from more blue-collar backgrounds. Most were abused as children—sexually, physically, and/or emotionally. The majority grew up in families in which addiction already flourished, including alcoholism, compulsive eating, and compulsive gambling. Most grapple with other addictions as well, but they find sex addiction the most difficult to stop.

Yet, great hope exists in their stories. Sex addicts have shown an ability to transform despair and chaos into confidence and peace. During our research couples shared realistic ways to regain trust and to restore sexual vitality to their relationships. Participants in our survey showed dramatic improvements in almost all spheres of life, including finances, health, job, and family. When addicts gave us their "best advice" about what worked for them, most evident was the deep spiritual quest created as a result of overcoming addiction. Part of the antidote for the emptiness of addiction is finding meaning in suffering.

Sex addicts define recovery as the transformation from a life of self-destruction to a life of self-care. In order to further understand the recovery process, I directed a group of researchers to start a project to investigate systematically the nature of sex addiction and recovery. Starting in July 1986, a team of twelve people worked for over three years to make this project happen. Some were professionals in data analysis, some were clinicians. Some were recovering sex addicts without whose extraordinary networking efforts the data gathering would simply not have been possible. All worked long hours, some in addition to regular full-time professional commitments.

We started by developing two twenty-eight-page surveys: one for sex addicts, the other for their codependent partners. We piloted and refined them. We learned early in the testing that for most sex addicts and coaddicts, the actual process of completing the survey was extremely painful and time-consuming (four to eight hours). Most reported that while the process was useful, yielding important insights and information, it was also emotionally draining. This knowledge helped us prepare people for taking the surveys and prepared us for the tremendous amount of follow-through work needed to overcome their natural resistance.

Fifteen hundred copies of one survey were distributed to sex addicts, targeting those with three or more years of recovery. Five hundred copies of the other were distributed to coaddicts. We wanted people with sufficient recovery history to illuminate the problems encountered in the recovery process. We also believed that a longer recovery period would result in more accurate data. For example, repression of memories about childhood sexual abuse is very common in early recovery. Our hope was that by working with more experienced recovering people, key issues would be clearer and better defined.

Finding these people proved to be a tough assignment. While recovery groups have been active since the late seventies, the number of people who have had successful recoveries over a significant period of time is still small. In addition, because of the anonymous nature of those groups, locating the people and getting them to complete long, painful surveys required the use of an informal network of therapists and recovering addicts. The success of the project in many ways testifies to the extraordinary trust among members of that network and people in those groups.

No fellowship officially endorsed this survey; to do so would be against their traditions. We received generous support, however, from individual members of all four of the fellowships: Sex and Love Addicts Anonymous, Sex Addicts Anonymous, Sexaholics Anonymous, and Sexual Compulsives Anonymous.

Twenty percent of the surveys were returned, for a net count of 289 addicts and 99 coaddicts, some with recovery records of ten to twelve years. We believe that some who received the survey were too early in their recovery to be able to respond or found the task too painful. Those who did complete the survey were incredibly generous. It was not unusual to find page upon page of added detail stuffed into the forms. To further our effort we asked over six hundred additional sex addicts to complete a portion of the survey as part of their admission to the sexual dependency unit at Golden Valley Health Center. While not adding much in terms of extended recovery history, they greatly deepened our ability to comment about sexually addictive behavior in general. Throughout the book, unless otherwise specified, the data reported is from the initial group of 289 addicts. In the appendix, we include a table listing the baseline behaviors of 932 addicts to show that the differences between the group with advanced recovery and those entering recovery are minimal. The survey group tended to be white, educated, and professional—not surprising given that the early members of AA came from similar backgrounds. Also, 19 percent of survey participants were women; this figure is paralleled in alcoholism recovery to this day.

Another phase of the project was an intensive interview of 89 recovering sex addicts and 37 coaddicts. All had created enduring and successful recoveries. Many of these are the true pioneers in sex addiction recovery—they did it when help was extremely difficult to locate or entirely unavailable. Again, finding them, gaining their commitment to be interviewed, and interviewing them at points all over the country required an enormous amount of energy and time. The result was many thousands of pages of their words, which add depth and wisdom to the numbers and comments gathered from the surveys.

To create data files, run statistical analyses, tabulate open-ended questions, and make meaning out of many thousands of pages of interview transcripts was a gigantic task. That it was all done within two years was possible only because the research team and the recovering people who supported us shared a sense of urgency.

We all know sex addiction can be a life-and-death struggle. As the extent of the AIDS epidemic became clear, we knew we were in a race against time.

This book is divided into two parts. Part I (Chapters One through Five) examines sex addiction in all of its various aspects, including the powerlessness associated with the illness, its unmanageability, its causes and patterns, and the impact on the family. Part II (Chapters Six through Twelve) shares the wisdom of people in successful recovery on topics including the decision to get help, the evolution of recovery over time, how healing of damaged relationships occurs, how to reclaim healthy sexuality, and how to overcome obstacles to recovery.

This book synthesizes the story of nearly one thousand addicts and their families and represents the combined efforts of many. I wish to acknowledge my deep gratitude to all who filled out surveys and completed interviews. Without you we could never have verified what we knew to be true or discovered all that we learned. Throughout the book, identifying details and names were altered to protect our survey respondents. Their words and the facts of their life experiences appear unaltered. Stories were selected because they were typical for most sexually addicted people. More unusual or extreme experiences were not emphasized because they did not represent common aspects of sex addiction.

Similar gratitude goes to the research team, without whose ingenuity, perseverance, research skills, and ability to build trust we would never have finished. Team members include Larry D., Jeanne O'Gorman, Barb DeWitt, James Blix, Rob Berger, Judy Weedman, Nancy Skilling, Debra Nonemaker, Cindy Larsen, and Perry Ferguson. I am especially grateful to Tammy Horstman, project coordinator for the research team. Her organizational skills and enthusiasm sustained us all. Much help was also received from the Advanced Studies Group of the Institute for Behavioral Medicine and the staff and administration of Golden Valley Health Center. All of us are profoundly appreciative of the many recovering people in the network who helped us arrange the interviews.

In preparing the manuscript, a number of people were key: Becky Thorvig, my office manager; Ann Poe, my editorial consultant; Jonathon Lazear, my agent; Toni Burbank, my editor at Bantam; and Randee Falk, my copy editor. Without their support, patience, and belief, this very complex effort would never have happened.

Two special friends guided me: Melody Beattie, who always seemed to call at my darkest moments as an author, and John Bradshaw, who can affirm his friends like few people I know. Together they were like a safety net for me. This book is a testimony to their support.

This book is a gift prepared by many. I am privileged to have been able to witness the generosity, sacrifice, and commitment of all involved in this task. In this effort, I truly feel that my role has been as a scribe to tell a significant story about recovery—and our culture.

Patrick J. Carnes
The Institute for Behavioral Medicine
Golden Valley Health Center
Golden Valley, Minnesota

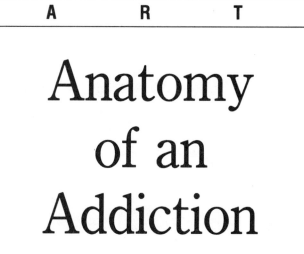

P A R T I

Anatomy
of an
Addiction

The Signs of Addiction

- A woman uses a vibrator so intensely she burns herself and has to go to the emergency room.

- A thirty-one-year-old man, married and the father of three small children, has been having sex with men in "hot johns" since he was seventeen. He got married to stop. He went through treatment for alcoholism to stop. Now he has AIDS. So does his wife. They are both dying.

- The priest has a thousand-dollar-a-week prostitution habit. His only way to support the habit is to steal from the parish he serves.

- Their children and friends knew. But his wife was in the dark until she discovered three volumes carefully annotating his sexual encounters with fifteen hundred women.

- A thirty-eight-year-old dentist is furious about his wife's sexual unavailability. He secretly drugs her to have sex with her.

- A thirty-five-year-old schoolteacher is stunned as she watches *Looking for Mr. Goodbar* and recognizes that it fits her life with frightening accuracy.

- A thirty-three-year-old woman leaves her toddlers alone while she goes off to meet her lovers.

- A sixty-six-year-old man is arrested for the third time for stealing lingerie.

- A minister is confronted by the bishop, who has heard about his affairs with parishioners.

- A corporate technical guru has been the subject of seven sexual harassment complaints in two years. Now there is one from a major customer.

- A youth leader has sex with yet another boy. He plans suicide if ever discovered.

The signs of addiction. Some would say these cases are matters of sexual excess or bad judgment or accidents. Others would dismiss them as bizarre or perverted, part of the ragged edge of life. In reality, they represent a much more serious problem: a life-threatening obsession with sex. These situations involved people whose lives were dominated by a pattern of out-of-control sex. Such people are sex addicts. They have experiences that others don't have, at least not in the same way or to the same extent. The patterns of their lives signify the presence of an illness we are just beginning to understand.

We are surrounded by the signs of sex addiction yet still resist its reality. We can accept that people can be sick with alcoholism or can destroy themselves with gambling or food—but not sex. There are some who see the problem clearly but hesitate to call it an addiction. They choose words like "compulsive" or "hypersexual"— yet they have absolutely no problem calling compulsive gambling an addiction. Why is there so much resistance to recognizing the clear signs of sexual addiction? The answer resides in the central role sex plays in all of our lives.

1. *Sex is essential.* Sex is key to the survival of our species, and some of our richest cultural symbols relate to the meaning and beauty of sex. Our songs and literature testify that some of our best moments as human beings are sexual. The first statement made about every one of us is a sexual statement: It's a boy! It's a girl! Our sex—male or female—is a fundamental definition of who we are and strongly influences how we live out our lives.

2. *Sex is powerful.* People in passion will murder, betray, and exploit others. Sex sells products from cologne and cars to newspapers

and talk shows. Sex changes our mood and relieves tension. From migraine headaches to arthritis, medical research tells us, sex can be a significant force in healing. But most important, sex for many becomes a bonding force; it sustains relationships through some of our most significant and difficult moments.

3. *Sex is frightening.* Current estimates suggest that one out of ten men will commit date rape and that one million women will be raped this year, over half of them by someone they know. Over forty million American adults were abused sexually as children. Each day an average of three thousand teenage girls in the United States become pregnant. Our fears of sexual excess emerge in religious teachings, legislative action, and zoning ordinances, which together express an unwritten cultural code suggesting that sex is dirty and bad. Most adults can confirm that this is the cultural judgment by recalling myths told them as children to prevent sexual play. Our fear of sexual excess serves as a sad counterpoint to our own profound fears and self-doubts about our sexual adequacy. The irony, of course, is that performance anxiety and sexual exploitation are driven by some of the same fear-based sexual assumptions rooted in our culture.

This book is about sex addicts but also about the fear, the power, and the importance of sex. From the stories of addicts who have committed themselves to a program of recovery, painful questions emerge about public policy, church practice, and family life. We learn about the damage of child abuse, family dysfunction, and multiple addictions. Sex addiction may be the extra insight we have needed to generate a global picture of a cultural crisis: ours is an addiction-prone culture which is, moreover, becoming increasingly vulnerable to addictive illness. And sex addiction is one of the most destructive.

For many, this book will be painful to read. You may recognize patterns in yourself, your family members, your friends. Yet the stories shared here offer extraordinary hope. The journey to recovery starts with being able to identify the common characteristics shared by sex addicts. On the basis of our research and clinical experience, there are ten signs that indicate the presence of sexual addiction:

1. A pattern of out-of-control behavior

2. Severe consequences due to sexual behavior

3. Inability to stop despite adverse consequences

4. Persistent pursuit of self-destructive or high-risk behavior

5. Ongoing desire or effort to limit sexual behavior

6. Sexual obsession and fantasy as a primary coping strategy

7. Increasing amounts of sexual experience because the current level of activity is no longer sufficient

8. Severe mood changes around sexual activity

9. Inordinate amounts of time spent in obtaining sex, being sexual, or recovering from sexual experience

10. Neglect of important social, occupational, or recreational activities because of sexual behavior

By exploring each sign in depth, we begin the anatomy of an addiction. We will also start to see how it has been obscured by the shadows of denial, misperception, and prejudice.

1. A pattern of out-of-control sexual behavior

To all outward appearances, Barb's childhood was a normal one. Barb came from a seemingly upstanding Roman Catholic family; she and the other children attended parochial school. No one guessed at the violence and sexual abuse pervading their family life. In fact, the mother, a social worker, brought home tales of such severe abuse that the children themselves thought they were an average family. Not until Barb's older brother was hospitalized after severely beating their father did the family's *Better Homes and Gardens* veneer start to peel off. Growing up in her family left Barb with many conflicting feelings.

For Barb, sexuality and violence fused early on; in fourth grade, she began to obsess about violent sex while masturbating, as a method for going to sleep. Barb's family, with its violence and sexualizing, structured the foundations of her coping patterns. The compulsive masturbation that started in grade school became the foundation of a lifelong pattern of being out of control.

An alert high school counselor saw that Barb was suicidal

because of what was happening at home. He managed to get her out of the house and referred her to a therapist. Unfortunately, Barb's therapist became part of her problem. She says:

> He physically and sexually abused me. So, I think that was when the covering of the sexual addiction came off. I was out of the house so I didn't have as many restrictions, plus my therapist was being real seductive and was hurting me—hurting my genitals and hurting my breast while he talked sexually explicitly with me. I knew it was inappropriate for me to be directly sexual with him, and even the therapist was telling me not to be sexually active, but was doing stuff to me. I would call him supposedly in distress while I masturbated. Some of the sex and love addiction started at that point.

Sadly, one of the discoveries that emerged from our survey is that women addicts seeking help are often sexually abused by their therapists. In Barb's case, the situation became even more complicated when she became romantically involved with one of her therapist's friends. She lived with him for about a year in a very destructive and obsessive relationship. When that ended, her sexual life became a blur of partners:

> I would go out and have sex with men I hardly knew. There were times when I had dates with up to seven men in a twenty-four-hour period. I can remember going through a week where I'd had eight partners including two at a time. When it was two partners at a time, both a man and a woman, I was doing cocaine, drinking quite a bit, and smoking marijuana. The next day when both the drugs and the sexual high wore off, I felt like I was completely empty, bankrupt, and black inside.
> Yet I would flirt with any man without having any control over it. It didn't matter how old someone was, it didn't matter if they were married, it didn't matter if they were a best friend's lover. I was embarrassed, but I couldn't stop myself. That was part of the way I set myself up for multiple relationships. And I was actively having sex when I had infections. I got herpes, of course, through acting

out. There was a relationship with a guy I had been trying to get out of for a couple of months. I didn't want to have sex with him at that point because of herpes. But I couldn't stop.

Barb's story underlines the first major sign of sex addiction—a pattern of out-of-control behavior. The amount, extent, and duration of behavior regularly exceeds what the person intended.

Addicts can even see they are endangering their life and yet still persist in the pattern. Many of us abuse our sexuality at some time or go through periods of sexual excess or make mistakes sexually, yet we learn and adjust our sexual patterns to comfortable or at least safe levels. Sex addicts are incapable of permanently making that adjustment by themselves.

Barb talks, for example, of being sexual when she had not known she was going to be: "I'd get involved with somebody and, before I knew it, we'd end up in bed. We never talked about what it meant or what it was—or what it wasn't. It was as if neither of us knew it was going to happen, but it would happen all the same."

A common scenario for sex addicts is to have cycles of disastrous love experiences followed by meaningless and self-destructive sexual binging. The short-term solution is another romance—or better yet, a number of romances. Sometimes the sex addict becomes obsessed with one or two particular individuals. These are relationships for which the addict gives up everything, including self-respect. For the addict to even be around these individuals becomes an emotionally supercharged event. The addict is preoccupied, unable to stop seeing the person, and in despair about the hopelessness of the relationship.

2. Severe consequences due to sexual behavior

Barb was not alone in her despair over the consequences of leading an addictive life. In our survey we found a seemingly unending array of ways that sex addicts harm themselves and others:

• Many sex addicts talk of near-death experiences from accidents, violence, high-risk situations, or rape.

- Sex addicts recognize AIDS as perhaps the most lethal complication to their illness.

- Many sex addicts have lost a partner or spouse (40 percent), and most have experienced severe marital or relationship problems (70 percent).

- Some addicts have lost rights to their children (13 percent), and some have found it necessary to cut their ties with their family of origin (8 percent).

- Women sex addicts report deep grief over abortions (36 percent) and unwanted pregnancies (42 percent).

- For a majority, addiction has had severe financial consequences (58 percent).

- Some addicts reported losing the opportunity to work in the career of their choice (27 percent).

- Most sex addicts (79 percent) talk of serious losses of job productivity; 11 percent were demoted.

- Many sex addicts repetitively pursue their behaviors to the point of exhaustion (59 percent) or even physical injury (38 percent).

- The majority of sex addicts say they routinely ran the risk of venereal disease (65 percent).

- A total of 58 percent have pursued activities for which they could be arrested; 19 percent actually were.

Barb's sex addiction led her to put herself in jeopardy with dangerous men. On three separate occasions men she slept with threatened her life. One told her stories of dismemberment while holding a knife to her throat; two weeks later he was arrested for first-degree murder. During these years Barb worked compulsively, sometimes at as many as four or five jobs. The only relief from work was men. The only way to avoid men was work. Barb estimates that she lost ten years of her life engaging in or running away from her sex addiction. At one point she saw a sex therapist to help her with the problem, but the therapist did not see her behavior as an issue. Rather, Barb was told that she needed to become comfortable with her sexuality.

Finally, like so many other addicts, Barb reached a point of deep despair because of the consequences of her illness: "I realized I could not make it through another year like this. I would either be killed by somebody or I would kill myself. I didn't know what my problem was. I just knew I couldn't continue on like this and that I needed help."

Suicidal feelings, lost years, dangerous situations, and sexually transmitted diseases—Barb experienced many of the common consequences of sex addiction.

3. Inability to stop despite adverse consequences

Mark, a physician, clearly knew the costs of his behavior and had much to lose. Yet the power of his addiction overwhelmed him. He began compulsively masturbating by the age of five and had sex with his first prostitute, courtesy of an uncle, at age sixteen. By the end of high school, he found himself caught up in a predatory type of promiscuity.

A few years later Mark got married. For a while his sexual acting out went underground. He would have sex with his wife once or twice a day and then channel his obsession into masturbation. "I became an obsessive masturbator. I knew every bathroom there was anywhere I went. I masturbated everywhere I went."

This pattern lasted until Mark was thirty-one and had completed medical school and a psychiatric residency. At that time Mark underwent an intense religious conversion and became an Orthodox Jew. Ironically, as his involvement in religion intensified, so did his sexual addiction and his alcoholism. Also at this time, Mark discovered homosexuality at the local YMCA. He became an active jogger, obsessively running eight to nine miles a day. With his running and his homosexual experiences, Mark's addiction quickly mushroomed.

> I started having lover after lover. It was getting too complicated at times. Then I started getting this gift as a jogger: I had this ability to pick people from the street, I would not even go to gay areas. I'd bring them to my office in the evenings or in the late afternoons. I started discovering bookstores, then buying male prostitutes. When the male prostitutes weren't around, I went to the girlie shows

and I bought the gals. The pattern was the same: one wasn't enough, I'd need two guys at a time. It finally got to two women at a time. These people would call my house. They'd bug me for money. My last lover I figured cost me about $30,000. I was not a wealthy man. My addiction cost me a fortune. And time.

I was spending hours a day pursuing lust objects, either going to the pornos, picking people up, trying to get my wife in bed, or masturbating. A great deal of time and money.

It was as if I thought I was invisible and I'd go to the pornos in the middle of the daytime. Here I was in a relatively small city, practicing a psychiatric profession and acting out my lust in broad daylight.

The complications in Mark's life became overwhelming. Banks were chasing him. He was bringing home diseases. He was seen at the Y—one of his patients heard about it. His sex partners were demanding drugs. Mark went to AA meetings for his alcohol use, but the chaos worsened. Mark, like other sex addicts, knew he faced disaster, but he was not able to stop his compulsive behavior.

4. Persistent pursuit of self-destructive or high-risk behavior

A step beyond inability to stop behavior despite adverse consequences is the actual pursuit of self-destructive or high-risk behavior. To have sex with someone you know has AIDS is a self-destructive act. To consistently pursue high-risk behaviors is in itself symptomatic of a loss of control.

Consider the story of Peter, a forty-five-year-old gay man who lives in a large southeastern city. He described himself as "careening through life" and "constantly running away" from intimacy and from himself. Highly successful in his career, he was always pushing himself harder. He compensated by medicating himself with sex, alcohol, and prescription drugs. His sexual behavior was by far the most dangerous. Violent, anonymous sex kept him on the edge. Yet, like Mark who talked of being "invisible," Peter felt almost invulnerable to the risks he took. He told us:

I felt that I was immune. I was so successful in certain areas and had, in a sense, proved that by my career accomplishments. My ego was so abnormally large that I felt that I was going to be impervious to any kind of exposure to something like AIDS. I think that, just from the statistical standpoint, because of the number of contacts I've had, I very likely have been exposed to the virus. I still haven't had the test yet. . . . I would try and cut down on my anonymous contacts, but I couldn't do it. I couldn't do more than maybe three days at a time. I felt that I needed to have whatever energy sex was providing me so that I could maintain these other balls in the air.

Change the circumstances and Peter's words give voice to the experience of many. Sex addicts find themselves doing things that are dangerous. Yet, addicts ignore the reality, distort the reality, and at times lose touch with reality. Addiction specialists call this denial. The result is that the dangerous behavior continues.

At a recent workshop that I conducted, the role of denial and danger was brought to life by one of the attendees. This participant was a Ph.D. psychologist, highly intelligent and recognized in his community for his competence and kindness. He is also a sex addict. He had been in therapy for eighteen months, was active in a Sex Addicts Anonymous (SAA) group, and had a sponsor. The problem was he continued to act out in high-risk situations. He could not admit, however, to his therapist, his sponsor, or his group that he was unable to stop. He felt that he should have been able to change by himself. Once he had lied, he then could not admit his dishonesty. Secrecy and pride kept him at risk.

Attending the workshop, however, brought home the incongruity between his beliefs and his behavior. He was so upset that he did what addicts do: he acted out because the pain was overwhelming. On the second morning of the workshop, he stopped at a park on the way to the conference center and had oral sex with a man he'd never seen before. He knew the risk of AIDS. All he could do to minimize his exposure was to induce vomiting as he drove, to rid himself of the ejaculate. While vomiting, he crashed into a truck, two blocks from the workshop site. When we saw him, he was traumatized by the accident and in total despair over his behavior. Here was a smart man who knew all the risks. Further, he had all kinds of support. Yet he persisted anyway.

5. Ongoing desire or effort to limit sexual behavior

Almost all addicts make promises to themselves to quit their behavior. They tell themselves they'll stop "from this moment on" or "after this time." It never happens.

Our workshop participant wanted to stop and had sought help to stop. Peter also made attempts to stop, although he could last no longer than three days. These two men share a characteristic with all other sex addicts: an ongoing desire or effort to limit sexual behavior. Sometimes this means trying to stop totally; sometimes it just means trying to cut back. Yet the more efforts the addict makes to control behavior, the worse the problem gets. The attempts to stop work much the way diets do. People who compulsively diet often end up starving and then bingeing, seesawing back and forth in an endless attempt to control food intake.

Sex addicts will go to similar extremes to limit their sexual activity. The exhibitionist who buys a new car that will be difficult to expose himself from, the businessman who gives up a career path that he has worked years to achieve in order to avoid a woman he can't stop being sexual with, the woman addict who joins the Marine Corps so she can be more disciplined—all are driven by their desire to stop experiencing the pain and consequences of their addiction. Often addicts will use geographic or job changes in an effort to "start over." Some addicts immerse themselves in religion in hopes of leaving their problems behind. As most pastoral counselors who work with sex addicts know, this is not a spiritual journey. Rather, it is a way to take care of shame.

Whatever the strategy, most addicts attempt to control their behavior. In our survey, 71 percent reported periods of sexual "anorexia," where all sexual urges and behaviors were tightly controlled. These efforts, however, simply fueled the addiction.

Don and Kim's story shows how both partners may try to control the sex addict's behavior. Don is a forty-four-year-old administrator of a chemical dependency treatment facility in the Midwest. He is a victim of incest, which left him with essential confusion over nurturing and sexuality. He is also chemically dependent, but as with so many addicts with more than one addiction, sex is by far the strongest. He comments, "Intercourse was the greatest discovery of my life. I was instantly hooked. It was very much like a drug experience only much better than any drug I had ever taken."

Don's relationship history plays like a country western song of busted romance and broken hearts. As soon as he became involved with someone, he became infatuated with someone else. When he did finally marry, within ten days he was already preoccupied with thoughts of affairs. Within two years he was having outside relation-ships and felt terrible about his behavior yet powerless to stop. The woman he had married was herself an incest victim and the daughter of an alcoholic. She was very dependent and extremely unhappy about his behavior. Sex was creating problems in other areas as well:

> I started having sex with patients. It really bothered me—I had lots of guilt—and I made lots of promises to quit, but I couldn't. During that first marriage, I also started collect-ing pornography. I would bring it out inappropriately at parties, talk about it, and try to keep the focus on sexual topics with a lot of inappropriate sexual humor. I tended to sexualize every situation I was in.

Eventually, Don talked his wife into an open marriage, hoping that would help. The marriage failed, and Don felt great pain at the loss of his three daughters, ages five, six, and eight. Still, the unending sexual quest continued.

One of the last affairs he had when married was with Kim, who eventually became his second wife. The pattern repeated itself. Almost immediately he was fantasizing about affairs. Within two years he was again having sex outside the marriage. Don uses the word "white knuckle" to describe his behavior at that time. "White knuckling" is a phrase commonly used by alcoholics to describe a person who is not drinking but who has to hold on so tight to keep from drinking that the knuckles become white. In Don's case this meant some substitution as well: "As part of my white knuckling, I tried to keep my sexual focus on the fantasy level, looking at pornography, collecting it."

Yet he still had affairs. He became involved with a patient and was fired from his hospital. Don and Kim decided to move in order to make a fresh start. Within a few days of moving Don was involved again. But Don was not alone in his desperation to control his behavior. He now had a partner in Kim. She describes her frustration:

> It's like living with a drug. It's like he was shooting every day and I had to check the stash to see if he was shooting up. Or, in my case, check the Kleenex in the garbage to make sure that, yes, he was masturbating. You do all these crazy things. Once I confronted one of the women that he was having some relationship with and said, "What is going on?" And she said, "Who, me?" And then I knew that the move didn't make everything all better, because that was what my idea of that move was—it was going to make everything okay because we were leaving those relationships in another city.

Finally, the bottom fell out for Don on the new job. One of the women he was involved with was a colleague at work. Two of his male colleagues confronted him about his sexual addiction.

One of the central paradoxes of addiction is that when addicts believe they can stop their out-of-control patterns, they wind up compounding the patterns instead. Only when addicts admit to being out of control can they and their family members end the deadly cycles. Throughout this book this unalterable fact about addiction will surface again and again.

Don is clear that for him the turning point was giving up his effort to control and finally admitting his need for help. He says, "It brought me right to my knees. I felt humiliated and humbled—like somebody had punched me." Kim echoes her belief in the importance of stopping the game of trying to control what you cannot: "I did the healthiest thing that I could do for myself when I decided I would not check his stash of pornography again. That was my first step in breaking away from his addiction."

6. Sexual obsession and fantasy as a primary coping strategy

Sexual preoccupation becomes an "analgesic fix" for the sex addict. Obsession and fantasy become a primary coping strategy. Planning, thinking, searching, intriguing, and looking for opportunity become a way to get through each day. Sexual addiction presents special difficulties both diagnostically and in treatment, since the addict can escape into an altered state simply through obsession and fantasy. For days on end, sex addicts may spend most of their time in a sexual stupor. Losing one's self in obsession is very different from what most people experience during sexual stimulation. All human beings during the course of a day see people they find attractive, have sexual thoughts, experience arousal, and fantasize. What makes addiction different is that sex becomes a primary tool that addicts use to regulate their emotional life. They become dependent upon it to the point that sex is no longer a choice or an option—rather, it is a coping mechanism that for the addict is connected with survival. Without sex the addict's world unravels.

Obsession becomes the dominant factor in the addict's world. Behavior then becomes a focus for the obsessive energy. Clinicians use the term "acting out," which means that the addict relieves tension and reduces anxiety by seeking sexual release. Acting out might mean starting a new affair or compulsively masturbating in the car or exhibiting oneself. The addict seeks a pleasurable high or sexual focus which temporarily obliterates all problems. Thus, acting out defuses anxiety. Yet obsession itself is pain relieving. Addicts talk about how sexual preoccupation keeps a level of arousal going constantly. In fact, almost all addicts agree that most of the time lost to the addiction was spent in obsession and fantasy.

Many ask how sex can be an addiction when no drug is ingested. Drugs, in fact, *are* involved—in the form of naturally-occurring peptides such as endorphins which govern the electrochemical interactions within the brain. These peptides parallel the molecular construction of opiates like morphine, but they are many times more powerful. We know that when experimental rats are habituated to morphine or heroin, they will go through much pain in order to obtain more. However, when the pleasure centers of the brain are stimulated, releasing endorphins, rats will go through even more suffering than they will for morphine or heroin.

We have made tremendous progress in understanding the neurochemistry of sexual and other addictions. Yet science is just beginning to appreciate the pain-deadening characteristics of sex. For example, the time-honored excuse for not having sex is having a headache. Researchers, however, find that sex gives significant symptomatic relief of migraine headaches. Similarly, research into arthritis finds that sex gives relief in a number of the more painful forms of that illness. It is no wonder that sex addicts use medical language to describe their illness, referring to sex as their "pain reliever" or their "tension reliever." (In the novel *The Seduction of Peter S.*, the opportunistic heroine describes sex as "the thinking women's Valium.") Sex addicts use their sexuality as a medication for sleep, anxiety, pain, and family and life problems.

7. Increasing amounts of sexual experience because the current level of activity is no longer sufficient

A classic trait of addiction is that the addict will require more and more of the substance or activity in order to maintain the same level of emotional relief. Mark, for example, kept having to add behaviors whether with men or with women. It is a misconception, however, that addicts get worse at a steady rate, in an inevitable spiral downward. In sex addiction, as we have noted, an addict may go through periods of excessive control before eventually returning to or going beyond old levels.

The experience of Steve illustrates this classic pattern:

For as long as I can remember, things have felt scattered, or off center. Through the years I've come to seek sexual experiences that would either make me forget about that off-centeredness or bring it together. When I left home and went into the navy, what was a normal pattern of masturbation with soft-core pornography became escalated into a pattern of sex shops and bookstores where I would seek hard-core pornography. I began also to use prostitutes. I got out of the navy hoping that I would outgrow this sort of thing. I was never comfortable with it.

I would much rather have spent fifty or so bucks on sex than getting myself a set of decent clothes. I'd rationalize that by acting as if I identified with a nonmaterialistic culture. But the fact is, I really wanted nice clothes and I didn't have any. And I didn't know how to not spend money acting out sexually.

Steve married in his late twenties. He hoped that marriage would be a solution to his problem. Within months, however, it became worse in terms of both pornography and prostitution. When his first child was born, his behavior took yet another leap.

Now, when at adult bookstores, he looked for other men to have sex with. Because he felt so shameful about his new sexual behavior, Steve withdrew emotionally from both his wife and his young son. Within his isolation, he found himself binge eating and using alcohol heavily after his sexual bingeing "because it was just better than facing the pain of it." He also developed a rhythm of alternating between rigid control of his sexuality and sexual excess. The more he tried to control himself, the more he acted out. He comments that "fear and anger also fit into the rigidity and release." When he became fearful, he'd tighten up his effort to control; when he was angry, he'd look for sexual release. Fear supported the rigid control; anger underlay the sexual release.

8. Severe mood changes around sexual activity

Steve's withdrawal from his family underlines the addict's experience of severe mood changes around sexual activity. Filled with shame and self-hatred because of his behavior, Steve could not let his family in on why he was hurting. He started living a double life. And as his behavior escalated, his double life deepened. Sometimes Dr. Jekyll, a decent husband and father, he was also subject to the capricious appearances of Mr. Hyde in the form of the willful, exploitive addict.

The emotional life of the addict parallels the proverbial roller coaster. If unable to stave off the pain with sex, the addict plunges into despair. When another sexual binge occurs after the addict has promised to stop, the addict despairs again. When he or she has to invent more lies, or if somehow the lies are unmasked, the addict despairs again.

Shame drives the sex addict's behavior, and shame is also the reaction to being out of control. There are several reasons for these feelings of shame. First, addicts feel shame because other people seem able to set appropriate limits about sex. Addicts wonder what is wrong with them that they cannot be "normal."

Second, sex addicts believe that no others exist like themselves. They believe they are unique both in the kinds of activities they engage in and in their excesses. In a culture that denies the

)eration at the thought

d with family messages
.r evidence that there is
.ve they are bad simply for
negative religious messages
.ve sexual self-image. Many
) be good, it has to be bad—
.percharged.
. pleasure during the incest have
of violence and sexual abuse who
, pain, and shame also are unable to
.itement. The very factors that con-

tribu. .xual behavior even more compelling,
in the sense .n is somehow better.

The final ingre. the addict's despair is the withdrawal experience. Addicts repor. symptoms that absolutely parallel the withdrawal experience of the cocaine addict. Physical symptoms— including dizziness, body aches, headaches, sleeplessness, and extreme restlessness—are very common. Many addicts who have recovered from a chemical addiction and a sex addiction say that recovery from sex addiction was more difficult. They generally agree that while the initial physical symptoms are less severe, the withdrawal experience is more prolonged and more painful.

Sex addicts, then, live a life on the edge, only a few steps ahead of their pain. They push themselves harder and harder until they drop. In our survey, 89 percent reported regularly bingeing to the point of emotional exhaustion. Further evidence emerged of the strength of the despair. Seventy-two percent of survey respondents contemplated suicide as a way out of their addiction and pain; 17 percent attempted suicide. When addicts feel isolated and different from everyone else, they feel hopeless, and when the pain is so great, suicide seems acceptable.

9. Inordinate amounts of time spent in obtaining sex, being sexual, or recovering from sexual experience

For sex addicts, sexual obsession becomes the organizing principle of daily life. Everything revolves around it. The basics of living—clothes, food, sleep, work—become a lower priority. Most of the addict's time is devoted to initiating sex, being sexual, or dealing with the aftermath. Almost universally, addicts count as one of their major losses the extraordinary amount of time they spent on their addiction.

Barb with her multiple relationships, Mark with his prostitution and anonymous sex, and Steve in the bookstores—all the addicts described thus far diverted their energy and time from other things for the pursuit of sex. Few were more eloquent about this than Peter, whose addiction had become his life-style:

> Food was something I would think about only periodically. Sleep became passé. I would rush from work on Friday afternoon and change clothes and pick up a bag of cos- tumes, I called them—sleazy Levi's, torn shirts, things like that—and jump in the car and rush to the city. Then check into a bathhouse and be there all weekend long and get maybe six hours sleep the whole weekend. Catnaps in the bathhouse at times when they weren't very busy between 6:00 and 9:00 in the morning. I'd rush back home Monday morning at 6:00, jump in the shower and shave and put on a suit and go off to work. I would do that week after week after week. During the week I would frequently rush out on Tuesday night or Thursday night because I couldn't stand not doing it. It was all this rushing, rushing, rushing.

Another major time drain stems from dealing with the conse- quences of the addiction. Lies have to be covered. Upset and exploited lovers need to be calmed down. Money shortages have to be faced and diseases dealt with. Outraged spouses, arresting offi- cers, disappointed bosses, neglected children—all take time. Fur- ther subterfuges are required to prevent more discoveries. Addicts become even more depleted by these problems—and then attempt to restore themselves with sexual behavior.

10. Neglect of important social, occupational, or recreational activities because of sexual behavior

Friends, family, work, and hobbies are all placed on a back burner, subordinated to the pursuit of sex. Consider the business person who makes business trips organized around sexual prospects rather than business prospects, hires on the basis of sexual potential and not business competence, or puts off business priorities because of sexual priorities. Decision making comes out of sexually focused priorities rather than sound judgments.

Nowhere is this fact of addictive life more clear than in the addict's relationships. As their illness progresses, sex addicts put energy only into relationships with sexual potential. They invest in few or no nonsexual relationships. Relationships that once had meaning are neglected. Long-term relationships of active sex addicts are often stormy and unsuccessful. More likely, short-term relationships, whether personal or professional, are the norm. Addicts, because of their sexual overextension and avoidance of intimacy, tend to leave interpersonal transactions unfinished and relationships untended, left to wilt or die. Further, addicts typically search for people who will take care of their neediness or for people who will be vulnerable or dependent upon them. Finally, the quality of emotion is affected. The degree of shame surrounding the double life prevents addicts from being emotionally present, especially at critical or meaningful times.

For Rebecca, a freelance artist and single parent, the state of her relationships became apparent after she completed treatment for her chemical dependency.

At that point Rebecca's sexual addiction dramatically increased in its intensity. She spoke of sex addiction as her "core addiction" and believes that in many ways it simply had been masked by her chemical dependency. She was involved in an obsessive relationship with a man named Gerry:

> Wanting to be sexual with Gerry became primary in my life. The compulsion to be sexual with him rose above all else, including taking care of my daughter, who is the most important person in the world to me. What I wanted to do and what I did were different. . . . I would go over to his house, and I would say that I couldn't stand his behavior. I would stay there anyway on the chance that we could be sexual. If there was a slim chance for sex, I still hung around. He was verbally abusive to me, and I still hung around so that I could be sexual. He was shaming and I still hung around. There was cruelty when we were sexual, which I was appalled by, but I still hung around.

After breaking up with Gerry she had many successive encounters, which left her empty and alone:

> The pattern was, I would meet a guy and there would be an attraction. We would immediately start going together. If we weren't being sexual, we were talking about being sexual or thinking about being sexual or planning to be sexual. The energy was based on sex. I didn't really know these people, and I really didn't care to know them. I just went from one to another to another and lied to myself all the time.

For some addicts the fear of losing important relationships is a catalyst for change. Like many others, Rebecca was finally pushed to do something about her sex addiction through an event involving a loved one. She describes it this way:

> One of the things that tipped me over the edge was when my daughter in the second grade wrote a note in school to a boy that she wanted to have sex with him. The teacher showed me the note and I in turn showed it to my therapist. My therapist said, "How long do you want to continue to give those kinds of messages to your daughter?" That was the clincher for me. I went to SAA, and I've been there ever since. . . . The two key factors were the note that my daughter wrote and the constant confrontations from my therapist. At one point my therapist said she wasn't sure if she was going to be able to continue to work with me. That was the conversion experience. I wasn't willing to lose my therapist or my daughter.

Many adults will take huge risks for their children that they would not take for anyone else, including their spouses. Sex addicts have an additional incentive to do so in that they often have extreme pain around the abuse and deprivation they experienced as children. Rebecca knew she did not want her child to experience what she went through growing up. So she took the risk to change. Rebecca was like many others who found that the neglect of the most important parts of life—family, friends, work, talents, and values—was a sure sign of addiction.

WHEN IS SOMEONE A SEX ADDICT?

No one sign is proof that sex addiction is present. But as these stories show, usually many of the signs are present concurrently. Taken together, they form a pattern revealing the underlying illness. Sometimes people focus on specific behaviors. As one reporter put it, "How many affairs do you have to have before you are a sex addict?" The question parallels asking how many drinks it takes to be an alcoholic or how many bets to be a compulsive gambler. The answer is not one of quantity but rather of pattern. For example, drinking ceases to be social and becomes problematic and then addictive as out-of-control behavior becomes the norm in the alcoholic's life. The same standards apply in sex addiction.

Important barriers exist to our acknowledging the signs of sex as an addiction. In our culture, we find it difficult to talk about sex in a straightforward, serious fashion without sensationalizing, making jokes, or somehow discrediting the value of the discussion. Also we fear what would happen if a part of our population was out of control sexually. Perhaps most important remains our persistent view of sex as always a matter of self-control or choice. In that sense there is a direct parallel with concepts of alcoholism in the forties and fifties. Alcoholism was perceived as a problem of character and not as an illness that afflicted millions. Now we know that alcoholism is often transmitted across generations. In the stories that follow we shall also see examples of generation after generation of out-of-control, destructive sexual behavior.

Sexism and sexual stereotypes also affect our acceptance of sexual addiction. The cultural expectation that "boys will be boys" obscures sexual addiction with popular notions of sexual conquest and the good life. In contrast, women addicts report that one of their greatest obstacles to getting help was not being believed because women are perceived as the guardians of morality and not prone to sexually excessive behavior. In earlier times it was also deemed to be manly to be able to control one's liquor. Many men had trouble admitting they had a problem with alcohol because of how they perceived manhood. Women, on the other hand, were not supposed to have a problem with drinking. It took years before there was wide acceptance of women alcoholics in the health care system. Our cultural stereotypes prevent us from seeing that people are in desperate trouble.

HOW CAN IT BE AN ADDICTION WHEN NO DRUG IS INVOLVED?

People ask how sex can be an addiction. It is not like a drug or alcohol which is foreign to the body. For professionals in addictionology (the science of addiction), this is familiar territory, already traversed in the areas of compulsive gambling and compulsive eating. We have learned that addictive obsession can exist in whatever generates significant mood alteration, whether it be the self-nurturing of food, the excitement of gambling, or the arousal of seduction. One of the more destructive parts of sex addiction is that you literally carry your own source of supply.

By focusing on external chemicals like alcohol, we have missed the significance of being able to get high on our own brain chemicals. We find that compulsive gamblers, for example, have abnormally low beta-endorphin levels. Like alcoholics who experience an opiate deficiency, they manufacture a state of excitement to make up for the deficit. Prolonged use alters these individuals' brain chemistry until they "require" the excitement in order to feel "normal." Similarly, Harvey Milkman and Stanley Sunderwirth summarize research on sexuality in their book *Craving for Ecstasy: The Consciousness and Chemistry of Escape:*

> It is becoming more evident that orgasm is not so much a function of the genitals as it is of the brain. As early as the sixteenth century it was known that opium ingestion decreased sexual activity and in some cases could cause impotence. Opiates occupy endorphin receptor sites on the presynaptic terminals of neurons in the central nervous system. In this way opiates mimic the pain-killing and the euphoric effects of our own endorphins. The inference is obvious: endorphins (and the limbic system) must some-

how be involved in the ecstasy of sexual activity and
orgasm.

The relationship between endorphins and orgasms was
demonstrated by a group of neuroscientists who showed
that the level of endorphins in the blood of hamsters
increased dramatically after several ejaculations. This finding would account for the well-known decrease of pain
during and after sex. . . . The rush of endorphins into the
central nervous system could also explain the euphoria
usually experienced immediately following orgasm and loss
of romantic interest just after sex.

Beyond the pleasurability of love, there also exists the "rush"
or intoxication experience during the attraction stage of new love.
Dorothy Tennov described the pursuit of this experience as "limerance"
—the state in which one finds oneself romantically compelled. Michael Liebowitz describes the compulsive pursuit of this condition as
"hysteroid dysphoria"—a "common pattern of repeated intense romantic involvements." In Liebowitz's book *The Chemistry of Love*,
he underlines the importance in romantic attraction of the peptide
called phenylethylamine, or PEA.

According to Liebowitz, PEA is critical to the chemistry of
courtship. Its molecular structure parallels that of amphetamines
and creates a high-arousal state. The mood-altering effect of
PEA is immediate but short-lived. Its intense impact tapers off
as the romance gets past the initial "limerance" stage to the
bonding of the long-term attachment phase of love. The impact
also may be affected by context. For example, monkeys injected
with concentrations of PEA demonstrated hypersexual or super-
erotic behavior—but only in the presence of other monkeys. So
the psychobiological connection is crucial. For PEA to result in
excessive sexuality in primates, the object of affection has to be
present.

Considerable evidence also indicates that PEA and sexual arousal
are highly affected by the presence of fear, risk, and danger. For
instance, PEA concentrations have been measured as extremely
high in connection with divorce court trials. Experiments with attraction have shown that fear serves as an important escalator of
desire. For example, in one study students were interviewed by an
attractive interviewer. Those who were (falsely) told they might

receive an electric shock rated the interviewer more attractive than those who were not given this "warning."

Two important contexts must be considered to put PEA research in perspective. First, PEA is probably but one of many brain chemicals that exist in the chemistry of sexuality and love. Of the over three hundred chemicals involved in the chemistry of the brain, we have a working understanding of only about sixty. Breakthroughs in neuroscience are occurring almost daily, but we still have much to learn. Some experts like Milkman and Sunderwirth, as well as Liebowitz, speculate that designer drugs that go by street names like "Ecstasy" and "Love" have molecular constructions that will serve as models for expanding our knowledge base. For now, the isolation of PEA is but one significant contribution to our ongoing quest for knowledge.

The second context is that PEA research fits with other efforts to link danger or fear to addiction. Skydiving, shoplifting, and gambling share the emotions of high risk. Pioneering work in the risk-taking personality has been done by Marvin Zuckerman, whose research on the biological basis of sensation seeking amplifies what is occurring in the neuroscience of addiction. Many studies he underlines show the existence of low levels of monoamine oxidase (MAO) as a biological factor in seeking high risk; MAO is an enzyme that regulates the neurotransmissions of arousal in the brain. In compulsive gambling, we are already able to link alterations of brain chemistry with different levels of risk. Perhaps we will be able to do the same for sex.

Some people object to breaking down love and sex into chemical components, believing that such analysis takes the magic away. However, it is now commonplace to talk of the neurochemistry of stress reactions. Almost everybody can describe a Type A personality: the hard-driving, goal-oriented, high-risk individual. Few of us would have difficulty understanding the role of adrenaline and its impact on the heart. Yet we are reluctant to accept the same kind of analysis of love and sexuality. The reality of neuroscience exists. We will all become neurochemists to some degree as the emerging science helps us to understand our behavior. Neurochemistry does not invalidate anything we know about addiction. It simply helps us to understand the mechanisms of what addicts have been telling us about for years.

Over and over in our survey we heard addicts talk about their

withdrawals

see as a drug.

- wife as a drug.

- neory

sexuality as a potent drug. Mark, the physician sex addict described earlier in this chapter, really became clear about this when he was told that masturbation was part of his problem. On learning that he would have to stop masturbating, he reacted strongly: "I said that's impossible. Nothing's wrong with it—I'm a physician, there's nothing wrong with masturbation. Then I realized masturbation had been my trouble all my life. That was my drug. From that moment on I worked my AA approach on my masturbation. One day at a time I stopped masturbating, and as soon as I stopped masturbating, my life started getting better."

Almost immediately Mark was able to see how sex was like a drug for him.

One day I walked into the hospital. Someone had died and two people started crying. I walked down the hall and all of a sudden I started to weep. Spontaneous weeping. I believe that all that masturbating I did in college and medical school kept me going. It helped me numb an enormous amount of feeling. When my father died and when my brother died, even though it's against our religion I immediately had sex with my wife. She knew if there was any way to get me calmed down if I was upset, it was to have sex with me.

Similarly, Peter described the pain and anguish when he stopped his sexual bingeing:

I can remember many, many, many times during withdrawal when I was crying and howling like a wounded animal in my condominium and I was lying prostrate on the floor in the living room pounding my fist into the carpeting and I would call someone up—usually my sponsor, but I would call other people, too. They would pick up the phone and say hello, and I would just start bawling. Bawling uncontrollably. Those people loved me unconditionally. After the numbness wore off I started to have a lot of feelings come up, as so many people do, feelings of rage, anger, hysteria at times. . . . I realized what I was grieving for was that life as I had known it up until then was dying. I would no longer be able to do the things I had been doing in order to get the anesthesia I was so desperately looking for. That was a very mournful period for me.

To suggest that addiction can involve only chemicals external to the body is to dismiss the sex addict's reality. Such misperception also overlooks a rapidly expanding body of scientific literature.

SEX AND THE OTHER ADDICTIONS

One common scenario is that of the recovering alcoholic who finds that his sexual behavior increases dramatically. He may even discover that he rationalized earlier excessive sexual behavior as a result of the drinking. When his drinking stops, his sexual behavior not only continues but escalates. Many individuals have entered recovery from sex addiction by first committing to a program of recovery for chemical dependency.

People who experience dual dependencies like chemicals and sex often make this striking observation: chemical abuse is easier to stop than sexual addiction. They point to several factors explaining why this is so. First, sex addicts often begin sexually compulsive behavior early in life. Compulsive sex, as we already have seen, can start in childhood. So a thirty-year-old addict who started abusing chemicals at the age of seventeen may have been using sex to cope since he was five. In fact, many sex addicts in our survey talked of using chemicals as a way to kill pain they felt about their sexuality. Second, unlike an alcoholic, who can avoid alcohol, a sex addict carries the source of supply within. A more difficult recovery is one of the prices of getting high on one's brain chemistry.

Ironically, one of the cofounders of Alcoholics Anonymous clearly struggled with this pattern: the venerable Bill Wilson found his sexual behavior a source of great pain. Pultizer Prize–winning author Nan Robertson describes this story in detail in her book *Getting Better: Inside Alcoholics Anonymous:*

> Wilson's marriage to Lois Burnham in 1918 lasted until his death at the age of seventy-five in 1971. She believed in him fiercely and tended his flame. Yet, particularly during his sober decades in A.A. in the forties, fifties and sixties,

Bill Wilson was a compulsive womanizer. His flirtations and his adulterous behavior filled him with guilt, according to old-timers close to him, but he continued to stray off the reservation. His last and most serious love affair, with a woman at A.A. headquarters in New York, began when he was in his sixties. She was important to him until the end of his life.

There are those whose rigidity about alcoholism precludes their accepting addictions beyond alcohol. The tragic truth is that the patterns of dual dependency recovery may have existed from the very beginnings of AA.

Nor are dual addictions limited to sex and chemicals. We have noted the role of eating disorders, compulsive "busyness," and other addictive behaviors. In our survey, less than 17 percent of respondents reported only sexual addiction. Dual addictions included:

Chemical dependency	42 percent
Eating disorder	38 percent
Compulsive working	28 percent
Compulsive spending	26 percent
Compulsive gambling	5 percent

For many sexual addicts, these multiple out-of-control paths exacerbate feelings of powerlessness.

Two recovering addicts, Kevin and Sue, were asked at a professional conference about the interactions among addictions. Specifically, they were asked, "If a sex addict is also an alcoholic, how can sexual performance occur when we know that alcohol is a depressant and inhibits sexual performance?" Their articulate responses echo the findings of our survey.

Kevin: Most of us began our sexual addiction at an early age; in my case, age eight with masturbation. My first drunk was age sixteen. I used alcohol, not only to feel good, but it also medicated my fear and pain of my "sinful" acting out, having been raised in a strict Catholic family. I used enough alcohol to feel good and to give me the courage to "chase" for sexual partners, and at the same time to remove "morality" issues. Later on I found amphetamine that would enhance my acting out so that I could go for hours in my sex addiction while the alcohol kept me from thinking about what I was doing. I also was an addiction binger and addiction trader so that I could satisfy my craving needs through food, work . . . anything to feel normal.

Because of threats from my wife, I went to AA and found relief from alcohol but still felt I was leaving half of me outside the doors of AA for my secret addiction. I was convinced it was a result of being an alcoholic. I then decided that my problem was overeating and went to OA. My acting out decreased only to find it rage again. I now faced it without alcohol or food and found the pain of this addiction was killing me after having been exposed to the principles of the 12 Step programs. I also felt this was a "character defect" as shown in the 4th Step of AA. I finally found a 12 Step program for sexual addiction. Since then I've found out my use of food with sex is a common story.

I would lose weight to be physically attractive to gain sex partners and when I would binge out, I would get into my self-hatred, loathing myself. I used food to not only medicate myself, but gained weight in order to be non-attractive to others. When I got tired of that, I would repeat the cycle over and over again . . . a lust machine to eating machine and vice versa.

Susan: I did much of the same thing, except, as a woman, I was deeper "under the gun" because of society's pressure to have the "perfect" shape along with the burden of being mankind's guardian and caretaker of morality. Overweight men can get by easier, attracting more partners than women can who are heavy. We women tend to suffer bulemia more than men which is a major clue that we were sexually abused as children and suffer from sexual addiction. Many eating disorder units do not even address these issues. I also agree with Kevin regarding the use of alcohol, cocaine and amphetamines, that to the sex addict, at least perceptually, does greatly enhance the pleasure of sex addiction. Why not cocaine and sex for the best synergism of sensual pleasure? Those who insist that the pharmacology of these drugs have the opposite effect do not understand sex addiction.

If the role of multiple addictions is not understood, the pattern of sex addiction is likely to be ignored.

THE DENIAL OF AN ILLNESS

People can admit that sex addiction exists but still deny its impact. One way to do that is to argue that "sex addiction exists, but it is exceedingly rare." Professionals who have expressed this opinion have been hard pressed to explain the growth of twelve step groups like Sexaholics Anonymous, Sex Addicts Anonymous, Sex and Love Addicts Anonymous, and Sexual Compulsives Anonymous. Most major cities and many rural areas have active, growing programs. They are not advertised; they get their members from referral services or therapists or by word of mouth. Estimates by the various fellowships indicate that over two thousand groups meet every week and that the number is growing exponentially.

As we found with alcoholism, it is easy to identify the skid row drunk in the last stages of hitting bottom. Yet, there are many whose lives are in profound disarray because of their drinking who can nevertheless maintain appearances. From the outside, things look fine or even great. The same is true of sex addiction. Until we understand how hidden sex addiction can be and yet thrive, we will continue to see it as a rare illness, affecting other people, not ourselves or those we know and love.

Another way to deny the illness is to say "sexual addiction may be widespread but it is not serious." One of the common jokes about sex addiction is that "if you are going to have an addiction, this is the one to have." The perception is that you cannot hurt yourself by too much sex. Suicide, unwanted pregnancies, family disintegration, violence, dramatic health care costs, and child abuse—all consequences of sex addiction—can be denied. But as a culture we will have to come to terms with another illness we are just beginning to understand: AIDS.

Shortly before this chapter was completed, one of the members of our research team died suddenly of AIDS. He was a recovering sex addict who was one of the gentlest of souls and a good friend to have. He worked extremely hard and excelled at solving problems with research in the real world. The clarity of some of the data presented in this book represents his diligence and creativity. We miss him very much.

When you experience losses like this, it is hard to hear jokes about sex addiction. This is not to say that funny things never happen. They sure do. Rather, it is that, as when you truly understand racism or ageism or sexism, some jokes cease to be funny. They become a commentary on our cultural denial and our collective ability to ignore human suffering.

As Nietzsche said, we give things power when we deny their existence. So it is important to proceed with our anatomy of this addiction. It is essential to understand the inner workings of this illness and all that it touches before we explore the transformation of recovery. Two key concepts from Alcoholics Anonymous are useful here: powerlessness and unmanageability. Chapter Two begins our in-depth exploration by focusing on powerlessness.

Powerlessness: The Eleven Behavioral Types

"Powerlessness"—the word has become a touchstone for recovering people the world over. It captures the essential nature of addiction: not being able to stop. In fact, usually the harder addicts try to stop, the worse their addiction gets. Addicts often know they should not pursue the high they are after. Sometimes they make dramatic efforts to stop. Yet time after time, they find themselves in the situations they've intended to avoid. Time and again, addicts' stories reflect their poignant realizations of having lost their way.

Every addict remembers moments of being out of control that were particularly painful. Consider the person who has been invited to give a guest lecture to a prestigious audience and fails to show because he was acting out sexually. Or think of the beloved high school principal, married with children, whose arrest for soliciting a young male prostitute became front-page news. Or reflect on the pain of the woman who realized her lifelong pattern of indiscriminate sex started in the seventh grade with multiple partners and an abusive affair with the school custodian. Different moments exist for each addict. All have times of profound shame and pain in common.

In our interviews and surveys, we asked addicts to describe these moments of powerlessness—moments of being sexual when they did not really want to or when they knew it would be perilous for them. A partial listing of their answers is given below. It shows the painful variety of ways addicts can be out of control.

ADDICTS' STATEMENTS OF POWERLESSNESS

Ending up in massage parlor when I promised myself I wouldn't.

Not being able to refuse sex with women—felt no right to say no.

Unable to hold marriage commitment.

In high school I had sex with older women for money.

Sleeping with serial partners in one night.

Out six nights a week to pick up or be picked up in bars.

Took sexual risks with employees.

Would masturbate in library and never study.

Attempted to start an affair with sister-in-law.

Lost two close friends because I tried to seduce their wives.

Involvement with total strangers.

Exchanged sex for drugs.

Being sexual in public places like bars.

Masturbating in car despite accidents and near accidents.

Stole money to keep sexual relationship.

Accumulated heavy debt to "buy" person.

Whenever I was alone, I felt compelled to be sexual.

Arrested for lewd behavior.

Every time I went shopping I felt compelled to go to rest room for sex.

Involved in more than one intense relationship at once.

Many anonymous partners.

Could not form friendships/only find sex partners.

Hitchhiking at night hoping to have sex.

Went to a bookstore after getting negative HIV test.

Exhibiting self while driving.

Could not practice safe sex even when trying hard to do so.

Sex with married men.

Calling guy who tortured me—went over and had sex with him.

Dangerous situation with strangers.

At age fourteen already having multiple lovers in daytime.

Stole woman's clothes for crossdressing.

Masturbating on porch in the middle of the night nude.

Sex on a passenger train with a stranger.

Took risks with pimps and prostitutes.

Sexualizing clients on the job.

Brought men home in the middle of the day while children were there.

Slept with circle of one man's friends to stay close to him.

Waking up to strangers.

Could not say no to husband's suggestion of wife swapping.

Physician masturbated me during examination and I could not say no.

THE BEHAVIORAL TYPES

As part of our survey, our research team developed an assessment instrument to help us be more specific about the behaviors that characterize sex addiction. As often happens in science, what you expect to find and what you actually find can differ dramatically. Although many of the categories of addictive behavior we used were confirmed, other new categories emerged once the data was analyzed.

When we administered the same instrument to the general population—that is, to people not identified as sexual addicts—we found that the differences in behavior between the two groups were extreme. Sex addicts did many more of the behaviors, did the behaviors more frequently, and reported the behaviors as being much more powerful.

As part of our analysis, we examined what kinds of behaviors clustered together. Out of one hundred and four behavioral categories, eleven behavioral types emerged. Each type had a specific sexual focus with common characteristics. When we look at the differences and the commonalities among the eleven types, behaviors that have puzzled us for years begin to make sense. By adding the context of culture, family, and neurochemistry, we can make significant strides toward understanding sexual addiction. The eleven types help pinpoint those behaviors most vulnerable to addictive patterns. Equally important, we are taking important steps toward defining sexual health and understanding what is positive, appropriate, and nourishing. Sex addiction becomes a clarifying prism, revealing the spectrum of healthy elements in our sexual lives.

PATTERNS OF POWERLESSNESS— ELEVEN BEHAVIORAL TYPES

1. FANTASY SEX
Behavior Examples: Thinking/obsessing about sexual adventures; inordinate amounts of time spent losing self in fantasy about future and past; neglecting commitments because of fantasy life; dramatizing a particular role in your fantasy; creating sexualized or seductive atmospheres that you prefer to keep as fantasy and not act on; spending a large amount of time preparing for sexual episode.

2. SEDUCTIVE ROLE SEX
Behavior Examples: Having many relationships at the same time or one after another; using seduction to gain power over others; thinking that sex will give power over another; flirtatious or seductive behaviors; hustling in singles clubs, bars, or health clubs; maintaining open calendars or failing to make commitments in order to be available for sex; bringing sex or sexualized humor into conversations; having to be sexual in order to feel good about self.

3. ANONYMOUS SEX
Behavior Examples: Engaging in sex with anonymous partners; cruising beaches, parks, parking lots, rest rooms, and baths; having one-night stands; participating in group sex.

4. PAYING FOR SEX
Behavior Examples: Paying for sexually explicit phone calls; using an escort or phone service; paying someone for sexual activity; using the personal columns to find sex partners; patronizing saunas, massage parlors, or rap lounges.

5. TRADING SEX
Behavior Examples: Making sexually explicit videotapes and photographs; posing for sexually explicit videotapes and photographs; exposing yourself from stage or for hire; pimping others for sexual activities; receiving money for sexual activity; receiving drugs for sexual activity; administering drugs to force sexual activity.

6. VOYEURISTIC SEX
Behavior Examples: Using sexually explicit magazines or videotapes; having collections of pornography at home or work; patronizing adult bookstores and strip shows; using binoculars or telescopes to watch people; looking through windows of apartments and houses; sexualizing others in public places; sexualizing materials not sexually explicit.

7. EXHIBITIONIST SEX
Behavior Examples: Exposing yourself in public places, such as parks, streets, school yards; exposing yourself from your home or car; being sexual or dressing and undressing in public; using choice of clothing to expose yourself; belonging to a nudist club to find sex partners.

8. INTRUSIVE SEX
Behavior Examples: Making inappropriate sexual advances or gestures; touching or fondling others without permission; using sexually explicit stories, humor, or language at inappropriate times or places; using power position (e.g., as professional, clergy, or employer) to exploit or be sexual with another person; forcing sexual activity on any person, including your spouse or partner.

9. PAIN EXCHANGE

Behavior Examples: Receiving physical harm or pain during sexual activity to intensify sexual pleasure; causing physical harm or pain to partner to intensify sexual pleasure; willingly giving up power or acting out the victim role in sexual activity; using sexual aids to enhance sexual experience.

10. OBJECT SEX

Behavior Examples: Masturbating with objects; crossdressing to add to sexual pleasure; using fetishes as part of sexual rituals; engaging in sexual activity with animals.

11. SEX WITH CHILDREN

Behavior Examples: Sharing inappropriate sexual information with children; exposing children to adult sexual activities; forcing sexual activity on a child within or outside the family; engaging in sex with a consenting minor; watching child pornography.

Engaging in behaviors that fit within a specific behavioral type does not necessarily make a person a sex addict. The pattern of loss of control does. In order to use the signs of addiction to identify those patterns of powerlessness, we must explore each behavioral type in depth. Note, however, that few addicts focus on one behavioral type. Most mix three to four orientations and some as many as six or seven. Addicts always have a preference for some behaviors or combinations of behaviors over others.

FANTASY SEX

Our nonaddict and addict populations agreed on two items: everyone *thinks* about sex and *fantasizes* about sex. Some members of our sex addict population, however, took their fantasy life much further than did their addicted and nonaddicted peers. This group was especially characterized by neglect of responsibilities and commitments and by inordinate amounts of time spent in preparation for sexual episodes. Often their fantasy life was anchored in a specific role, one that was sexually supercharged for them. Typically, they equated sex with love and believed that they had special sexual needs. Often sex addicts will use terms like "love addict" or "romance junkie" to describe someone lost in endless intrigues and obsessions.

Ironically, when it came to actually being sexual, they either would pass or would find it very disappointing. They preferred the fantasy. They might create sexualized atmospheres and opportunities for seduction and then not act on them. They were most likely to feel depressed, hopeless, or unworthy following a sexual encounter, to have sex even though they did not feel like it, and to deny or suppress their sexual feelings for significant periods of time. Not surprisingly, they also reported themselves as more into mind games of rationalization and denial.

While their sexual encounters with others were disappointing, their sexual contact with themselves tended to be extremely intense. As a group, they were most likely to masturbate to the point of injury. In our survey, almost 45 percent of men and 33 percent of women reported having injured themselves through masturbation. Most of these addicts were in the fantasy sex category. Intensive masturbation enabled these addicts to preserve a heightened fantasy life and be sexual without involving others.

A very important characteristic of fantasy sex addicts is that they most often are victims of covert incest in their families. Covert incest occurs when a parent sexualizes a child or initiates sexual transactions with a child but no sexual touching occurs. Because the child has not been touched, the sexuality can be denied even though the impact is still there. In fact, the denial adds to the feelings of confusion the child already has. As adults, victims of covert abuse are prone to be stuck in the initiation or romance stages of relationships and unable to move into the consummation and attachment stages. They tend to lose themselves in fantasy.

Alicia, for example, lived in a very sexualized family where uncles would be very sexual with her and her twin sister. They would comment on the girls' bodies, touch them near their breasts, and play games like trapping and tickling them. Alicia and her sister lived in fear that something more overt would happen. Alicia's addiction as an adult took the form of elaborate fantasy and romance and stopped just short of being sexual. She had all the traits of a fantasy sex addict: multiple romances and intrigues, compulsive masturbation, preference for fantasy over contact, and periods of compulsive nonsexuality. She lost extraordinary amounts of time to fantasy. At one point, her therapist confronted her and she spent the weekend bingeing. Describing that event she told us, "My fantasies started to go wild. In the morning I had a hangover kind of thing. I felt physically sick. I could really see that this was a problem. I couldn't stop."

We heard a similar story from Sean, who described his mother's sexualization as "one of the dominant forces in my life." He remembers being lost in fantasy:

> I just was mesmerized. I would go into a trance, go to my room, go through my rituals and masturbate. Then I would have the feelings of hopelessness and despair. I'd go through cycles of that. Even at work I was not able to say no to masturbating because it was such a sedative for me. The only thing that seemed to get me any relief was by using fantasy and masturbation.

Sean sought what he called "sex vibe games," which were flirtation and intrigue. "I loved the power that a sex vibe game would give me." Many times while driving his car, Sean found himself preoccupied by flirtation or lost in fantasy while masturbating secretly. He said, "I was an accident looking to happen."

Sean and Alicia represent a type of sex addiction often overlooked and not taken seriously. While dangerous to themselves and even, inadvertently, to others, they are not having multitudes of partners, seducing children, or spreading AIDS. So they are viewed as being harmless and in their own world. Yet they experience the losses all addicts face: intimacy, time, energy, and productivity. They also have the shame, pain, and physical risks.

Fantasy sex addicts share one other characteristic with the other behavioral types. The form their addiction takes is strongly preconditioned by childhood experience. This fact becomes tremendously significant in understanding the varieties of sexually addictive behavior and vital to recovery from the illness.

SEDUCTIVE ROLE SEX

Seductive role sex usually involves having many relationships at the same time or successive relationships one right after another or affairs outside of a primary relationship. A number of attitudes characterize this category. Many of these addicts believe that if you have sex with someone, you will have that person in your power. They are sexual with the intent of gaining power over another person. Women addicts talk, for example, of the Mata Hari syndrome, named after the famous spy who would use sex to gain enemy secrets. Similarly, men talk of scalps or notches. People in this behavioral group tend also to feel compelled to be sexual because they have been seductive, not because they really want sex. They are the group most likely to be found "hustling" in bars, singles groups, or health clubs.

Seduction means being emotionally engaging while being misleading about your intentions. Therapists use the phrase "high warmth with low intention" to describe seductive behavior. (Protestations that "I didn't mean anything by it" parallel such other classic dysfunctional lines as "Her no really means yes" and "Promise her anything.") If sex occurs, no one has to take responsibility for something that "just sort of happened." The game of seduction is to get someone to be sexual with you when they are not ready or don't want to. The conquest is everything. Between trusted partners, seduction scenes can be fun and revitalize romance. When it is part of a predatory effort to use sex to medicate pain, the behavior becomes destructive and degrading.

Joanna provided us with a classic description of seductive role sex. Her seductions and entangled relationships led to a blur of partners:

> I was living with a man, Bill, about whom I was very serious; we were talking about getting married. Then I started a sexual relationship with another person. I think in a way it made it easier for me to get out of the relationship with Bill by having another one to go into. And then while I was in that one, I got in another one. I definitely leapfrogged from one to another. . . . I can remember spending a lot of Sunday mornings getting out of bed and feeling really ashamed. And in a fog. I can remember feeling like that every weekend. I would go home to where I lived with my roommate and I would feel like I was in a daze. And I didn't know what to do about it.

Joanna's experiences help clarify how addicts' behavior is different from that of most people. A key point of addiction is its *use to regulate emotional life.* Many times that emotional process remains hidden from even best friends. Joanna describes her process this way: "My addiction has always been about surviving. While I'm acting out, I don't feel lonely or angry. And I'm one of those people whose acting out is very hidden and controlled. In fact, some of the people closest to me say they would never know. If I tell them the feelings they can tell."

Seductive role sex is disguised by cultural images of male conquest and female seduction. But addicts know that what they do is different, that it has a power of its own, and that they are no longer in charge of their lives.

In our survey we found noticeable differences between how men and women were distributed into the various categories. To make definitive statements about those differences is risky, since we were able to sample only a small population of addicts who have achieved recovery and since the sample included far fewer women than men (18 percent as opposed to 82 percent). A clear trend that emerges is that women tend to be more involved in seductive role sex than men. The table below provides a comparison of selected items illustrating the difference. This is in marked contrast to the next two categories discussed— anonymous sex and paying for sex—in which men clearly predominate.

TABLE 2-1
GENDER DIFFERENCES IN SEDUCTIVE ROLE SEX

	% MEN	% WOMEN
Having many relationships at the same time	41	74
Having successive relationships one after another	39	72
Having affairs outside your primary relationship	53	77
Using sexual seduction to gain power over another person	39	74
Hustling in singles clubs, bars, or health clubs	29	42
Thinking that if you are sexual with someone, you will have them in your power	50	79
Using flirtatious or seductive behavior to gain attention of others	52	79

ANONYMOUS SEX

Father John, a fifty-two-year-old Catholic priest, was known for his leadership in the church and his pastoral ability. Given that he was a public figure, his powerlessness was underscored by his willingness to run the risk of recognition. When his compulsive sex with men spilled out into the street, he knew he was out of control. He describes his growing awareness of powerlessness:

> I picked up somebody on the street in another city and attributed that to grief over my father's death the year before. I said, "That'll never happen again." A year later I picked up a young man in the town where I was a public person right on Main Street. A year or so after that, I went into a porno shop for the first time in another city. I said I'd never do that and vowed I'd never do it in my own town. Soon I was frequenting porno shops at home. These were clear signs of real powerlessness, and somehow, deep down, I knew it.

Anonymous sex often involves "cruising," hanging around places where anonymous sexual contacts can be made: rest rooms, beaches, public baths. This cruising is different from hustling in bars in seductive role sex. In anonymous sex there is no pretense of emotional contact. Sexual contact is the goal of all parties involved. Closely associated with cruising are group sex and one-night stands. What these two have in common is the absence of an emotional relationship. Most of our survey participants report that cruising for the sexual opportunity creates a trancelike state in which they spend endless hours. Father John describes his last major cruising episode before he sought treatment:

> I arranged to take about three days off, to travel over the Memorial Day weekend. I no sooner got on the highways than I was in a cruising state, checking every public rest room. When I got to the city, I cruised the shopping centers and the parks and everything else for two or three days. I was like a sleepwalker. Finally, I parked for a longer period than I ever had in a porno shop and had a

sexual encounter with another man. At that moment I
came out of the trance. I decided to go home and disclose
what was going on. I knew I simply had to get help. But
even on the way home I was still out of control, cruising
rest rooms all along the way.

Table 2-2 summarizes responses by gender to some anonymous sex categories. Note that men reported cruising more than
women whereas women had the edge in one-night stands. What
these statistics do not reveal, of course, is that anonymous sex is a
high-risk category because of the danger of disease and violence. A
consistent finding in our interview process was that danger and the
unknown were, in fact, part of the excitement.

TABLE 2-2
GENDER DIFFERENCES IN ANONYMOUS SEX

	% MEN	% WOMEN
Engaging in sex with anonymous partners	53	46
Cruising beaches, parks, parking lots, or baths	59	23
Participating in group sex	32	30
Having one-night stands	63	75

PAYING FOR SEX

The quintessential form of paying for sex is prostitution. Money
becomes the medium of exchange. The addict does not have to
seduce anyone, search for anyone, wait for anyone, or engineer or
manipulate anything. Nor are there any aftermath problems, such as
tearful scenes, upset lovers, or lingering obligations. Sex is immediate and contained, with little emotional risk. Simply pay and go on
your way.

This behavioral type includes patronizing massage parlors, saunas, and rap lounges, as well as using escort services. All often
serve as fronts for prostitution. Whether the person picks up an

adolescent runaway who is working the street or uses an expensive service that specializes in a high-class, exclusive clientele, the exchange remains the same.

A related behavior is paying for sexually explicit phone calls, by using "dial-a-porn" services. Phone sex of this type is an important subcategory. Participants who used prostitutes and/or paid for phone sex also tended to make obscene calls or use the phone inappropriately for sexual purposes. This might mean sexualizing legitimate phone calls or simply masturbating while on the phone talking to someone who is unaware of the sexual activity on the other end of the line. Interestingly, also highly associated is the use of personal columns to find sex partners.

So addicts who use prostitutes regularly as part of their addiction are likely also to have paid for phone sex, used the phone for a sexual connection, or scanned the personals for quick sex. What these behaviors have in common is immediacy and anonymity.

We live in a convenience culture, and sex is no exception. You can charge prostitution or phone sex on your VISA, Master-Card, or American Express credit cards in virtually any hotel, office, or home in America. In fact, for frequent travelers, there are services with representatives in almost any midsize to large city in America. The costs, of course, can be dramatic. In our survey we heard from addicts who spent fifteen to twenty thousand dollars a year on prostitutes. One very wealthy person reported several years of spending forty to fifty thousand dollars. His vast— but dwindling—wealth allowed for daily and expensive prostitution use.

But for most addicts who pay for sex, limited finances create great anguish. Family needs are subordinated to addictive acting out; addicts feel tremendous guilt and shame over secretly draining cash while spouses and children are scrimping and making do. Phone sex and cruising the personals are, for many, a cheaper way to make a sexual connection. Some report, however, that phone sex is part of their preparation for seeing a prostitute. Many also talk of how credit cards made it easy to charge much more than was intended, ultimately leading to financial disaster.

Users of prostitutes run many risks, including danger of violence or robbery, exposure to disease, and arrest. The risk of public exposure may also loom. While phone and escort services promise confidentiality, many public figures become compromised when there is a police raid. Somehow the press ends up with selected names, usually well-known ones.

Perhaps the greatest risk today is the risk of AIDS. Studies of prostitution show a direct relationship between the number of sexual partners and conversion to a seropositive state. In 1989, Center for Disease Control AIDS expert Elizabeth Connell, M.D., wrote, "In New York City, there are currently estimated to be 200,000 IV drug abusers, 50–75 percent of whom have HIV antibodies; 25 percent, or 50,000, of the drug abusers are women. Many of them turned to prostitution in order to support their drug habits; they transmit it to spouses and other sexual partners."

Similar estimates exist for other cities like Newark, Seattle, and San Francisco. Prostitution has become one of the gateways for the epidemic to spread to the heterosexual population in America.

Beyond cost and risk, addicts report a fundamental sense of betrayal of themselves. Father John did many things he felt shameful about apart from anonymous sex. For example, he injured himself many times masturbating with a vacuum cleaner. Yet, the internal pain and powerlessness he felt around his use of prostitution was the worst. He says:

> There was a force in me that was moving towards com-
> plete destruction. I felt deep shame and guilt. I used
> money that had been given to me for religious purposes for
> pornography and prostitution. It was a terrible misuse of
> gifts—not just material gifts, but my own gifts as a human
> being—to have put them in the service of my addiction. I
> felt a lot of shame and self-hatred.

Money in exchange for sex represents an age-old dynamic that has damaged sexual relationships in male-dominated cultures since the beginning of time. Sexual harassment suits notwithstanding, trading sex for jobs continues to thrive as a dynamic in present-day corporate America. It serves as material for TV sitcoms, *Playboy* cartoons, ad campaigns, and jokes among friends.

For our purposes, though, the cultural and social issues con-
nected with prostitution, important as they are, are secondary. Of primary importance to us is that paying for sex is quick and people who use this type of behavior, by phone or in person, are looking for a quick fix. Here, gender differences are significant. Whereas 45

percent of the men in our survey paid people for sex, only 6 percent of the women reported doing so. Similarly, paying for sexually explicit phone calls is more a male activity. Female percentages rise significantly with sexualizing phone calls and inappropriate use of the phone, activities that don't involve money.

TABLE 2-3
GENDER DIFFERENCES IN PAYING FOR SEX

	% MEN	% WOMEN
Paying someone for sexual activity	45	6
Using an escort or phone service	13	0
Participation in phone sexual activity	34	23
Patronizing saunas, massage parlors, or rap lounges	32	4
Making inappropriate sexual phone calls	21	12
Using the personal columns to find sex partners	18	11
Paying for sexually explicit phone calls	17	4

TRADING SEX

In the movie *Looking for Mr. Goodbar*, Theresa is a character who leads the classic double life. By day she teaches retarded children. In the evening she cruises bars to pick up men in a style not unlike that of many of the women in our survey. She invites a bartender to have a drink with her, but he says that he does not drink because he can never stop at just one. "I know," she responds, "I have that trouble with men."

At one point in the movie a man who has just had sex with her and who is very much in a hurry to leave offers her money. Poignantly she refuses, not comprehending why he would offer it to her, totally missing the cultural meaning of the "quick fix" transaction. But in the real world many female sex addicts say they've received money for sex (22 percent) or exchanged sex for drugs (25 percent versus 10 percent and 6 percent, respectively, of the men).

Related activities include making sexually explicit videotapes, pimping, and stripping for stage or hire. One of our survey participants developed a business selling lingerie and sexual aids to groups of middle-class women in their homes. On the surface, it was an innocent activity, providing titillating resources to housewives. However, in the context of her life—which included thousands of partners, a preference for dangerous men, and two abandoned illegitimate children—the business loses its innocence and becomes an extension of her addictive pathology. She saw it as a way to get high talking to women about their sex lives and telling them about her own exploits. She loved to talk frankly in order to shock her customers. For her it was simple: another way to be erotic, avoid dealing with the pain of her life, and make money.

Another woman, Monica, told us one of the most moving and courageous stories of the whole survey—a story of high finance and sex. Monica had built and lost several empires selling sex for money. Her story started with all the classic precursors of sex addiction including a rigidly moralistic and punitive home, sexual abuse, problems with drugs and alcohol, and an eating disorder. At nineteen she found herself pregnant by a boy six years younger than herself. Abandoned by her family, she was supported by a wealthy man, who gave her money in exchange for sex. In order to be independent from him, she started to work in massage parlors and earned incredible amounts of money.

At twenty-one (with a two-year-old at home), Monica noticed that although her earnings were good, pimps were making money off of her and other women. So she studied the business, and by the time she was twenty-four, she owned a chain of massage parlors. Her accumulated wealth and success attracted the attention of state officials, who eventually closed her business down. She moved to another state and started a very successful escort service. A special irony for Monica, looking back from the perspective of recovery, was that her family who had abandoned her finally started to be supportive when she undertook her "entrepreneurial" ventures.

Monica's life was totally absorbed by her business. Her alcoholism and drug abuse often raged out of control. Her weight fluctuated by sixty to eighty pounds. But she was most out of control sexually. Monica called herself an obsessive "crotch watcher." She had a series of damaging fantasy sex relationships with men that she made into romantic obsessions, committing herself to them no matter what the cost or danger, while always avoiding physical sex with them. It was prostitution, however, that was Monica's biggest high.

Change came for Monica when she started attending AA meetings. She became a real estate agent so she could live a more normal life and seem like a normal mom. Her main income, however, still came from prostitution. Her thinking at that time reflected the toll her addictive life had taken:

> By that time I had decided that I was not going to pimp anybody. I wasn't going to turn out people. Turning out people is when somebody has not worked in the business before. That was just kind of a no-no in the business. You do not turn somebody on to this business and get them started in it. By then I had also come to realize that it was not a victimless crime because an employee of mine had committed suicide. A lot of people I knew had died and/or been hurt. I was seeing that the girls were the victims. I had enough of the twelve step program at that point to say no, if I'm going to hurt anybody, it's going to be myself. I'm not going to drag anybody into this with me. Also, at that point just because of the length of time I had been in the business, learning to hustle, the talk and everything else, I had a pretty exclusive clientele and so my pride was just really high. It was people who owned companies, presidents of companies, and they would fly in. It was an exquisite clientele with a real high price tag. I can remember during those times like I would have a real estate closing which was a big closing and go out and be with a trick and just have gobs and gobs of money, stuff it into my pocket, and maybe stop at a supermarket on the way home. I felt so much emptiness and so much pain.

Finally Monica found Sexaholics Anonymous and was able to leave the life she had led. Today she is clear that danger and risk combined with sex and money was a powerful, exhilarating high. She is clear that to have continued would have meant the kind of tragedy for herself that she had witnessed in the case of so many others.

VOYEURISTIC SEX

Noticing that people are attractive and being drawn to them is one of life's pleasures. Sometimes you meet someone whose presence makes you weak at the knees, out of breath, and filled with adolescent uncertainty. Married, single, old, young—everyone has such encounters. On these occasions we can be philosophical and celebrate the diversity and beauty of the human species. Or, we can indulge in speculation as to what it might be like to have a sexual experience with this person. Or, we can use the occasion to create an intensely sexual, even orgasmic, fantasy.

In voyeurism, passion degenerates into pathology. Watching people through windows of their houses or apartments, using binoculars or telescopes, or hiding in secret places to watch or listen—all these activities violate the personal boundaries of others. The victims did not ask to be watched. Today, the classic Peeping Tom has been transformed by technology. Survey respondents used videocameras with telephoto lens to record for repeated viewing neighbors undressing. Patrons of tanning booths used mirrors to view other customers, whose eyes were shielded to prevent eye damage.

Intrusive voyeurs report great excitement associated with the risk and a phenomenal amount of time invested in it. Often, as Don reports here, voyeurism starts quite young:

My mother used to leave home to run up to the store. I would watch the car leave so I could act out until she got back. I can remember when I started coming to what I now call a dry orgasm. Sex was the perfect drug in my childhood. I could use it for hours and hours and hours and there was no end to it.

Peeping in windows started by hanging around childhood playmates' houses by the time I was starting second or third grade. It wasn't too long before I was peeping into their window. That was when I nearly got caught. I remember for the first time questioning whether all my masturbation was healthy. There was this debate going on inside of me. I wondered if I should try to control it.

Don combined his voyeurism with exposing and crossdressing, both of which added to his isolation:

> I came to live totally alone, in constant fantasy of one type or another about all sexual things. At one point I realized that the regular world of people, work, families, school, and caring about those things seemed completely foreign to me. The only life that seemed normal to me was the life of searching for one more sexual high after another. I believed that I was living a life-style that other people were missing out on; they just weren't as high as I was. Meanwhile I ignored the fact that I was absolutely bankrupt inside.

Voyeurism can take forms more subtle than traditional peeping. Some addicts sexualize others in public places or sexualize people or materials that are not sexually explicit. Undressing people in your mind, masturbating using the lingerie ads in the Sears or Penney catalog, or staring at people's sexual parts to the point of embarrassing them—these are samples of a vast array of voyeuristic sexualization.

Our survey showed that pornography and voyeurism were very highly related. Watching strip or peep shows, patronizing adult bookstores, using sexually explicit videos and magazines, or keeping collections of sexually explicit material at home or at work are connected to voyeurism. They are all forms of visual sex.

As a culture, we have an extended tolerance of the pornography industry. *Playboy* and *Penthouse* have served to desensitize us to a large and extended "cottage industry" with gross annual revenues of somewhere between seven and ten billion dollars. We spend more on pornography in one year than the annual sales of the Coca-Cola corporation.

The debate about pornography goes far beyond this book. But two highly relevant facts emerged from our study of sexual addiction. First, among all addicts surveyed 90 percent of the men and 77 percent of the women reported pornography as significant to their addiction. Second, for some, the costs were staggering. Among those whose acting out was primarily visual in nature, it is not unusual to hear reports of pornography collections with cumulative costs in six figures. Consider Al, a physician who had dedicated a full third of the floor space of his home to an elaborate minitheater for viewing video pornography. Over the objections of his wife, he had plunged hundreds of thousands of dollars into elaborate electronic gadgetry and films. The secret did not come out through two alcoholism treatments. When Al could not stay sober and when several women patients filed complaints about inappropriate touching, the costs of his sexual addiction began to appear.

EXHIBITIONIST SEX

The average person's image of the exhibitionist is a trench-coated figure exposing himself to women passing by. Trench-coated exposers are comparatively rare, but exhibitionists are fairly common. Using home, car, public places, or choice of clothing, exposers seek arousal through sexual attention to their body. The means for exhibitionism are extremely varied and include:

- removing the liner from your swimming trunks so that your genitals are exposed

- cutting holes in crotches of shorts or jeans and pretending unawareness

- leaving your pants zipper down and riding elevators to see who notices

- unbuttoning your blouse and acting as if you were forgetful

- opening your curtain so people can see in

- pulling your skirt up while driving next to truckers as if you were unaware

- ignoring the hotel maid's knock so that she walks in on your feigned sleep

As the examples indicate, exhibitionism is not an exclusively male phenomenon. Table 2-4 compares percentages of men and women addicts who use exhibitionism as part of their addictive patterns.

TABLE 2-4
GENDER DIFFERENCES IN EXHIBITIONIST SEX

	% MEN	% WOMEN
Exposing from home	25	34
Exposing from car	23	25
Exposing in public places such as parks, streets, schools	22	14
Exposing by being sexual or dressing/ undressing in public	26	33
Exposing through choice of clothing	30	59

Note that women addicts responded in higher percentages than the men to our questions about exhibitionistic behavior. Women addicts report pursuing their exhibitionism with the same obsessive and compulsive rituals men use. They are more able to do so—even while breaking social and legal codes—because men do not report women. Women do not get arrested for exhibitionism. And, in some cases, women are rewarded for it.

In many ways women are trained to be exhibitionists. Sexual politics and roles precondition very different responses to men and women. To expose your genitals from a moving car invites different risks for each sex. For men the risk is arrest; for women the risk is the danger of chase.

The naked body is beautiful. In some cultures very little clothing is worn, other than adornments with symbolic value. Yet even these cultures have significant taboos around body coverings. The issue is not nudity per se but rather arousal. Those who would dismiss exhibitionism by pointing to these other cultures fail to realize that sex addiction is not about being different or deviant. It is about excitement rooted in the forbidden and hazardous.

INTRUSIVE SEX

Intrusive sex occurs when someone is sexualized or touched without their permission—in some cases, without their knowledge. The characteristic of intrusive sex is violation; intrusive sex is sex whether someone wants it or not. Sometimes intrusive sex can be extremely subtle, so that the victim is unaware or, if suspicious, uncertain enough not to protest. Subtle intrusions include:

- touching people "inadvertently" in crowded public places such as shopping malls, subways, and airports

- brushing against people in dance situations such as discos or other night spots

- professionals sexually touching vulnerable persons in what seem like unintended ways (e.g., during psychotherapy, health exams, or crises such as accidents)

- telling sexually explicit stories or using sexually explicit language in an inappropriate context so people feel violated but don't know why

More obvious intrusions are making inappropriate sexual advances or gestures, sexual touching or fondling, or the use of force. Rape—including date rape and wife rape—is the most violent form of intrusive sex. The use of a power position to exploit or be sexual with someone is highly intrusive and terribly damaging. This includes more subtle violations. We found that indecent liberties are often connected to more serious forms of sexual exploitation and abuse, which corroborates findings in an earlier study, discussed in *Contrary to Love*. What is clear is that if addicts are willing to violate the boundaries of others in overt ways, chances are they will do so in subtle ways as well.

Danny is a case in point. His background is typical: addiction runs in his family, and he suffered abuse as a child. Familiar, too, are the consequences, beginning with his being fired from a job at the age of eighteen because he took indecent liberties with a customer. Later, he lost his family and his business. He blames the death of a daughter partly on his addiction.

During the height of Danny's acting out, the family went on a bike trip. Because he was so anguished by his acting out behavior, Danny lost his temper with his daughter. He slapped her for straying from the family. She ran away from him straight into the path of a passing car.

Danny's pattern started with compulsive masturbation and then developed into frequent, coercive sex with his wife. He describes it this way:

> From age thirteen I masturbated regularly until I got married at twenty-one. I'm sure I missed very few days during that time, although I remember a period when I was about sixteen years old when I tried to stop. I thought it wasn't good for me, but I wasn't able to stop. After I married I transferred that urge into having intercourse with my wife every day. It accomplished the same kind of release of energy and calming effect. After I was married, I masturbated in my wife's vagina to numb out and get to sleep.

Wife rape is perhaps one of the most common forms of sexual violence. Note that the presence of coercion or violence may in fact increase the mood-altering quality of the sex.

Our image of a violent sex offender is a stranger who attacks a woman in the street—an event that occurs three times a minute in North America. We need to broaden our focus to include date rape (committed by one out of ten American men) as well as the rape of friends, acquaintances, and partners. The actual numbers are difficult to document. Street rape is problematic to prove in an adversarial court system; when rape involves existing relationships, documentation becomes even more murky. Fully 30 percent of the men in our sample, however, used force with their partners to gain sexual access.

It's also important to note the distinction between sex offenders and sex addicts. Some sex offenders are sex addicts, and some sex addicts are sex offenders. Although there is an overlap, the populations are not the same. Sex offenders rape and molest out of a complex mosaic of motivations, one of which is an eroticized, addictive pattern. Other factors include sociopathy, personality disorder, and familial disturbance. Our survey clearly reveals, however, that the use of force in the name of addictive relief occurs with some sex addicts.

Danny first went to a therapist whose prescription was "to desensitize myself by going to massage parlors and porn shops. It fed me further into the system and wasn't good treatment for addictive sexual behavior." He finally got the help he needed when his wife and children went to a shelter. He sought in-patient treatment for chemical dependency, and the hospital chaplain led him to Sex Addicts Anonymous. His description of his early days in recovery underline his emotional reliance on sex: "I committed to abstain for a while and it was just astounding how depressed I got. I felt an enormous sense of loss. Even though I was making the choice to not be sexual with anyone, at the time it felt like I had lost a friend."

PAIN EXCHANGE

Related to violence is the use of pain to escalate sexual excitement. Chains, whips, sadomasochistic games, self-torture, self-strangulation—how can these be pleasurable? The answer is that often they are not. But the associated emotions of fear, risk, danger, and rage are very mood altering. We can make fun of people who are "into pain"; media portrayal of "s and m" roles often involves humorous exaggeration. Grim reality exists that we, in our cultural denial, attempt to avoid and deflect with humor. For most of us, the combination of pain and sex is as repugnant as violence.

How does an individual start associating pain and sex? A particularly poignant example of how the process works emerged from our in-depth interview with Caren, a thirty-five-year-old industrial psychologist. Caren's sexual addiction started at the age of twelve and included extreme promiscuity, compulsive masturbation, and pornography. Most shameful for her was sex and pain.

I remember masturbating nightly as early as five; this continued all through my life. I had a lot of practice because my mother was an alcoholic and she'd put my sister and me to bed really early at night. I'd listen to kids playing outside and it would still be light out. I don't recall feeling any shame then, but some events occurred that fueled my fantasies and fostered a fetish in me that I still have. My father and mother disciplined my sister and me frequently and in a humiliating, ritualized kind of way.

They would have whoever was going to get hit go locate an article to get hit with and then undress and get hit in front of the family. If it was both of us, then we would alternate. I say hitting, because the word "spanking" is real sexual. I can't hear it or see it or say it without it triggering a lot of sexual feelings in me and also a lot of shame. So I stick to "hitting."

When I was about six, I witnessed an incident where a

neighbor man who was drunk appeared to be touching his three-year-old's genitals while he was hitting her, punishing her for wetting herself. And so at that age, I started masturbating to that fantasy of the image of that scene. And that has stayed with me.

The family environment was supercharged with pain and sex. One night when Caren was about twelve, her mother was drunk and invited Caren into her bedroom. She started to undress and asked her daughter to hit her. Caren refused and went to her room. They never talked about it. But it was with her father that Caren most closely connects pain and excitement:

> I remember having a lot of fear, but somewhere along the line, a lot of that fear turned into a kind of excitement. It was like a ritual—always after I got hit, I'd go right to my room and masturbate. And my father would always disappear about that time too. I don't know if he was doing the same thing—if it charged him up or not. But it seemed like he would manufacture excuses to hit me.

Caren's history illustrates a number of commonalities important to remember: early childhood experiences, family environment, and associated emotions are critical in understanding the nature of sexual addiction. For Caren, those factors also led her to behaviors associated with our next category—object sex.

OBJECT SEX

Object sex involves the use of specific articles that have become eroticized. Masturbating with objects, crossdressing, and fetishism fall into this category. Also included is sexual activity with animals. Again, if our survey respondents did one of these behaviors, they probably did others.

Caren reported that the objects that she was required to find to be beaten with became sexualized. Later, just being around those articles caused her to feel sexual and shameful. She describes bingeing by herself, using a combination of objects and self-violence:

I did a lot of self-abusive stuff while masturbating. I had these rituals (I called them orgies with myself) where I would block out time and take care of my loneliness. I would haul out whatever pornography I had and wander around the house masturbating and collecting articles to hit myself with. Then I would always fall asleep and wake up amidst all this paraphernalia and pornography and feel like dying. I was living with a roommate and I would do these things when she wasn't home. I was sexual with her dog a lot. It was a female dog, but I could have an orgasm with the dog. Then I would take these long baths. I felt so dirty.

Notice that in Caren's description she mentions loneliness and how her activities temporarily filled the void but did not make it go away. Instead, the pain and secrecy of what she was doing added to her isolation.

Many stories, like Caren's, include specific objects that have intoxifying effects, objects that people become intensely attached to and would sacrifice anything for. However, just because people use objects as part of their sexual life doesn't mean that they are sex addicts. Again, addiction must be measured in terms of powerlessness.

One of the more eloquent descriptions of the tremendous power given to objects comes from Tom, a forty-two-year-old minister whose crossdressing was a source of extreme pain. Like Caren, his story begins early in life with an alcoholic parent:

I remember going upstairs to the attic with my brothers and we dumped out a seabag full of clothes. There was an army and a navy uniform and all kinds of stuff. We tried that stuff on, until finally, the only thing left to try on was my mom's slip. In fun I tried that on. It felt good and I got an erection. It wasn't that it was planned, it just happened. After that, every time I felt hungry, angry, lonely, or tired I went upstairs and put on my mom's slip and fondled and played with myself.

As an adult, Tom's secret life intensified. He hoped that being married would end his obsession. He burned all of his stash of women's undergarments and said good-bye to the old ways. But, within six weeks of his ritualistic burning, he knew he could not go without. So he approached his wife. At first, she got into it with him to be supportive. Ultimately, it almost destroyed his marriage. Tom's words reflect the feelings of many:

> I found this lifeboat. It took care of me, it nurtured me and gave me life. But later it demanded much of me. It got progressively worse and worse. Not only when I was hungry, angry, or tired, but every time I wanted to relax I needed the slip. It was a very powerful addiction, a very powerful high. I never did other drugs, I've never done cocaine or even marijuana. But this was so deeply embedded into my system that when a trigger occurred—it could be the newspaper (women in their underwear) or just wanting to have fun and relax—I would want to do this. The feelings would kind of start in my neck and go down into my chest. It was almost like an outside force, beyond my control. I realize now that I will probably always have this addiction. I will always be in recovery. I think the best way of describing this is that it's kind of like the old Marlon Brando movies of having malaria. Once you get malaria, some stress or whatever will fire that stuff up. I will always have it. I realize that I will never be recovered. I will always be in recovery.

Caren's and Tom's stories both show the tremendous power object sex can have for sex addicts. Nor is this rare. For example, 54 percent of the men and 66 percent of the women reported the use of objects as part of masturbation. Although 31 percent of the men and 23 percent of the women engaged in sexual activity with animals to some degree, women ranked it as more powerful in their addiction.

SEX WITH CHILDREN

To most people, as unimaginable as violence, pain, and object sex may seem, sex with children is most repugnant of all. Yet 30 percent of the men and 14 percent of the women surveyed indicated having sex with a consenting minor. If an addict had an intense child focus, that addict probably was sexual in front of children, shared

inappropriate sexual information with children, and used child pornography obsessively. A minority of that group also forced sexual
activities on children in or outside their family.

Our professional distinction between pedophilia and incest often
obscures a reality that emerged in our survey: some people are
sexually oriented toward children in general. Complex reasons exist
for a sexual orientation toward children. And the sexual abuse of
children does not necessarily mean addiction is present. However,
sexual abuse of children violates one of our culture's greatest taboos, which invests it with danger, fear, and excitement—key esca-
lators of erotic excitement. Vulnerability and a history of having
been abused as a child are also important elements.

Abused as a boy, Nick was extremely promiscuous as a teen-
ager and obsessed with young boys as an adult. He told us of his
first encounter:

> My first victim I was involved with over a four-year pe-
> riod, and I was totally "in love" with this young boy. I
> spent countless amounts of money, time, and energy work-
> ing on him and manipulating him into performing sexual
> acts with me. I had a lot I was gambling with, including my
> career and my family.

Knowing there could be consequences did not stop him. For five
years Nick worked for the Boy Scouts of America and thus had
constant access to boys. He reported, "I would sneak in touches and
have a lot of horseplay and mess around with the boys." Some he
was able to be sexual with. This was followed by an eighteen-month
stint as a volunteer in a Big Brother program.

On April 3, 1982, Nick was married. On May 4, 1982, he was
arrested for his behavior. The marriage survived both treatment and
prison. In recovery, his marriage thrives. He is a father to one
daughter, and his career is a success—none of which he would have
believed possible. Yet he acknowledged that "for the rest of my life I
will have to live with the pain of what I did and how I victimized
those boys."

Nick's story underlines the importance of understanding the
sexual orientation toward children. He reported that if he had had
access to child pornography, he knew he would have been hooked
on it. We heard a similar statement from Caren, who was described

earlier. Her obsession and shame around her desire for child pornography helped her to identify her powerlessness: "I never used any kind of pornography about children, but that's what all my fantasies revolved around. If that had been available to me, I'm sure it would have been my favorite kind of pornography. I felt a lot of guilt about that." We found child pornography highly related to other forms of sex with children.

In Chapter Three we will explore extensively the role of child abuse in the genesis of addiction. Here our focus is on the role that eroticization of children can have in addictive obsession.

ADDICTION-PRONE, DEVIANT, OR HEALTHY SEX?

The eleven behavioral types raise questions about what constitutes a healthy relationship to sex. That individuals deviate from the norm doesn't make them bad—nor does it make them sex addicts. Only an out-of-control pattern along with the other classic signs of addiction—obsession, powerlessness, and use of sex as a means to relieve pain—indicate the presence of sexual addiction. The eleven behavioral types are addiction prone, that is, they tend to lead to compulsive patterns. In particular, six characteristics, shared by many of the behavioral types, create vulnerability to addiction:

1. *Exploitation of others*. Many of the behaviors take advantage of vulnerability or victimize through intrusion or the use of power. The sexual addict repeats his or her experiences of childhood victimization, now becoming the perpetrator.

2. *Nonmutuality*. The behaviors involve inequality or isolation. They typically do not result in intimacy or increased emotional closeness.

3. *Objectification*. Many of the behaviors dehumanize others, making them into objects. Sex objects are easier to exploit, allow for greater risks, and do not disrupt an addict's sexual trance by requiring a response.

4. *Dissatisfaction*. The behaviors often leave people in despair, yet wanting more. This dissatisfaction stems partly from the lack of

meaning inherent in impersonal sexual contact and partly from the fact that sexual pleasure only anesthetizes the pain, without ever healing it.

5. *Intensification of shame.* The behaviors create shame and secrecy, key ingredients in addiction. With a diminished sense of self, addicts are less able to set appropriate boundaries, except those that reduce the risk of being discovered.

6. *Basis in fear.* Dangerous, risky, and illicit behaviors generate fear. Excitement and arousal are directly related to how much fear exists.

Consider the following pairs of examples. Imagine sexually touching an unknown person in a crowd and acting as if it were an accident. Then imagine sexually touching someone who has asked you to touch them, someone who clearly is sharing your excitement. Or, contrast exposing yourself to people who do not wish to see you with undressing in front of your partner before having sex. Common to each situation is excitement. But sexual addiction always involves exploitation, dissatisfaction, shame, fear, objectification, and a lack of mutual consent. Healthy sex almost always involves the opposite.

In addition, many of the behaviors discussed are conducive to addicts falling into trances. Crossdressing is a good example. In many cultures men wear clothing that is feminine by Western standards. There is nothing particularly erotic about such clothing. Even in our own culture, women may wear men's clothing and appear highly fashionable. So what is it about crossdressing that can be so addictive? Says Tom: "I wonder why women don't have the equivalent fetish of getting turned on by wearing men's clothes? Maybe it's because they're perfectly capable of wearing men's clothes in our society without it being shameful."

The answer is that the behavior itself isn't bad or wrong. Rather, an individual's belief system makes his or her behavior emotionally loaded. If people see their behavior as shameful or fearful, that can propel their eroticism into a compulsive spiral. Addicts literally enter a trance which objectifies others and isolates themselves. While searing in its pleasure, such a trance is profound in its lack of satisfaction. And the addict is profoundly powerless to sop. An addict will violate his or her own values as well as the rights of others in order to maintain the behaviors.

Some critics of the concept of sexual addiction assert that labeling undesirable sexual behavior as an illness is simply pathologizing deviance. They see sex addiction as a concept rooted in an intolerant medical establishment ignorant of sexual practices in other cultures. Worse, they fear, it is an expression of the fundamentalist, conservative, and sex-negative attitudes of the eighties, an example of the pendulum swinging too far away from the sexual liberation of the sixties. These critics have failed to see or have misunderstood significant breakthroughs in our knowledge of human sexual behavior and of addiction. Moreover, they miss the desperate need of hundreds of thousands of people.

In order to clarify the issues as well as underline the significance of the behavioral types, we need to see sex addiction as part of the general evolution of our knowledge of addiction.

THE BEHAVIORAL TYPES AND THE ADDICTIVE PROCESS

In *Craving for Ecstasy*, Milkman and Sunderwirth synthesize much of the progress in the neurochemistry of addiction by describing three basic types:

1. *The arousal addictions*—including compulsive gambling, stimulant drugs, sex, and high-risk behaviors

2. *The satiation addictions*—including compulsive overeating, alcohol, and depressant drugs

3. *The fantasy addictions*—including psychedelics, marijuana, and artistic and mystical preoccupation

They characterize sexual love as the "pièce de résistance" of the addictions because it spans all three major neuropathways:

It is love's unequaled capacity to profoundly influence each of the three pleasure planes—arousal, satiation, and fantasy—that qualifies it as the *pièce de résistance* among the addictions. While the human inclination toward intimate

pairing affixes a territory within which mating can occur, it
also holds the trigger to the most primitive impulses on
earth. An instant of reflection on love's hearty contribution
to homicide and suicide reminds us of the horrifying consequences of uncontrolled passion.

Milkman and Sunderwirth crystallize a major concept in addiction emerging out of the intense scholarly activities of the eighties:
different addictions tap into the same brain chemistry. And sex is one
of the most potent.

The eleven behavioral types span the three types of addictions.
Some sex addicts are lost in fantasy. Others become caught up in
high levels of arousal because of danger, shame, and risk. Yet
others use sex as a sedative to medicate personal pain and anxiety.
As research efforts unfold, we will probably discover that sex addicts mix and match behavioral focuses to fit their neurochemical
ends of escape, stimulation, or release.

Further, we will notice that shifting from one addictive behavior
to another also shifts neuropathway patterns. New questions will
emerge about the relationships among the addictions. Notice that in
many of our examples, addicts had more than one behavioral focus
and more than one addiction. For example, the exposer experiencing high arousal because of increased risk may use a mixture of alcohol
and fantasy sex as a way to medicate and escape the profound
shame. The addictions offer multiple ways to regulate personal
emotions. Sex addiction is perhaps the most flexible.

ADDICTION ACROSS GENERATIONS

To complete the picture, we asked our survey respondents
about their families of origin. This information further expands our
understanding of both the addict's addiction and larger addictive
patterns within families. We asked addicts with significant recovery
(three-plus years) to indicate who else was addicted in their family.
Table 2-5 summarizes their answers to questions about sexual addiction, alcoholism, and compulsive overeating. In these three areas
alone, there is an extraordinary pattern of multiple addictions, with

22 percent of the mothers, 40 percent of the fathers, and 56 percent of the siblings having more than one addiction.

TABLE 2-5
ADDICTIONS OF OTHER FAMILY MEMBERS

ADDICTION	% MOTHERS	% FATHERS	% SIBLINGS
Sexual	18	40	50
Alcohol	25	38	46
Overeating	43	24	37
More than 1	22	40	56

Here is clear evidence of the transgenerational power of addictive patterns. Early in alcoholism research, the question emerged of whether the illness stems from nature or nurture. Is it a matter of genetics or of family environment? Studies of genetic transmission in alcoholism, such as research in adoption, clearly show a genetic factor. Very clear documentation of the power of family environment also exists. In summarizing research into addictions, Milkman and Sunderwirth observe that parents are responsible for both genetics and environment, so one "must pick one's parents very carefully."

In view of brain chemistry and the coexistence of multiple addictions, we can suggest a model for a common pattern of acquisition:

Genetic predisposition—inherited genetic structure

↓

Neurochemical vulnerability—neurochemical deficits are created

↓

Neurochemical change—prolonged abuse of excessive "highs" alter neurochemical balance

↓

Neurochemical imbalance—addiction serves to preserve imbalance so addict can feel normal

Genetic predisposition leads to the creation of neurochemical deficits. These deficits make a person particularly vulnerable to situational and environmental stress. The potential addict may excessively use "highs" over a period of time to combat the stress. The prolonged abuse of the highs then alters the neurochemical balance. The continued use of highs to compensate preserves this imbalance, and addiction results. The addict now needs the highs to feel normal. To reverse the process—that is, undergo withdrawal—is too painful. Of course, multiple addictions can serve as multiple pathways to preserve the imbalance. Such a model would help explain what we observed among sex addicts: they used sex to regulate their emotional lives; they became powerless over their sexual choices; they used sex in a number of different ways; they used different types of sex; and they augmented their use of sex with other addictions.

CHAPTER THREE

Unmanageability: Costs and Consequences

The founders of AA created the twin pillars of our understanding of addictions when they described how addicts had to admit both that they had become "powerless" and that their lives had become "unmanageable." For most sex addicts this means that their sexual behavior has started to cause trouble. Usually this trouble comes in the form of consequences or losses. Something happened that stripped away the secrecy, compromised them in some way, or affected their health.

Sometimes the trouble becomes public. Recent stories from across the country include these:

- A teenage boy was discovered dead by his mother; he was in the bathroom hanging nude from his belt. His death was among the up to one thousand deaths a year from autoerotic asphyxia. Like other victims, he was enhancing his masturbation by reducing the oxygen flow to his brain. He misjudged and strangled himself.

- A Catholic priest attending a national conference visited an adult bookstore. He stumbled, fell, and died of a traumatic injury to the head. Newspaper accounts described him as specially loved by family, friends, and parishioners but also indicate he was tormented by feelings of unworthiness to be a priest.

- A noted sex therapist in a major industrial city, well-known for his work with sexual dysfunction, was arrested in an adult bookstore for soliciting an undercover police officer for sex. His colleagues were uncertain of how to proceed, because of his professional standing and because his behavior did not involve patients.

- A respected clergyman assumed leadership of an antipornography commission in a southeastern state and developed a following as an effective speaker on the issue. He was arrested for the distribution and production of child pornography. Stunned readers of news accounts tried to make sense of the difference between his public and private behavior.

- An employee of a large retail chain won a sexual harassment suit of 3.2 million dollars because of her former manager's behavior. A federal government study of civil service employees documented 267 million dollars in lost productivity and turnover in two years because of sexual harassment.

- A state board for licensing physicians in a northeastern state was forced to bring separate charges of sexual misconduct against nine psychiatrists. Five of the psychiatrists were heads of agencies or hospital programs, and four were associated with a prestigious Ivy League medical school.

Political figures, religious leaders, Hollywood stars, and re-spected business leaders have had stories appear about their sexual escapades: womanizing, paying prostitutes, buying pornography—being caught doing the wrong thing at the wrong time. Many people regard these stories with the cynicism of the times, saying that is the way things are or that the incident was unfortunate.

Those who understand this illness recognize patterns that es-cape the attention of others: ongoing risky behavior, revelations of other addictive behavior, losses because of sexual acting out, and pain at living a double life. After a friend told the Catholic priest described above, for example, about all those who loved him, he could only respond, "I just don't feel good. If they really knew what was inside of me, they couldn't love me." Such statements provide the perceptive reader with clues to the existence of the double life of addiction. Media stories become more than isolated events. They represent the tip of a pathology that runs through our culture.

Public awareness of alcoholism and drug dependency has given us new lenses with which to view public events. An expanded awareness would allow us to see other ways addiction works to compromise the lives of some of our most competent and admired public figures. However, powerful cultural forces keep us all in denial. We live in an addiction-prone culture, in which the unmanageability of an addict's problems does not stand out. To confront that denial we have to face some of our most basic social and cultural assumptions.

THE ADDICTIVE CULTURE

If we were to design a society in which addiction could optimally thrive, many of the components required already exist in our own. An often-asked question is whether we are seeing more addiction because of our increased awareness or because the number of addicts is increasing. The answer is probably both. But many of the factors that contribute to the growth of addiction also block our awareness. Here are some of the key components of our society that allow addiction to thrive:

- Ours is a *convenience-oriented culture* dedicated to removing obstacles to satisfaction. Everything from oil changes to food preparation can be done with little effort. Driven by the convenience ethic, the addict simply extends *quick-fix* logic to reducing anxiety.

- Our culture emphasizes *sophisticated technology* and assumes that technology can resolve all problems. Oil spills, cancer, AIDS, or the ozone layer—whatever the crisis, we do not face the realities, because of our misplaced confidence that someone will come up with a technological breakthrough. *Easy solutions* have become a way of life in the postindustrial society.

- Our culture seeks *entertainment and escapism* rather than searching for meaning. Storytellers in other cultures and in earlier stages of our own told tales that were not only entertaining but also created meaning or imparted skills or history. Most important, as they were told and retold, the stories bonded people to the community. Contemporary storytellers most often seek only to entertain. They create unreal scenarios which have little to do with the lives most of us lead. Movies, television, novels, and magazines that do not provide meaning or bonding contribute to a *lack of meaning*, which the sociologist Durkheim termed *anomie*, the state of meaningless that precedes suicide.

- Our culture is experiencing massive *paradigm shifts*, which means that our view of the world is constantly changing. Every time we have a technological breakthrough, our view of the world is in some way challenged. We still, for example, are intensely at odds over birth control. Gene splicing, supercomputers, nuclear power, surrogate mothers, and space technology all challenge traditional value systems. The result is an ongoing *values confusion*, which adds to the difficulty of living.

- Our culture reels from *disrupted family life*. Two out of every three first marriages end in divorce. Fifty-four percent of all marriages are dual career (which for many means that the woman does two jobs, family and work). We still have significant gaps in our ability to provide day care. Worse, this is the first time in history we have asked just two people (a couple) to raise children, let alone single parents. Parents in the eighteenth century had more child care options than we do now. The result is pervasive feelings of *abandonment*, which is the core of addictive longing.

- Our culture is experiencing *the loss of community*. The average executive changes jobs every eighteen months, and the average family moves every three years. Sociologists tell us that it takes three years to build a support network in a community. The disintegration of community networks results in *isolation*, a precondition of child abuse, battering, and addiction.

- Ours is a culture of *high stress*. People live overextended, overcommitted lives or, alternatively, are in a bitter battle to eke out survival. The context for this personal stress is national economic struggle, international competition, and global tension. This context is underlined by our news media, which tend to focus on crisis, disaster, and threat. The result is a chronic *anxiety*, which commingles with our shared existential dreads and our unique individual fears.

- Our culture is *exploitive* of others. Wherever oppression or economic disadvantage exists, there is ingrained cynicism about people's concern for others. Even if we are not victims, our experience parallels that of the sibling in the abusive family who himself was not abused. Being in the environment promotes distrust, and it is *distrust* upon which addiction feeds.

- Our culture essentially *denies limitations*, including even death. Denial of human limits gives us unrealistic perceptions of what we can handle or achieve. Mental health and addiction problems thrive when there are *no limits*.

- We live in a culture in which there are *many addicts*. Start with gambling, sex, food, and chemicals, take into account that many addicts have more than one addiction, then include all those affected by addicts, such as the 28 million adult children of alcoholics. A recent estimate of all the addicts in our culture places addicts and those affected by addiction at over 131 million people. When over half the population is involved with addiction, *addictive norms* become central to the cultural experience.

Table 3-1 summarizes cultural characteristics and the corresponding addictive characteristics. We need to acknowledge not only that our culture supports addiction, but also that the most troublesome trends are increasing in importance. This connection becomes absolutely crucial in understanding how addiction evolves. It is not simply neurochemistry or family impact but a complex ecology, one of the most significant elements of which is culture.

When it comes to sexual issues, cultural influences are obvious. The glamorization of sex extends far beyond women's magazines in which a female's self-worth is contingent upon her looks and men's magazines in which a male's self-worth is contingent upon his ability to seduce good-looking women. It extends beyond commercials which use sexual turn-ons to sell, soap operas with unending sexual sagas, and gossip-oriented media with the latest tales to tell.

Glamorization can be seen in the portrayal of prostitution as a high-paying, exciting career option for those who dare to risk their reputations. The Mayflower Madam epitomizes this image of the sexual entrepreneur who hobnobs with the power brokers and lives in high fashion. The movie *Nuts,* with Barbra Streisand, powerfully portrays the connection between sexual abuse and prostitution, but

TABLE 3-1
CORRESPONDENCES BETWEEN THE CULTURE AND THE ADDICT

CULTURE	ADDICT
Convenience	Quick fix
Confidence in technology	Easy solutions
Entertainment before meaning	Lack of meaning
Paradigm shifts	Values confusion
Disrupted family life	Abandonment
Loss of community	Isolation
High stress	Anxiety
Exploitation	Distrust
Denial of limitation	No limits
Addicts in population	Addictive norms

also a posh lifestyle that looks very attractive. Similarly, TV series that portray the good life as the pursuit of excitement typically use sexual excitement as a counterpoint to the adventure.

More subtle is when sexual excitement becomes a solution. In a recent study, alcoholism researchers found that in the average episode of *Dallas* characters had a combined total of thirteen drinks to cope with anxiety. What the researchers did not count was the use of sex to cope with crisis and fear. When J. R. Ewing's empire is on the brink of disaster, he finds a woman he has some control over and has sex with her. At the conclusion of the sexual episode he does something "dastardly" that puts distance between himself and the woman. J.R. can smile once again, for he has regrouped psychologically to face the crisis.

Beyond being glamorous, then, sex becomes a solution, a way to cope with life's challenges. We have made extraordinary progress with sexual liberation, helping people to talk frankly about sexual functioning and to overcome obstacles to their sexual happiness; we have supported sexual growth as part of a more holistic approach to medicine. Yet with all the positives, we have failed to see that the glamorization of sex can mask compulsive preoccupation.

With all addictions, the most concrete form of cultural support is peer support. Peer support draws upon both healthy and unhealthy forces in the culture to make what the addict is doing okay. With sex addiction, peer support can include:

- sexual partners who are part of the acting out

- friends who are conspiratorial in their affairs

- a group of professional colleagues who hire teenage prostitutes for a party

- swinging groups whose purpose is to develop a network based on sex encounters

- patrons of bathhouses used for anonymous sex

What the peers do not see is just how out of control the addicts and their problems are. The addicts' shame—also derived from cultural standards—keeps the true extent of their behavior hidden. Consider a married woman who is having affairs. With each of her partners, she has a "meaningful" discussion of the legitimacy of the affair and how they cannot deny their feelings for each other. They may discuss the inevitability of the affair given the nature of marriage, the problems in their own marriages, the fact that 74 percent of married people have affairs, or even the conviction that they must have been partners in a previous life. What her partners do not realize is that each is one of five men having the same conversation with her that week. If each knew about the others, those rationales would look very different. But she knows and feels very alone in her secret knowledge.

Consider a group of attorneys who regularly gather for lunch and play the "rating" game over lunch. They scan the room, rating women on a one-to-ten scale. They even pull the waitress into the game by flirting with her, rating others in front of her, and giving her a high rating if she is responsive. The group with the right waitress finds it very titillating to tell her she is a 9.5 on their scale—sort of a fantasy gang rape they share. For most of these men, it is "harmless" chauvinism and "male bonding." The waitress is likely to feel violated and angry inside, yet she goes along with a smile because that is what management requires and what waitresses endure for good tips.

One of the attorneys, however, always finds himself super-stimulated. Lunch with the guys is followed by a visit to the massage parlor for a "hand job" or "topless local." The masseuse responds just as the waitress did. She is angry on the inside but smiles because she can make five hundred dollars for a day of part-time work. So somehow she feels "familiar" to him. When finished, he feels shameful. Upon returning to work he has neither the energy nor the time to prepare adequately for his court appearance the next morning. As a result, his court appearance goes badly, which adds to his feelings of inadequacy and isolation.

If his peers knew the costs to him—up to three hundred dollars a week, untold losses in his practice, and a pain which he is unable to communicate to his spouse or friends—they might view the lunches differently. The male fellowship takes on a different cast. But the only person knowing the whole story is the addict, who feels shame at not being able to limit his behavior.

The irony is that culture is what people have in common. When addicts draw upon the culture and their peers for support, their own denial and justification for the behavior is reinforced. They end up in isolation, estranged from others. Addicts draw upon their peer group to support their denial but remain isolated because of the secrets they have about their behavior. Support turns into estrangement because addicts use the support to feel better about what they know is self-destructive. The result is that pressures from the addictive culture are focused by the peer group but transformed by the addiction into intense loneliness:

Addictive culture—supports out-of-control behavior

↓

Peer support—draws on cultural values to reinforce addictive behavior

↓

Isolation—comes from secrets addicts keep from peers and others about how bad things are

WHEN DENIAL FAILS

While peers and countervailing cultural winds may defuse and obscure the desperation of addicts, they do know they are in trouble. Denial evaporates when there is a catastrophe or near catastrophe. When the costs become so great that the outlines of unmanageable behavior are unmistakable, the addict truly knows his or her powerlessness. The addict may make new resolves and fresh starts, but despair about past failed attempts eats like acid at hopes for change. The following statements from recovering people describe moments when consequences of their behavior brought them to a bottom point. Remember, these are but isolated events of larger, painful stories. But these events are those very painful moments when each addict realized the costs were too great.

ADDICTS' MOST UNMANAGEABLE MOMENTS

I found people were lying for me at work to cover for my absences.

I lost a job at eighteen for sexual liberties with a customer.

I had a crisis with the promiscuity of my daughter who at age fifteen was doing exactly what I did.

I lost our family business.

I had two pregnancies in two years, giving up both children for adoption.

I was rejected by roommates several times because of sexual behavior.

I realized that my exhaustion from sexual cruising was seriously affecting my work.

I realized I lost three marriages all because of affairs.

I had six abortions.

I became suicidal because of multiple intense involvements.

I was being sexual with my therapist and two of my graduate professors at the same time.

I was kicked out of bars because of being publicly sexual.

I had to drop out of school because I could not concentrate because of my obsessive fantasies.

I could not come straight home from work without cruising—sometimes all night.

I spent money on sex when I needed it for children's clothes.

I would be exhausted from loss of sleep from masturbating all night.

I lost so much time cruising for hookers.

I did not know which man was the father of my child.

I could not tell my husband about abortions during our marriage.

I failed my senior year of high school.

I believe that my compulsive masturbation created circumstances leading to the death of my infant twins.

I stayed in my marriage despite destructive sex.

I went to porno movies during work time although I did not want to.

I crossed professional boundaries with my patients.

I got herpes and gave it to my spouse.

I was married in September and arrested one month later.

I made a series of bad business decisions because of sexual stuff.

I had no girlfriends due to stealing their boyfriends.

I lost promotion opportunities and a special scholarship because my co-workers found out about my sex life.

I had two lovers show up at work, one at the back door and one at the front.

I was constantly late for work or too tired to work.

I stayed out all night and slept all day with kids to care for.

I realized I had a pattern of changing jobs every two or three years because of sexual complications.

I lost whole weekends in bed with multiple partners.

I took minimal jobs to have more time to obsess.

I had a Ph.D. and was working as a cleaning lady vacuuming offices.

The list shows the tremendous array of problems caused by addictive behavior. Work, friendships, family relationships, school, health, and finances were all affected by the addiction's unmanageability. From the addicts' point of view, there is a definite hierarchy of losses in terms of the amount of pain involved. Our survey revealed that out of the many losses addicts experience, ten were the most painful. In order of priority they are:

1. Loss of primary relationships

2. Loss of children (including abortions, deaths, and loss of custody)

3. Loss of significant friends

4. Unavailability to children (including neglect)

5. Financial losses

6. Guilt of having hurt others (including victims and sex partners)

7. Loss of productivity and creativity

8. Career losses

9. Loss of integrity (including violations of personal values)

10. Loss of self-esteem

Notice that all but one of the top six have to do with key relationships. Of the top four, two have to do with children. One of the most common themes that emerged from our research was grieving about children. Addicts were very clear about the damage to their offspring, especially through neglect. If loss of children and neglect were combined, this would be the number one source of pain for addicts.

Other problem areas, which may not have ranked as high in personal pain, were nonetheless critical for getting help. Physical complications like sexually transmitted diseases or personal injury often were the first step toward getting help. Financial losses and productivity or career problems also forced addicts to look for assistance. While we are nowhere near being able to estimate the cost to society in health care or business losses, our research helped develop a clearer picture by documenting personal costs. We can start with what sex addicts reported about their physical well-being.

PHYSICAL PROBLEMS

Many addicts receive care from health professionals and their secret world remains intact. Physicians who specialize in sex addiction report that when training urologists or OB/GYN specialists, they often hear, "I have three people like that in my practice right now." Doctors in clinical settings focus on the biological issues and tend not to explore the behavioral.

Sexually transmitted diseases are a common problem among addicts. In our survey 38 percent of the men and 45 percent of the women contracted venereal diseases as part of their addictive behavior. Furthermore, 64 percent of the addicts reported that they continued their sexual behavior despite the risk of disease or infection. Knowing the probabilities does not stop the behavior. This characteristic of sex addicts is one of the more frightening aspects of the AIDS epidemic. In our sample, 3 percent had AIDS or were seropositive. It should be kept in mind that our survey respondents were a group who had already modified their behaviors considerably. The fear is that those still active in their addiction will contribute to the spread of AIDS. The 3 percent in our sample may be but a foreshadowing of things to come.

Pregnancy is another reality of sex that addicts in their denial would choose to ignore. In our sample, 40 percent of the women had unwanted pregnancies; 36 percent of them had abortions. As mentioned, grief over children lost was a recurrent theme. Although often children had been lost through divorce or death, clearly this sense of children conceived in obsession and the resulting high abortion rate exacted a high level of shame, rage, and guilt.

One woman told us, "I had two illegitimate children I relinquished for adoption. I felt like that labeled me as this horrible person because I couldn't control myself. Add to that the loss of

having two children [and] you don't even know if they're dead or
alive or what's going on with them."

Almost 70 percent of the women routinely risked unwanted
pregnancy by not using birth control. Fern, a forty-six-year-old
Catholic nun. tells a very painful story about the unmanageability of
her sex addiction. Pregnancy did not fit with the vow of celibacy—
yet she lived with the fear. Addictive denial kept her unprotected.
She told us, "I was so fearful of being pregnant yet I never took
precautions against pregnancy because I was never going to have
intercourse again. I never took birth control because that would
have been permission for me to have sex." Yet she had sex, over
and over again.

At one point she was having an affair with a married man who
belonged to the parish and whose children attended the parochial
school where she taught. She also was having affairs with a woman
in the parish and a Sister in the convent. She describes the extremes she was willing to go to:

> Feeling so much guilt and shame about it and yet sneaking
> out of the convent at night and seeing him, lying and also
> being so confused because I was being sexual with a
> woman and then being sexual with him and being obsessed
> with sex. Thinking about it all the time. Then there was a
> Sister that I was with, too, in that very same house; I
> introduced being sexual to her. I wanted to stop. This was
> like over a year and a half period of time. In my desperation,
> I made many promises to myself that I wasn't going to do
> this anymore, but then I would always be breaking them. I
> just thought if I had a more strict reminder. I took a razor
> blade and cut crosses on the inside of my thighs. On each
> thigh, just to help me realize in some way that I had said
> that I would not be sexual, and so I had a double guilt of
> not only sinning but breaking my vow. So for me that was
> more mountains of shame for what was happening. It was
> very, very painful because I was living a real hypocritical life,
> on the outside being a Sister and going to Mass every day,
> at night being very sexual.

Fern's story introduces another element of physical damage
stemming from the addiction. Fern had been sexually abused in

childhood, and she cut herself. Many addicts use self-mutilation as a way to control themselves sexually. The ultimate expression of sexual self-hatred, these self-destructive efforts create even more problems. Nor are they the only types of physical harm. Some sexual activities caused physical harm because of their violence, use of objects, or inherent danger. Sometimes accidents occurred because of sexual behavior (driving while masturbating, for example). Table 3-2 summarizes some of the physical harm documented in our survey.

TABLE 3-2
PHYSICAL HARM

	% MEN	% WOMEN
Physical injury to genitals, breasts, colon, etc.	30	38
Victim of rape	7	50
Self-abuse (e.g., cutting, burning, bruising)	9	36
Victim of physical abuse by another person	16	60
Involvement in potentially abusive or dangerous situations	44	79
Vehicle accidents	19	21

Addicts reported various ways in which their addiction affected their health. Almost one-third related serious health problems, such as ulcers or high blood pressure, connected to addictive acting out. They also repeatedly made the connection between being physically exhausted and being vulnerable to sickness. Fifty-seven percent of those in our survey reported such periods of physical depletion.

One of the more remarkable health facts to emerge is that sex addicts have serious problems with sleep. Sixty-five percent of addicts reported sleep disorders. Usually the pattern involved not being able to sleep because of stress and shame around the addiction and also the use of sex as a way to reduce tension in order to sleep. Many addicts are relieved to learn that they are not alone in their disrupted sleep patterns. As most therapists familiar with the illness are well aware, sleeplessness becomes a very severe problem during the withdrawal period. In fact a key research question is how the addict's sleep disorders are connected with the neurochemistry of the addiction.

Pregnancies, abortions, injuries, accidents, AIDS, disease, other addictions, major health problems—no one knows the cost to our health care system. It took decades for us to understand the extraordinary health care costs of alcoholism. Even now alcoholism professionals have difficulty convincing health care providers that many physical problems can be traced to compulsive drinking. We are at an even more primitive stage with sex addiction. Surveys such as this however, are beginning to document the extraordinary cost to all of us.

FINANCIAL COSTS

Sex addiction costs addicts in many ways. The most direct expenses are sexual. Prostitution, massage parlors, bathhouses, pornography, sex toys, and dial-a-porn services can be very expensive. This kind of spending was done mostly by men. It was not unusual for male addicts in the survey to have a thousand-dollar-a-month prostitution habit; one spent as much as four to five thousand dollars a month. Nor were pornography collections valued in six figures unusual. To support such cash outlays, many addicts stole from employers or from family funds.

Addicts also reported spending on extravagant gifts for lovers, repairs for car accidents, car expenses for cruising, divorce expenses, moving expenses for geographic changes, and trips to meet lovers. Frequently mentioned were expenses for therapy and treatment which did not help. There were also tales of blackmail, theft, and credit cards stolen from victimized addicts who often were too shamed to report the losses. In all, 56 percent of our respondents experienced severe financial difficulty because of their addiction.

By far the biggest losses recorded were in the workplace. Although the main loss in the workplace was time some addicts lost their jobs and some even lost whole businesses. Impropriety on the job cost some people opportunities; others, such as physicians, nurses, and therapists, lost professional licenses. Almost all talked of not being able to function up to their potential. A few very highly trained persons ended up doing menial tasks, such as the Ph.D. who worked cleaning offices. Eighty percent of sex addicts reported a loss of productivity. Eleven percent said they were actually demoted. The statements listed below give some sense of the costs of sex addiction in the workplace.

JOB UNMANAGEABILITY

Twice I lost jobs because of involvement with the boss.

Could not stop an affair with husband's professor which led to his being fired.

Left work for three days to rest. Came back exhausted from cruising.

Masturbating on the job.

Would forget important messages because of preoccupation.

Work took longer; accuracy suffered.

Disciplined at work for too much tardiness and too much personal time on phone (because of multiple affairs).

Fantasizing about men I had, I lost ability to concentrate.

Phone calls to partners interfered with work.

Put off tasks because of fantasy life.

Was unable to work (sometimes for weeks) because of obsessions about women at work.

Left "must" work undone to act out.

Abandoned work frequently to pursue sex.

Neglected ordinary duties, blamed others, and dumped responsibilities on others.

Exhausted, angry, and full of shame, I wasn't able to work.

Unable to travel for work without losing control.

Loss of sleep caused work to suffer.

Unable to keep appointments because of watching movies or cruising.

Obsessing about and sexualizing people I work with professionally.

Planned week's schedule around affairs.

Emotional and physical absence from work caused problems.

Unmanageability crosses over many categories. Physical problems have an impact on work. Consider the story of Cathy, a thirty-seven-year-old manager of a boutique chain, who was married and the mother of a child. Cathy's unmanageability made her aware of how powerless she was:

> I got syphilis and herpes. I went to all the men I slept with and talked to them about it, which was very difficult and painful. Realizing how many there had been in the past three months, I knew it would all have to stop and I couldn't do this anymore. But I couldn't stop. I felt like a little bird looking in the snake's eyes. I just couldn't move, couldn't tell someone to stop, or not touch me, or not do something.
>
> I was into risk. Dressing seductively, dancing exhibitionistically. I considered being a topless dancer. Like once having an affair with my husband's best friend and, while my husband's asleep upstairs, screwing the guy on the sofa downstairs. A lot of risk-taking sorts of things like that. Or being sexual in my office at work, with the door open.
>
> Realizing after I had syphilis, I had to deal with all that, saying "Hey, this has got to stop," I said to the man I was involved with four years, "Hey, this is reality, you're married you have kids, you can't do this." And both of us not being able to stop.
>
> At that point my job situation was a disaster. I was so far behind in my paperwork, I thought I could never catch up. I would get more and more depressed about that. I functioned less and less at work. I'd spend a half a day sitting just sort of staring into space. I would be either writing love letters or be spaced out or be exhausted because I'd been up all night. I wasn't sleeping. I was up till three dragging into work or not dragging into work.

Cathy, like other addicts, found that physical problems like herpes and syphilis added to the sleeplessness, exhaustion, and inability to function.

The nature of the survey population underscores the impact of sex addiction on the workplace. As noted earlier, survey respondents tended to be highly educated professionals. So we know that people functioning at high levels can be affected. At the same time, over one-fifth of the respondents linked their sexual addiction to failing grades, dropping out of school, and lost opportunities. For both high performance and low performance groups, the same key questions emerge. What potential is lost by society or individuals because of sex addiction? What will it take for us to be able to identify patterns when we see them in the workplace or in the health clinic? How can we document the damage?

EMOTIONAL COSTS

Yet another area of unmanageability is incalculable in its costs. The emotional damage to the addict provides fundamental energy to the addictive process itself.

Jeanine taught school in a small, conservative midwestern town, but her life was far from conservative. She participated in the basic double life of the sex addict and felt the penetrating sting of the addict's loneliness:

> Total, total loneliness. My phone never rang unless it was somebody who was calling me to be sexual. I didn't have friends. I had two lives. One was sexual. In the other I had a professional life where I was known in many towns and through my course work and my graduate work and through belonging to organizations. I was known for my devotedness to my profession and my energy and my workaholism. At that time I was really a workaholic. It was the only thing I had.

Jeanine was so ashamed of her life, she felt undeserving of a loving partner. Many addicts struggle with an image of what they want in their lives but feel too unworthy to have. When they meet someone who seems to represent the life they have always wanted, they find a myriad of obsessive ways to reject him or her. Their damaged self-concept and feelings of unworthiness stem partly from messages addicts internalize from the dysfunctional families in which they were raised. Addiction confirms these feelings and deepens them in profound ways. Addicts are not able to accept real intimacy because of a core certainty that they will be rejected. They opt instead for the neurochemical highs of danger, risk, abuse, and pain and the temporary relief of escape. Becoming further isolated because of their shame, they become even more desperate for relief. Jeanine describes the form this dilemma took for her:

One of my biggest personal losses was no intimate friendships. I kept just selling myself out. I knew in my heart of hearts that this wasn't what I wanted. I mean, I always had this fantasy of meeting this wonderful man, that I would be sexual with him, and it would turn out that he'd be good, good to me. And I finally did find a man who was a nice man and I couldn't stand him. Because he was too nice to me. It just made me furious that he didn't threaten to sexually abuse me or beat me up or shame me or belittle me or make fun of me.

And I saw him as sort of a eunuch. I just could not stand to have him touch me. I thought if he knew what sort of a whore I was—I really saw myself as a whore that didn't get paid. Actually I thought I was better than a prostitute because I didn't take money. I thought if he knew that's what I really thought of myself that he would not have anything to do with me. So I canned the relationship. I started seeing this other man, who I didn't even like, just to be sexual. Just to get that part satisfied.

I thought I was trash. I knew that he was valuable, but I knew he really belonged with someone else. I refused any attention he would give me. I remember sleeping with him once, and he just wanted to touch me—just lie by me and touch me and not be sexual. I couldn't receive that. And yet that's what I always wanted. Every time I was sexual with these men what I wanted was for them to just hold

me and touch me, and here's this man that will do it and it
was like you're not a man, because you don't want to fuck.
It was really—really black-and-white thinking.

When Jeanine talks of her loneliness she gives voice to the
experience of many addicts. Over half said they were not able to
sustain important friendships and had few nonsexual friends. Developing friendship is basic to intimacy.

If you cannot sustain friendships, you also cannot get the help
and support you need. Jeanine at one point was furious with one
lover for lying to her about his use of condoms. With that twisted
and perverse thought process so common in addictive thinking, she
retaliated by having unsafe sex with another man two days later.
The cosmic irony was that she got pregnant—out of rage at his
failure to use birth control.

She decided to seek an abortion because she did not wish to
face the judgment of a small rural town. She had no one to go with,
so she called a therapist, who was so moved by her plight that she
offered to go with her to the clinic. Jeanine never called her back.
She drove to the clinic in a major city ninety miles away, had the
abortion, and against the clinic's advice drove back home by herself.
She describes how terrifying it was to sign the waiver demanded by
the clinic. But she saw no choice except to leave alone.

Almost immediately there were complications to her surgery.
She was frantic to conceal her condition because she was now living
at home with her mother. While hemorrhaging, she drove in the
middle of winter to various pay phones to call the doctor to see what
she should do. So the terror and the loneliness continued.

Later, Jeanine became involved with a very violent man. He
would back her into a corner, beat her, or threaten her in some
way. And she kept going back because, as she said, "I knew I
wouldn't survive without the kind of sex I had with him. It was the
highest escalation of excitement, danger, and fear." Finally, Jeanine
sought the solution many addicts end up seeking: suicide. She ate a
bottle of aspirin and drank a jug of wine.

As she lay on her couch waiting to die, her father came over to
see if she was all right. Jeanine went into what she called her
"Barbie doll" routine and convinced her father she was okay. But it
was enough of an expression of care that she phoned the therapist
she had called when she was facing the abortion. This therapist—

whom she still had not gone to see—motivated her to survive. So she vomited, stayed home from work, and went right back to her abusive lover. Only this time it was different. "From that point on it was like an internal surrender. It was kind of like 'Kill me. It's okay.' "

Suicide and the desire to die became a haunting specter for many: 17 percent of addicts surveyed attempted suicide; 72 percent were obsessed with the idea. Over 50 percent of hospital in-patient admissions for sex addiction are due to severe depression. Table 3-3 summarizes addicts' responses to items concerning the emotional costs of their addiction. Taken together, they create a profile of desperation. While the percentages are consistently high, note that they are highest for loss of self-esteem, strong feelings of guilt and shame, and strong feelings of isolation and loneliness. What Jeanine and other addicts are telling us is that the unmanageability of their lives creates profound despair. Their lives are unraveling and they are ashamed. This sense of shame, intensified when their behavior becomes known by others, is one of the essential dynamics of sex addiction—and, indeed, of all addictions.

TABLE 3-3
EMOTIONAL COSTS

CATEGORY	% YES
Loss of self-esteem	97
Strong feelings of guilt and shame	96
Strong feelings of isolation and loneliness	94
Feelings of extreme hopelessness or despair	91
Acting against personal values and beliefs	90
Feeling like two people	88
Emotional exhaustion	83
Strong fears about own future	82
Emotional instability	78
Loss of life goals	68

THE SHAME DYNAMIC

Shame emerges from addiction. Shame causes addiction. Whichever way the shame is flowing, whether consequence or cause, it rests on one key personal assumption: Somehow I am not measuring up. This belief starts early in life. The addiction deepens the conviction.

At the same time our understanding of addiction has been growing, so has our understanding of shame and the shame-based personality. In fact, the expanding knowledge of addiction has been one of the principal factors in our full appreciation of the role shame plays in people's lives. The reason is simple. Shame-based people are particularly vulnerable to addiction and codependency. Sex can be one of the greatest sources of shame anyone has. Sexual addiction and sexual shame are interwoven at the most fundamental levels.

The great psychologist Erik Erikson defined the various stages of development that all of us pass through. He described each stage as a series of tasks that a person either does or doesn't work through. For example, the first stage is "trust versus mistrust." Children in the first year of life need to decide that their parents are trustworthy. Mistrust at this stage can haunt people across their life span. The second stage, equally significant, comes in the next two years of life, when the child faces the conflict of "autonomy versus shame." Basically children need to have a sense of mastery or competence. They need to be assured that they can do things for themselves. They get that assurance from people who care for them who acknowledge the simple things they do. If children succeed in developing this sense, they are on the road to independence or autonomy. If they do not, they will be plagued by self-doubt and vulnerable to dependency problems. The chief dependency problem, of course, is addiction. People who are addicted look for something to rely upon. And one thing about drugs, sex, food, and excitement, they always do what they promise. You can depend upon them. With them you learn to feel okay and competent. But then without them, you'll feel empty and defeated.

The shame-based child asks the question, "Why is it other kids can know the alphabet [substitute any task] and be accepted and I can't?" The question is replayed by the adult addict who asks, "Why is it others can drink appropriately [substitute eat, have sex, work] and I can't?" For addicts, the lack of success erodes even further any foundations of trust they may have had. And as their unmanageability is noticed by others, they become even more "ashamed."

All of this starts with the family environment. Parents need to be encouraging, supportive, and realistic about what a child can do. They also need to affirm standards that respect the internal life of the child. John Bradshaw, one of the pioneering voices in addiction and family life, makes this key point: "To be shame bound means that whenever you feel any feelings, any need, or any drive you immediately feel ashamed." In other words, if as part of mastering your little world as a child you were told that it was unacceptable to have feelings, to have needs, or to have drives—especially sexual drives—you were bound to end up shameful. Parents give their offspring significant gifts when they accept their emotional life and help them to meet their needs and regulate their appetites through affirming guidelines and reasonable expectations.

To fully understand the shame process, we must explore three aspects of the shame-based personality: doing things right, conditional love, and the amorphous ego.

DOING THINGS RIGHT

Shame is about lack of acceptance—acceptance of who you are and what you do. Some families get so focused on what children do, they miss who the children are. Worse, their expectations become too high because they want the best for them. Loving motivations become shaming demands. These are families in which performance counts more than the person. People are measured only by what they do. To use John Bradshaw's phrase, these families "turn human beings into human doings." Children in these families internalize the basic belief that they are what they do—and that they'd better do it right.

One of the ways children are taught to "do it right" is by not being allowed to make mistakes. The classic example is the child who is coloring in the coloring book and goes outside the lines because it looks better that way, then gets told that he has to stay within the lines. When the only acceptable standard of performance is perfection, perfectionism is what children learn. They add to their belief system the idea that if they blow it, people will not accept them.

A twist on that theme occurs when parents upbraid children suggesting that they cannot do it right because they always do it wrong. This response teaches children to be failure prone. They will grow up to live out self-fulfilling prophecies about how things never work out for them.

Some parents always insist that the child do better, no matter how well the child has already done. Their logic is that if they do not keep pointing out areas of improvement, the child will stop trying. The myth underlying this logic is, of course, that if you give out too many compliments, it will "go to the kid's head."

Children growing up in such an environment can become over-achievers. As adults they can string together an incredible list of accomplishments which would make any parent proud, but they are still uncertain if they have done enough. They are characteristically overextended and overcommitted, jealous of others' successes, and starved for recognition. What they desperately wanted was a parent to say, "What a great job," without any conditions, reservations, or critiques.

Sometimes parents fail to validate their children's efforts because they reserve praise for the exceptional. When their children do well, parents may not comment because that is what is expected. Children then worry whether they have any impact at all.

Such parenting strategies are particularly devastating when extreme standards of performance are demanded. Children literally face the intimidating message that anything less than the best means that they have not tried hard enough. By such standards, however, no effort is good enough. Children can only conclude that they should try harder. With these high performance standards, parents can have "hardening of the categories." This judgmental emphasis on doing things the right way versus the wrong way precludes the child doing anything different. Alternatives are not acceptable. Creativity is squashed. Children learn to evaluate their behavior with categorical black-and-white thinking. They tell themselves, "It should be only one way."

This type of rigidity was reflected in our survey. We used a widely-accepted instrument developed by Dr. David Olson of the University of Minnesota's Family Social Science Department. Olson has pioneered in the measurement of how families work at each stage of their development. Measured against national norms we found that 73 percent of sex addicts came from rigid families. And in rigid families, 'doing it right" is one of the highest priorities.

Rigid families in our sample were further characterized by being extremely judgmental and disapproving of anything sexual. That is, beyond giving their kids unrealistic expectations in general, these parents were particularly judgmental and rigid about sex. Danny, a forty-three-year-old social worker from California with four years of recovery, told us, "Sex was something that was regarded as very dangerous. My father was a minister who when teaching young people likened it to high voltage electricity—something to be handled at a distance and very carefully." Or consider Mona, a thirty-year-old graduate student from Georgia with five years of recovery:

> I grew up in New England in a repressive household. My mother's a practicing alcoholic. She's Danish. My father was Jewish American. Second generation. Highly competitive. I think both of my parents were sex and love addicts. And they married to keep each other and to keep themselves off the streets. . . . The subject of sex was never raised. My parents feigned a great deal of disgust for the whole subject. They slept with their door open all the time. My sister told me we were born by artificial insemination, and I believed her because the atmosphere in the household was such that it was something that seemed entirely logical and if it wasn't true was at least something I can imagine my parents wanting us to have believed. So I believed that until I went off to college. Both of my sisters have been anorexic. My older sister still is suicidal.

Children in families with rigid, repressive environments, especially sex-negative ones, are prime candidates for evolving profound shame about themselves and their sexuality. In all of our surveys few stories were more moving than Jim's. When we talked to him, he was a fifty-year-old member of a Catholic religious order. As an adult he struggled with exhibitionism, pornography bookstores, prostitution, and for the period of time he was married, affairs. His family typified the rigid expectations we routinely found in the families of addicts. His family enforced this rigidity with violence. Jim used sex to cope:

> I still can't live with the reality of how much they beat my sister. I can almost deal with mine, but I still can't deal with the fact of what my mother did to my sister. There were ten of us in the family and she beat us all—all the way down. I remember not wanting to go home with a report card because I got a licking for everything under a C. I got straight Es and Fs. So I'd get fourteen or fifteen beatings I'd have to face every three months—it was more than I could handle. Once I realized what masturbation was I was already being sexually abused by my uncle. Once I realized that that's sex—I didn't give a damn. I lived out on the street; I didn't care what happened to me. I walked around with my penis out of my pants all the time. My penis was always out. It was like it numbed me totally.

Here is where shame connects with unmanageability. Shame is partially about excessive emphasis on "doing it right." Jim's early solution, dealing with the shame by numbing himself with sex, only deepened the shame because sex was especially disapproved of. Jim said that for him shame "triggered acting out and acting out triggered pain." Like many abuse victims he said, "I had to hurt myself more and more to get aroused." Disapproval and abuse became connected with arousal. But as he got into more and more trouble, his life became unmanageable because he was not "doing it right."

CONDITIONAL LOVE

Jim, like many addicts, came from an emotionally impoverished family. Love was nonexistent, not expressed, or at best conditional. Unless conditions like "doing it right" were met, there would be no support or care. When children do not experience approval for tasks or affirmation for who they are, they have no internal way of feeling okay about themselves. Self-worth becomes contingent on others' opinions. As long as others approve, the child is all right. Self-worth evaporates with disapproval.

Some families give no affirmation. Compliments are seen as dangerous. Parents with this perception operate out of fear—fear of intimacy, fear of overinflating egos, fear of breaking the family rules by which they were raised. The result is low self-esteem; the children are convinced they are bad, unworthy persons. Sometimes parents try to show kids that they care by what they do. They assume children will conclude for themselves that they are cared for. This is simply not true. Children need to hear it said. When it is not, the child is desperate for approval, always wondering, "Am I acceptable?"

Some parents extend the logic to the point of abandonment and neglect. Sometimes abuse is disguised as "tough love." Healthy tough love is when parents set clear-cut, consistent boundaries with predictable and reasonable consequences. Abusive tough love is when children have to figure things out for themselves. Often it is found in families where parents felt that they, too, had to take care of themselves as children. These parents have not understood that being loving and supporting is as important as, and different from, instilling responsibility. Some parents are emotionally incapable of being there for their children; some are simply mean spirited. And some simply leave. Whichever was the case in their family, addicts fear being abandoned and conclude that people will leave them because they are unlovable. And they are ashamed.

Perhaps most damaging to a child's sense of self-worth is when parents are hypercritical and attacking. They label their children, calling them lazy or spoiled. Children learn to be self-critical and self-hating, using damning labels for themselves, like "I am selfish [lazy, weak, undisciplined, etc.]." Parents who escalate this tactic by scapegoating or blaming children for the family's problems will have children who take responsibility for everything that goes wrong. And their children will be ashamed.

Shame can also start when the family has a low "us" concept. Just as individuals can have a poor self-concept, families can have a collective sense of unworthiness. Race, ethnic heritage, skeletons in the closet, family problems—whatever the underlying cause, family members feel they have to try harder. They each work to overcome what they perceive as the opinion of the outside world. And they are each ashamed.

In families in which love is subject to all these conditions a profound emotional emptiness exists. Jim describes how he connected the loneliness of his family with sexual behavior:

> The thought of going home always set off my addiction after I was eight years old. Then as an adult, going home to an empty apartment every night would start my addiction. I couldn't go home to an empty apartment. I had to block that out somehow. I would end up going to a movie or buying a bunch of books or whatever. Then I could sort of go home. I didn't have to face the emptiness alone. I definitely have to say the top priority thing that sets off my addiction is being alone in a room or the fear of being beat up. As a child, even the thought of going home after school and knowing that I was going to get beat up—I'd have to act out before I went home. I think that's mostly my whole life. It's a real powerful thread. The first thing I would do before I could visit my family or even friends, I'd act out first. . . . I'd say that's number one. That's the first thing that sets me off is my fear of being rejected or being alone.

Gershen Kaufman, one of the great contributors to our understanding of shame, wrote years ago about the connection between sex and emotional deprivation:

> A young boy who learns never to need anything emotionally from his parents . . . is faced with a dilemma whenever he feels young, needy or otherwise insecure. If masturbating has been his principal source of good feeling . . . he may resort to masturbation in order to restore good feelings about self at times when he is experiencing needs quite unrelated to sexuality.

Kaufman's words provide a vital insight into sexual addiction that many miss. People tend to think sex addiction is about sex; it is not. It is about core feelings of loneliness and unworthiness. Many addicts, in fact, encounter their sexuality for the first time as part of recovery when they experience sex without shame.

We were able to concretely document this type of family environment as key in the making of an addict. Again using Olson's instrument, we found that 87 percent of sex addicts in our survey came from "disengaged" families. These families operate with detachment and distance, with low affirmation and approval, and with high levels of criticism and disapproval.

THE AMORPHOUS EGO

"Doing things right" and "conditional love" combine to create an amorphous ego. Consider an amorphous rock: it is sturdy and hard like other rocks, and yet it is filled with pores and holes. Similarly, addicts have areas of "emptiness" in their egos where they lack a sense of their own goodness or ability to do good things. Addicts attempt to fill those holes with "feeling good," but it never works because the holes remain.

There are ways in which families unintentionally add to the holes. Parents who criticize their children for having feelings that are difficult or challenging teach them to constrict all feelings. Comments like "Don't wear your feelings on your sleeve" tell kids that feelings make one too vulnerable. Children learn to block out those feelings and don't know how they feel about events in their lives. This lack of awareness becomes a "hole" in their personality structure.

Painful, unresolved issues continue in the family because no one addresses them. When children express feelings about these issues, they are told they are exaggerating or being dramatic. From this, children learn to tolerate pain. As adults they will respond to the dictum "when the going gets tough, the tough get going." They will ignore how much they hurt—more holes.

Many of these families have anticonflict rules as a way to control disruptive feelings, especially anger. Parents quote the famous imperative introduced in Walt Disney's *Bambi*, where Thumper's mother tells him, "If you can't say something nice, don't say anything at all." Children who have learned conflict avoidance live by the rule "Don't rock the boat." Worst of all in these families, there are unprocessed, unmentionable, secrets that have great power and generate much shame. Children know about them and feel their impact, yet parents say, "It is in the past, so there is no need to talk about it." Why dredge up old problems? they ask. Yet children fear the unknown; they fear what is not understood and not resolved. Children learn to keep secrets and to live with the fear of discovery. Their deepest fear is that if people really knew their secrets, they would be abandoned.

Children's needs may also be denied or criticized. Some parents feel so overwhelmed or overburdened that meeting needs or comforting a child may be beyond them. Some needs create fear in parents by touching their own unresolved issues. Children who play with themselves sexually get told, "Only bad kids touch themselves there." Those children are left with conflict about needs because what feels good also feels bad. They learn to deny those needs, since "doing it right" means they should not have them. But they also want to feel better. To avoid the conflict they simply detach from the needs—yet more holes.

For many shame-based persons, the toughest battle of all is over boundaries. Parents violate the personal boundaries of their children in many ways. Attitudes such as "kids don't have rights" allow parents to force kids to do things that don't feel good or safe. These children's boundaries become permeable. They grow up feeling that they have to give whatever is asked: explanations, help, information—and sex.

Family therapist Marilyn Mason speaks of boundaries as a zipper. Most people are able to control the zipper from the inside. They limit other people's access to themselves. If somebody wants something, they are able to say no and risk disapproval. Shame-based people have their zipper on the outside where anybody can access it. Boundary problems create more holes.

SHAME CHECKLIST

Check the characteristics of shame in your family and yourself which are appropriate. Use the sample phrases as clues. For the characteristics you checked, write down examples of phrases from your own life. Match phrases you heard in your family to statements you make to yourself.

×	YOUR FAMILY'S STATEMENT	×	YOUR OWN SELF-TALK
____	1. Performance over person "You are what you do." ➡	____	1. Human doing versus Human being "I am what I do."

✕	YOUR FAMILY'S STATEMENT	✕	YOUR OWN SELF-TALK
___	2. Cannot make mistakes "Stay within the lines."	→ ___	2. Perfectionism "If I blow it, people will not accept me."
___	3. Cannot do it right "You always do that wrong."	→ ___	3. Failure prone "Things never work out for me."
___	4. Must always do better "Never give full credit because they will stop trying."	→ ___	4. Overachieving "Have I done enough?"
___	5. No validation of effort "Why comment about what is expected?"	→ ___	5. Self-doubt about effort "Do I have any impact?"
___	6. Extreme standards of performance "Anything less than the best, and you have not tried hard enough."	→ ___	6. No effort is good enough "I should try harder."
___	7. Judgmental emphasis on right/ wrong "I don't want to listen because it's wrong."	→ ___	7. Categorical black-and-white thinking "It should be only one way."
___	8. No affirmation "It's dangerous to give compliments."	→ ___	8. Low self-esteem "I am basically a bad, unworthy person."
___	9. Scapegoating and blaming "You caused all this."	→ ___	9. Responsibility for everything "When things go wrong, it is my fault."
___	10. Limited expressions of care "They should know that I care because of what I do for them."	→ ___	10. Desperation for approval "Am I okay?"
___	11. Conditional support "If you do things right, I'll support you."	→ ___	11. Self-worth contingent on others' opinions "I am only okay if you approve of me."
___	12. Abandonment, neglect "I had to take care of myself when I was a kid."	→ ___	12. Fear of abandonment "People will leave me because I am unlovable."
___	13. Attacking, hypercritical "You are ungrateful [spoiled, shiftless, etc.]."	→ ___	13. Self-critical, self-hating "I am selfish [self-centered, lazy, etc.]."
___	14. Low "us" concept "Because of our background, we have to try harder."	→ ___	14. Heightened sense of unworthiness "I am a [family name or nationality label] so I have to overcome people's opinions."

✕	YOUR FAMILY'S STATEMENT	✕	YOUR OWN SELF-TALK
____15.	Anticonflict rules "If you can't say something nice, don't say anything at all." →	____15.	Conflict avoidance "Don't rock the boat."
____16.	Undiscussed issues, secrets "It is in the past, so there is no need to talk about it." →	____16.	Fear of discovery "If people really knew about me, they would leave me."
____17.	Constriction of feelings "Don't wear your feelings on your sleeve." →	____17.	Unaware of feelings "I don't know how I feel about it."
____18.	Refusal to address painful issues → "You are exaggerating how serious this is."	____18.	Tolerance of pain "When the going gets tough, the tough get going."
____19.	Needs denied, criticized "Only bad kids touch themselves there." →	____19.	Conflict about needs "What feels good feels bad."
____20.	Personal limits not respected "Kids don't have rights." →	____20.	Permeable boundaries "I owe you an explanation [help, information, sex, etc.]."

THE SHAME CYCLE

In their book, *Facing Shame,* Merle Fossum and Marilyn Mason describe the internal shame experience of the addict as a shame cycle. Addicts go from one extreme to another in alternating rhythms. These rhythms go back to their early experiences of "doing things right" and "conditional love." They try to reach the impossible norms of their parents, family, and culture. But the feelings, needs, and drives they have been taught to ignore keep reasserting themselves. As with a dam no longer able to contain the floodwaters, there is a collapse and none of the waters are held.

This release of the floodwaters we call "acting out." It relieves the tension, pain, and deprivation that pervade all parts of the addict's life. In that moment of relief, there is total absorption in the behavior and a numbing to all judgment and expectations, real and imagined. Almost immediately, however, shame reasserts itself and the addict feels like a failure. Once out of control, the addict scrambles to regain control. This "acting in" becomes even more intense because the feelings of failure reinforce the preexisting feelings of shame. Addicts' lives are governed by two primary directives that seem irreconcilable: to do things right and to feel better. They have never learned how the two can work together. No one showed them how they could fulfill their normal human needs, and still be appropriate in their behavior.

Addicts, then, become immersed in their "control-release" cycle of acting out and acting in. They tend to have many such rhythms in their life. One of our survey respondents described how when she was out of control sexually, she was also anorexic, and when she was in control sexually, she compulsively overate. For her, one hundred pounds more or less was an index of where she was sexually.

All addicts have shopping lists of ways to be excessive. To act out, they can be compulsive with sex, eating, alcohol, drugs, spending, gambling, risk taking, and working. To act in, they can be compulsive with dieting, saving, sex avoidance, religion, teetotaling, and risk avoiding. Addiction is much bigger than any specific compulsive behavior, because it can manifest itself in any number of ways and still be the same problem. If we compartmentalize addictions, we miss the core issue of shame. When we talk of the addictive personality, we are really talking about this core of shame.

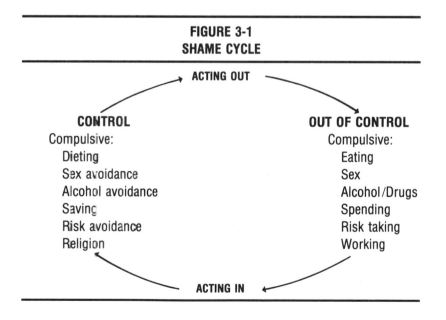

FIGURE 3-1
SHAME CYCLE

ACTING OUT

CONTROL
Compulsive:
 Dieting
 Sex avoidance
 Alcohol avoidance
 Saving
 Risk avoidance
 Religion

OUT OF CONTROL
Compulsive:
 Eating
 Sex
 Alcohol/Drugs
 Spending
 Risk taking
 Working

ACTING IN

In recovery, addressing shame becomes central because, as we learned with many years of alcohol treatment, stopping one behavior does not mean the problem is over. The addict may simply have shifted the rhythm. And the essential dynamics remain.

Addicts are very clear about being out of control and in control. They also are very specific in recognizing the connections with the early family environment. Jim, who did a great deal of acting out with his automobile, described it like this: "The car automatically represents a real feeling of loneliness, insanity, and powerlessness. It was my bike when I was little and my car now."

The diagram below, adapted from Fossum and Mason, summarizes the development of the shame cycle. The rhythms start early, in family environments that are rigid and disengaged. If the child becomes shame based, he is then vulnerable to the destructive shame cycles of acting out and acting in.

Family environment—rigid, disengaged

↓

Shame-based personality—self-doubting, desperate for approval, afraid of discovery, unaware of feelings, etc.

↓

Shame cycles—acting out, release; acting in, control

This picture was confirmed by Olson's instrument, which showed less than 2.5 percent of those surveyed as coming from families in the normal "healthy" ranges. Over two-thirds of those surveyed came from dysfunctional families that were *both* rigid and disengaged.

Focusing on early family experience reveals another key factor in the making of an addiction. The clearest way to engender shame in children is to abuse them—sexually, physically, or emotionally. Our research demonstrates that child abuse is an essential cause of addiction. As professionals are just beginning to appreciate, addiction starts with vulnerable children—the topic of our next chapter.

CHAPTER FOUR

Vulnerable Children: The Legacy of Abuse

Children: trusting, inquiring, needy, dependent, and most of all, vulnerable. Their vulnerability is so compelling that most adults are moved to protect, to teach, to help, and to nurture them. Unfortunately, their vulnerability also leaves children open to exploitation, misuse, and neglect—in other words, to child abuse.

In the fields of alcoholism and drug addiction, evidence has started to emerge showing the impact of abuse on chemical dependency. A recent study showed that women alcoholics were much more likely to have experienced childhood sexual abuse, experienced it in more ways, and experienced it for longer periods of time than nonalcoholic women. Another study found that of drug-abusing adolescents, up to 45 percent of the boys and 77 percent of the girls had been sexually abused. A study of abused adolescents showed that they used drugs and alcohol to cope with sexual victimization and that rates of use were high. Related studies show that sexual abuse victims in general have more "acting out" behaviors, including school problems, conflict with authority, eating problems, and sexual promiscuity.

Sexual addiction provides a larger context for looking at the effects of the abuse of children—especially sexual abuse. As in other areas, sex addiction has been the key that connects abuse with the addiction process. When we conceived our survey, we were determined to document this connection. We were not prepared for the overwhelming results. Simply stated, the more abused you are as a child, the more addictions you are likely to have as an adult.

The path pointing to this conclusion has existed for some time. Many sexual addicts have reported sexual abuse as part of their history. In a 1982 study, we were able to document sexual abuse as a factor; 39 percent of the men addicts and 63 percent of the women addicts reported being sexually abused. The amount of abuse was probably underreported because the study included people new to recovery as well as veterans. People just starting their recovery process are often still in significant denial. It takes years of recovery for most to have real clarity about the kind and extent of abuse in their history.

Another problem implicit in the statistics was that male sex addicts, while reporting much higher incidences of abuse than men in the general population, reported lower incidences than female sex addicts. While lower incidences for males fit a stereotype of girls and women being abused more often than men, it did not fit the clinical experience of most therapists. Therapists find that men have extraordinary difficulty in admitting they have been victimized. That problem is rooted in the macho ideal: men do not admit to pain or vulnerability. In addition, men often see sex in terms of their power over women, so they are blind to being exploited themselves. When a boy is thirteen years old and his first sexual experience is with the thirty-nine-year-old woman next door, he does not see that as victimization; he sees it as a "score."

Consider the movie *Summer of '42,* a poignant romantic film about a woman whose husband dies in World War II. A young lad who happens to be helping her around the house when she learns of her husband's death ends up spending the night. For her it was a night of comfort in her grief. For him it was an initiation into adult sexuality. Reverse the roles, however, with a twenty-seven-year-old man taking a fifteen-year-old girl to bed. Would we still think the movie was poignant and romantic? More likely, we would see the girl as a victim.

If the double standard exists for us, it also exists for the courts. In a southwestern state, a thirty-four-year-old male language arts teacher had an affair with an eighth-grade girl. He received a sentence of fifteen years in prison. A female librarian, also in her early thirties, had an affair with an eighth-grade boy. She was sentenced to probation only. Yet it was the same state, the same judicial system.

Another factor in male denial is homophobic responses. If a boy was abused by a man, the fear is that talking about it will be an admission of homosexuality. One way to deal with homosexuality is to deny it exists. One way to deal with abuse is to deny it exists. Taken together, they become mutually reinforcing reasons to not talk.

In our survey, we wanted as much as possible to avoid inaccuracies stemming from insufficient recovery and from male denial. So we focused on data concerning the 233 men and 57 women with the most advanced recovery. Even here denial existed. For example, in one interview, a man with five years of strong recovery was asked if he had been sexually abused. He responded, "I am one of the lucky ones. I know that many of us have, but it didn't happen to me." When the interviewer later asked for his earliest sexual memory, she was astounded when he said, "That was when my uncle started masturbating me at the age of five."

Even with those limitations the results were striking. We asked about physical and emotional abuse as well as sexual abuse. Identical percentages of men and women in our survey reported having been abused:

Emotional abuse	97 percent
Sexual abuse	81 percent
Physical abuse	72 percent

With a few notable exceptions, men tended still to report somewhat lesser amounts and durations of abuse. But the grim outlines for both men and women were extremely clear.

This chapter profiles the abusive conditions in which sex addicts were raised. In many ways it can serve the reader as a guide to how abuse occurs. Most important, the chapter shows how abusing children contributes to addictions, sexual and multiple. Being a victim intensifies all the factors we have already identified, including neurochemistry, culture, and family.

SEXUAL ABUSE

- A thirty-eight-year-old attorney tells of the oral and anal sex he experienced with an adult friend of the family whom they would visit regularly. As an adult he would use the memories to "trigger" his addiction. He knew even as a child that this was a violation of himself, but because he participated he felt responsible. He told us, "I had no instruction, explanations, or guidance from my parents and had no background to judge these experiences. So I just stumbled along caught between fear and ignorance."

- A forty-five-year-old reading teacher remembers when her father abandoned her and her mother when she was six. Her mother had to work, and she was alone much of the time. As a little girl starved for attention, she was easy prey for an uncle who was sexual with her until well into high school. As a recovering sex addict with a full understanding of the impact of abuse in her life, she struggled with denial. "I adored the uncle who was so abusive to me. I even named one of my sons for him. I'd like to give the SOB a kick in the nuts now."

- A fifty-year-old college professor was sexually abused at an early age by a baby-sitter. She abused him for six years. (This started a whole chain of sexual experiences not only in his family but in hers as well.) He remembers his sadness when his baby-sitter "got serious" with a boy her own age. He felt profoundly abandoned. And he remembers with pain that when he got older and baby-sat for others, he did to them what had happened to him.

- A very successful newspaperman talks of his boyhood experience participating in activities sponsored by a local men's voluntary organization. One of the sponsors was a policeman who sexually molested him over a number of years. As an adult professional, the newsman was rabid in his suspicion of organized groups like the Lions and the Shriners. His articles were scathing. As a recovering sex addict, he now traces the distrust back to the original events. Until now, he had stereotyped all such groups "as dirty old men with fezzes on who drove up and down alleys on their motorcycles looking for little girls."

The legacy of sexual abuse persists for most sex addicts. The further problem for most of them was to identify that fact. Many were not able to remember until they stopped acting out and, even then, often only with the assistance of therapy. Also, they had many ways of denying the impact of their experiences. They told themselves that:

- since they consented they had no right to complain

- it was their fault because of some action of theirs

- it was normal and therefore to be accepted

- they enjoyed the experience so it was not damaging

- they felt loyalty and/or love for the person who abused them

- it was not that bad and was best forgotten

- it had no impact so there was no need to upset everybody

- it was understandable given what was going on with the person

For most people, much clarity about their addiction came with expanding their understanding of abuse. Part of powerlessness is being vulnerable to exploitation over which you have no control.

What constitutes abuse is a difficult question. Complex legal definitions exist as well as clinical ones. We also have varying community and cultural standards. But six standards stand out as generally accepted measures of the sexual abuse of children.

1. *Intention or response of the actor.* If a parent or care giver intends or cultivates a sexual response, it is abuse. Most parents will at times have sexual reactions during routine parenting tasks, but will set them aside. To seek or develop those responses is abusive.

2. *Victim's response.* When a child feels violated by a parent's invasive or inappropriate behavior, abuse occurs whether the parent intended it or not.

3. *Involvement of assault.* Use of force to gain sexual pleasure with a child is abusive.

4. *Involvement of exploitation.* Because children are dependent upon their care givers for information, support, and survival needs, they can be easily manipulated. Such exploitation constitutes abuse.

5. *Lack of consent.* Children do not have sufficient awareness or information to give consent.

6. *Developmental prematurity.* Sexual activity and expectations that do not match the developmental stage of the child are abusive.

We found in our survey that sexual abuse had occurred in a wide variety of ways. Table 4-1 provides percentages for men addicts and women addicts of selected examples of the types of abuse.

TABLE 4-1
SEXUAL ABUSE OF SEX ADDICTS

CONTACT FORMS OF ABUSE	% MEN	% WOMEN
Inappropriate holding, kissing	25	56
Sexual fondling	43	58
Masturbation	28	35
Oral sex	25	36
Forced sexual activity	15	58

NONCONTACT FORMS OF ABUSE	% MEN	% WOMEN
Flirtations and suggestive language	21	60
Propositioning	22	51
Household voyeurism/exhibitionism	25	36
Sexualizing language	17	44
Preoccupation with sexual development	13	44

As we have noted above, the same percentage of men as women reported being sexually abused; in individual categories, however, the percentages were lower for men. The question remains as to whether that is because of underreporting. Even so, percentages for men far exceed what typically is reported. In fact, the rule of thumb offered by many professionals is that one out of ten men has been sexually abused. In our study of addicts it was eight out of ten.

Child abuse professionals single out the age at which the abuse began as extremely important. The earlier the abuse starts, the more dysfunction occurs. Among the 290 people we focused on, we found that age of onset varied by behavior. Sexual fondling, for example, started on average at age eight for boys and at age six for girls. By contrast, forced sex started much later, at eleven for boys and twelve for girls. Many addicts noted that their compulsive sexual behaviors started shortly after the onset of the abuse experience. We compared the age when sex addicts perceived their addiction starting with the age at which they reported being abused. The most common profile showed abuse occurring concurrently with or shortly before the beginning of the addiction. For boys the average age was ten, and for girls it was nine.

NONCONTACT FORMS OF ABUSE

Sex addicts find it important to their recovery to distinguish between contact and noncontact forms of abuse. Table 4-1 provides five examples of noncontact forms of abuse, in which there is no touching yet sexual transactions occur. For example, consider the father who talks to his daughter about her developing breasts in order to become aroused. The daughter feels violated and does everything she can do to change the subject. Yet he persists. Has he touched her? No. However, his preoccupation with her development exploits her vulnerability. Professionals use the term "covert incest" to describe this behavior.

Many sex addicts were abused as children simply by being in the presence of an adult sex addict. When a parent is sexual with strangers in front of a child or explicitly sexualizes others in front of a child, an essential boundary is crossed. Beyond being poor modeling and inappropriate, this behavior eroticizes the child's environment in damaging ways. The child may experience arousal at a premature age and may start to sexualize other relationships, as well.

Often noncontact and contact forms of abuse intermingle. Georgeanne, a thirty-two-year-old office manager from a northern city, first experienced contact abuse when her grandfather regularly fondled her as a preschooler. At that early age she fell into a pattern of going along and never saying no. "I loved him a lot," she said, "and figured that's what people you love did." Contact abuse continued as she grew up, and in fact, shortly before the survey Georgeanne's mother had grabbed her breast under the pretext of checking out what size she was. The various noncontact forms of abuse she had experienced ranged from her father's sexualizing language and sexual stares to her mother's "falling in love" with her fiancé. She commented on the covert aspects of her relationship with her father:

> Prior to recovery and in early recovery I perceived my father's explicit talk about my body in sexual terms to be sexist. I was both annoyed by it and turned on simultaneously. Later I realized the inappropriateness and felt invaded, abused, and appalled. I recognized that my previous reaction to it was a way to deny the abuse I felt. The inappropriateness fed my addiction.
>
> I also recognize that the many ways in which my father was "open" about nudity and his sexually explicit conversation with me were forms of incest, since I now recognize both his preoccupation with sex and the turn-on he derives when engaged in this. (It continues to this day, requiring limit setting from me.) I also now recognize how "icky" I feel when I'm around his sex talk, which underscores the power of this abuse.

WHO WERE THE ABUSERS?

In the child abuse literature, the abusers most frequently reported are stepparents, foster parents, and fathers. We found, however, significant patterns by abusers not typically discussed in the literature. There tended to be more blood relatives as opposed to step- or foster parents, significant numbers of women, and adults outside the family. Part of the difference has to do with sex addicts being a special population, part has to do with the recovering person's greater sophistication in these issues; yet part may also have to do with our tapping into populations who were less likely to report abuse.

We found over twenty-six categories of abusers, including family members, family friends, and professionals. In the survey we had included a category called "others," intended as a catchall. As it turned out, however, almost all of the abuse fell in this category. About half of the incidents involved adult strangers; occasions of abuse were rare but were very traumatic. The other half involved adults who were known to the family but not family friends; generally, these adults were neighbors or business associates. This abuse tended to be long-term and to have great impact.

TABLE 4-2
ABUSER PATTERNS FOR TWO TYPES OF ABUSE

	SEXUAL FONDLING		FORCED SEX	
	% MALE	% FEMALE	% MALE	% FEMALE
Father	4	21	3	9
Mother	15	9	11	3
Other adults	20	36	41	34
Professionals	9	6	8	3
Family friends	11	18	5	9

Table 4-2 contrasts sexual fondling and forced sex in terms of the abusers most often involved. Note that gender patterns emerge, with more boys being abused by mothers and more girls being abused by fathers. Also note that although in general the percentages were lower for forced sex than for sexual fondling, for boys with abusers in the "other adults" category, the percentage for forced sex was actually double that for fondling. When violence occurred outside the family, the leading target was vulnerable boys.

Another way to look at abusers is to total the number of incidents of all types of sexual abuse and then rank the categories of abusers by the percentage of incidents they were involved in. For women addicts the five worst abusers were:

Other adult	19 percent of incidents
Father	16 percent
Brother	12 percent
Mother	11 percent
Male juvenile	10 percent

For men addicts the five worst abusers were:

Mother	17 percent of incidents
Other adult	15 percent
Male juvenile	13 percent
Family friend	8 percent
Father	8 percent

The same pattern emerges: opposite-sex parents and other adults are at the top of the list for each gender.

Abuse does not occur in isolation. Usually the sex addict's profile includes a number of abusers and of types of abuse. Paula's story is a good example. She described how her abuse started in her family at age eight with a brother who was six years older. They began by showering together and by the time Paula was thirteen were going to bed together. She was also sexual with their family physician from the age of thirteen until she was twenty-seven. She talked to us about the "hole in her soul":

> There was a hole in my soul that I was able to fill up with the sexual contact of another human being. I think it had a lot to do with that person finding me desirable and wanting me sexually. It gave me the ultimate feeling that since this person is willing to go to bed and make love to me, then I am a worthwhile, lovable person. That was my belief. This would fill the hole in my soul.

In another case of abuse by a brother, Fran talked of how it started out as special. Fran and her brother were neglected by their parents, partly because her father had a prolonged illness that absorbed much of her mother's time. When her father was well, her mother would contract very unusual illnesses which were difficult to identify. The result was that the kids would rely on each other. Further, Fran idolized her brother. Everything he touched turned to gold. She was the dyslexic kid who had braces. When he paid attention to her and was sexual with her, she was grateful. She said, "It was our sexual secret. Like Christmas presents were hidden and secret, but they were neat and were okay." Fran believes to this day that all the early sexual stimulation caused her to develop early. Other kids teased and harassed her unmercifully. But, as she says, "the sex was a matter of survival.

It was not until she was with some cousins and her brother was being sexual with them that she realized that sex with her brother was not unique and special. In fact, he was routinely sexual with lots of people. When she started to pull away, he became more violent and manipulative. "For example," she said, "we had chores that we had to do and if I didn't clean the bathroom he would say, 'Well, I'll clean the bathroom for you if . . .' knowing that I had lots of homework." Sometimes they would go out with their parents who were working as real estate agents. While the parents showed the homes, Fran's brother would drag her into a closet and feel her through her clothing. She felt violated and angry, but she asked, "How do you deal with that when you are ten years old?"

Most kids get protection from their parents, but Fran's support from her parents was minimal. Fran describes this event with her parents which, sadly, was a story often repeated in our survey:

The night our incest was discovered, my parents had gone out for the evening and Father came home early because Mother wanted a sweater because she was cold. They weren't that far from our house. We heard the garage door open, and I jumped up and ran into my bedroom to act like I was getting ready to go to bed so that was why I was undressed. My father was not stupid. He didn't buy it for a minute. He went back and picked Mom up at the party they were at. They came home and they sat us down and they said, "We are not going to punish you for what happened because we can't change it, but we're never ever going to discuss it. No matter what, you don't talk about this to anyone anytime, okay? That's the law. That's what you do. No problem." They turned around and left and went back to their party. Leaving us there all alone together.

Many abused children grew up with a no-talk rule. David Calof, a specialist in child abuse, talks about the universal bind that these children experience: "Do not see, hear, feel, sense, or address what is real, but rather accept what is unreal and proscribed in the interest of your very survival." He adds, "Disbelieve the obvious, but accept the improbable."

Fran's story, of course, did not end here. Her life was a long line of men. At one point the police tried to intervene because her house had the reputation for the best sex in town—but since she did not charge, they could not do anything. Fran, like many addicts, pinpoints her addiction as beginning with the abuse. She told us:

> After I found out about my brother and my cousins, I discovered how to masturbate. Because all of that need for the affection and the tenderness and the warmth was suddenly gone. I had to do something to survive to take care of me. Also the house was a ranch-style house. It was very long and there was a furnace for the bedrooms and a furnace for the kitchen, dining room, living room areas. The back furnace was kept at sixty-two degrees, so the bedrooms were always very cold, and I didn't have an electric blanket. I found that by masturbating I could warm the bed and warm me enough to fall asleep. I didn't realize then what I was doing, I just knew it worked. Mother never understood why so many pairs of my panties were ruined and had holes always in the same spot of the panel. It was because I was digging at my body, masturbating. She never figured that out.

Fran's story is typical in one more way. Seldom is sexual abuse isolated; it is generally accompanied by physical and emotional abuse. In Fran's case, her brother used blackmail and violence. To get a clear picture of the sex addict's childhood, we must look at the impact of these other forms of abuse.

PHYSICAL ABUSE

Like sexual abuse, physical abuse is surrounded by denial. Many in our survey reported that their lives were affected by violence they were unable to acknowledge until they entered recovery. One addict said, "I did not realize I was severely abused because I thought it was my fault. I used to say my mother would pick up a knife and 'cut me.' Only in recovery could I say 'stabbed me.'" Another commented, "I didn't consider myself an abused child until I got sober. I thought everyone was slapped or spanked every day." Walt, a forty-two-year-old engineer from a southeastern state gave perhaps the most articulate description of denial as a process:

> Before I got into recovery, I thought that the beatings, whippings, baiting, harassment, sarcasm, name-calling, and weeping over my "black heart" were normal forms of punishment and were completely deserved by me. I grew to feel that when anything bad happened in my relationship with another person I was at fault, or at least that accepting blame was the preferred consequence to losing a relationship.
>
> During my recovery one of the most difficult tasks has been to validate my experiences of abuse. I struggle against voices inside me which tell me that I am exaggerating, that I am being cruel and unfair, that I am merely trying to pin the blame for my problems on someone else. I have slowly begun to get in touch with the anger and hurt and personal reality that I have been abused by my parents and my older brother.

When such "personal realities" are reduced to numbers, the collective story sex addicts tell is overwhelming. Table 4-3 gives figures for some of the types of physical abuse they endured. For boys, physical abuse started early, usually around age five. While girls tended to experience the beginning of such abuse later, usually around age ten, they were much more likely to be physically injured.

Of the women we surveyed, 18 percent had been cut or wounded as children, 13 percent had bones broken, 7 percent had damage to internal organs, and 11 percent had permanent injury.

TABLE 4-3
EXAMPLES OF PHYSICAL ABUSE

CATEGORY	% MALE	% FEMALE
Shoving	30	45
Slapping or hitting	45	62
Scratches or bruises	12	38
Beatings or whippings	36	44
Pulling or grabbing hair, ears, etc.	19	36

As Table 4-4 shows, the major perpetrators of abuse were the same-sex parent followed closely by the opposite-sex parent; brothers and sisters played lesser roles. Taken together, most of the physical abuse that occurred happened within the family. (Not surprisingly, 21 percent of women addicts were later battered by husbands.)

TABLE 4-4
FAMILY MEMBERS RESPONSIBLE FOR PHYSICAL ABUSE

FAMILY MEMBER	% MALE	% FEMALE
Father	36	20
Mother	27	31
Brothers	9	7
Sisters	4	3

Physical abuse takes a toll in other ways. Simply being in the presence of violence in the family is a form of emotional abuse. Being forced to watch the beatings of other children or physical fights of parents is traumatic for children. Having to hide injuries or wounds from others is also emotionally upsetting. Not receiving medical attention for physical damage is a form of neglect. Consider the man who demands from his teenage son confirmation that his

ex-wife is seeing another man. The son knows he has two choices.
If he confirms his father's suspicions, his father will beat his mother.
If he doesn't, his father will accuse him of lying and beat him. Such
blackmail is in itself cruel torture. Again the patterns of abuse do not
exist in neat categories. Without losing these interconnections, we
must shift our focus to emotional abuse.

EMOTIONAL ABUSE

More than anything else, emotional abuse is about deprivation—
the lack of essential nurturing, protection, and care. Sometimes it
extends beyond such deficits to mean-spirited, cruel, or malicious
treatment of children. Addicts told us about abusive conditions like
these:

- living with threats to kill me and the whole family

- parents choosing a favorite son while the rest of us were neglected

- father wanted me dead at birth

- constantly subjected to sadistic teasing and tricks

- often was locked out of the house for extended periods of time

- lived in unnurturing, harsh seminary for most of my teenage years

- my mother's favorite saying was she was sorry she adopted me

- parents would humiliate me by making me stand at supper while
  they critiqued my failures

- father made me watch him attempt suicide

Table 4-5 provides an extensive list of ways that sex addicts reported being emotionally abused.

TABLE 4-5
EMOTIONAL ABUSE OF SEX ADDICTS

EMOTIONAL ABUSE	% MALE	% FEMALE
Inadequate medical attention	5	29
Inadequate food or nutrition	7	13
Neglect	71	71
Harassment or malicious tricks	29	47
Being screamed or shouted at	56	69
Unfair punishments	36	44
Cruel or degrading tasks	13	24
Cruel confinement	20	25
Abandonment	44	47
Touch deprivation	45	58
Overly strict dress codes	13	20
No privacy	28	38
Having to hide injuries or wounds from others	11	22
Being forced to keep secrets	30	55
Having to take on adult responsibilities as a child	42	60
Having to watch beating of other family members	21	36
Being caught in the middle of parents' fights	43	36
Being blamed for family problems	27	60

Notice that one of the major forms of emotional abuse was touch deprivation. Some pioneers in child abuse research have postulated that lack of touch is a key ingredient in sexual abuse and physical violence. James Prescott created considerable controversy when he demonstrated that violent and sexually aggressive cultures could be predicted by how little children and adolescents were touched. The responses in our survey further confirm the significant role of touch deprivation in abusive behaviors.

Closely related to touch deprivation were neglect, abandonment, and inadequate food and nutrition. Neglect and abandonment can take many forms, including lack of protection when there is danger, lack of guidance when direction is needed, or lack of help when the child faces a crisis. Sometimes they take the form of parents "warehousing" kids, that is, finding places to put them because they don't want to deal with them. Parents can "specialize" in one child at the price of neglecting the others. Sometimes parents bring children to inappropriate or jeopardy settings like bars. Whatever the form, the fundamental conclusion children come to is that they are unimportant and their needs will not be met.

Another significant area of emotional abuse was asking children to take on adult responsibilities. Developmentally, children need to feel cared for. If they don't, they miss forming certain assumptions that are crucial to living a healthy life. Forcing children to face the world like adults gives them a sense of being able to depend only on themselves. Parents do this whenever they require or allow their children to:

- baby-sit for younger siblings too early and too often

- take on adult roles, such as that of a surrogate spouse

- work excessively, either inside or outside the home

- date people who are significantly older

- do something before they are ready or when they say no out of fear

- conform to adult standards regarding food, work, play, or sex

When he was four years old, Joe contracted polio. He was taken away from his family to a strange hospital. This was before the days of physical therapy, so he was strapped down and held immobile for extended periods of time. No one from his family talked to him or supported him. He felt this was punishment for ruining his family by catching the disease. He was expected to face his illness as an adult.

Joe characterized his family as one "never to touch, hold or hug, or show feelings—and never express 'I love you.' " He was physically and sexually abused in his wheelchair by a group of sadistic older boys. The leader of that group later married his sister. Joe's father was a violent alcoholic, who abused everyone over his frustration at the boy's illness. He died in a fight with another alcoholic. Neglect, abandonment, and unreachable expectations fueled Joe's addictions. In fact, he was clear that his sex addiction and drug addiction masked his "suppressed anger and rage."

Again abuse compounds abuse. Like many addicts, Joe experienced physical, sexual, and emotional abuse. Ted was another example of commingling patterns of abuse. His family parallels Joe's in being unresponsive. Ted was never held or given signs of affection; the only attention he got was criticism. Simply put, he said, "I just couldn't get the attention I needed." However, there was an elderly male neighbor who would pay attention. The abuse started with the man enticing him into hidden areas and inducing him to masturbate him. He was eight years old. This man then introduced him to a group of senior high boys who joined together regularly for mutual masturbation. Until he entered a recovery program, Ted felt responsible for all this. Now he sees that his vulnerability as a child was exploited, that he was emotionally and sexually abused. He still avoids those abusive boys, who are now adults in his town.

Walt, the engineer mentioned in the physical abuse section of this chapter, described the interplay of various patterns this way:

> I have been able to recognize the intense emotional intrusiveness that existed in my family and the constant physical violence that pervaded our private family life. It still shakes me to the core to write or speak of it. As I write now, I feel a knot in my abdomen and the old familiar feeling of being cornered. I first got in touch with the many spankings—with my mother's recurrent term, "You have a black heart"—and with a memory of my father beating me when I was about five years old. Later came additional memories—my brother's attempt to have sex with me, my father's strict authoritarianism, and his absence from my life, his having never played with me. Later came other memories, and most recently the one that has been significant is that of his "playing" with me by slapping me around, all the while saying, "Think fast now, think fast," and putting my head between his legs, squeezing hard and jumping up and down, or putting me in a headlock and "scrubbing" my head with his knuckles—all done "in fun."

Perhaps one of the saddest facts to emerge from our research was the interconnection among the various patterns of abuse. We contrasted sex addicts who abused children with those who did not. We found no differences in terms of severity of sexual or physical abuse. What we did find was that those addicts who molested children had been the most severely abused emotionally.

CHILD ABUSE: A FACTOR IN ADDICTION

When most sex addicts start recovery and stop acting out, the memories start to return. Those feelings about painful experiences have been blotted out by early compulsive behavior. A concept that helps us better understand the returning memories, as well as the connection between abuse and addiction, is that of posttraumatic stress disorder (PTSD).

Posttraumatic stress came first to public attention through the plight of Vietnam veterans, who were still having reactions to the war years and even decades later. Thus a former marine might wake up in his hallway at 2:00 A.M., wearing his battle fatigues, with no idea of how he got there but with the same feelings he had in battle. Essentially, what had happened in battle was so horrifying that he could not let himself fully experience the terror until later. The stress reaction comes long after the trauma—hence the term *posttraumatic stress*. These stress reactions resulted in disrupted families, lost jobs, and severe addictions.

In fact, addictions were a way to cope while in Vietnam. Drug use in Vietnam was unparalleled in American military history. Many vets told us that sex addiction was also vital to their survival. One, for example, shared a story about the extraordinary risks he would take going AWOL regularly in order to see prostitutes. Yet, the stress continued for these people, and so did the addictions.

Posttraumatic stress exists also in child abuse victims. Decades later they are having reactions to the trauma from their childhood. Some started to use compulsive behavior when the abuse was happening. Many used it later when the stress continued.

By examining the characteristics of posttraumatic stress disorder, we can see how addiction becomes a central coping mechanism. Essentially, there are ten characteristics:

1. *Disassociation.* Many victims develop an ability to detach from their abusive reality. This detachment borders on feeling disembodied. Kids will report, "I imagined myself watching us in bed from the ceiling." They literally cultivate the ability to disconnect from pain. Their susceptibility to trance and their search for escape make them vulnerable to the ultimate form of escapism: addiction. Disassociation is also a precondition for multiple personality disorders.

2. *Flashback.* Time collapses for victims, so that they mistake the present for the past. The Vietnam vet who wakes up in battle gear and the incest victim who wakes up terrified share a loss of reality: the past appears as if it is the present, especially under stress. They fear being insane and do not trust their ability to know what reality they are in.

3. *Confusion.* Situations in some way parallel trigger a fundamental inability to function. When circumstances or personalities remind victims of earlier traumas, they close down emotionally, physically, and intellectually. Victims use this "freezing" as a way to survive. Although under normal stress they can respond well, when something is reminiscent of the abuse their capabilities leave them. Addiction is an alternative when they cannot cope.

4. *Displaced anxiety.* Victims live with the fear of future victimization as well as unresolved anxiety from the past. Because the fear may have no current focus, it surfaces in other forms: insomnia, nervousness or jumpiness, and unexplained irritability. Many times the victims have absolutely no sense of where their discomfort comes from. They do seek relief from it, however.

5. *Exaggerated distrust.* Many victims who felt loyal and loving toward those who abused them cannot acknowledge their betrayal except by exaggerated distrust of partners and friends. Sometimes victims have no consciousness of the origins of their misgivings, since they long ago repressed their traumatic memories. Those close to them are left wondering how they earned this distrust or why they have to keep proving themselves trustworthy. If you do not trust people, you look for what you can rely upon—many find it in sex, food, and chemicals.

6. *Fusion of sex with associated feelings.* If early arousal patterns are connected to fear, loneliness, vulnerability, or neediness, victims as adults will always connect those feelings with sex. Many victims have trouble separating fear from the erotic, and, as noted earlier, fear is a powerful escalator in the neurochemistry of this illness. When nurturing has been sexualized for you as a child, as an adult you will see nurturing as sexual.

7. *Tolerance for pain.* Victims of sexual and/or physical abuse sometimes deliberately cut or burn themselves. These episodes are sometimes acts of self-hatred, other times reenactments of early trauma. For some victims, pain has been eroticized to the point where sexual pleasure can be escalated only by more severe pain, piercing, or flailing. In certain cases (e.g., the woman described in the previous chapter who cut crosses in her thighs), self-mutilation is a familiar way to control—the way one was controlled as a child. More common than many would think, self-injury is one of the most dangerous forms of sex addiction. In a prison of their own memories, addicts torture themselves.

8. *Perfectionism.* One way to avoid abusive attention to yourself is to avoid mistakes. Be adult, competent, and grown up, and you will not be hurt, judged, or exploited. People who try to such an extreme to control all outcomes deny their own dependency needs. We humans need help, make mistakes, and have limits to what we can do. Those who use the perfectionist solution are vulnerable to addiction, since compulsivity is the only way they can be out of control.

9. *Dependency avoidance.* Victims do not ask for help, nor do they trust love or care. They act as if they do not trust anybody. In therapy, victims will be flooded with painful emotions, then moments later collect themselves and speculate about whether they need therapy. What happens is that once having trusted the therapist enough to share some of the pain, their fear of needing the therapist takes over and they distance themselves. Part of recovery is for a victim to learn that dependency can be safe.

10. *Shame.* Many victims are profoundly ashamed. They see themselves as unworthy, immoral, destructive, and sinful. Abuse is often accompanied by messages designed to shame children into

submission or secrecy. When a man forces oral sex on his three-year-old daughter and then tells her she is sinful and bad for having allowed that to happen, that girl will make the message part of her personal reality. Self-conclusions about unworthiness are central to the addictive process.

Maxine's story illustrates the role posttraumatic stress may play in addiction. Her earliest sexual memory was of a man fondling her and raping her mother. Her early years were filled with violence and sex, but worst of all was the abandonment. She told us:

> First my grandpa got kicked out of the house, and I was his favorite. Then my mom left soon after he did, and then my dad couldn't take care of us so we ended up in foster homes. I was just totally alone, and the masturbation filled that emptiness. In the foster homes there was more physical abuse and more sexual abuse. For me I think a key piece with the addiction stuff was being so isolated, being so abandoned. It was the only way I knew how to feel in any kind of way that I was loved or belonged or worth something.

As an adult, her sexual behavior was indiscriminate, at times anonymous, and often with multiple partners. She would hang around strip shows and porno theaters and mingle with pimps and prostitutes. Danger and violence were central to her acting out.

It was her children who brought home to Maxine her own unmanageability. "I'd stay out all night and then sleep all day, and the kids would be up wanting to eat, wanting attention, and I'd just be tired. When I would get up, I'd be planning whatever I was going to do that night." She realized she was recycling the dynamics that had victimized her.

Maxine went to chemical dependency treatment and her therapist identified her primary addiction as sexual—she drank to block out her pain about her sexual acting out and the abuse. She said, "I did not want to feel." Further, she reflected, "It was realizing that I had never been innocent. I had never known what it was like to look at life and be amazed and awed at the world. I was managing to just survive. The drinking and sexual stuff were just more survival skills."

For many addicts like Maxine, the abuse events become critical incidents from which their addiction derives energy. The addiction may have any or all of the following characteristics:

- Addiction becomes a way to "survive" or cope with crisis.

- Addiction becomes a way in which the abuse events become internalized; fantasy and behavior "reenact" the childhood events.

- Addiction becomes a way to deaden or escape from the pain.

- Addiction becomes a way to fill the hole, to nurture oneself to make up for the deficit or the damage.

- Addiction becomes triggered by memories or parallel situations.

Essentially, the addiction is part of a maladaptive response to stress. The child abuse experience led to posttraumatic stress. Posttraumatic stress in turn evolved into one or more patterns of maladaptive response to stress. These patterns laid a foundation for the addiction:

Child abuse—sexual, physical, and emotional

↓

Posttraumatic stress—disassociation, flashbacks, confusion, anxiety, distrust, etc.

↓

Maladaptive response to stress—impaired coping, including addiction

This three-phase process gives us a framework for comprehending one of the most startling results to come out of our survey. We compared how severely each person was abused as a child with how many addictions they had as an adult. For the people in our survey, severity of abuse was an extremely accurate predictor of the number of addictions.

Sexual addiction has provided us with an essential key to understanding addictions in general. To study the connection between sexual abuse and sexual addiction was an obvious research goal.

That effort, important in itself, also helped further our knowledge of addictions in general. Three implications of tremendous importance have become clear:

1. All addicts, including sex addicts, must confront any denial they have about the role their child abuse experiences may have played in their addiction(s).

2. Our culture must make an even greater effort to confront the denial that we have collectively about child abuse and its damage.

3. We must construct a model of addiction that includes child abuse as a factor along with other factors relating to neurochemistry, shame, culture, and family.

CONFRONTING PERSONAL DENIAL

Maxine, like most who talked to us, emphasized how vital it was to be clear about what happened. She had to stop drinking and acting out first, but once stabilized, she had to see the reality. "I kept seeing the memory of my mom's rape and him fondling me in the bed. I kept setting myself up in those same situations where I would repeat what happened. Circumstances were different, but the scene was the same. That's what most of my fantasies were about. I was thirty years old before I made that connection." In fact, for Maxine, one of the more powerful discoveries she made with the help of her therapist was that many of her most driven fantasies were repressed memories. For example, her fantasies of being raped or watching rape were really memories of her early experiences.

All victims must evaluate their experiences in terms of frequency and degree of trauma. Just because abuse happened only once or twice does not mean it was not serious. Some of the most traumatizing events reported to us were one-time events. Similarly, abuse shouldn't be dismissed just because its form seems relatively trivial. A father's sexualizing stares may seem of little importance when compared with an experience of forced intercourse. But if this sexualizing is constant over time, trauma accumulates. These two extremes are apparent in Figure 4-1, which shows how trauma and frequency interact to determine the impact of the abuse.

FIGURE 4-1
IMPACT OF ABUSE

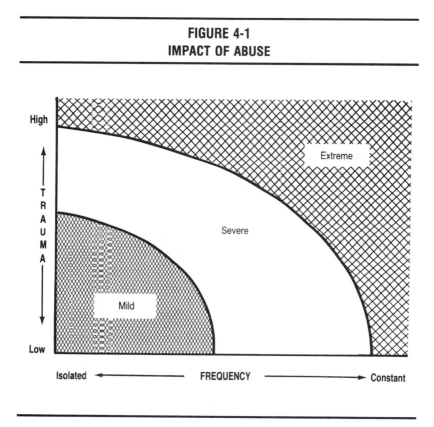

In a later chapter, we will detail strategies that addicts found successful in coming to terms with their abuse experiences. Now might be an appropriate time, however, for the reader to think about his or her own abuse history. You might want to complete the Abuse Survey, in Appendix A, adapted from our study, including the section on posttraumatic stress, before continuing with the chapter.

CONFRONTING CULTURAL DENIAL

John is a tall, thin Native American who works as a social worker and is certified as an alcoholism counselor. He also is a recovering sex addict and alcoholic. He describes sex addiction as one of the most shameful secrets of reservation life. He describes a pattern in which children are abused as part of the severe addiction problems of their parents. When the children's behavior becomes a problem, they are taken from the home and placed in a regional reservation school. There the older kids abuse the younger ones. The staff flagrantly abuse them all. Having come from this system, he says it is no accident he ended up an alcoholic and a sex addict. When he exposed the problem with documented cases, white Bureau of Indian Affairs managers refused to respond, saying it was a matter internal to the reservation and tribe. Angry tribal leaders buried the problem and ostracized him. John, one of many inspiring people we met in our study, is a genuine hero, committed to exposing the secret of sexual abuse.

Father Dominic is a specialist in canon law in the Roman Catholic church and frequently represents the church in corporate legal matters. But now a great deal of his time is taken up with a different sort of case. The Catholic church in America faces a great crisis in the growth of sexual problems among its clergy. Beyond affairs, the abuse of counseling relationships, homosexuality, and homophobia, and the double life around celibacy, there are dramatic problems with pedophilia. One diocese has a priest with 163 counts of sexual misconduct with children; out-of-court settlements in this case alone thus far exceed twenty million dollars. Thirty-two other priests in the same diocese are under indictment or investigation. Most archdioceses have six to nine current cases. Father Dominic fears that by the mid-1990s settlements will exceed a billion dollars.

In working with bishops and provincials, Father Dominic finds that many focus mainly on matters of financial liability. He seeks to expand their vision to the broader necessities and opportunities of the situation. Congregations ripped apart by such incidents need a healing process that reflects gospel principles. More generally, attitudes and information about healthy sexuality need to be infused into the life of the church. Celibacy closes off significant ministerial resources, draws into the clergy people with wounded sexual selves, and drives out talented leadership. There are increasing numbers of recovering sexually addicted clergy. These people could serve as a tremendous resource for the healing and vitality of the church—if the church leaders would accept them. Father Dominic's greatest fear is that the hierarchy's response will be based not on values or theology, not on building community, but rather on money concerns and the desire to maintain secrecy.

John and Father Dominic are authentic voices in a chorus that will crack the silence of denial. Yet competing voices exist. In a recent interview, a reporter from a national news magazine challenged me by suggesting that child abuse claims were exaggerated, in that seventeen-year-olds, for example, were really old enough to know better. Later in the interview he "apologized" for some rudeness by saying, "I'm sorry. I keep forgetting you guys take this seriously."

Cultural denial persists in many forms. *Sassy* is a slick magazine aimed primarily at junior high and senior high schoolgirls. In its August 1988 issue there was an article called "Hot for Teacher." This article describes problems confronting female high school students who have affairs with their teachers. The article treats these relationships as being a "hassle" and not going anywhere, rather than as being exploitive. It even concludes with a section entitled "You and Your Teacher Are Getting Married." The author extends the hope that such romances can have success:

> It can happen. Just ask Susan, who married her sexy junior-year French teacher. He was only 28 and she was 16. She had a crush on him the entire year and she knew he liked her back. "He let it be known that he was interested," she says, "by kissing my hand and looking up my skirt." This subtle approach really melted Susan's heart. So the summer after junior year she made her best friend call him up. He invited them to his apartment, and they both went. Things sort of accelerated from there. "I saw him three to four times a week my senior year—secretly. My best friend was the only one who knew."
>
> After her senior year, Susan finally decided to tell her parents about the French teacher. She lied and said he was 24 (he was 29 by then), and they told her she could go out with him

They eventually moved in together and then (drum roll) they got married. But even now, they have to lie about their relationship. Like, he doesn't want anyone else to know that she used to be his student because he's afraid people will think "he's a lech," says Susan.

Well, what's a few white lies compared to true love, right? (At least that's what Susan says.) And yes, there are occasions when fate and true love and all that will throw you and a teacher together into eternal bliss. But I think the experiences of these girls demonstrate that doing anything about a crush on a teacher is mega-dangerous, and not usually worth all the trouble.

But don't get discouraged; it's always safe to fantasize about your teacher. It's fun, easy to do at home in your spare time and causes very little wear and tear on the emotions. (Like me and my creative writing teacher, for example. God, he is so amazingly talented and a total babe. And I'm practically sure he'll propose to me any day now.)

While the author does express concerns, she gives explicit permission for the "special situation." Further, she models a fantasy that is intended to be tongue-in-cheek but really encourages a crossing of boundaries. The article clearly supports relationships that would be prosecutable.

George Michaels wrote and sang a song entitled "Father Figure." For many weeks it was at the top of the charts. It was well executed, rhythmical, and easy to dance to. Walkmans, radios, and videos everywhere played the compelling refrain. Probably, very few people thought about the words of the song, which are openly sexual and clearly state an incest theme.

One could say that the song is metaphorical, that it talks about a father figure rather than a father. But references to how love can be confused with "crime," and to holding the girl's "tiny hand" sound very familiar to therapists who see abused children—children who also believe their father when he says he will love them "until the end of time." According to the song, a girl needs the love and guidance of a superior, more knowledgeable, and more experienced male—a "daddy" who is also a "preacher teacher." The fact that the father image is extended to include male professionals like teachers and preachers intensifies the irony.

With some contemporary songs, no ambiguity exists. The rock group Oinga Boinga sings a song called "Little Girls," which tells of being sexual with underage girls, discovering that they are too young, and getting in trouble for it. The haunting refrain states, "I don't care."

Commercials also blur boundaries. Child abuse professionals at professional conferences always gasp when I screen a widely used gum commercial that depicts a series of romantic, suggestive scenes of adults kissing and holding one another. Inserted into the midst is a single scene of a father kissing his three-year-old daughter. While neither the father/daughter scene nor the scenes of adult trysts are in themselves bad, putting them together is jarring and suggestive.

Today, however, a new consciousness is emerging as courageous artists approach this difficult topic. The movie, *The Legend of Billie Jean* portrays a teenage girl who refuses sexual advances and then is set up by adults as a thief. The story shows how she and her friends take their own power and validate their reality. The Aerosmith song "Janie's Got a Gun" and the Mission's "Amelia" dramatically portray the damage of sexual abuse. "What's the Matter Here" by the group 10,000 Maniacs shows the powerlessness of concerned adults who want to help but are prevented by the abusive family. Suzanne Vega's "Luka" poignantly shows how hard it is to share the abuse story.

We live in a culture that responds to the drug problem with campaigns that teach kids to Just Say No. We who are concerned about addiction in light of what we have learned need to see that much more is done. We need to support the artists who are making positive statements to kids about the problem. We need to support child abuse prevention programs so children will help break the silence of denial. A key step is to build a model of addiction that incorporates child abuse as a contributing factor.

AN ADDITIVE MODEL OF ADDICTION

Often people ask addiction specialists what is *the* cause of addiction. Of course, no single cause exists. Rather, addiction, like any illness, can only be understood as an ecology, with many complex systems involved. Throughout these early chapters, we have underlined a number of key factors in addiction. In this chapter, we have shown how child abuse generates posttraumatic stress, resulting in addiction as a maladaptive response to stress. In Chapter Three we pinpointed how early family experiences could create shame-based personalities, which in turn were prone to self-defeating shame cycles.

We also acknowledged the role of an addiction-prone culture and peer group influence in promoting the addict's isolation. Earlier we made a case for a genetically predetermined neurochemical vulnerability as a foundation for addictive disorders. Addicts, we determined, underwent a neurochemical change, resulting in an imbalance, which the addiction preserved. Figure 4-2 summarizes factors causing the addictive process. By integrating these factors, we can perceive the pattern in the growth and development of addictions. A three-phase process unfolds: vulnerability, initiation, and addiction.

FIGURE 4-2
FACTORS IN THE ADDICTION PROCESS

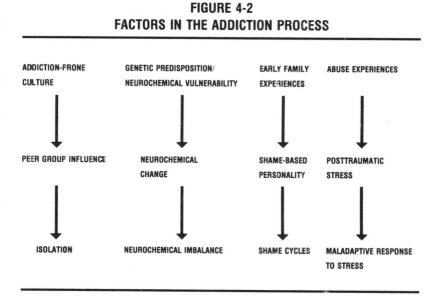

VULNERABILITY

Certain children are especially susceptible to the addiction process. These children live in our addiction-prone culture. They probably have parents who are addicted to one or more behaviors and/or substances. They come from families that are dysfunctional, and—at least in the case of sex addiction—probably also rigid and disengaged. Most often the children are abused, probably in several ways. These children are the vulnerable children.

Vulnerable children under these circumstances seek to feel better. They are not bad children, but rather children in pain who seek relief. They will use "highs" to feel better—food, sex, TV, whatever it takes to numb the pain. For most potential sex addicts, masturbation will be a key coping mechanism and source of comfort. Certain sexual experiences they have in their family may also serve this purpose. Figure 4-3 graphically represents the relationship of this pool of children to their environment. No one knows how many such children there are. We simply know they exist.

FIGURE 4-3
VULNERABILITY

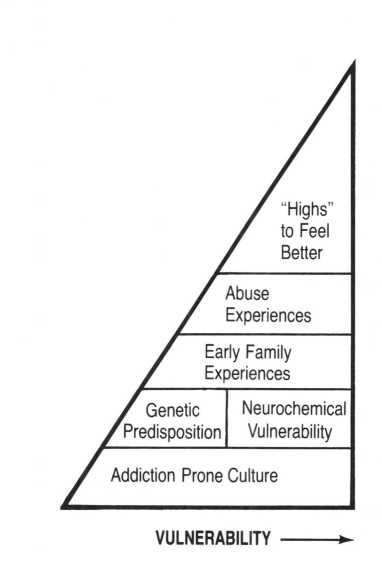

INITIATION

As they mature, some of these children do not get the support and care they need. They start to use the "highs" excessively or abusively. They probably find new, alternative highs as well. Their excessive use of highs is rooted in stressors, which they cannot handle. In this way, stressors serve as a catalyst to the addictive process. What initially was used to feel better now becomes a prerequisite for survival. This isn't surprising, since for these people, current traumas are compounded by posttraumatic stress. They have also developed a shame-based personality, which precludes fully normal development. They seek peer group support for their excessive use. What they do not realize is that this excessive use causes a neurochemical change. Without the highs, they start to not feel normal.

This initiation phase can be clear-cut and occur as soon as early adolescence. More likely, it will occur over time in a series of bouts of excessive behavior associated with stressful situations or life transitions. Without some significant intervention such as therapy, this ebb-and-flow pattern can extend indefinitely into adulthood. In such cases, addicts tend to see this initiation period as if it were merely a matter of circumstances or accidents. In retrospect, it is more reminiscent of a heat-seeking missile. Figure 4-4 graphically represents both the vulnerability and initiation phases of the addictive process.

ADDICTION

At some point excessive use becomes compulsive use. The highs become so compelling that the person loses control. Usually the loss of control means serious consequences. Yet the highs remain so compelling that the addict starts to distort, ignore, or lose contact with reality. The addiction now regulates the emotional life of the addict. The addict cannot act "normal" without the high. Nor can the addict deal with stressors without the maladaptive response of the addiction. The inherent shamefulness of the addict brings on self-destructive shame cycles, in which the addict's efforts to stop seem only to intensify the failures. The brain achieves a new neuro-

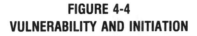

FIGURE 4-4
VULNERABILITY AND INITIATION

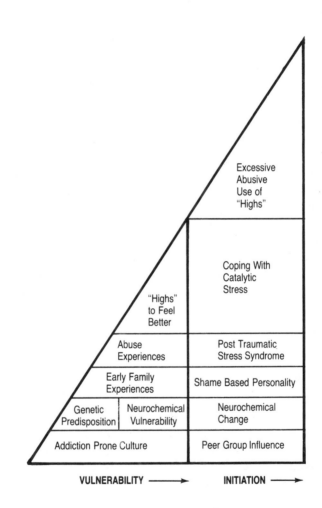

FIGURE 4-5
VULNERABILITY, INITIATION, AND ADDICTION

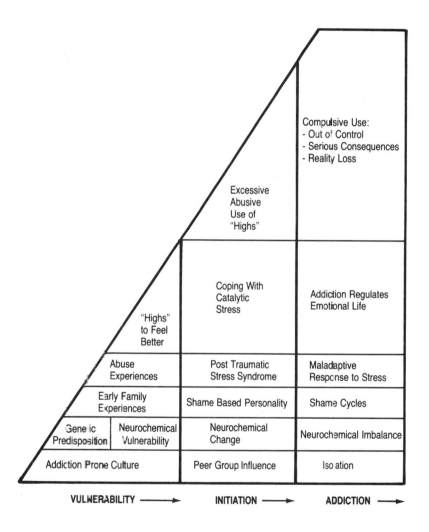

chemical imbalance, which can only be relieved by compulsive use. The addict ends up isolated and alienated.

Once this point is reached, addicts cannot undo all the damage even with help. Significant shifts have occurred which leave them forever vulnerable to their addiction. Since the addiction draws its strength from so many sources—abuse experiences, shame, neurochemistry, and culture—compulsive use always remains as an option. Illness occurs when an organism has become impaired in its functioning. Addictive illness becomes chronic, flaring up like herpes or diabetes when stress occurs and the body is depleted. But when addiction emerges, it becomes the organizing principle of the addict's life. Figure 4-5 graphically represents the addiction phase as it evolves from the vulnerability and initiation phases.

In short, addiction emerges from the interplay of various factors. How much does each factor contribute? We have no way of measuring this. More than likely their relative contributions vary with each child. Yet we can say that these are the factors involved and that each adds to the illness.

A critical factor in the transition from one phase of the process to the next is how the family reacts. In fact, in some cases, family reaction is pivotal to the development of addiction. Family members can prevent the addiction or become coparticipants. That is the final focus of this anatomy of addiction—and the topic of our next chapter.

CHAPTER FIVE

Addictive Partners: Mirrors of Obsession

- Ellen found out about her husband's affairs when she discovered three journals describing sexual encounters with over fifteen hundred women during their twenty-five-year marriage. Her friends knew. Her children knew. But somehow, during all those years, what was obvious to everyone else eluded her.

- Jan found out about her husband's pornography collection when someone called about a garage for rent. She had not known they owned a garage. In fact, she believed they were a family of very modest means. She had worked hard to manage on little. To make every dime count, she had even, for example, asked her children to wear shoes that no longer fit. When she found the garage, she was stunned to discover a twenty-year collection of pornography, which when adjusted for inflation represented an investment of three-quarters of a million dollars.

- On a hunch, Nancy followed her husband around for a full day. He had insisted they make love that morning, but it was a transaction, like many of late, for which neither seemed to be present. Even so, he stopped at a woman's house for lunch, visited another woman after work, and had dinner with a third. When he came home, he grumbled about his hard day. Hurt and angry, she said nothing about it for four months.

- Fran's path to treatment for coaddiction started with her neighbor's discovery that on some nights she slept outside in the family car. When confronted about it, she started sobbing in her neighbor's arms. Her husband's sexual demands were so excessive, it was the only way she could cope. The neighbor brought her to her pastor. He in turn got the couple into treatment.

- Although they lived together, Joe was always getting jealous. She would keep talking him out of it, saying he should be "liberated" and have a "higher consciousness." He felt there was something going on with those male friends of hers, but he would set his intuitions aside in order to gain her approval. Then he caught her in a couple of suspicious incidents. Each time they had a dramatic fight followed by a passionate honeymoon period. Finally, she admitted to an affair with a man who was a model in her art class. Joe had a painful talk with the man, hoping that he would back off when he realized Joe's pain. Two days later, he discovered they were together again.

- Fran was stunned. She was pregnant with her first child and about to deliver, when her husband informed her that he had a sexually transmitted disease. The only reason he was telling her now was that his physician had explained that without treatment the child could be damaged coming through the birth canal. In fact, to ensure the safety of the baby, he recommended a cesarean.

- John and Suzie were the model couple. Good-looking and successful, they were the type that should be in a family magazine photo essay. Their image collapsed when she discovered his thirteen-year affair with her sister. Worse, she found there had been many others. In therapy, she righteously punished him for over a year until her therapist astutely sensed there was something else wrong. On exploring her sexual history, he found that her behavior outside the marriage made her husband look like a neophyte. Her coaddiction was a screen for her sexual addiction.

These were the coaddicts in our study. Most were in their mid-thirties, but they ranged from the early twenties to late fifties. The majority were women, but some men participated, too. Like the addicts in our survey, the coaddicts were well educated; over half had college or postgraduate degrees. Many had their own addictions, and almost all came from families of addicts. They, too, were abused as children. They were the spouses and lovers of sex addicts—many of whom were in our survey.

They were clear about their own illness as coaddicts. They had an obsession with people who were out of control sexually. If their relationship was not with one sex addict, it would have been with another. For some, sadly, there were relationships with a number of sex addicts. The good news is that on the average the coaddicts had been in recovery for four years. Not only were they doing well, but they gave us great help as well.

The most startling part of talking to the partners of sex addicts was that coaddicts are mirror images of the addicts themselves. We discovered that there is a pool of people who are very much alike, that unerringly they find each other, and that they form dysfunctional relationships. Many coaddicts early in recovery resist the notion that they have anything in common with the addict. Those with significant recovery, however, insist on the importance of owning to the commonality. It is, they say, the place to start.

Our research absolutely validates that perception (see Table 5-1). To start, addicts and coaddicts in our survey came from the same type of families. Approximately two-thirds of addicts and of coaddicts come from families that are both rigid and disengaged. As already discussed, disengagement promotes fears of abandonment and low trust, while rigidity leads to feelings of shame and dependency. For addicts and coaddicts alike, relationships that are controlling and emotionally unsatisfying create comfort in that they are familiar.

As we reported earlier, 87 percent of sex addicts had parents or siblings who were addicted or multiply addicted. Almost all coaddicts came from such families as well. So living with out-of-control family members is familiar to both. Children raised with addicts learn ways to cope that are dysfunctional. Sometimes that means addiction itself. Over one-third of the coaddicts had eating disorders, 15 percent were alcohol or drug dependent, and 20 percent were sex addicts themselves.

Another similarity was histories of abuse. Patterns of sexual, physical, and emotional abuse for coaddicts were almost identical to

TABLE 5-1
CHARACTERISTICS REPORTED BY ADDICTS AND COADDICTS

	% ADDICTS	% COADDICTS
FAMILY HISTORY		
Disengaged	88	75
Other addicts in family	87	98
Rigid	77	77
Rigid/disengaged	68	63
ABUSE HISTORY		
Emotional abuse	97	91
Physical abuse	72	71
Sexual abuse	81	81
EMOTIONAL HISTORY		
Acted against own values	59	59
Emotional exhaustion	79	86
Emotional instability	76	83
Hopelessness and despair	87	87
Living double life	85	63
Loss of life goals	68	61
Loss of self-esteem	91	86
Self-abuse (e.g., cutting or burning)	11	11
Strong fears regarding future	78	80
Strong feelings of loneliness	90	87
Suicide attempts	17	8
Suicidal thoughts/feelings	69	54
PHYSICAL PROBLEMS		
Extreme weight loss or gain	25	38
Physical exhaustion	58	63
Physical problems (e.g., ulcers, high blood pressure)	25	29
Sleep disturbances	62	70
CONSEQUENCES		
Financial problems	55	58
Loss of career choice	25	20
Loss of important friends	49	53
Loss of interest in hobbies/ activities	65	61
Loss of work productivity	75	54

those for addicts. Posttraumatic stress characterized their lives as well. Their emotional complications in general paralleled those of addicts, ranging from suicidal obsession to self-abusive behaviors like cutting oneself.

Finally, addicts and coaddicts necessarily share some of the same consequences, including unwanted children, venereal disease, and AIDS. In addition, both experience other adverse physical consequences, including extreme fluctuations in weight, stress-related physical problems, sleep disorders, and exhaustion. And, for both, key areas of life, like work, friends, hobbies, and finances, become adversely affected.

If the coaddict's life is woven from the same threads as that of the addict, in what ways are the patterns that emerge different?

WHAT IS COADDICTION?

We start with the story of Sunny, a beautiful Amer-Asian woman in her mid-thirties. She was born in Japan; her mother was Japanese, her father an American GI. From the outset, her mother struggled with being accepted in America. In particular, she would go to extraordinary lengths to please her in-laws and would use Sunny in her efforts to gain approval from her mother-in-law. So the dynamics of placating were quite familiar to Sunny.

As the oldest, Sunny was often left with the responsibility of taking care of her sister and two brothers. In retrospect, she feels that she was harsh with them:

> It was the only way as a little kid I knew how to take care of three littler kids. A lot of times I was left to set an example, or make sure so and so didn't get into trouble. I always chose force and that was the way that was shown to me, too. My parents used physical abuse as a disciplinary measure. I was alone a lot in the sense that even though there were a lot of people around me, I felt like I had to be real responsible for a lot of things, all the time. With nobody else to share that responsibility with, I was a lonely child.

Living in an abusive, rigid, and disengaged family environment, she learned to cope with her overwhelming feelings by control and domination.

Other dynamics were generated by her father's sex addiction. He had gotten several girls pregnant before he married Sunny's mother. He was constantly collecting and hoarding pornography. The pornography had a special impact on Sunny. From grade school on, she told us, "I harbored a secret, shameful desire to be a stripper, to be in the same magazines that Daddy read." She would hear her mother berate the magazines, but in her head she concluded that "this is what men liked and this is how I wanted to be loved." So, from her father, she learned that sex was the most important sign of love. And by watching the way her mother manipulated her father, she concluded that women can control men by sex.

Sunny's sexual abuse by her father started when he gave her a copy of *Lolita,* the famous incest novel by Vladimir Nabokov. She and her father intellectualized their own sexual experience as an affair and an outgrowth of the Lolita role. She felt responsible for it because at times she initiated sex with her father, but she felt good about it, since she had something special that "other girls didn't have." By the time she was sixteen, however, she was clear that it no longer felt good. After watching early episodes of Rowan and Martin, she started to call her father a "dirty old man."

In college, Sunny got caught up in a whirlwind of sexual promiscuity and drug abuse. "I kept looking for being loved and connecting and for getting self-esteem needs by being able to attract many men into bed." Sunny felt that up to this point her history was very similar to that of many sex addicts. But then she met her husband and things changed dramatically.

She was attracted to him because he was bright, witty, and because he could tell jokes, especially sexual jokes. Now, she sees clear parallels with her father and his sexual humor. They had a romance of three months and moved to his hometown in the Midwest. On their honeymoon, he took her to some porno movies and a strip show. She was upset. She was confused because she had had fantasies about doing the things he wanted to watch. Yet she felt also that there was something wrong with him. "That's when the controlling started. I started saying that's too much and defining what the limits were for his sexual acting out." For Sunny, an essential line had been crossed. She now started to obsess about her husband's obsession with sex. Basically, she did what many coaddicts do—she switched one obsession for another. The only difference between the obsessions was who was doing the acting out. She told us:

> Coaddiction won out over the sexual acting out. From that point on, when I started realizing that he was too much into this, that became the dominant role that I played in our relationship. And that went on for maybe six years. I did the whole classic thing of finding the stash, throwing the stash out, giving him a lecture, saying "I'm going to leave forever unless you clean up your act." He cries and does the whole thing of "I'm sorry, I'll never do it again." It was just like the whole classic alcohol scene, where you find the bottles and pour them down the drain.

For all of Sunny's efforts, the problem became worse. In the process of moving she found in the trash a record of a recent loan her husband had received. It was for eight hundred dollars and she knew of no reason that he needed the cash. When confronted, he said it was for pornography—but she knew then it was not true. She extracted a promise that he would see a psychiatrist when they were settled. Then the detective work really began. Sunny was checking everything:

> Searching pockets, going through bills with a fine-tooth comb. Searching the premises. Turning over every mattress, I mean everything. Looking in every place. Looking in storage areas downstairs, looking through closets, under things, just tearing the place apart. To find what I knew I usually would find. But that was my craziness.

At one point she kept a record of her husband's mileage, not knowing that every time he drove into the city to sexually act out, he disconnected the odometer.

They went through a number of psychiatrists. One physician insisted she come in for a session. During the session he suggested that maybe part of the problem was that she was too prudish. "With my history," Sunny pointed out, "that was a big joke." So they searched for yet another doctor. At one point she thought her husband was seeing a doctor but in fact the physician was mythical and the trips were to act out.

With each new therapist, things would settle down, however, and Sunny would refocus on the family and managing their children's lives. She thought of herself in terms of a line she had read in a cookbook called *Laurel's Kitchen* about the traditional role of women as the "keeper of the keys." She said, "It just felt like so much power. I was what I believed and what I did."

Finally, Sunny's discovery of an extensive stash of pornography in his business office forced them to seek help one more time. They were referred to a hospital-based outpatient program for sexual addiction. In addition to his receiving treatment, she was asked to attend meetings of Co-SA, a twelve step program for spouses and partners of sex addicts. Co-SA, like S-Anon and Co-SLAA, is a nationwide fellowship enabling coaddicts to develop a recovery program for themselves. Sunny started her recovery when the hospital insisted she join Co-SA.

Sunny had to address her powerlessness over her husband. She could not control him or manage him. She told us, "That's my number one powerlessness issue—not being able to stop controlling him—even though I had many, many opportunities to see that it did not work." She added, "I kept thinking that maybe this would be the time."

She found that her coaddiction took many forms, including behaving in ways she did not like. She tried to be sexually more attractive to her husband. This involved, she reflected, "a lot of things that were not me"—underwear, garter belts, and lots of makeup that were all designed "to keep his sexuality at home."

Sunny also did not like the rageful person she was becoming. She used her rage to act out her feelings of being a victim and a martyr. She would rage at her husband and that would precipitate physical violence in which they both participated. She would also get him by "exposing" him to ridicule in the family by telling some of her discoveries. She tried to shame him in front of others and also used shame as a tactic to manipulate him into doing things she wanted, even if it was only the dishes.

Most painful for Sunny was the fact that the primary recipients of her rage were her children. They became "garbage cans" for her feelings and for her sense of shame about herself. If her daughter did something that reminded her of her own flaws, she would "explode in rage at her." These explosions reflected not only her frustration about herself and her husband's acting out, but also general "hysterical rage against all men and against the whole world." She described her losses this way: "My losses have been that I hurt my children. And that I'd been in a self-destruct cycle for so long, I mean those neuron pathways are etched into myself, and it makes it very difficult to live any other way. It makes it hard to let go and to have space and to fill myself up with good things."

Sunny had become disconnected from herself and what she wanted to be. She existed either in a reactive mode or in a care-taking mode. Her own needs and wants were discarded. She was doing what she did not want to do, and she could not stop herself. She felt caught with no escape. She was an addict, but her obsession was another person. So, to the other characteristics that coaddicts like Sunny have in common with addicts, we can add self-destructive behavior that they want to stop but can't.

COADDICTS' DEFINITIONS OF COADDICTION

Being addicted to the addict.

Taking responsibility for people, tasks, situations I'm not responsible for.

Being "good" enough to earn love of others.

Reacting to someone else's behavior instead of from my own motives.

Being all-consumed with another person and putting yourself on hold.

Due to the reaction to your addict you are just as crazy and just as sick.

A coaddict is so emotionally tied to another they cannot admit the other's illness.

I lost all sense of myself, how I feel, and what I need. Being obsessed with another person as a way of not dealing with my own life—my own pain, shortcomings, joy, and growth.

Being obsessed with the addiction and all my spouse's feelings and behaviors—trying to fix him, keep things smooth, while neglecting myself and not looking at my own difficulties.

Controlling another person's behavior, and the preoccupation is energy draining and draws attention from self.

A common definition emerges: coaddiction is an obsessive illness in which reaction to addiction causes the loss of self. Like addicts, then, coaddicts lose an essential sense of themselves. They may put up a front for the world, but the reality of what is happening proves the lie. The front has little to do with the coaddict's true self; it is just an image used to shield the reality of what both addict and coaddict have become. The coaddict is part of the addict's double life. As Sunny summarized:

> I would have died if I had stayed in the codependency, but it just seemed safer. There's something more secure in it, other people involved, and it's not so lonely. It's a better front. It fits culturally. It looks real good. It looks like we have a family and that we're all functioning well, and I didn't want to be skid row anything. You know, I wanted to be very presentable and I had just in mind how I wanted to appear, and so that was the facade that I contrived to arrange.

The preserving of appearances does not prevent the erosion of self, however. Terri, another coaddict, did all the same things Sunny did. She obsessed about her husband, where he was, what he was doing. She did all the detective work. She would not leave home for fear of his having someone in the house. She became paranoid about other women, saw them through his eyes, and compared herself with them. She rationalized that he was more liberal and open-minded about sex than she was. She risked diseases because of his sexual habits. She felt embarrassed to go out with him because other people knew about his exploits. Out of her experience, Terri wrote a definition of coaddiction that reads like a coaddict's creed:

> The loss of self. I never questioned if I loved him, only if he loved me. I never thought about being happy, only

could I keep him there. I never thought about my needs, only could I meet his. Feeling less and less because nothing I did was enough. Thinking there was something wrong with me that I could not meet his sexual needs. Hating myself for being "weak," having no pride, putting up with abusive treatment. Thinking the best solution was if he were dead, then wishing I was dead. Having no interest outside of the relationship. Feelings of absolute nothingness when he left me. Willing to do anything to get him back. And always the pain. The extreme difference between what I projected myself to be and what I actually was.

Another of our coaddicts said, "The old song—'Sometimes I'm happy, sometimes I'm blue. My disposition depends on you'—was written for me."

COADDICTS' POWERLESSNESS AND UNMANAGEABILITY

Sunny told us that in treatment one day she suddenly "got it": "Not only am I not in control of his behavior, but I'm not in control of wanting to control his behavior. That's something I can't stop and it's a real compulsion for me." Essentially, she admitted her powerlessness. Usually, clarity about the illness comes from a "first step" in which coaddicts look at their powerlessness. This first step requires very specific and concrete examples that when strung together shatter the coaddict's denial. Usually these examples of powerlessness include extreme acts of attempting to control the addict. But they also include more ordinary attempts at control that had become excessive.

COADDICTS' STATEMENTS OF POWERLESSNESS

I listened in on my husband's phone calls.

Checking bank account statements and phone bills and reading his journal.

Looking for the addict at his "favorite spots" in a city of 1.7 million.

Checking his underwear for signs and clues.

Feeling so powerless and victimized by his "secret life" that my anger exploded at my children.

Feeling restless when he's not home—watching from the window.

Checking on him when he disappears at parties.

Asking for reassurance all the time that he is not acting out.

Looking through his papers and mail.

I would not travel away from home (because I feared my husband would act out) for fourteen years.

I would not speak up about things in our relationship because I was told "If you don't like it, leave."

Driving 70 + mph home from work when he didn't answer the phone in the A.M. to see if he was home.

Checking the phone bills for long distance calls to strange numbers as evidence of acting out.

I would take the phones when I left for work every day so he could not call certain "services."

Riding by the home of his "lady friend" to see if he was there.

Following him when he acted out and waiting parked next to his car until he came out.

Looking at these examples of powerlessness, readers might wonder why anyone would keep doing such things. What the coaddicts share with addicts is preoccupation. Sex addicts spend almost all their time being preoccupied with sex, whether or not they are acting out. Coaddiction is also an obsessive solution. As long as coaddicts obsess, they do not have to deal with their own feelings, limits, or flaws. They do not have to face themselves. The loss of self is, in fact, the payoff—as in any addiction. Over two-thirds of coaddicts in our survey clearly were able to identify with the concept that they obsessed about the sex addict as a way to avoid their own pain.

Also, playing roles of caretaker, detective, or superorganizer feels powerful. Coaddicts think they can change things. Addicts get stuck in self-destructive cycles because they believe that they ultimately can control their addiction—if they just try harder. Similarly, coaddicts believe that with greater effort they can turn things around. In their powerlessness, they believe themselves to be powerful.

Sadly, they learn. Consider Herb, a thirty-eight-year-old production manager from New England. All of his growing up had led him to some fundamental conclusions. He felt sex was bad and shameful and had great self-doubt about his own sexual adequacy. His frustration at being unable to form sexually intimate relationships led him to select women who were dependent upon him and unable to be emotionally present for him. He found women who were unfaithful, deceptive, manipulative, and promiscuous. His last major affair was with a prostitute. What he told us of his motivation could be a refrain for most coaddicts:

> I became attracted to women who were less capable than I, women I could take care of and receive some feeling of self-importance from. These women were emotionally abusive to me. I put up with the abuse, I took on their pain, I focused on their lives and what I could do to make their lives better—took the focus off my life and what I should do for myself to make me better and happier. I became frustrated, angry, self-pitying—I felt shame when they were promiscuous or unfaithful. I felt unworthy of anything better—I had lost my self and my goals and aspirations by trying to save unsalvageable relationships.

Saving the unsalvageable becomes harder as the coaddict's life becomes more unmanageable. Unmanageability, together with powerlessness, is the fundamental determinant of the individual's being out of control. Thus, as a first step toward recovery, coaddicts must admit not only to powerlessness, but to how unmanageable things have become. As with powerlessness, they must face the very concrete, specific facts of what they were willing to tolerate for their obsession.

COADDICTS' STATEMENTS OF UNMANAGEABILITY

Periods where anger was so out of control, I set up the addict to do things I did not want, approve of, etc.

I became so depressed when I first learned I took off work for three weeks and went to bed.

Inability to concentrate and accomplish tasks to meet deadlines.

Habitual irritability.

For comfort, I spent money and ate.

I shut down sexually and denied myself pleasure to deny him pleasure.

I had an automobile accident on the way to police station when he was picked up.

I would get overly mad and hit our dog.

I couldn't concentrate on work and made more mistakes.

I paid so much obsessive attention to the addict, I was very unavailable to my children, and I didn't even notice that.

I lived in daily depression, anxiety, and self-hatred.

I took on all the financial responsibilities of the addict.

I smoked pot with the addict to try to regain some form of common ground— even though I hated it.

I became very disorganized and found small tasks too large.

I felt distraught and nauseated when I felt the addict was acting out.

Behaving in ways you don't like, violating your own values and standards, emotionally bingeing so you hurt innocent loved ones, having accidents, being in jeopardy situations, becoming overextended emotionally, financially, and in other ways, losing your own life goals hobbies, and interests—the list of unmanageables grows and grows.

A picture emerges of the addict and coaddict living parallel lives, progressively more obsessive and more unmanageable. The difference lies in the objects of their obsession. Some would suggest that another difference is that addicts are men and coaddicts are women. We found this to be untrue about addicts; it is also not true about coaddicts.

GENDER DIFFERENCES

What is true is that most coaddicts *who seek help* are women. Clinicians have long noticed that coaddicted men are difficult to involve in treatment—for many of the same reasons men do not talk about abuse they experienced as children. To be coaddicted runs contrary to cultural images of what it means to be manly. The fact is that both men and women draw heavily upon cultural stereotypes for coaddictive preoccupation. Coaddiction takes some of the worst sexual and family pathology our culture has to offer and transforms it into obsessive illness.

When growing up, coaddicts learn from their family rules that later provide energy and support for their dysfunctional patterns. We asked women for examples of rules that kept them stuck in their coaddiction. Examples they gave were:

- Women need men no matter how awful the man is.

- Sex is a valuable tool for females to use to control males.

- Women need to dress sexy but not be sexual.

- Boys could want sex, while girls were either virgins or "bad."

- Family togetherness is everything.

- Keep odd behaviors a secret; do not even discuss them within the family.

- A woman simply is no good without a boyfriend.

Provide sex but don't be sexual; without a man, you are not a person; keep the family waters smooth—these served as prime directives for many women coaddicts. These rules also reflected family shame. One woman told us, "Sex was never discussed openly. I remember feeling shame about our family and thought it was because we were poor and a large family. I found out recently that my grandfather was in prison for asking little girls to pull their pants down." Further, she added, "My mother absolutely fit the description of codependency." Secrecy, sexual negativity, no-talk rules—the patterns start early.

Men's lives, too, are shaped by strong cultural stereotypes and family experiences. That became very clear as we listened to the story of Jason, a thirty-two-year-old physician from the Northwest.

In retrospect, Jason looks at his high school dating and sees the patterns already there. His first sexual involvement started when he "dated a girl who was probably chemically dependent and known to be kind of loose." He found women who were needy and had problems. He remembers at one point having a choice between a girl who was stable and healthy and one who made him feel needed. He chose feeling needed. He said, "I think that's when I really fine-tuned my codependency."

His dating reflected patterns that already existed in the family. He described his parents:

> My dad was a great codependent caretaker. He took care
> of his mom, his aunts, and his grandmother after his dad,
> who was an alcoholic, left. His brother and sister became
> alcoholics, and he was kind of the one stable factor in the
> family. He really took care of them. He moved next door
> to them and really did an awful lot of things for them. He
> was also raising a family.
>
> My mom, I think, was also a real caretaker. She's a
> nurse, in kind of a care taking field. She was also one that
> had a great knack for making you feel guilty about disap-
> pointing her or not living up to certain expectations or
> whatever. She would not be openly honest about her
> feelings, about feeling sad or mad. She would just let you
> know in many ways that this was not quite right with her
> and you better make it right.

In college Jason started dating a woman named Patti, and they married before his senior year. Like the women he had dated in the past, Patti had a problem-filled life and a family history of addiction. The first incident occurred while he was still in college. Patti worked as a waitress in a café that served a lot of railroad crews. She developed friendships with railroad people and took some trips with them. He found out she was also sleeping with them. He remembered, "It was just like somebody kicked my world out from under me. I didn't know what to do or who to turn to. I was just lost. So lost."

And so the episodes began. There was the man she saw during her first pregnancy. There was the man she brought home while her husband was away at a church retreat. There was the photographer she did "shoe modeling" for. The pattern following each discovery was the same. First, there was always the shock. Then there was a period of blame and recrimination, which often started with Jason telling the family what she had done now. Then there would be a period of reconciliation and promises to change.

But Jason could not share how his anger deepened with each episode. He said "I think it came out by telling her she wasn't good enough." He would criticize the "way that she spent money, her lack of involvement in bed, the way she would communicate to our friends and say the wrong things." Surprisingly, Jason's behavior received some support from one of the first of many therapists Jason insisted his wife see. The therapist advised, "This wife of yours is not grown up and she'll act like a child and there may be times when you need to treat her like a child. You may need even to spank her." Jason never spanked her, but he observed, "It kind of set me up as the adult and her as the rebellious child, and that's the way things developed."

Finally Patti found a therapist who worked on her sexual addiction. Jason remained an "observer" for some time but eventually started therapy and a twelve step program for himself. "That's when I started looking at myself rather than Patti. I started looking at my extreme need to be needed, the need to take care of, and the need to control." He also started owning how medical school and medicine "was some built-in escape" because he would be away so much. In fact, he admitted that coaddiction was one of the driving forces that led him to become a physician.

Jason and other men coaddicts share control, shame, anger,

escape, and self-destructive behavior with coaddicted women. They differ in that they draw mainly upon those cultural rules that say they must be the rock and the guiding hand for the unreliable, emotionally unstable partner. Like women coaddicts, however, they also are not to rock the boat or create waves in the family. So they are just as stuck.

PROBLEMS WITH SEX

Over half of the coaddicts identified with the statement that sex was the most important sign of love. If someone was sexual with you, that meant they loved you. This belief spurred coaddicts to be seductive, to be cooperative in sexual behavior they did not like, and to use sex as a way to control the sex addict. However, when the addict was sexual with others, the belief turned coaddicts into driven people: since sex meant love, this sexual acting out was equated with abandonment. And coaddicts will do almost anything to avoid abandonment, including giving up their own sexuality.

It helps to contrast sex addiction with other addictions. When your alcoholic partner chooses a bottle over you, you can detach. When your partner chooses other sexual partners, the sword cuts deeper and detachment is much more elusive.

Coaddicts become sexually very volatile; their reactivity to the addict's behavior showed a wide range of sexual responses. Of the coaddicts in the survey, 21 percent had affairs to retaliate against or punish the addict and prove that they were still attractive. A more common response, reported by 37 percent, was to become "hyper" sexual for the addict. Coaddicts would join with the addict in his activities and fantasies and collude in his behavior—at least as long as they could handle it. Joining in is better than abandonment. By far the most common response was to close down sexually; 74 percent of the coaddicts reported that ultimately they lost touch with their own sexuality. Some did all three things—had affairs, became hyper-sexual for the addict, and became asexual.

Disassociating from oneself sexually is a "solution" in that, by not being sexual, the coaddict deadens the pain. The coaddict does not have to deal with betrayal, secrecy, or risk—or with how much it matters. Nor does the coaddict have to deal with feelings and memories from an abusive past. And for those who had bouts with promiscuity, it is easier to turn off their sexuality than to deal with the issues it presents.

Many coaddicts become sexually "anorexic" in order to control the addict. Sunny, earlier in this chapter, described how she turned from promiscuity to sexual rigidity to limit her partner because he was "too much" into it. Typically, coaddicts go to a compensating extreme in order to balance the relationship. Often, the more out of control the partner is, the more closed down sexually the coaddict becomes. It is as if there were an equation for the relationship that required one extreme to be balanced by another. The coaddict's sexuality is sacrificed in service of the marital system.

To further complicate matters, sexual issues become entangled with other addictions. Consider the sex addict who is married to a compulsive overeater. He watches her to see if she is sneaking food (his coaddiction to her food addiction). He is angry because her weight repels him sexually, yet uses that to rationalize his acting out (a common trait among coaddicts). When he catches her, he says, "Did you really need that?" And she is immediately angry—and hungry.

She, too, is an addict watcher, always looking for some evidence that he is doing something sexual. The more she works to catch him, the angrier he is and the "hornier" he feels. She uses food to escape her pain from "the problem." And, in fact, her weight is a sexual statement. She does not want him to be sexual with her in the ways he has been. Her commitment to not being sexual emerges as a key dynamic in the addictive dance.

Sexual anorexia, sadly, speeds up the rhythms of the dance. When she changes clothes out of his sight so as not to "stimulate" him, he interprets that as a judgment of him and his sexuality. He feels more shameful and wants to escape pain. The familiar way to deal with shame and pain is to sexually act out, and in doing so, he'll feel fortified with justification by her sexual nonavailability.

The variations on this theme are endless. Sexual reactivity and multiple addictions provide a staggering array of ways for partners to destroy their sexuality together.

Consider the story of Dave and Mary. Dave saw the intimate connection between his sexuality and his drinking almost from the start of treatment. He was committed to not being sexual because, he said, "I knew in the past that my pattern had been that if I got involved in extramarital affairs I ended up drunk. I really wanted to be sober." For a long time he struggled with talking about the issue in AA but got little support. Not until he found a Sexaholics Anonymous group was he able to work on the connection between his alcoholism and his sexual addiction.

Meanwhile, Mary, too, had gotten into affairs, and when she did, she started to use prescription drugs. As a nurse she had easy access to this way of dealing with the pain. She told us that her addictions evolved parallel to Dave's:

> I think I was very lonely because he was drinking all the time. He was always drunk when I came home. I did not know about all the sexual affairs he was having, but I felt quite shut out of his life because he had other things to do that weren't mine. That's when I got involved with one gentleman. Then I became involved with about nine different guys in two years. I really lost control there I feel totally.

Mary says she felt so guilty about what was happening, she had to have a gastorectomy: "Part of my stomach had to come out because my nerves were just shot."

In recovery, Dave and Mary realized that, as they acted out with other people, their sexuality with each other had dwindled. Their chemical dependencies had built further walls, partly because the chemicals were different and partly because addictions always build walls.

Contrast Dave and Mary's experience with what happened to Esther. Like most coaddicts, Esther grew up in a rigid, nonsupportive environment with many negative messages about sex. Esther says her parents didn't validate her sexuality in any way. Their message was not only that sex was bad, but also that she was not "feminine," not "good-looking," and not "capable of attracting a man." Further, her father told her, "You've got to hide your brain from men. You'll drive them away if you let them know how smart you are." There were even suggestions that she get a job with the Union Pacific, which has a good pension, since no man would take care of her.

Esther did get married. She also became alcoholic. The man

she married was the perfect match for her addiction. She told us about meeting his family during their courtship:

> At Easter he had me fly down to meet his mother in Fort Lauderdale. She was a very severe alcoholic and he wanted me to see his family as it really was. His grandfather was also an alcoholic. The first thing his mother said to me when we came in the house practically was "Why don't you two go in the bedroom and have sex." She had been giving him this message since he was about twelve years old. She herself was married five times, and his aunt was married six times. And she was an alcoholic. Her husband was one that stopped through Christian Science, and his brother was also. I mean the family was riddled with every kind of addiction and abandonment, I now know.

She found a man who was familiar with alcoholics and who himself became a sex addict.

Esther's history as an alcoholic was painful and traumatic. Her husband's work involved their living overseas for periods of time. At one point her behavior was so bad he had to send her back to the United States in order to save his job. When their second child died of crib death, she became suicidal. She ultimately got into treatment and began a successful recovery.

Several years later, while her daughter was home from boarding school, Esther found, lying on the bedroom rug, a picture of a woman. On the back was her husband's name, the words "I love you," and the woman's name. She confronted her husband in front of the daughter. The discovery and confrontation precipitated another bout with suicide. But this time she had the support of her daughter, her AA network, and her therapist. After the crisis her sexual reaction was very typical of coaddicts:

> What I did then was totally try to change myself to recapture his love. I mean I really went into the codependency like crazy. I also bought books on sex because we'd had very little sex in our marriage. It was an anorexic kind of thing. He just denied me sex because I'd been so awful when I was drunk. And I didn't know he had all these affairs all these years. So what I did was buy this book on

sex and it said that you should fantasize and masturbate and I did. And I went crazy masturbating. I mean I was just as compulsive as could be. And it really scared me. So I put that away and stopped that. Then he told me that he had given up the girl and we seemed to be having a very good time. He really had not broken off all his relationships, but I didn't know this, and it seemed like we had this new life.

As so often occurs, alcoholism, sexual addiction, and responses of sexual anorexia and hypersexuality are all mixed together. The pattern fits, right down to the honeymoon period of starting over.

After six years of sobriety came the event that finally got them into treatment. Esther received an anonymous letter saying, "Your husband's having an affair." She had had no clue that anything was going on, aside from the fact that he was not being sexual with her. She immediately blamed herself, recycling all the shame-based responses she had used since childhood: "I thought it was my fault as you always do. There was something wrong with me. I wasn't sexy enough. I wasn't pretty enough. I wasn't as fancy as the rich women in the hotels and the career women that he ran into all the time. And it was my fault. I was doing it all wrong. And if I could get it right and I could improve myself in every way, then he would love me and give me sex."

What Esther, Sunny, Jason, and Mary have in common is sexual reactivity, one of the clear signs of coaddiction. Ultimately, coaddicts' extreme and volatile sexual responses draw on the shame-based dynamics of addictive families. To understand how sexuality becomes the hostage in these relationships, it is necessary to take into account the sex addiction itself, the interplay with other addictions, and the deep roots in family history.

Sexologist Ginger Manley of Vanderbilt Medical School stresses that she will never again treat inhibited sexual desire without first checking for sex addiction in the family. Too often she has found that inhibited desire is a coaddictive response—or that (as in Esther's case) it is the addict whose acting out prevents connection with the partner. She asks her patients to complete a family genogram in which they map out all the addictions and abuse experiences in the family. This larger picture has been often overlooked by clinicians who focus on the immediate problem.

A very common experience in sex addiction treatment is that when partners of sex addicts come into the program, they report that they have not had sexual feelings in years. As soon as they learn that the addict has embraced celibacy as the first stage of the treatment process, they are flooded with sexual feelings. Their sexuality has been on hold as a pawn in the game of addiction. Manley and other sexologists recognize this phenomenon as a key to helping people reclaim their sexual selves.

NINE PATHS TO COADDICTION

All coaddicts share nine processes in common. These processes are paths to powerlessness and unmanageability, and thus to coaddiction. They are signs that coaddiction is present.

1. *Collusion.* Most coaddicts actively support the addiction by covering up for the addict in some way. Powerful childhood rules about family image and secrecy have helped make them unwitting partners in the addictive process. Over two-thirds of our survey respondents kept secrets about the addict. Over one-half actually lied to cover up for the addict's behavior. Nearly three-quarters said that they actively worked to present a united front to the world. Another form of collusion was evidenced by the 37 percent who reported becoming "hyper" sexual in an effort to join with the addict.

2. *Obsessive preoccupation.* Coaddicts obsess about addicts and their lives. Thus, 62 percent of our survey respondents found themselves constantly thinking about the addict's behavior and motives. Moreover, 58 percent actually played detective, by checking mail, purses, and briefcases. A similar percentage found themselves so obsessed they would forget about other things. Over two-thirds clearly saw that their obsession was a way to avoid their own feelings.

3. *Denial.* When not obsessing, coaddicts lapse into ignoring the realities around them. In our survey, 83 percent mentioned setting aside their intuitions, while 43 percent said there were

periods in which they totally denied the problem. Almost three-quarters indicated that they would keep extra busy and overextended to avoid the problem. Despite failures, over two-thirds maintained the belief that they could eventually change the addict.

4. *Emotional turmoil.* Life for a coaddict is an emotional roller coaster. Approximately three-quarters of our coaddict respondents indicated that they went on emotional binges, that at times their emotions were simply out of control, and that they experienced free-floating shame and anxiety. Almost two-thirds agreed with the statement that they always had a crisis or problem.

5. *Manipulation.* Coaddicts become manipulative in their drive to control their partner. Of the coaddict respondents, 61 percent recognized that they had tried and failed to control their partner's sexual acting out. The same number admitted using sex to manipulate their partner or patch up disagreements. Over half made threats to leave but never followed through. Almost all saw themselves as having played martyr, hero, or victim roles.

6. *Excessive responsibility.* In their obsession, coaddicts were extremely tough on themselves. Over three-quarters blamed themselves for the problem. Sixty-two percent believed that if they changed, the addict would stop. The same number took responsibility for the addict's behavior. In addition, many would actually seek extra responsibility; 59 percent indicated that they created dependency situations where they would be indispensable.

7. *Compromise or loss of self.* Coaddiction involves a constant series of compromises, which erodes one's sense of self. Thus, 59 percent of our coaddicted respondents acted against their own morals, values, and beliefs. A full 61 percent gave up life goals, hobbies, and interests. Over half changed their dress or appearance to accommodate the addict. Forty-three percent accepted the addict's sexual norms as their own.

8. *Blame and punishment.* Coaddicts become blaming and punishing in their obsession. Almost two-thirds of coaddicts in our survey perceive themselves as having become progressively more self-righteous and punitive. Twenty-one percent had affairs to punish the addict or to prove that they were worthwhile and attractive. Over half saw their behavior as destructive to others. Perhaps

the best indicator of coaddictive vengeance was the 36 percent who admitted to homicidal thoughts or feelings.

9. *Sexual reactivity*. Coaddicts went to various extremes in reacting sexually to their partner's behavior. Predominant, however, was the impulse to close down sexually. Over two-thirds of our respondents reported numbing their own sexual needs and wants. Over one-third would change clothes out of the addict's sight. Forty-three percent would make excuses not to be sexual. Two-thirds rarely felt intimate during sex.

Table 5-2 summarizes the preceding list and gives data from the survey for the nine characteristics of coaddiction.

We have defined coaddiction as an illness in which reactivity to addiction causes the loss of self. These nine characteristics serve then as signs of the presence of the obsessional illness. Yet, substantial confusion persists over what coaddiction, or codependency, is. First, we need to sort out sex, love, romance, and relationship addictions from coaddiction. Second, we need to examine how the word "coaddiction" gets used.

TABLE 5-2
NINE CHARACTERISTICS OF COADDICTION

COADDICTIVE CHARACTERISTICS	TYPES OF BEHAVIOR	% COADDICTS
1. **Collusion**	Joined addict to present united front	71
	Kept secrets to protect the addict	66
	Lied to cover up for the addict	53
	Became hyper sexual for the addict	37
2. **Obsessive preoccupation**	Focused totally on addict to avoid feelings	67
	Constantly thinking about addict's behaviors and motives	62
	Checked addict's mail, purse, briefcase, etc.	58
	Forgetful	57
3. **Denial**	Denied personal intuitions	83
	Kept overly busy and overextended	72
	Believed I could eventually change addict	68
	Totally denied the problem	43

COADDICTIVE CHARACTERISTICS	TYPES OF BEHAVIOR	% COADDICTS
4. **Emotional turmoil**	Emotions were out of control	79
	Went on emotional binges	78
	Experienced free-floating shame and anxiety	74
	Always had a crisis or problem	63
5. **Manipulation**	Played martyr, hero, or victim roles	92
	Used sex to manipulate or patch disagreements	61
	Failed efforts to control sexual acting out of partner	61
	Made threats to leave but never followed through	54
6. **Excessive responsibility**	Blamed myself	75
	Believed if I changed, addict would stop	62
	Took responsibility for addict's behavior	62
	Created dependency situations where I was indispensable	59
7. **Compromise or loss of self**	Gave up life goals, hobbies, and interests	61
	Acted against own morals, values, beliefs	59
	Changed dress or appearance to accommodate addict	53
	Accepted addict's sexual norms as my own	43
8. **Blame and punishment**	Increasingly more self-righteous and punitive	64
	Destructive to others	54
	Homicidal thoughts or feelings	36
	Had affairs to punish the addict or prove worth	21
9. **Sexual reactivity**	Numbed my own sexual needs and wants	68
	Rarely felt intimate during sex	66
	Made excuses not to be sexual	43
	Changed clothes out of sight of addict	34

LOVING TOO MUCH?—
OR COADDICTION?

The *Journal of Polymorphous Perversity* has for a half-dozen years been providing spoofs of academic and scholarly foibles. Written by academics, the parodies provide perspective in professions prone to pomposity. In the fall of 1988, the journal published a review by Dr. Michael Shaughnessy entitled "A Book Review of Three Contemporary Popular Psychology Books: *Men Who Hate Women and the Women Who Love Them; Men Who Can't Love;* and *Women Men Love, Women Men Leave."* The following excerpt captures the spirit of the review:

> The authors address the issues of leaving and loving, living and learning, and hating and loving. These books fill a major void in the psychology of loving and leaving, and hating and leaving. Those who desire insight into the women men hate, the men who love them, the women who can't love, leave, or hate, and the men women love and the men women leave, will be very inspired by these pages. Those therapists who work with women who hate women, men who hate men, women women love, and women women leave, as well as men women love and leave, as well as leave and love, will be richly rewarded by the wisdom in these pages.

Shaughnessy's humor does what all good satire does: it reveals the comedy of our tangled efforts to deal with real problems. Our confusion about the addictive aspects of loving too much has been overwhelming to scholars as well as to the general population.

Anne Wilson Schaef, one of the current pioneers in addiction, has provided a clarifying voice. Her book *Escape from Intimacy* sorts out the differences among the "love" addictions: sex, romance, and relationships. She insists at the outset—and I think rightly so—that we ought not to use the word *love:* "I believe that no interpersonal or pseudo-relationship addiction has anything to do with love. These addictions may have something to do with the illusion of love, and they have nothing to do with true loving and, in fact, are ways of avoiding love and intimacy."

She then defines sex, romance, and relationship addictions as separate, but often intermingling, obsessions. The sex addict focuses on specific sexual behaviors. The romance junkie is hooked on the exhilaration of falling in love and all the magic that goes with it. Relationship addicts, from Schaef's perspective, are powerless in two ways. First, relationship addicts become involved with a specific destructive relationship and are unable to leave it on their own initiative. Second, relationship addicts are drawn into such destructive relationships over and over again even though they see their self-defeating characteristics. In many ways, Schaef's distinctions are reflected in our empirical findings. Her romance addict shares characteristics of the fantasy addict described in Chapter Two. The relationship addict parallels some of the characteristics we described as seductive role sex. In effect, we are getting closer to discerning the outlines of various forms of sex addiction. What has made it hard has been the overlap that often exists among the forms.

On the subject of coaddiction, Schaef makes the very important point that many persons define themselves as codependent who are really sex, romance, or relationship addicts. She suggests that people think it is somehow cleaner and nicer to call themselves coaddicts rather than addicts. She even urges that a new term be devised to eliminate the *co,* so it can stand as the obsessive illness it is. Coaddiction is clearly another addiction. Throughout this chapter we have underlined the vast similarities between addict and coaddict.

What remains difficult from a definitional point of view is that coaddiction is obsessive *in reaction to* another addiction. Hence, I have continued to use the prefix *co.* Schaef's point that it diminishes its role as an addiction is accurate. Yet the illness is about reactivity. A new model of coaddiction is needed to make these relationships clear.

THE THREE PARTS OF COADDICTION

One way to clarify how coaddiction works is to think about how the coaddict's experience parallels that of the addict. This focus on parallel development allows us to see the co part without losing sight of the addiction. It also serves to clarify some misconceptions that exist in the addiction field.

A common assumption among professionals and recovering persons is that coaddiction also underlies addiction. Usually the statement is made to show how in the addictive family, everyone, including the addict, is coaddicted. While this is probably true, seeing everyone as coaddicted further confuses an already muddled situation, as Schaef and others point out. In practice it means that people label behavior as coaddiction when it is not.

Coaddiction and addiction have the same roots. We have already noted the many commonalities between coaddicts and addicts. By comparing the addiction and the family life of coaddict and addict, we gain a clarifying perspective that enables us to see more precisely what is the same and what is not. Coaddiction has three parts: family shame, family dysfunction, and family obsession.

In Chapter Three, we explored the nature of family shame. This shame originates in a low "us" concept plus overwhelming secrecy. Shame is connected with an emphasis on doing things right and conditional love. It leads also to an amorphous ego, an ego full of "holes." Addicts and coaddicts alike come from shame-based families.

We also noted ways in which families with addicted members are dysfunctional. Such families do not do what they must do in order to produce healthy, whole human beings. These families are extremely rigid and extremely disengaged. They are also characterized by inability to resolve conflict, to solve problems effectively, or to cope well with change, stress, and loss. Similarly, they fail to support the individual through life's fundamental transitions and fail to provide a consistent process by which the individual can derive sense and value from experiences.

Thus, family dysfunction and shame characterize the families of both addicts and coaddicts. When people refer to addicts as also being coaddicted, they are referring to the characteristics of shame and dysfunction. It is obsession—the third characteristic—that distinguishes the coaddict from the addict. While both are obsessed, the coaddict's obsession is with the addict.

TABLE 5-3
THREE COMPONENTS OF COADDICTION

FAMILY SHAME	FAMILY DYSFUNCTION	FAMILY OBSESSION
Low "us" concept	Extreme rigidity	Collusion
Secrecy	Extreme disengagement	Obsessive
"Doing things right"	Inability to resolve	preoccupation
Conditional love	conflict	Denial
Amorphous ego	Ineffective problem	Emotional turmoil
Feelings are bad	solving	Manipulation
Needs are bad	Poor coping with	Excessive responsibility
Sex is bad	change, stress, or loss	Compromise or loss of
Pain is tolerated	Impaired development	self
	Failure to find meaning	Blame and punishment
		Sexual reactivity

In particular, the coaddict's obsession is about the addict being out of control. The coaddict's addiction is powerlessness over the powerlessness of others. This explains the characteristics of coaddictive obsession we explored in this chapter: collusion, obsessive preoccupation, denial, emotional turmoil, manipulation, excessive responsibility, loss of self, blame and punishment of self and others, and sexual reactivity.

The relationship between addict and coaddict is thus a merging of obsessions. What each partner does furthers the obsession of the other. The addict reacts to the coaddict's worry, control, and manipulation by increasing the addictive behaviors. The coaddict then responds by intensifying the obsessions.

A useful analogy is to think of the partners as sharing an electric blanket with dual controls. Unknown to the partners, the controls have been reversed. One partner feels a little cold and so turns up the thermostat. The other partner, feeling warm, turns down the thermostat. The cold partner feels even colder and turns up the thermostat. And so the cycles continue until each thermostat is jammed in its extreme position.

In the same way, out-of-control sexual behavior and sexual anorexia each in part represents a *response* to the partner. For example, when Esther's husband made comments about her alcoholism, his coaddiction thermostat was turned up. Notice, however, that it also served his own addictive acting out. The interweaving of one's own powerlessness and preoccupation with a family member's powerlessness and preoccupation creates the complex rhythms of family obsession.

In the last chapter, we developed a model of addiction with three stages: vulnerability, initiation, and addiction. Each of these stages corresponds with one of the aspects of the coaddictive family environment.

Vulnerability/Family Shame

The shame-based family environment serves as a catalyst to all those forces that make a person vulnerable to addiction. Family shame is key to the formation of the shame-based personality. When the influence of culture, abuse, and neurochemistry interact with individual and family shame, we have a total human ecosystem vulnerable to the addictive process.

Initiation/Family Dysfunction

When addiction-prone persons struggle with the forces that transform vulnerability into addiction, they desperately need a functional family. They need help and support with crisis and change. The impaired family becomes a contributing factor, rather than a bulwark of prevention.

Addiction/Family Obsession

Obsession by family members becomes an intensifying factor in the addiction. Worse, it deepens both the family dysfunction and the family shame.

FIGURE 5-1
AN ADDITIVE MODEL OF RECOVERY

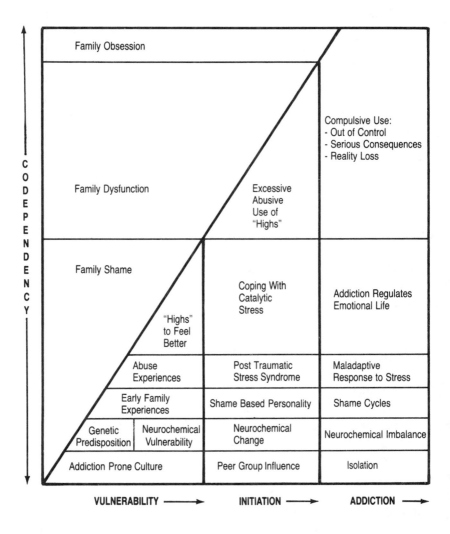

By connecting the family processes with the development of addiction, we see how each part interacts with the others. Like a kaleidoscope constructed of reflecting mirrors, the entire addictive system creates reciprocating images reflecting individual struggles in the larger patterns of the family. Whether we are looking at addict or coaddict, the patterns always fit. Figure 5-1 shows our addictive model with the corresponding family phases.

With the problem of the electric blanket, the obvious solution is for the partners to exchange controls, so that each can take responsibility for regulating his or her own temperature. In the same way, all those who are caught in the web of obsession and addiction have to take responsibility for their own behavior and recognize they are powerless over the behavior of others. Recovery begins with self-responsibility, as we shall see in the next chapter.

Transformation of an Illness

The twelve step fellowships for sex addiction have patterned their programs on the Twelve Steps of Alcoholics Anonymous. Each fellowship has adapted the Twelve Steps in a slightly different way. For those who are not familiar with the steps, we have reprinted the original version here.

THE TWELVE STEPS OF ALCOHOLICS ANONYMOUS

STEP ONE
We admitted we were powerless over alcohol—
that our lives had become unmanageable.

STEP TWO
Came to believe that a Power greater than ourselves
could restore us to sanity.

STEP THREE
Made a decision to turn our will and our lives over to
the care of God *as we understood Him.*

STEP FOUR
Made a searching and fearless moral inventory of ourselves.

STEP FIVE
Admitted to God, to ourselves, and to another human being
the exact nature of our wrongs.

STEP SIX
Were entirely ready to have God remove all these defects of character.

STEP SEVEN
Humbly asked Him to remove our shortcomings.

STEP EIGHT
Made a list of all persons we had harmed, and became willing
to make amends to all of them.

STEP NINE
Made direct amends to such people wherever possible, except when to do so would injure them or others.

STEP TEN
Continued to take personal inventory, and when we were wrong, promptly admitted it.

STEP ELEVEN
Sought through prayer and meditation to improve our conscious contact with God *as we understood Him,* praying only for knowledge of His will for us and the power to carry that through.

STEP TWELVE
Having had a spiritual awakening as the result of these steps, we tried to carry this message to alcoholics and to practice these principles in all our affairs.

The Twelve Steps reprinted with permission of Alcoholics Anonymous World Services, Inc. The program described in this work is not associated in any way with Alcoholics Anonymous.

The Stages
of Recovery

- Sally had sex with four men in her AA group the first year she was there. They were all friends and talked to one another. One night at a dry bar she ended up sitting with all four of them at a table. One of them asked her who it was going to be that night. She was filled with shame and felt pain at the loss of the relationships. The next day at noon in the AA club the men decided to go to the beach. She wanted to go, but they left her. When they drove off, Sally fell apart. A woman she barely knew asked her out to lunch. She poured out her story to this stranger. She told us, "I spilled my guts, and she carried the SAA message to me. I was in a meeting the next week, desperate for recovery."

- Jeremy's wife was fed up with his lack of interest in sex and insisted he seek help from his physician. He went to the doctor already knowing what his problem was. His masturbation and pornography use were so excessive he had no sexual energy left for his spouse. During the examination, Jeremy admitted he was "hooked on porn." Finding no physical reasons for impotence, his physician gently urged that he see a therapist and join an SAA group. The following week he went to his first meeting.

- Bernie saw her life as a whirlwind. Even treatment for her alcoholism had not stopped the problem. After two and a half years of sobriety, she had not stopped the affairs or the compulsive masturbation. In desperation, she decided to move to another state rather than face the pain she was inflicting on her family. So she went, leaving her husband and two children behind. Yet moving did not help; the sexual chaos continued. She finally gave in to her husband's pleas to return. Upon returning, she was standing in a hotel lobby when she heard the words "Sexaholics Anonymous." She remembers, "I knew, almost immediately after it was explained to me what the fellowship was for, that that's what had been wrong. I'm a sex addict. I came into the program already surrendered."

- Fred was sitting in a chair in the living room of a small one-bedroom home he had rented after leaving his wife. His sexuality, especially his use of prostitutes, was way out of control. He gazed at his wall, at a piece of contemporary art in which black and white shapes swirled to the center. He told us, "My life was that painting and it all spun toward the black center. I remember saying if I don't change I'm going to die." He went to a walk-in crisis center. A counselor helped him to see the common threads relating to his sexuality and recommended SLAA. He remembers walking into his first meeting, feeling the warmth, the gentle laughter, and the care. He said, "I knew I was home."

- Mike's sexual behavior in the workplace was costing him clients, business opportunities, and ultimately lots of money. What really pained him, however, was being sexual with his daughters. An incest victim himself, he found himself doing the same things to his children that his parents had done to him. His moment of truth came when a police sergeant called to tell him that he was being charged with sexual misconduct, that he needed to talk to an attorney, and that his daughter could not come home until he was out of the house. He told us, "There was a certain sigh of relief when I got that call because I had tremendous fears that the call wouldn't come. It took off my shoulders the responsibility to take action on my abuse and my addiction."

- For one addict, it was as simple as lying in bed and realizing he did not want to do it anymore. For another, it was being awakened by his wife at six-thirty in the morning and asked to come out to the living room. There he found his boss, pastor, two friends, adult children, and an intervention specialist. At first he was furious that they were talking about his sexual behavior. By eight o'clock, he realized their care and the truth of their words. By ten o'clock, he was in a hospital treatment program.

Each has a different tale; all come to a point of surrender. Their problem is bigger than they can handle. They are not powerful; rather, they are powerless. Yet for the addict the myth of being in control and capable of coping is very deeply ingrained. Addicts have a feeling of invulnerability, a feeling that nothing can happen to them. In their addiction, they are without limits others must observe, can take risks others can't, and can live on the edge where others cannot survive.

A telling metaphor occurs in Tom Wolfe's novel *The Bonfire of the Vanities*. Sherman McCoy, a central character, perceives himself as a "Master of the Universe":

What was he, a Master of the Universe, doing down here on the floor, reduced to ransacking his brain for white lies to circumvent the sweet logic of his wife? The Masters of the Universe were a set of lurid, rapacious plastic dolls that his otherwise perfect daughter liked to play with. They looked like Norse gods who lifted weights, and they had names such as Dracon, Ahor, Mangelred, and Blutong. They were unusually vulgar, even for plastic toys. Yet one fine day, in a fit of euphoria, after he had picked up the telephone and taken an order for zero-coupon bonds that had brought him a $50,000 commission, *just like that,* this very phrase had bubbled up into his brain. On Wall Street he and a few others—how many?—three hundred, four hundred, five hundred?—had become precisely that . . . Masters of the Universe. There was . . . no limit whatsoever! Naturally he had never so much as whispered this phrase to a living soul. He was no fool. Yet he couldn't get it out of his head. And here was the Master of the Universe, . . . Why couldn't he (being a Master of the Universe) simply *explain* it to her? Look, Judy. I still love you and I love our daughter and I love our home and I love our life, and I don't want to change any of it—it's just that I, a Master of the Universe, a young man still in the season of the rising sap, deserve *more* from time to time, when the spirit moves me.

The Master of the Universe theme emerges in addicts' lives in many different ways. But constant is the rationale that all is justified because of the addict's uniqueness, specialness, or superiority. In their addiction, they are set apart from others, either made of "the right stuff" or having some special right or need others don't have. Being out of control requires that you have no limits. Overextension, denial, sexual acting out, trouble, and unmanageability mingle in the addicts who live on the edge. For Sherman McCoy, the sexual logic was as follows:

> Sherman resumed his walk toward First Avenue in a state of agitation. It was in the air! It was a wave! Everywhere! Inescapable! . . . Sex! . . . There for the taking! . . . It walked down the street, as bold as you please! . . . It was splashed all over the shops! If you were a young man and halfway alive, what chance did you have? . . . Technically, he had been unfaithful to his wife. Well, sure . . . but who could remain monogamous with this, this, this *tidal wave* of concupiscence rolling across the world? Christ almighty! A Master of the Universe couldn't be a saint, after all. . . . It was unavoidable. For Christ's sake, you can't dodge snowflakes, and this was a blizzard! He had merely been caught at it, that was all, or halfway caught at it. It meant nothing. It had no moral dimension. It was nothing more than getting soaking wet.

Greek playwrights warned of such pride. Their tragic heroes were often characterized by *hubris*—the excessive pridefulness of one who sets himself up over other men, making himself into a god. Ignoring their own human limits was always the undoing of the Greek heroes. It is the undoing of addicts as well. For addicts, the theme of invulnerability postpones the decision to get help. Recovery means the unraveling of Masters of the Universe.

RECOVERY AND THE DEMISE
OF MASTERS OF THE UNIVERSE

Brought to a point of surrender, addicts wonder, Can this change? Can I build a better life? Professionals have wondered this as well and been skeptical. In the scholarly literature, nymphomaniacs, exposers, Don Juans, pedophiles, and many sex offenders have generally been labeled incorrigible and untreatable. Indeed, historically professionals have had at best limited success. For the addict who wished to surrender before being destroyed, the professional community until recently has offered little hope.

A significant parallel exists between what is occurring now for sex addicts and what happened for alcoholics in the forties and fifties. Initially, Alcoholics Anonymous was greeted by professionals with disdain. A 1939 issue of the *Journal of the American Medical Association* provided a devastating critique of the "Big Book" of AA and of the concept that alcoholism was an emotional, physical, and spiritual illness. Yet the opening sentence of the 1985 American Medical Association manual for the treatment of alcoholism describes it as an "emotional, physical, and spiritual illness."

The pioneers who started Alcoholics Anonymous modeled with their own lives the successful use of peer support. Once it was shown that AA worked, professionals like E.M. Jellinek initiated an effort to combine the twelve step process with clinical findings, in order to accelerate recovery. Today, there is an unparalleled system of help for the alcoholic, along with an extensive body of scholarship documenting every stage of recovery.

The pioneers of alcohol recovery paved the way for those working in other addictions. Many professionals were quick to understand the significance of what sex addicts were saying. This was true despite academic entrenchment and the highly evocative, symbolic, and politicized nature of sex.

Unfortunately, professionals in sex addiction do not yet have the extensive longitudinal studies that exist for alcoholism. At this point, more than anything else our task was simply to document that some sex addicts can achieve recovery, there is a possible solution as well as a problem. We had to find a large enough sample of people who had actually transformed their lives and who could tell us about it. Comparative, longitudinal studies will follow. The story of those who initially succeeded had to be told now.

To piece together the recovery process, we asked recovering sex addicts and their partners to complete a number of instruments, including an extensive life status inventory and a month-by-month history of their recovery. We also interviewed people with extended recovery in a stage-by-stage fashion and analyzed their responses. We then adopted two strategies to obtain a pattern of recovery. We developed a pattern from the retrospective information provided by the surveys and interviews, and we asked people with different periods of recovery (six months, one year, eighteen months, etc.) how things were going for them now. The two strategies yielded the same pattern. The following overview of a five-year recovery process is based on changes in classic quality of life indicators:

The first year. There was no measurable improvement, and yet most addicts reported that life was definitely better. This apparent contradiction might be explained by one respondent's comment that "when you are hitting your head against the wall, even stopping the hitting helps." In fact, according to our assessments, some things got worse. Most slips, if they occur, will occur in the second six months of recovery. Further, all health indicators—accidents, sickness, and visits to physicians—show the second six months to be the worst over the five years. The first year appears to be characterized by extraordinary turmoil, which really tests the recovering person's resolve to change. Some of the consequences of addiction continue, and the change is wrenching.

The second and third years. If the recovering person can get through the first year, significant rebuilding starts. There is measurable improvement occurring in many areas, including finances, ability to cope with stress, spirituality, self-image, career status, and friendships. Our survey documented improvements in finances, coping with stress, career status, and friendships continuing over the five-year period. These indicators reflect a period of intense personal work, which results in higher productivity, stability, and a greater sense of well-being. Stopping the acting out appears to give people the energy they need to reconstitute their lives.

The fourth and fifth years. Once the personal base is established, healing occurs in the addict's key relationships. Improvements, often dramatic, occur in relationships with children, parents, siblings, and partners. There are, however, some exceptions. About 13 percent found that a breach with their family of origin could not be healed because the family was abusive or threatened recovery. Also, some marriages were casualties to the recovery process. Most important, sex addicts reported a significant shift toward more healthy and satisfying sexual expression. With the healing of relationships, overall life satisfaction improved dramatically.

RECOVERY OVER TIME		
WORSE SECOND SIXTH MONTHS	BETTER SECOND/THIRD YEARS	BETTER THREE YEARS PLUS
Sex addiction relapse Health status	Financial situation* Coping with stress* Spirituality Self-image Career status* Friendships*	Healthy sexuality Primary relationship Relationship with family of origin Relationship with children Life satisfaction

*Continue to improve three-years plus

What addicts, family members, and professionals want to know is, does it have to take three to five years to rebuild one's life? Could the process be speeded up? No answers exist at this time. When the people in our survey went through recovery, the groups they joined were generally small and inexperienced. There were no treatment programs, and therapists who tried to help were learning as they went along. It is possible that, with the advent of treatment, the greater experience of therapists, and the growing maturity of the fellowships, recovery can move faster. Nonetheless, some aspects of recovery address core developmental issues which take time to heal. We will have to wait for longitudinal studies to tell us what is possible.

Nor was the process the same for everyone. Some people took

longer. Some had great difficulty in stopping their behavior. We learned there were critical factors that helped the process and others that undermined it. Before we can describe the essential tasks each recovering person faces, we must explore in-depth the stages addicts who succeed in their recovery go through. We found six stages of recovery.

THE DEVELOPING STAGE

Marty was a classic Master of the Universe. He was an executive responsible for the commercial loan business of a large, conservative bank. He told us, "I had power and control over people's lives. I could make or break a company by a decision I made. Ninety-five percent of the staff were women and I had control over them." His double life as an addict, however, was where he truly was the master of it all. In one life, he was exposing himself to women—from cars, in the streets, and in shopping centers. On the other hand, he worked to be the favorite boss of women in the bank. He commented, "Women loved working with me because my mother is a feminist. I knew all the lingo and issues around the feminist movement." He added, "I lived in both extremes." He abused women, yet he championed against the abuse of women. Only a Master of the Universe could pull that off. Obviously, one does not have to be a high-powered executive to have the addictive pride that says you can manage the unmanageable, that you can do things others can't. It is this addictive arrogance that pushes aside realities like AIDS, family commitments, and work priorities.

Things come apart, however, for Masters of the Universe. In *Bonfire of the Vanities,* the downfall of Sherman McCoy starts with a phone call. Intending to call his mistress, he dials his wife by mistake, and his wife figures out what happened. From there events unfold like the plot of a contemporary Sophocles. For Marty, the process began when he was arrested for exposing himself.

After the arrest, Marty went to court alone. He chose not to engage an attorney; he wanted the "rush" of being able to handle things by himself. He asked to see the judge in his chambers, admitted he had a problem, and asked to see a therapist. He went to a psychiatrist, who listened to Marty's stories about his family and his wife and, at the end of six months, wrote a letter to the judge saying Marty was doing well. As soon as the letter was submitted, Marty stopped therapy. He did pursue some couple therapy with his wife. But he had not accepted that he had a problem—or at least one he could not handle.

We call this the developing stage. Unmanageability and powerlessness force the addict to acknowledge the problem, but he or she continues actively in the addiction. True recovery begins only after this stage, which typically lasts up to two years. For Marty the developing stage lasted about a year and a half. Like many, Marty made efforts to curtail his activities but the addiction remained.

Below are listed some typical comments addicts made about this stage of recovery. From the comments it is clear that the following are key characteristics of the developing stage:

- Many addicts seek help but discontinue it or find it not helpful.

- Many therapists fail to see the problem or, if they see it, fail to follow through on it.

- Addicts have a growing appreciation of the reality of the problem but tend to counter this realization by minimizing the problem or thinking they can handle it by themselves.

- Some addicts temporarily curtail their behaviors or substitute other behaviors. (Marty, for example, escalated his prostitution use.)

- Most addicts fear that stopping would mean giving up sex.

THE DEVELOPING STAGE

My isolation and inability to believe I could get help kept me stuck.

Confronted by a colleague in a supportive way, I went to a twelve step group, but then left it.

Two DWIs caused me to stop drinking and I ended all relationships for four to five months. Then I fell into a new relationship, drinking returned, and things got crazy again.

Unconsciously sought help—suicidal at times.

First I hoped that divorce would cure my addiction. I turned to pornography and affairs as a less shameful way to act out.

When a friend said, "You are choosing death and I won't stay with you," I started to realize the problem.

I recognized in therapy what was going on but only increased my control.

It seemed I was always waiting for something or someone to rescue me.

I assumed the problem would go away as I got older or if I found the "right" person.

At the end of a very long and insane relationship, death looked better.

I went to SAA to please my therapist. I thought he was making too much of the problem. Then I dropped out for a year and a half.

I realized I had the same issues as an SAA member in my therapy group. I waited one year to explore SAA because I was afraid I would be asked to give up relationships and I didn't want to.

I went to a therapist for help who told me I should accept that I was a "party girl."

For most addicts, the addiction is closely connected to survival. It has been a trusted friend, relied upon for years. It has always delivered what it promised—but at a price. As the price grows intolerable, the addict prepares to face the fact that something has to change.

THE CRISIS/DECISION STAGE

Marty had not counted on one thing: his second arrest. This time the message was inescapable. His attorney told him about SAA. Worse, the judge told him he had to go to SAA for six months. And the therapist he saw for couple therapy said that further treatment would be contingent on Marty attending SAA meetings.

The therapist also insisted that Marty tell his wife of the arrest and of the SAA meetings. Marty resisted. His way of handling the meetings initially was to tell his wife he had joined a Thursday night computer club—another lie by a Master of the Universe. The problem was his therapist would not budge. Marty had to be honest.

Marty had entered the crisis/decision stage—the stage at which a commitment to change is made. This stage can occur within a single day or can take up to three months; in any case it marks the beginning of recovery. There can be a substantial time lag between when the behavior stops and when a commitment is made.

The following list presents typical comments addicts made about their crisis/decision stage. These comments reflect the variety of ways in which addicts come to this stage. For some addicts, there was a growing consciousness that something needed to be done. Others were frightened into action by the escalation of their behavior. Yet others were so overwhelmed by their behavior that they would do anything to fix it. In fact, several in our survey had admitted themselves for chemical dependency treatment, even though they knew that was not the issue.

Most addicts were forced to do something by events or by people—family members, partners, friends, or therapists. Because of the addicts' denial, the pressure often had to be continued over a long period of time. Actually, this process of breaking through denial continues throughout recovery.

THE CRISIS/DECISION STAGE

I didn't get what sex addiction was about—felt I was just a mild case. Spent two weeks doing my first step and then I "got" it.

Unable to stop until I was sexually assaultive. Scared me so much I was ready.

Learned about sex addiction from people in ACA and started paying attention. Husband pushed me to look at treatment.

Got arrested: October 1983.

Wife took off wedding ring (after thirty-five years) and said, "You can't come home."

A sexual episode at work [mental health] was reported by a patient.

Couldn't deny it after apartment supervisor ordered me to move within twenty-four hours.

There was a spiritual awakening for me just prior to my first meeting.

I wrote to Dear Abby to learn more about Sexaholics Anonymous.

Lost chemical sobriety because of sexual behavior.

Did a "lifelong" inventory in AA in 1981 which dealt with love obsession and sexuality. One month later went to first SLAA meeting in Boston.

Arrested at work with much publicity and lost job. Someone sent me information in the mail having seen my address in the newspaper.

Acting out the night after getting a negative HIV test was sign of my total insanity. My life had become total chaos.

Newspaper article about sex addiction hit me like a bull's-eye. I took it to my therapist. Later, when I was feeling suicidal, therapist made me go to SLAA.

Six weeks of crisis before finding SLAA. Literally a typhoon of bingeing with AA people. AA sponsor said: "Get some help or go crazy."

Went into chemical dependency treatment even though I'd been sober four years, because I was going crazy.

Found out about syphilis and then I joined a group.

THE SHOCK STAGE

Marty told us, "When I was court-ordered to SAA, it was a major shock. I knew I had to be there but I wanted to minimize the consequences of being there. I didn't want anyone to know." The shock stage is a time of emotional numbness, extraordinary disorientation, and efforts to control the damage. On the average, addicts spend the first eight months of the first year of recovery in this shock stage. We suspect that the primary reason that we were unable to detect any significant movement on quality of life indicators is that addicts in this early stage are operating at a subsistence or survival level.

What we found simply validates conventional AA and Al-Anon wisdom which says, "Nothing major the first year." Simply entering recovery and dealing with the implications of the illness are so stressful that to undertake significant change would overload the system. Time-honored fellowship slogans like "A day at a time" or "Keep it simple" appear to be appropriate prescriptions for this stage of recovery. As shown by the addicts' comments, the following experiences are characteristic of the shock stage:

- Addicts describe physical symptoms of withdrawal that are at times unbearable.

- Addicts experience disorientation, confusion, numbness, and inability to focus or concentrate.

- Addicts have periodic bouts with despair and feelings of hopelessness, which become more intense as their sense of reality grows.

- Addicts react with angry feelings about limits set by therapists, sponsors, or family members.

- When addicts join a recovery group, they experience a sense of belonging along with the realization that recovery was the right decision for them.

- Feelings of relief and acceptance are common once the double life is over.

THE SHOCK STAGE

Felt gradually like I was coming to.

Became absentminded.

The program was disorienting, painful, scary, and relieving, but I knew I belonged.

Felt crazy but determined to get better.

Numbness and grief over loss of my job. Despaired and felt no hope.

Relief was the main feeling but felt at home immediately. Took a long time to get abstinent with some painful slips.

I separated from my husband and felt really dark but not entirely hopeless. Raw, vulnerable, and exposed.

I felt very anxious—and decided to act "as if."

Was numb over breakup with last boyfriend. Cried off and on for weeks. Was in a fog. Felt nauseated. Brutal withdrawal.

Frozen with pain. Withdrawal very painful. Believed no part of me was okay—I was only an addict.

In treatment I realized my inadequate ability to be close and intimate. I was angry, depressed, and helpless. Felt my life was over.

I felt stunned, shocked, anxious, and depressed.

Felt physically as if hit on head with a two-by-four.

Sexually shut down, emotionally dead, I felt like my body was plastic.

Terrified because I was afraid I would have to qualify to belong. After that, withdrawal hit and I was terribly anxious.

Stopped professional job and worked in a deli. I felt like someone punched me.

Perhaps the biggest struggle during this period is for addicts to be honest with themselves about the extent and nature of their addiction. Marty, like others, began to bargain and argue about his addiction. He described this process to us:

> I remember how intellectual I was and how argumentative I was. As I look back on some of the arguments and discussions I had, the only addictive behavior I acknowledged was that I exposed myself. Prostitution, bookstores, my own relationship, setting up and feeling out my wife's affairs—I didn't own any of that. None of that was a part of my addiction. That was okay behavior. The fact that I kept getting busted all the time was a problem for me.

With time, however, and with support, clarity emerges about the addiction. When there is sufficient clarity and acceptance of reality, the addict enters a stage of profound grieving.

THE GRIEF STAGE

Grieving typically involves denial or bargaining, anger at the loss, acceptance of the reality, and sadness. Actually, some aspects of grieving, particularly bargaining and anger, first emerge in earlier stages and simply continue in the grief stage. What really distinguishes the grief stage are the sadness and pain felt when losses are finally acknowledged. The grief stage lasts from four to eight months and for most occurs at the end of the first year and the beginning of the second.

By specifying the timing of the grief period, we could better understand why slips were most likely to occur in the second half of the first year. Addicts use acting out to avoid pain. When the pain becomes overwhelming, the addiction brings relief, just as an old friend brings comfort and aid. During the earlier shock stage, addicts were more numb than anything else.

Similarly, we could understand the decline in health noted in the second half of the first year. The high stress associated with the grief stage impairs the immunological system and makes the addict more vulnerable to illness. Stress and preoccupation together reduce the ability to function normally, increasing vulnerability to accidents. These effects on health status provide potent testimony to the power of the pain.

Marty's grieving period began suddenly. He had just acknowledged that his wife's affairs were part of his own obsession, when he was involved in a brutal car accident. In his own words, "I was literally screaming down the highway, much faster than anybody else in a snowstorm—on my way to an SAA meeting, ironically. I lost control of the car and sideswiped a utility pole." He was in the hospital for two months, with injuries including a pelvic bone fractured in eighteen places and a ruptured bladder.

The powerlessness of being in the hospital triggered Marty's grief. He told us that during much of his stay he "sobbed and cried" about all the pain of his addiction. The accident was the last straw—once he started crying, the proverbial dam burst. Hospital staff, especially the hospital psychologists, were very important sources of support. Also important was the support from his SAA group. Almost every day his "SAA brothers" were there. Marty tells the poignant story of his sponsor's visit right after the accident:

> Norm came the very first night I was in the hospital and I was drugged out of my mind. No one could get through to me; I was out cold. I don't remember, but my family and Norm tell me that Norm came up and kissed my forehead and said, "Marty, I love you," and all of a sudden I woke up and said, "Norm, I love you too," and went right back into my coma. My family just fell apart, they were so moved.

The need for support as the pain and the despair finally hit full force was by no means unique to Marty. Below are listed some comments sex addicts typically made about the grief stage. Note a number of characteristics common to this stage:

- The anger and defiance of the shock stage continue in the grief stage.

- Sadness and pain are punctuated with periodic bouts of despair.

- An extraordinary sadness exists about the losses incurred because of the addiction.

- Addicts experience a profound loss as the addiction ceases to serve as friend, comforter, and high.

- Addicts tend to take general stock of their lives, inventorying now beyond the addiction.

THE GRIEF STAGE

Tears about loneliness, about the loss of my life to addiction. Tears seemed endless.

Often grieved the loss of my addict and of what I was. A lot of sadness . . . self-hatred. Hard to forgive self.

I went through a rebellion period and felt very defiant.

I went through a hard withdrawal and had to learn to cry. I was angry and asked myself, "What sexual chances am I missing?"

I felt overwhelmed and bitter.

Incredible sense of loss over addiction. I had to learn about nurturing myself.

Lost days just crying, which overlapped just feeling numb. I stayed like in a cocoon if not at work or at a meeting.

Enormous grief at loss of sexual high although I felt relief. Grieved the loss of self. Felt empty.

I could not remember a good to go back to and build on—I felt the loss of never being innocent.

Great pain and sadness recalling daughter screaming, "Why do you hate me?" I wondered if I would ever be able to repair damage. Felt suicidal and full of remorse.

I was in mourning, crying all the time, afraid of my own shadow, angry at God, angry at having to stop, and had very little energy.

Real sadness for an old affair and grief over loss of the high.

Cried a lot with a new kind of tears. These tears felt like I was getting bad stuff out of me.

As in all grieving, the expression of sadness shared with others leads to the acceptance of new realities. The irony of the accident was not lost on Marty. He was driving through a snowstorm faster than anybody else would. The accident brought home to him his feelings of invulnerability and arrogance, fueled by his addiction. It was more Master of the Universe stuff—living on the edge where others cannot handle it. Marty told us:

It was like the universe finally said, "I'm going to take my hand on this little car and I'm going to ram it up against this tree bad enough that it jars your attention." My concept of a Higher Power isn't God took his hand and hit me like that. I'm real clear that I set these lessons up. That the universe keeps putting these lessons in front of me and up until then I was unwilling to learn the lessons. So the lessons had to get a little more intense in order for me to finally say, "Okay, okay, I give up, I see the lesson, I'm ready to learn."

When that final acceptance occurs and addicts own to being vulnerable—to being human, ordinary, not unique—then significant change can begin. As part of the acceptance, addicts must clearly admit to the extent and range of their addictive behavior. Awareness of the addiction will expand and deepen over many years. At this stage it seems important that addicts perceive the broad outlines of their addictive behavior and that they grasp that the addiction is more than just behavior. They must see the addiction as involving beliefs, attitudes, and distorted thinking which preserved the denial and delusion. With that growing acceptance, the addict enters into the repair stage.

THE REPAIR STAGE

For Marty, the real watershed between the grief and repair stages was when he left his wife. She had continued her sexual acting out with other men and had made sexual demands on him even though he had not yet recovered from his accident. As Marty described it:

> I was in traction at night to pull my legs out of joint just slightly so the bones would continue to filter back into their natural places. I was literally tied to the bed. I could have said no because it was painful. Yet I endured the pain and I don't know why. Well, yeah I do. I felt bad because she kept pumping me with "When did you see prostitutes? Was that the same night that we made love?" type of stuff. She continued to act out during this time period. One night I came out on crutches to go to the bathroom, which was just outside the master bedroom, and she was naked on the couch with another man. Even then I was saying,

"Well, I deserve this type of stuff." Finally I said to myself, "This is nuts. I've got to get out."

Marty said, "I had to sort out my codependency issues from my addiction." He revealed the significance of his decision when he added, "I had never, ever, ever chosen to leave a female before." That is when chaos stopped and the rebuilding began.

Marty began to build sobriety. He no longer exposed himself, although he had slips with masturbation and pornography. Marty pointed out that "by this time I was connected. I had good SAA friends and daily contact. We did things socially and I involved myself in meetings, as a sponsor, as 'trusted servant,' and as our intergroup representative." He also involved himself intensively in therapy, including a weekly men's group. The result was that Marty was able to set aside his old behavior and put together a year and a half of celibacy.

"When I got on my own," Marty concluded, "sobriety didn't come easy, but it came. That's when I began to grasp the spiritual nature of the twelve steps. Before that it was pretty black and white." For survey respondents, this stage was generally marked by at least sobriety, if not celibacy, intense spirituality, and personal growth. For most, spirituality was the primary factor, the main basis for change. Marty told us about his experience:

> It started out first with a definition that I heard from Father Leo Booth, who called spirituality a "search for completeness within ourselves—mind, body, and emotions—and a connectivity with others." When it was taken out of the religious context and put into that definition, I realized that's what I had been doing. I then started to pursue it and a lot of other things. I began to experience what I now call miracles—miracles being connections. Choosing to love, choosing to believe, choosing to be willing, choosing to grow. That came from that sense of powerlessness in the hospital and turning around. I learned by experience the joy and the peace and the serenity that brings me.

Marty developed a nice metaphor for the repair stage by comparing the twelve steps to the foundation of a house: "It's made out of bricks, it's sunk in the ground, it's set on footings—nothing real neat, just gray, cement blocks." He added, "I also have built a house on top of it that is in color—three-dimensionally in color."

The sense of productivity and renewal that typifies this stage is evident from the comments below. A number of crucial changes characterize the repair stage:

- There is a new capacity for joy, although addicts often have to work to see humor in things.

- Central to all progress is the deepening of new bonds with others.

- Addicts take responsibility for themselves in all areas of life, including career, finances, and health.

- Addicts learn to express their needs, to accept that they have them, and to work to meet them.

- Addicts during this phase work on completing things (degrees, projects, work, etc.) and on being dependable (being on time, following through, and responding to requests).

- Addicts live less on "the edge" and learn to choose low-key options over high-excitement options.

THE REPAIR STAGE

Started taking care of my health, meditating, went back to school. Worked on boundaries.

Was a very private person so had to work hard on connecting through therapy and twelve step groups.

Decided to stay out of relationships and work on self.

Could wake up without feeling afraid; could laugh with people.

Told brutal truth in meetings and learned from failing my comprehensive exam in grad school.

Able to trust people as never before. Learned how hard it is to be balanced and that it's okay to be bored. Used calendar, kept dates, no longer late.

I took more responsibility for myself. I decided to work outside of the home and worked on my talents.

Began to do writing, got in touch with talents, went back to school, got in graduate program in addictionology, and accomplished things for myself.

Learned to eat and clothe self well. Even bought furniture to make my own identity. Started friendships with older women who could be mentors.

Felt a sense of accomplishment going through treatment and halfway house and keeping celibacy for a year. Started working on independence, financial responsibility, and friendships.

Learned to have fun by myself without the constant search for a man.

I found friends I could really count on.

Old spirituality was a crutch. New spiritual life allowed me to accept consequences and be human without shame.

Started to take care of myself, dressed better, exercised, and ate better. Took time to express my needs to counteract denial of physical and emotional needs.

For the first time in my life I got to finish projects, like on my house and my master's thesis. Own a store I love.

A common goal for addicts during this time is to achieve balance. Things have been out of hand for so long that they must focus on the basics. Working toward completion and staying low-key feels good after all the unmanageability. But the repair stage also requires developing new skills and forging new bonds. Many addicts are thus forced to face fundamental issues that made them vulnerable to the addiction in the first place. The addiction can be arrested, but those profoundly personal problems of distrust, victimization, and shame remain. Few are successful dealing with these on their own; most require therapeutic support.

Essentially, the task at hand is for addicts to learn to "reparent" themselves. One of the major contributions of the Adult Children of Alcoholics movement has been to demonstrate how family addiction damages children so that they remain dysfunctional as adults. Pioneers like John Bradshaw, Peter Cermak, and Claudia Black have talked about "healing the child within" in order to restore adult functioning. Few concepts emerging from contemporary addictionology have been more helpful. In many ways it provides a powerful metaphor for the therapeutic process.

Marty learned from his therapist that he could be cared for and not be exploited. His therapist also taught him how to reparent himself when he was feeling vulnerable. He could set safe boundaries and find healthy ways to meet his needs. Marty found the image of taking care of the child within an effective and appropriate one. For him the repair period was literally a time of rebirth. Being celibate meant he was not enmeshed in a relationship. He could truly be himself, learning about his values, preferences, and needs. Even before they get to this level of therapy, most addicts intuitively know they need to reparent themselves. For example, when Marty was still living with his wife, he knew that he was getting his emotional needs met by his children. They were safe, trustworthy, and available. Marty poignantly described for us his relationship with his daughter Bonnie:

> I was asking her at many levels to take care of my needs. I remember many times when Joanie, my spouse, and I would argue and I'd go up and get Bonnie out of the crib and hold her and cry. She was like my teddy bear. She was meeting my need. That is the first thing that I knew that was not right. This was what my mother had done with me. That's the first thing I knew I needed to work on in therapy. That is what I wanted to let go of. I wanted to set up boundaries, I wanted these needs met elsewhere.

During this period of reparenting and renewal, clarity about addictive behavior continues to grow. Most addicts start to have in-depth understanding of their behavior. They identify the governing themes and scenarios which connect all the addictive behaviors. This increased awareness facilitates reparenting, since the behavioral themes are deeply connected to childhood events. Marty, for example, was hooked on both voyeuristic and exhibitionist sex—two behavioral types that often occur together. Marty saw at this stage how his behavior connected with his childhood even to the point of recognizing that he had seen "reenacted on the faces of women my stuff as a child." Further, he now saw his behavior as a mosaic of acting out visually—either viewing or exposing:

> The behavior that I was most highly involved in was adult bookstores. I could make contact with prostitutes outside

those bookstores, could masturbate to the videos inside, and watch live women behind screens and masturbate to that. Yet there were tons and tons of other behaviors. It was constantly, what variation on this theme can I get a new high from? It would be window peeking, it would be exposing myself in many different ways, walking down the street in a long football jersey, football socks, and tennis shoes, and it looked like I had shorts on but I didn't, masturbating in the woods while looking down on a field of girls playing softball. Tons of variations on a theme.

Marty not only had a clear picture of his addiction, but also a fuller sense of his mental state. He told us about how his boss, the bank president, used to go to a strip joint during lunch. Marty, in a porn shop across the street, used to watch him go over there. Sometimes Marty himself would watch the strippers, even though he had had several encounters with his boss there. Marty lived in fear of his boss's reaction: "The president of the bank system knew I knew he spent his lunch hours watching strippers. Only he's the one in power, so I felt like he could yank my chain at any point." Something happens to addicts when they are no longer living in fear. They acquire a vital perspective on their powerlessness.

Marty, like all recovering addicts, had moments in which his addiction was triggered. But now his response was entirely different:

> Instead of beating myself with "How can I have that thought? I've got so much recovery right now," I would think, "Oh, thanks for that thought. It's a real clue that something's not going on or not going well with me at this moment." The gentleness that I've experienced toward myself is phenomenal.

At this level of self-care, many addicts nurture themselves into the growth stage.

THE GROWTH STAGE

Empowered by recovery, addicts enter a stage in which they explore new options and restructure relationships. The changes that have occurred enable addicts to open up what has been a closed system. Addiction offered only decreasing options. Recovery creates an open personal system that allows for the expansion of options. This period of growth usually occurred during years four and five of recovery. And the good news is that once a system is open, it has the capacity to renew itself. We talked to many addicts who experienced growth spurts after ten to twelve years of sobriety.

We were able to document that the quality of relationships improved dramatically. Relationships with children, parents, and partners all became richer and more sustaining. Many reported being able to be more emotionally present on the job as well. Addicts talked of more balance and intimacy, of an improved capacity to resolve conflict, and of being less judgmental and more compassionate. With the evolution of this new style of relationships, satisfaction with life dramatically improved.

Marty characterized these changes well: "The whole addiction was about me, me, me, me. In recovery, I flipped to the opposite extreme of really taking care of me in a healthy sense. Then I learned to be a conduit to allow this love that I'm receiving to flow through to others." Marty was very clear about the importance of creating a solid personal base. Of his current relationship, he commented, "Now it is two wholes sharing a life together instead of two half-entities coming together to make a whole."

Below are some comments typical of addicts who achieve the growth stage. Among the themes characterizing this stage are:

- Profound empathy and compassion for one's self and for others.
- Developing trust for one's own boundaries and integrity in relationships.
- Feelings of achievement over new milestones in love and sex.
- A new ability to take care of and nurture relationships.
- Old relationships are transformed or ended.

THE GROWTH STAGE

Feel connected to self and others. A totally new compassion for people with problems.

Today can say no. Can be safely sexual. Can now ask to make love. Can now say I love you.

Peace of mind. Finish my master's in fall. Holding a good job. I'm a father to a new baby.

Relationship rebuilt by taking ownership of my role. I make amends to my kids when I make mistakes. I feel close to my kids and husband.

Only later in recovery could I have healthy relationships.

To have partners with meaning. I needed to be able to make a commitment and not hang on to impossible relationships.

Sex isn't the requirement now; intimacy is.

I am no longer Princess Butterfly looking for Prince Charming—I have reclaimed my power.

I'm a much better therapist now. I've experienced deep healing myself.

I can talk about my present relationship, short-circuit shame and isolation, have boundaries with men, and trust my own reaction.

Another characteristic of this stage is a deep abhorrence of old behavior. Once addicts have enough distance from their old acting out, they often have very visceral reactions when they think about it. Many said they looked back almost in disbelief at some of the things they had done. One addict spoke, for example, of getting dry heaves when driving by places where he used to act out. Part of the reason for this reaction is remorse. Part is newly gained psychological health. Another part is finally acknowledging the depth of the fear and terror that they lived in. Yet another is their commitment to ways of living that do not leave them vulnerable to the addiction. Whatever the mix of reasons, there is an emotional response to the old behavior.

The growth stage provides a special perspective on the course of sobriety in general. It is clear that many addicts were not able to stop all their behaviors at once; sobriety occurred in chunks. Marty serves as a good example. He was able to stop his exhibitionism, then as his denial decreased, he realized that his other behaviors were addictive as well and that he had to eliminate them as part of his sobriety. Addicts tend to initially focus on what got them in trouble. Then, as their awareness grows, they see the variations on a theme. Sobriety moves the addict from crisis management to an evolved consciousness. This evolution takes time, because sexual addictive behavior is so often complex, pervasive, and shrouded in denial.

For some sex addicts, in fact, the process parallels that for alcoholism. We have seen for decades cases where the alcoholic would have to go through treatment several times before the old fears and beliefs broke down. Sometimes, an alcoholic would have to hit bottom several times before recovery could occur. There are many very similar cases in recovery from sexual addiction.

By the time sex addicts hit the growth stage, recovery no longer involves false starts. Consciousness of sobriety and consciousness of richer relationships have brought the addict to a new level of being. Addicts at this stage talk about addiction as a gift. They have experienced a depth of humanity that many people never achieve. Their addiction and recovery have given them a greater perception, compassion, and presence. They not only serve as models for recovering people who follow, but they are injecting new healing into our culture.

WHAT THE STAGES
OF RECOVERY TEACH

In our survey we focused on people who have been successful in recovery programs. We did not access those who were not able to initiate recovery; their perspective is an important one but difficult to document. Out of the thousand-plus people who participated in our research, only 293 were in recovery three or four years or more. So care must be taken in making generalizations.

FIGURE 6-1
THE COURSE OF RECOVERY OVER TIME

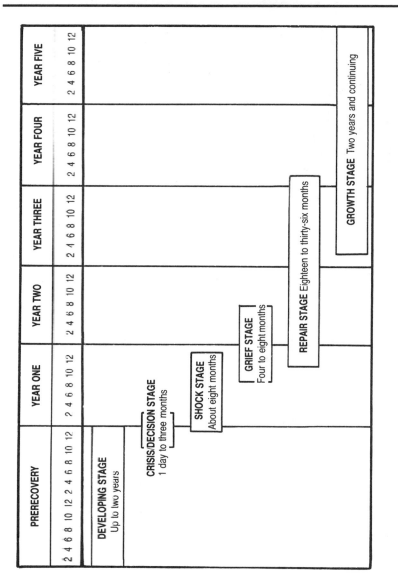

There were also many exceptions to general patterns. For example, we reported the average length of time of the stages. Some people had circumstances that prolonged the stages or changed

FIGURE 6-2
STAGE MIX IN RECOVERY

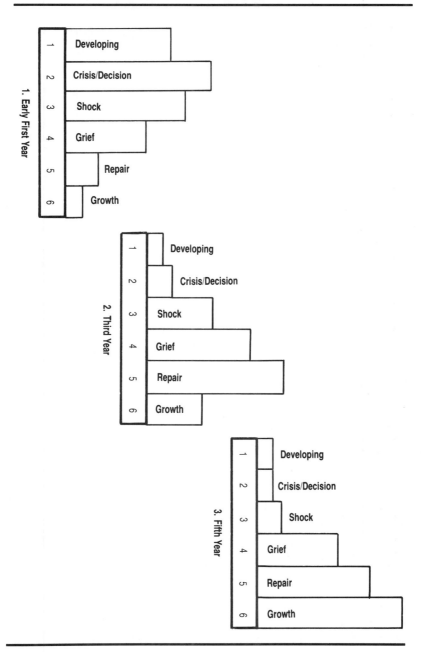

their timing. Even so, we were able to document the flow of the stages over time, as shown in Figure 6-1.

Of course, nothing in nature happens in neat stages. The eleven-year-old child, for example, often has some adolescent traits along with traits typical of elementary school children. Similarly, in recovery an addict can experience shock, grief, and repair in significant ways at the same time.

In fact, as is shown in Figure 6-2, all addicts have aspects of all stages at all times. Example 1 represents someone coming out of the crisis/decision period and into early recovery. Example 2 depicts an addict who is in the third year of recovery and focusing on repair work. Example 3 depicts an addict in the fifth year of recovery.

Slips and relapses may slow development or even send the addict back to the first stage of recovery. People who have been in recovery for some time can usually quickly return to where they had slipped from. Yet a slip still has an impact.

A number of specific factors can also impair development. Lack of family support is perhaps the most important of these factors. In an early study of patients in a sexual dependency unit, we found only one common denominator among those patients who slipped in their first year of treatment: their family had failed to come to Family Week, a specially designed program for coaddicts to learn about the illness. Each family member's recovery facilitates the process of recovery for the others. Lack of resources also slows down the process. Sometimes unforeseen happenings, such as the death of a parent, so overwhelm the addict that progress is slowed. Court involvement or lawsuits can prolong stages simply because of the stresses associated with the adversarial legal system.

The most important lesson that can be learned from the stages is that there are tasks appropriate to each stage. Addicts must focus on tasks appropriate to the stage they are in. For example, it is not helpful to work on reparenting during the shock stage. So we need to understand the tasks of recovery required at each stage, starting with the critical first year.

CHAPTER SEVEN

The Tasks of the First Year

The news conference was exceptionally somber. A well-known and widely respected state legislator was explaining that he had been arrested—not once, but twice—for soliciting male prostitutes. His wife and three children stood beside him as he confessed that he had no idea why he had the problem, and that he was desperate to understand it. Yet he himself offered a clue when he said that the legislature and city councils must "find a way to close the porn shops, put them out of business one way or another. They are addictive and are destroying people's lives daily."

Even the newspaper reports were restrained, a marked contrast to the steamy accounts given of another legislator's arrest for soliciting a female police decoy two years earlier. The difference reflected the very high regard in which this legislator was held. He had contributed markedly to the state and to the smooth functioning of the state house of representatives. He was, in fact, the leading finalist for a coveted state post paying seventy-eight thousand dollars a year. He had just completed his final interview when he was arrested. The second arrest occurred the day before his first court appearance, a mere two weeks later.

While this man did not talk about sex addiction, he did what many addicts are tempted to do in the early days of recovery: tell everyone. Basically this urge comes from relief at having the secret emerge and from hope that things will get better. To relieve the shame, the addict tells all. The underlying message is: "See how things are going to be different." Caught up in that almost euphoric vision, addicts are stunned when others react with judgment and ridicule. And even people experienced with addiction may greet such early statements about change with skeptical patience. The irony of all this is that the addict's intuition is right: the telling of the story will lead to healing.

Apart from the reactions of others, addicts at this point confront an enormous range of problems. Often the crises or problems that brought them to the point of recovery continue. Unresolved emotional issues that have been kept submerged by the addiction now come to the surface. There are often feelings addicts simply do not know what to do with and a loss of faith in oneself. There are also fears about a future without the addiction. Sometimes major and immediate career and life-style changes are required. For everyone there is the difficulty in stopping the behavior and facing whatever withdrawal symptoms occur. Here are some responses addicts made when asked what was the most difficult problem they faced in the early days of their recovery.

THE MOST DIFFICULT PROBLEMS OF EARLY RECOVERY

Being able to believe in myself and my gifts.

Wondered if I would ever be able to tell the difference between addiction, sexuality attraction, and simply liking someone.

Facing my fear of being known and becoming vulnerable.

Dealing with misplaced anger in the past and placing it where it belongs.

Accepting myself—I was very good at beating up on myself.

Difficulty staying in today, dealing with the problems and issues at hand.

Filling the void was a tremendous problem.

Feeling that I had to change everything right away.

Self-image was impossible for many months. Had to deal with seven separate crisis events that occurred all at once.

My job was unsuitable for recovery.

Not prepared at all for the profound effects that interruption of my sex addiction would have.

Feeling such guilt and shame over slips I wanted to give up.

This is a moment of great vulnerability. The addict's situation is not unlike that of the hermit crab who outgrows the old shell and is searching for a new one: as the crab struggles along the ocean floor to find a new shell, he is most exposed. Many addicts talk about that feeling of exposure and vulnerability. One addict stated the problem succinctly: "Letting go of the addiction, I was almost dead. I had nothing to replace it with except sheer tenacity or something. I didn't have enough experience or coping skills. I didn't even know what I needed." It is as if the crab has grown up in this shell until it became too painful to stay in it; now he has to find new shelter but has no idea what to look for or where to look.

Addicts were very clear about the challenges of their search for a new way to cope. They identified eight basic and universal problems listed here in order of importance:

1. Honest confusion about what was addictive behavior and what was healthy sexuality, with some deep resistance to setting boundaries between the two

2. Pain due to the loss or lessening of the sexual fix

3. Codependency, particularly emotional insecurity and fear of abandonment

4. Intense painful emotions, including sadness, loneliness, and anger

5. Difficulty surrendering to a program and making recovery a top priority

6. Feeling shameful and nonaccepting of oneself

7. Difficulty relating to family, spouse, and children

8. Lack of acceptance by community, family, and friends

In order to deal with these challenges, sex addicts face six tasks: breaking isolation, surviving withdrawal, reducing shame, working through emotions, resolving crisis, and defining sobriety. By accomplishing these tasks addicts lay a foundation for the repair work ahead.

BREAKING THE ISOLATION

"That group saved my life," Janis told us. "It was the only place I could go and people understood what it was like." In Janis's group there was another woman who had been married about the same number of years, had the same addictive patterns, and even the same patterns in her marriage. Janis commented, "It made me realize this was really true. This happens to people and they did the same thing I did. I was not a freak or crazy. I had an illness and here was a way to get well from it."

What happened for Janis was not unique. Our respondents found twelve step programs central to the progress they made. Their comments were echoed in almost every story we recorded. Five factors in particular seemed to contribute to the twelve step groups' success. The twelve step groups provided:

- An accepting environment from which to get support

- An opportunity to identify with others' stories and experience relief at not being unique

- Support and strategies to stop or diminish addictive behavior

- Healthy intimacy and friendship with others in the group

- A process and framework for recovering from addiction and building spirituality

THE IMPORTANCE OF
TWELVE STEP FELLOWSHIPS

Twelve step program led to honesty, honesty led to change.

Decreased isolation, increased male intimacy; increased self-esteem and spirituality; increased relationship skills; decreased self-pity.

I couldn't do it without my twelve step group. I practice real life with people in the program. Day to day, I share every problem with them.

I can share my deepest secrets, which haunt me, and I know they will be understood and accepted.

It helps me to see people who experience the same thoughts, fears, and problems that I do.

Acceptance by others has been essential. The group has been a laboratory where I can practice, and a stable place when things have been shaky. I get physical affirmation (hugs), and people share their lives and a good sense of humor with me.

The group has helped me to establish some connections with other men. The knowledge that I can be looked up to by other members gives me encouragement to maintain my sobriety.

SLAA and ACOA are great for sharing feelings. The main ingredient is being able to share experience, strength, and hope with people who understand and accept you. I never had that before.

Being in a room full of honest, trustworthy, recovering people is soothing to me. I feel accepted, no better or no worse.

It gives me a centering tool—a place to lay down my burdens. Members accept me and are willing to listen. I get wisdom, hope, and experience.

Allowing me to share my thoughts, problems, sexual urges, and slips, and being loved. Having healthy, male and female, intimate, nonsexual relationships, and enjoying good fellowship with friends at meetings and social outings.

Hearing others' stories helps me to remember that I have an uncontrollable disease and respect it. I can look around as the others get better and it gives me hope.

Ever since I began to share my vulnerability, wonderful things continue to happen. I'm closer to fellow addicts than anyone else—they are my true family. Sharing our vulnerability, and being accepted has been the key to hope and recovering.

By helping me to minimize my self-judgment; by providing a place to express feelings, by keeping the process ongoing by encouraging phone calls. We had an SCA retreat in May. It was at this time I truly saw the love of my fellow members, felt loved by them, and had an over-whelming experience of the love of God.

1. Seeing recovery in others. 2. Seeing others who will accept me. 3. Being able to help others. 4. Getting outside myself. 5. Being able to let go, and share. 6. Involving others in my family through family support groups.

I empathize with the triumphs/victories and defeats of the members in group—thus drawing object lessons from each individual experience. I find comfort in being with a group where I am accepted, feel secure, am able to render services and support to others. It is a "house" away from home.

They helped me with my biggest fear—"People won't love me if they know me."

It is the single most important element in my recovery. Gives me contact with others. Affirms my humanness. Allows spiritual growth.

The group was vital. I don't think I would have recovered without it.

This is not to say that there were no problems. All human endeavors have problems, and twelve step groups are no exception. To learn about these problems, we asked how the programs were *not* helpful. Some of the problems were typical of any group: jealousy, personality issues, gossiping, advice-giving, and judging. Generally, the traditions developed by Alcoholics Anonymous served well to minimize such problems. But some problems were unique to sex addiction groups.

By far the biggest problem was that most groups were new. They therefore lacked traditions, experience, and veteran members to supply leadership. Today the situation has changed quite a bit. Although groups are still new in some parts of the country, at least there are now national offices to provide groups with support. At national conventions new members can meet those who have been involved for a long time.

Another problem was the need for more positive support of healthy sexuality. In part, this problem stemmed from a lack of resources; with the growth of groups this is changing. In part, a fear of returning to old ways makes anything sexual seem suspect. Sexuality is central to humans yet sex addiction is highly damaging.

The survey respondents had to search, then—largely on their own— for ways to be sexual that were good for them. The solutions they found are at the heart of this book.

Many of our respondents had previous twelve step experience. They often noted, however, how much more intense it is to work on sex addiction. Talking about sexual issues creates a consistent level of vulnerability and intimacy rarely achieved in other twelve step groups. Further, sex is a difficult addiction to recover from. Sometimes, starting recovery from sexual addiction is really like starting all over again. One of the better descriptions of that process came from Charlene, an executive at a large foundation:

> I started going to SAA almost four years ago. Waltzed in, kind of scared, but thinking I was cool because I'd been in Al-Anon for four years by that time. I thought I was going to take the place by storm, and that everything I'd learned in Al-Anon was going to immediately translate to SAA. I was going to impress the hell out of everybody. Well, none of that happened. I was like a baby starting all over again, only it was like a cruel joke because I knew what recovery I had in Al-Anon and it just didn't mean beans in SAA. It was a great humbling. And yet I didn't come kicking and screaming the way so many women have. I came in with an immense state of gratitude and more serenity than I'd ever had before.

Another issue was the variations in groups. People new to recovery may have to look for a group that is a good match for them. Usually a good group will promote a fellowship life outside of the meeting, for example, through meals, retreats, and other events that bring everyone together. Good groups tend to have some structure for welcoming newcomers, such as temporary sponsors who meet new members in advance. Some offer "newcomers' groups." A clear sign of group health is a focus on step work and the basics of recovery, rather than getting lost in personal issues and conflicts.

We asked recovering persons for their best advice on critical topics. Their responses are presented throughout the remainder of this book in special lists entitled "Addicts' Best Advice." The advice is generally presented in order of importance; that is, the most frequently mentioned piece of advice is listed first, and so on.

Often, many other helpful ideas were suggested but to maintain our focus we summarized the "best advice" given most often. Addicts' Best Advice Number 1 is on developing support in the twelve step community.

ADDICTS' BEST ADVICE NUMBER 1:
Developing Twelve Step Support

---

1. *Find people with significant recovery to learn from.* If you cannot find people and groups in your area, call national fellowship offices for long distance contacts. (See pages 218–219 for addresses and telephone numbers.) Also, each fellowship has national conferences every year at which you can meet people.

2. *Remember that twelve step support is essential.* Twelve step support lays the foundation for the repair you need to do and sustains growth.

3. *You must use the phone.* Overcoming fear of using the phone is critical if you are to stay in touch with group members and sponsors. It is okay to call as many times as you need—even many times in one day or one hour.

4. *Be patient.* Going through the stages takes time There are no magic solutions—only time and constant use of program principles.

5. *Go to meetings consistently.* Find groups that are right for you and make a commitment to them. Remember, you are building a support network for yourself.

6. *Use your sponsor(s).* A sponsor is someone who knows the details of what has happened to you and coaches you on using program strategies. You can ask for a temporary sponsor. You can have more than one sponsor.

7. *Use program literature.* Find program materials. Study them. Ask about whatever you don't understand.

8. *Maintain contact outside the meetings.* Often more happens outside the meeting than in it. Groups often adjourn for coffee or supper. Some have standing breakfasts and lunches. Some offer

retreats and open meetings. Participate in the life of the fellowship by going to these events.

As already mentioned, in some areas finding a group may still be difficult. Below are listed key resources for people entering recovery or wishing to learn more information. Included are the main fellowships—Sex Addicts Anonymous, Sex and Love Addicts Anonymous, Sexaholics Anonymous, and Sexual Compulsives Anonymous. Some areas are fortunate enough to have groups representing all the fellowships. In such cases the problem arises of which group to join.

RESOURCES FOR SEX ADDICTION

Fellowships

Sex Addicts Anonymous (SAA)
P.O. Box 3038
Minneapolis, MN 55403
(612) 871-1520, (612) 339-0217

Sex and Love Addicts Anonymous (SLAA)
P.O. Box 119
New Town Branch
Boston, MA 02258
(617) 332-1845

Sexaholics Anonymous (SA)
P.O. Box 300
Simi Valley, CA 93062
(805) 581-3343

Sexual Compulsives Anonymous (SCA)
East:
P.O. Box 1585
Old Chelsea Station
New York, NY 10011
(212) 340-8985

West:
4391 Sunset Boulevard
Suite 520
Los Angeles, CA 90029
(213) 859-5585

Education (for training, materials, bibliographies, and resources)

National Council on Sexual Addiction (NCSA)
P.O. Box 3006
Boulder, CO 80307
(303) 494-5550

The Institute for Behavioral Medicine
Golden Valley Health Center
4101 Golden Valey Road
Golden Valley, MN 55422
(612) 520-1077

National Conference on Sexual Compulsivity/Addiction
Department of Education

University of Minnesota
Box 202, UMHC
420 Delaware Street, S.E.
Minneapolis, MN 55455
(612) 626-5525

Materials

Answers in the Heart—An excellent daily meditation book for sex addicts, published by Harper and Row, San Francisco.

Twelve Step Resources for Sexual Addicts and Co-Addicts—compares and contrasts the basic fellowships. Extremely helpful for new people. Published by the National Council on Sexual Addiction.

The Journal—Published by SLAA, intergroup monthly. One of the best sources for reflection.

The Plain Brown Rapper—Published by SAA. An excellent newsletter talking about recovery issues.

This problem originated in the mid-seventies, when SAA, SLAA, and SA were founded within a few months of one another in Boston, Minneapolis, and Los Angeles. The simultaneous foundings spoke to the need and readiness for these programs but also left those with choices confused as to which to join. In most significant aspects, the fellowships do the same things. They may emphasize different issues and have different terminology, rituals, and history. They each have their founders, "big books," and emerging bureaucracies. But they all follow the twelve step, self-help model of Alcoholics Anonymous.

Probably the major substantive difference among the fellowships is that Sexaholics Anonymous has a more restricted definition of sobriety than the other fellowships.' For SA, sobriety must take place within the context of a married relationship. In effect, this "sobriety imperative" rules out singles, homosexual couples, and couples in committed but unmarried relationships. This stance has been criticized from outside as moralistic and has also generated controversy within the fellowship. There is substantial support for moving to a more broadly defined sobriety, as in the other fellowships, where sobriety statements reflect each person's life circumstances and specific addictive patterns. Others, however, have argued that SA's hard line has helped them, especially early in recovery.

Undoubtedly, the diversity has a positive aspect. Each fellowship has its rich traditions, and many recovering people avail themselves of this richness by belonging to more than one group. It was not uncommon to find someone who went to a Sexaholics group on one night and an SLAA group on another. In some cities, like Denver, all the fellowship meetings are listed together to maximize convenience and choice. In other cities, individual groups maintain affiliation with several fellowships. Thus, a group in Philadelphia told us, "We are all three [SLAA, SA, SAA]."

Yet one of the clearest desires of survey respondents was that the fellowships merge or at least work more closely together. Some feel that the diversity simply fragments the overall effort. Real differences do exist but, according to many experienced twelve steppers, that is true of AA as well. Within a single city one can find tremendous diversity among groups, yet they all observe the steps and traditions of AA. Most important to everyone is that the best of each fellowship be preserved, and that the process of affiliating new members be simplified. As the dividing lines among fellowships become more blurred at the grassroots level, cooperation at a national level probably will follow. Out of that cooperative effort unity may emerge.

For many that we talked to, twelve step work was not enough. Over 87 percent pursued therapy as part of their recovery; 13 percent went to an in-patient facility. Professional therapists clearly were the persons addicts could talk to most easily. A therapist provides a unique perspective on the illness, structures experiences to support the addict, offers information about specialized groups and resources, and teaches important skills. The therapist also provides a relationship in which the addict can practice working through dependency and intimacy issues. This becomes the reparenting experience so many addicts need.

As with groups, there are now many resources that were not available when our survey respondents entered recovery. There are private practitioners who specialize in sex addiction, local clinics and treatment facilities that offer groups and out-patient programs, and hospitals and treatment facilities that offer in-patient programs. Yet, again as with groups, in many areas resources are still lacking. This can be tough for addicts who are looking for help.

It is best, when possible, to work with a therapist who is familiar with sexual addiction or with addiction in general. The next best solution is a therapist who is willing to learn with and from the client. A significant number of the addicts we surveyed had therapists who had successfully learned along with them. Some therapists become concerned about whether therapy is an adjunct to the twelve step group or vice versa. This is really a nonissue because it is all one recovery. The therapist becomes yet another resource to help the addict work through the stages of his or her recovery.

Some people need hospitalization. For example, Joe attended meetings several times a week, met with program people every day, and saw a therapist, yet could not stop acting out. In fact, his prostitution use reached the point where, to get money, he resorted to selling his car and to writing bad checks. His despair over his inability to stop made him suicidal. The failure of meetings and therapy, the danger of arrest, and the suicidal feelings all meant Joe needed hospitalization: if he was to move toward recovery he needed to be in a safe place with sufficient structure and a caring therapeutic community.

Beyond fellowship and therapy, there are few safe places for addicts to talk. Family members are seldom good sounding boards in early recovery. In fact, as we will see later, the family will need to go through a process of its own. We asked recovering addicts about discussing the addiction with others. Their advice, summarized below, the box, was essentially: go slow.

ADDICTS' BEST ADVICE NUMBER 2:
Telling Others About Your Addiction

---

1. *Be careful; tell only those you trust.* This was far and away the most frequent comment. Addicts say that in deciding whether to tell someone the key criterion is, how much do you trust that person.

2. *Wait.* Even after having decided to tell someone, take time to think your decision over before actually going through with it.

3. *Know your motives.* What payoffs do you seek? Do you want support or are you looking for approval?

4. *Do it if you can help others with the same problem.* Sharing with people who need to be in the program or who already are helps you, those people, and the group.

5. *Remember, it is not necessary to tell many people at all.* You don't have to tell—even when people pry or ask.

6. *You must tell your therapist, family, and the people closest to you.* It would be unfair to them if you were to not share something this significant. Besides, these people are all vital to your healing process. You might consult your therapist about appropriate points to talk to your family and friends.

7. *When in doubt, check it out with your sponsor and your group.* They can provide the support you need to make safe decisions.

8. *Mistakes will happen.* All addicts tell someone they later wish they had not told. It is okay to make a mistake.

SURVIVING WITHDRAWAL

At a Boston workshop on sexual addiction, a recovering professional stated in clear terms: "I have now experienced withdrawal from four addictions, including cocaine. By far the worst withdrawal was from my sexual addiction." This is a common refrain among sex addicts with other addictions. The withdrawal period seems to be difficult for all sex addicts. The SLAA "Big Book" describes it this way: "This unraveling was wrenching. We found it necessary to live through withdrawal in day-at-a-time, twenty-four-hour compartments. We would awaken in the morning, sometimes very early, and inwardly exclaim, 'Oh God! Another day of THIS!'" The same source also provides the best advice existing anywhere about withdrawal:

> We cannot go through your withdrawal for you, nor would we, if we could. Who would ever knowingly volunteer to go through it again? Certainly none of us! Yet the pain of each withdrawal is unique and special, even precious (although you probably don't now think so). In a sense, the experience is you, a part of you which has been trying to surface for a long time. You have been avoiding or postponing this pain for a long time now, yet you have never been able to lastingly outrun it. You need to go through withdrawal in order to become a whole person. You need to meet yourself. Behind the terror of what you fear, withdrawal contains the seeds for your own personal wholeness. It must be experienced for you to realize, or make real, that potential for you and your life which has been stored there for so long.

In a hospital study that is still under way, we have found there are fifteen symptoms addicts readily identify as characteristic of the early weeks of recovery. Listed by frequency of mention, these symptoms are:

1. fatigue

2. tenseness, nervousness

3. insomnia

4. headaches

5. shakes

6. high sexual arousal

7. low sexual arousal

8. body aches

9. increased food appetite

10. genital sensitivity

11. itchy skin

12. chills, sweats

13. nausea

14. rapid heartbeat

15. shortness of breath

Usually physical reactions last fourteen to fifteen days, but for some, they may last for as much as eight to ten weeks. Many who have withdrawn from cocaine report parallels in the withdrawal experiences. These parallels are intriguing, since cocaine appears to be one of the top drugs of choice for sex addicts. Researchers in cocaine have noticed a high incidence of sexual addiction in cocaine addicts.

Speculation exists about whether medication can alleviate severe withdrawal symptoms. Drugs ranging from lithium and Prozac to Depo-Provera have been used for sexual addiction withdrawal. Physicians confronting severe withdrawal also need to take into account the impact of concurrent personality disorders such as depression. Some leaders in the neurochemistry of addictive disorders urge the use of amino acid compounds to ease the transition period of recovery. Because there is not yet consensus in the field, decisions are currently made on a case-by-case basis.

For most addicts, one of the most disturbing symptoms is insomnia. Given that over two-thirds of sex addicts struggle with sleep disorders, it is not surprising that this problem intensifies in the early weeks of recovery. There are, however, simple life-style adjustments and concrete strategies that are very helpful for dealing with sleeplessness. Many of these are described in a book called *Natural Sleep*, written by Philip Goldberg and Daniel Kaufman and published by the Rodale Press. Addicts need to review their sleep patterns, determine their body rhythms, watch food intake, develop relaxation strategies, and exercise. With more severe sleep disorders they may need professional assistance.

Another problem that can be anticipated is changes in appetite. In one study 38 percent of sex addicts who went through treatment had eating disorders; half of this group found that their urges to binge-eat increased, while the other half actually found their urges decreased. There is no way to predict who will be in which group. What can be predicted is that recovery from sexual addiction will in fact have some impact—positive or negative—on other compulsive behaviors.

How, then, does one deal with multiple addictions? Some typical comments addicts made are listed below. Several principles emerge. To begin, the addictions that are the most life threatening should be dealt with first. Generally, this means that if chemical dependency is involved, the addict starts by detoxifying from chemicals. Then, if sexual addiction is the next most perilous addiction, sexual recovery becomes the priority. This continues until each area of compulsivity is addressed. Once recovery is established, a different hierarchy comes into play: the core addiction becomes the primary emphasis of recovery work. Recovery work transfers, however, in that a good recovery program in one area supports progress in others.

Most addicts, were they to go to every group they qualified for, would not have a life outside of group. In other words, it is important not to be obsessive about recovery. Gentleness and progress are vital. Priorities should be set.

When we asked what sustained people during early recovery, their responses were simple and clear:

- Once in recovery, many had a lower tolerance for pain and simply did not want to go back to active addiction.
- Many felt their emerging spirituality was key.
- Some knew that to return to their addiction would mean death.
- For a majority, the beginnings of a renewed self-esteem helped resist cravings.

- Many felt it important to keep their commitment to be faithful to their twelve step group effort.

HANDLING MULTIPLE ADDICTIONS

The same principles apply in every addiction. If sex addiction is the main focus, the others fall in line. Expressing feelings is what keeps me alive.

Find some people with similar compulsive patterns to check in with.

Compulsive behaviors are interrelated, like gears in a machine. If one gets active, the others are close behind.

Work on the most threatening addiction first, then after reaching some stability with it, work on the next most threatening.

When I become burned out with meetings and programs, I focus on the primary addiction.

Get sponsor for each addiction; have a solid home group in each program: remember, if you slip in one program, you don't have to slip in them all.

Learn how the addictions interact, and how each addiction is stimulated, and the reason for the behavior. Take one addiction at a time and allow the recovery from each one to strengthen the ability to stop the others.

They all are connected to shame—as shame is faced and worked, the addictions fade.

I must remember that sobriety in one program does not give me sobriety in another.

Trying to take it all at once is simply foolish. We need others to share in our struggles. For me, personal accountability to others is essential.

I cannot expect any one group to fill all of my needs; I take what I need from all my groups.

Keep a steady, even discipline—no big crash programs; I stay open to change and avoid a rigid mind-set toward a given concept of recovery.

REDUCING SHAME

Shame provides power to the addictive process. The shame cycle of bingeing and then feeling despair keeps addicts driven toward efforts to stop that are doomed to fail. One of the key tasks for all addicts is to reduce the shame that locks them into repetitive cycles.

The path out of shame, however, is often paradoxical. To see why, we need to understand what scientists who study systems call first-order change and second-order change. First-order change is best described by the saying, The more things change, the more things remain the same. A woman who keeps marrying abusive alcoholics changes husbands but not her life. If anything, the harder she tries to make her situation better, the worse it gets.

As another example of first-order change, consider the father who wants his son to avoid the painful mistakes he has made. He sets rigidly high standards in order to prevent his son from making those mistakes. The son, however, rebels at his father's extreme standards. The father believes that he has failed his son and that he needs to come down harder. The son becomes even more rebellious and alienated. Soon they are caught up in a destructive cycle, in which the harder the father tries, the worse the problem becomes. In first-order change, people fail as they try harder using solutions that don't work.

Addiction often exemplifies first-order change. Addicts believe they can control their behavior without help, and their shame keeps them from asking for help. Being a Master of the Universe, they want to figure it out alone. So they try harder, in secret, by themselves—and fail.

Second-order change means some essential change in the way the system operates. The woman who repeatedly marries alcoholics may need to stop being involved with men for a while. She can start to build a network of supportive women and learn to meet her emotional needs in other ways. The father can reach out to his son by sharing the pain and mistakes of his life. His vulnerability then becomes an invitation instead of an indictment or a demand. Second-order change often means solutions that involve vulnerability—and these are solutions people tend to rule out.

Addiction is no different. Addicts need to admit that they need help, that they have become powerless. To admit that you need help and are powerless breaks the shame cycle. You have an illness; you are not a bad person. Paradoxically what would seem not to work does. The key ingredient again is vulnerability.

Some have objected to the twelve step concept of illness and powerlessness. They see it as an abdication of responsibility, as letting people off the hook and granting them permission to behave irresponsibly. They feel addicts can and should be taught to control themselves. In essence, their thinking is like that of addicts, who also believe that it simply is a matter of self-control. These opponents overlook the twelve step messages of accountability to others and of taking responsibility for behavior by seeking help. They miss the paradox inherent in the solution of the problem; they don't understand that, by encouraging vulnerability to others, twelve step programs provide a way to escape shame.

Besides admitting their powerlessness, there are a number of strategies addicts can use to further reduce shame. First, addicts must learn to identify their own shame response. By learning to label their shame, they can then separate reality from their feelings of shame. They develop a capacity to detach from their shame so the feelings do not reengage the cycle of addiction. To start, addicts can focus on occasions when they are likely to feel shameful.

Addicts experience shame when they:

- feel like a failure

- despair over their struggle with destructive sexual feelings

- have suicidal feelings because things seem so hopeless

- feel like misfits—strange, unusual, or weird

- have a persistent sense of being judged by others

- fear they are not measuring up or doing things right

- feel "ashamed" about things they have done

- feel inadequate and unlovable

- feel that no matter what they do they cannot win

- consistently experience situations that fill them with dread

- obsess about what others would think if they knew the truth

Therapists working with people early in recovery often focus on identifying physical responses connected with shame. These responses include dryness of the mouth, rapid breathing, and tightness in the chest. Therapists focus on these responses to shame because people often find them easier to identify than the emotional responses.

Another strategy therapists and sponsors use is to teach about the addictive personality shift. This is simply another way of understanding the same cycle of control and release. All addicts experience themselves as if they were two people—the good and honorable Dr. Jekyll and the self-indulgent, out-of-control Mr. Hyde. Hispanic addicts sometimes refer to the *tecato gusano*—the junkie worm that rides within that you can't get rid of. Therapists build on this internal experience to reduce shame. They teach addicts to identify how their "addict within" operates. Addicts are asked, What does your addict do when things go right? What does your addict do when things are bad? How would your addict get you back to your old ways? How would your addict alienate you from your partner? your children? friends? How will your addict sabotage your recovery? your therapy? If you want, you can try this process for yourself by completing Exercise 7-1.

EXERCISE 7-1
WHAT WOULD YOUR ADDICT DO?

Addicts and coaddicts each have an "addict within" who will take over their lives with compulsive behavior. This addict becomes very predictable, always operating in certain ways and at certain times. Central to recovery is appreciating how predictable the addict can be. By knowing how your addict operates, you reduce the power of addictive demands. In each of the following situations, record what your addict's pattern has been:

1. When I feel great, like when I've accomplished something at work,

my addict will _____

2. When I am down and feel like a failure, my addict will _____

_____

3. When I have an opportunity to be intimate, my addict will _____

_____

4. When there are significant holidays or anniversaries, my addict

will _____

_____

5. When I am overextended and severely stressed, my addict will

_____

_____

6. When there is a crisis, my addict will _____

_____

_____

7. When I have a fight with a friend or family member, my addict

will _____

_____

8. When I have unstructured time, my addict will _____

_____

_____

9. When I am around my parents, my addict will _____

_____

_____

10. When I have a deadline or a project that must be done, my addict

will _____

_____

11. When I have conflicts with authority figures, my addict will _____

_____

_____

12. When somebody betrays a trust, my addict will _____

_____

13. When I can go on vacation, my addict will _____

_____

_____

14. When I am extremely tired, my addict will _____

_____

_____

15. When I am disappointed in something, my addict will _____

_____

_____

Your addict will tell you in certain circumstances that you deserve to—are entitled to—act out. List five times when your addict has told you this:

1. _____

2. _____

3. _____

4. _____

5. _____

In some circumstances, your addict rarely appears. List five situations that your addict avoids:

1. _____

2. _____

3. _____

4. _____

5. _____

Your addict has particular ways of sabotaging your recovery. List five strategies your addict might use:

1. _____

2. _____

3. _____

4. _____

5. _____

List three people with whom you should share this information about your addict:

1. _____

2. _____

3. _____

Before recovery, when the old compulsions would appear, the addict felt their inevitability. By identifying the addict within, addicts can now say to themselves, "Oh, that's just my addict trying to take

me down the path." The concept of an addict within transforms the
old pathology into the first step of relapse prevention. It creates a
psychological distance that allows recovering persons to ignore the
demands of the addictive system. Shame is now reduced because it
is about "my addict, not about me."

This internal process becomes concrete through sharing with
other addicts. On hearing others' stories, addicts understand that
they are not unique, not misfits or perverts. And when they tell
their own stories, they feel acceptance and care. They know there
are those who know everything and still welcome them. This exchange of stories reduces shame. Further, hope replaces hopelessness as those early in recovery meet others who serve as "models"
of recovery. These mentors or sponsors are people who have done
it. Their lives dispel shame because they show that there is a path,
that the condition is not irreparable.

The fundamental proposition of shame is that one is not acceptable. So people early in recovery often attempt to fight off or
discredit others' acceptance of them. They doubt the sincerity of
those who reach out. They dismiss compliments they receive and
see themselves as a burden. Isolation is so familiar that addicts run
to it when honest friendship is extended. Believing in abandonment,
addicts react with distrust. To deal with this barrier of shame,
therapists and sponsors work to help a person "act as if." When, by
going through the motions, addicts start to achieve connections, the
shame is further reduced.

Recovering people also use what neurolinguistic therapists
term "meaning anchors"—symbols or reminders of success and
progress. Oftentimes in twelve step programs these are medallions
that mark periods of sobriety or membership; some fellowships
give "desire" medallions for simply coming. Every victory is thus
celebrated in a concrete way. Recovering people can then learn to
create their own symbols of progress. These meaning anchors
further reduce shame, elevate self-esteem, and create confidence
in recovery.

WORKING THROUGH EMOTIONS

Another task facing addicts early in recovery is to deal with the many conflicting emotions that emerge at this time. First is profound grief, which reflects anger and sadness at the losses caused by the addiction. Another—often underestimated—is a sense of loss relating to the addiction itself, that is, to the addiction as a support system. Recovery requires a significant change in the addict's life, a change that means loss.

Competing with these feelings are all the feelings that were previously suppressed or numbed by compulsive obsession and behavior and that now reemerge. Because the feelings have been suppressed, addicts often cannot even identify them. Addicts will be flooded with emotions but have no awareness of where these feelings come from. Or they will magnify feelings. Feeling sad about the death of a pet may draw on sadness about a divorce. So a person may have feelings far beyond what the occasion warrants. This phenomenon stems from the backlog of unaddressed feelings.

A moving example of emotional backlog was given us by Joe, a forty-seven-year-old sales manager. When he and his wife got married, he was already heavily into acting out. In order to act out, he left his wife at home in a situation in which she was completely overburdened. Their six-month-old daughter accidentally choked to death. For twenty-two years Joe self-righteously blamed his wife for the child's death. Once in recovery he acknowledged and accepted his role. Now he and his wife could finally grieve their loss. He told us:

> I think grieving over Nancy's death has given me back my emotions. After all these years of blaming and anger and stuffed rage, I'm finally able to grieve. Very often I'll drive along and think about her and start crying. I just tell her I miss her and wish she were here. She's real for me now; she's not just some object I buried twenty-two years ago. She's alive in my memory. Sometimes I'll hear her say, "Daddy, I love you."

Grieving and emotional flooding can easily result in emotional overload. It is important for addicts to understand that they do not have to comprehend or label each feeling. At first it is enough simply to know the emotions exist—and to express them, rather than bury or avoid them. Our research shows that it is emotional overload that is most likely to lead to relapse. Addicts have always used their addiction to cope with pain. For some, facing the feelings becomes overwhelming, and so they relapse.

There are pitfalls other than relapse, however. In alcoholism treatment, the term "dry drunk" is used to describe someone who is still behaving like an alcoholic even though he or she is not drinking. Similarly, as we have noted, sex addiction can switch to anorexic forms, which are just as obsessive. To understand the problem, it is useful to recall the distinction between acting out and acting in. *Acting out* is the release part of the shame cycle. In acting out, rules are set aside, chaos and willfulness reign. *Acting in* is the control part of the shame cycle. Acting in involves excessive rigidity, self-denial, and control. This binge-purge cycle of shame can exist without compulsive behavior.

Rather than resolve the feelings that emerge in early recovery, some addicts will begin acting in. It is the only alternative they know to acting out, but it is still living in the extreme. Because acting in looks better, it is important for addicts not to mistake acting in for recovery.

The swing of the psychic pendulum from acting out to acting in appears in many areas of addicts' lives:

Boundaries—With acting out, boundaries collapse or do not exist. Acting in generates excessive boundaries which exaggerate separation needs.

Anxiety—By acting out, an addict seeks release of tension and anxiety. By acting in, an addict copes by making safety an inordinate priority.

Intimacy—When acting out, addicts are emotionally absent. When acting in, they can sense their feelings but do so in isolation.

Needs—Acting out is self-indulgent; needs are met to excess. Acting in minimizes needs but creates deprivation.

Feelings—Acting out is associated with feelings of anger. Acting in is most often based on fear.

Responsibility—Acting out is defiant: "I'll do it when I want to." Acting in is obsessive: "I have to do it right and ahead of time."

Presence—In the presence of someone who is acting out, others feel maneuvered or conned. Someone acting in appears to be a "fanatic."

Structure—Acting out activities are most often surrounded by chaos. Acting in activities require rigid structures.

Perceptions—Addicts who are acting out use no common sense or judgment, so their perceptions are unqualified. Acting in creates a mind-set that is excessively critical and extremely judgmental.

These characteristics are summarized in Table 7-1. Essentially, acting out and acting in can be seen as two different kinds of systems. Acting out is a system that is random, out of control, and chaotic. Acting in is a "closed" system highly resistant to change. Addicts in recovery need to avoid both extremes, working toward an open system that is flexible enough to accommodate change but solid enough to provide stability.

TABLE 7-1
LIVING IN THE EXTREMES

ACTING IN		ACTING OUT
excessive ←———————	boundaries ————————→	collapse
safety ←———————	anxiety ————————————→	release
isolation ←———————	intimacy ——————————→	emotionally absent
deprivation ←———————	needs ——————————→	excess
fear ←———————	feelings ————————→	anger
obsessive ←———————	responsibility ——————→	defiant
fanatic ←———————	presence ——————→	seductive
rigid ←———————	structure ——————→	chaotic
judgmental ←———————	perceptions ——————————→	unqualified

As the comments on the next page show, addicts are very familiar with the swing from being chaotic and out of control to being rigid and closed down. Over 92 percent of the addicts we interviewed strongly felt that this pattern had characterized their lives. It's not surprising that when they get into recovery, addicts believe their only alternative is to act in.

ACTING IN/ACTING OUT EXTREMES

I was at extremes always. Very controlling, then chaotic. Silent, then rageful. Judgmental and then not giving a damn.

I would go from one extreme to the other. Because I was so hard on myself, I threw the baby out with the bathwater.

In general my life was one extreme or another—trying to be the best or worst, shut down or acting out.

After and in between acting out (getting VD or badly hurt), I would swear off men entirely and go into acting in. I was acting in or acting out throughout my life until twelve step recovery.

Many years of the same pattern. Terrified of what was going on, I would decide to shut down and stay that way—no risks, isolated, shut down, rigid.

I would get into rigid rule setting for him and me in order to control the chaos. While acting out in rage, I made no pretense of "normal."

My acting in was the "straight" part of my double life. Conservative, middle-class banker, strict and short with my children, overresponsible provider for my family.

I went from totally denying my needs to being excessively needy. It was a continuous cycle throughout my life.

Mickey was a classic example of swinging between extremes. He entered a weight loss program and, using a liquid protein diet, went from 240 pounds down to 145 pounds. His sexual acting out stopped; in fact, he stopped being sexual with his wife. But within a year, the weight returned, and when it did, Mickey said, "I started sexually acting out again, hitting the bookstores and the rest rooms." After Mickey binged sexually, he became very afraid and shifted to acting in: "When acting in, some of the things that really stand out for me are the isolation and the fear. I was always afraid—afraid that I was going to be discovered. I was very rigid and judgmental to people." (Ironically, Mickey's wife told him that the periods of rigidity were some of the better times in their marriage. He said,

"She knew what to expect of me and what I would do. Whereas other times would be chaotic and she never knew when I would fly off the handle.")

Mickey's fears were well founded. He was arrested for being sexual with a man in a rest room. The story was front-page news, since Mickey was a well-known and popular high school administrator. He lost his job and found his way into SAA. Although he went to meetings and felt the acceptance of people there, he often found himself isolating and withdrawing, acting in as in the old days. The shock of what had happened seemed to reinforce his shutting down emotionally. The critical breakthrough came when Mickey started to grieve. He began to deal with the task of emotional resolution:

> The event that really brought it home to me was when a woman who had been a teacher's aide in my building and someone that I had liked a lot was killed in an automobile accident. I forced myself to go to that funeral. There was a lot of shame in going because this was the first time I was seeing some of these people that I had known prior to my arrest. I really wept at that funeral, and my feeling is now that I did cry for her and the pain that her family was going through but I think a lot of my weeping was for my own loss.

Many reported that the grieving period was critical to breaking through the cycle of acting in. In large part, acting out and acting in are both ways to avoid pain. By embracing the pain, addicts transform suffering into a new consciousness of themselves. They prepare themselves for the work they must do to achieve a complete recovery.

We asked addicts for their advice about how to get out of living in the extremes. Almost universally they referred to steps two through five of the twelve step program. Steps two and three help addicts to build a spiritual base and thus to trust outcomes and stay centered. Steps four and five assist addicts by inventorying areas of strength and weakness.

Many addicts also mentioned extra help they received by going to Adult Children of Alcoholics meetings. The list that follows summarizes other insights they offered. Note that clarity, balance, and gentleness are critical during this period of grief.

ADDICTS' BEST ADVICE NUMBER 3:
Avoiding the Extremes

1. *When in doubt check it out with your therapist, your sponsor, or a group member.* Living in the extremes is part of the old addictive mold that the Big Book of AA calls "cunning and baffling." Addicts and coaddicts need ongoing input from others to keep balanced and to have a check on their own denial.

2. *Be clear about your needs.* Many addicts emphasized that recovery offers human and spiritual resources to help people understand what they need and want. Take care of your basic needs: hunger rest, and support.

3. *Make balance an important goal.* Figure out boundaries that help you to maintain balance. Make those boundaries your priority.

4. *Learn to do kind things for yourself.* One addict told us, "Now I see a better way: we need to be more gentle with ourselves."

5. *Develop self-awareness.* Be an observer of yourself, using meetings, journals, and meditation.

6. *Work on the old hurts.* Your feelings will become important guides to the balance you need.

7. *Act "as if."* At first, not being in the extremes will seem awkward and unrewarding. In order to distance yourself from your fear, pretend that this is okay. Ask your sponsor about the Third Step.

8. *Leave cyclic, destructive relationships.* Avoid partners and friends who persist in old patterns of escalation. If they are not committed to pursuing balance, you must take action. Leave or at least separate from them until your recovery is solidified.

RESOLVING CRISIS SITUATIONS

One problem with living in the extremes is that addiction thrives in crisis. Crisis situations obscure accountability. They alter mood and generate adrenaline rushes. Overextended and overwhelmed, the addict is vulnerable to entitlement feelings: I deserve it because of all I'm going through. Moreover, crisis creates fear. We have already noted how for sex addicts fear, risk, and sexual arousal are all linked.

Part of the mystique of a Master of the Universe is being able to navigate through stormy, crisis-filled seas. For sex addicts, deceit, broken promises, and violated rules require a constant readiness to put out fires. And the energy expended maintaining a double life compounds one addict's feelings of depletion. In the addiction system, the addict still believes that the double life is the ideal life—or at least the only way to meet his needs.

Surrender and recovery are usually triggered by crises that have become overwhelming. Early recovery therefore requires facing and resolving crisis: arrest, public exposure, financial crisis, loss of job or marriage, disease, or accidents. One woman said to us, "In those early months, I had seven major crises at once."

In addition to dealing with their particular crises, addicts have to deal with their tendency to seek crisis. Addicts and coaddicts create crisis by magnifying, escalating, or catastrophizing an event. Like other forms of acting out, this helps the addict avoid pain or avoid tasks that need to be faced. Experienced therapists and sponsors will support addicts in resolving crises left over from acting out days. They are singularly unimpressed, however, by new crises that interfere with recovery tasks. Their hard-nosed, tough-love attitude provides a fundamental teaching about addiction.

Lance's experiences provide a good example of the role of crisis and the need to overcome crisis seeking. Lance is a thirty-eight-year-old minister who has been in recovery for four years. Danger was very much part of his addiction. He commented, "I constantly would set myself up for more danger. For example, one Halloween night I met a guy in a bookstore and went back to his house. The police were there. His roommate had murdered someone." His addiction caused many crises in his life, like the night he failed to show up to make a presentation to a group of forty because he was acting out.

Lance referred to himself as an "E-ticket" personality. Disneyland and Disney World used to have an E-ticket, which allowed purchasers to go on as many rides as they wanted, as many times as they wanted. Lance told us, "That's how I was and always had been. The more experiences the better." For Masters of the Universe, the E-ticket is the way to go. For Lance, the ride stopped when he failed his Ph.D. comprehensive exams.

Because of his tendency to seek crisis, the early part of recovery was especially hard for Lance. He commented that for a long time he hated going to meetings, hated the way he felt, and doubted recovery would ever get easier. Ultimately, however, balance provided Lance with a path out of constant crisis. He sees balance as the most important gift of his recovery. He was able to reconcile a balanced life-style with his need to be all he could be:

> I can have a balanced life and still be successful. I won't turn out to be a dull person. I have this incredible need to be known, to be something; and to be balanced seems to go against that. It's an ongoing, day-to-day, constant struggle to be balanced and to be everything I want to be at the same time—creative, energetic, alive, successful, artistic, bright, witty—all of those things and yet to be ever about it. It seems incongruous and yet people do it. I'm doing it, and it's working.

One of the key ways to achieve balance is by establishing and sticking to priorities. Wanda, a thirty-year-old beautician, describes how she did this:

> I really struggled because I was so used to the highs—the extreme highs and the extreme pleasure in the highs—that it was boring at first. Very boring to be on an even keel. I found myself creating problems. Crises kept coming up, and I could see it was really destroying my self-esteem. I had to work at that. It mostly was just a process, working a little bit at a time and scheduling and organizing my time. Putting so much time in for my son every day, so much time for my studying and if I didn't get it done in that time it was too bad I'd just forget about it. Sometimes I had to neglect my home, which was my big thing in my self-esteem. My home related directly to me, and if it wasn't clean, I wasn't clean. Dealing with that and saying, "It's okay. That's not number one on my list." My son is number one and I'm number one. Setting priorities. Getting them straight and then going from there.

Another key strategy is working to finish things. Addicts do not finish things. They in fact prefer to "keep options open." But in life some things simply need to be finished. Projects, arguments, conversations, and some relationships need to be ended. Addiction thrives in unfinished business. Starting much more than you can ever finish leads to crisis. Ending things adds substantially to recovery.

Rosalie is a twenty-seven-year-old whose life was marked by abuse, tragedy, and a frightening level of acting out. About seven months into her recovery, she realized she had given out a number of "rain checks." That is, there were people who had wanted to establish or continue a relationship but had agreed to wait until she was ready. Rosalie realized this was not healthy for her: "So I started to weed out those people, getting rid of those rain checks, tearing them up and starting over." For her it became the "fourth and fifth steps of my life," she told us.

In the fourth step, a person in recovery conducts a deeply personal inventory of his or her life and then in the fifth step shares that with somebody. Rosalie took stock of her life, and she then went on to finish what needed to be finished. She observed, "I didn't just go and say to somebody, 'Here, I did this: Say seven Hail Mary's.' I had to do some cleaning out of my life." For example, she still wore a ring given to her by her ex-fiancé, someone who was linked to her old addictive patterns. She now stopped wearing the ring.

One important ending had to do with Rosalie's childhood. Her father had abused her in many ways; in a jealous, incestuous rage, he had even attempted to murder her and her boyfriend when she was fifteen. In his house was a closet filled with Rosalie's things:

> My father told me to clean the closet out every time I saw him, but I couldn't. It was like the only tie I had left to this family, you know, since the contact I had with him was very little. He only lived five miles from me. He bribed me like he usually does. He said, "I'll buy you this stereo for Christmas if you clean out this closet." So I said, "Fine." I grabbed somebody in the program and we went over to clean this closet. In this closet was everything from Barbie dolls to birth control pills. All of my teenage-hood, grammar school, and nursery school stuff including big pictures I had drawn were in this closet. It took me about an hour.

I didn't spend time reading the stuff like I would have in the past. I went and put it in trash bags. I just went through the closet, got rid of all the clothes, got rid of all the junk, and I saved a handful of things. It was a physical fourth step, if anything, because my whole sexual history was in this closet. Barbie dolls and birth controls were one and the same. You know, I played with them while I was on the pill.

Grieving often involves acknowledging contradictions that intensify the sense of loss as when Rosalie recognized that she was playing with Barbie dolls and taking the pill at the same time.

Finishing, prioritizing, and balance all play key roles in resolving crises and avoiding the extremes. But perhaps nowhere are they more important than in the final task of early recovery: defining sobriety.

DEFINING SOBRIETY

A relatively new member of a program told us, "Before recovery I was obsessed with having sex, and since recovery I've been obsessed with avoiding sex. It's the only way I know how to deal with it. I have been absolutely on ice." Sexual acting in is a frequent complaint of those early in recovery. Frozen by the fear of creating more sexual havoc, they complain of having no sense of how to be sexual in healthy, rewarding ways. They are confronting one of the major tasks of the first year: how to develop a sexual sobriety and at the same time lay the foundation for a healthy sexual life.

How does sobriety lead to serenity and peace? Can there be sexual excitement in sobriety? How does one avoid simply acting in? The dilemmas here are very reminiscent of those facing people who have eating disorders. For the compulsive overeater, the familiar solution is obsessive dieting. The recovery solution, in contrast, involves choosing healthy foods while avoiding foods that adversely affect one's mood and body. The overeater needs to monitor when food becomes a "solution" for life's problems. Finally, for the recovering overeater and the recovering sex addict alike, few choices are simply black and white; every day presents an abundance of choices in myriad shades of gray. And similar questions emerge: Can healthy food be exciting or satisfying? Can healthy sex be exciting or satisfying?

Sobriety can ultimately become the basis for serenity. A great metaphor for appreciating this process was provided by a recovering addict who likened it to assembling a train. Sobriety is the caboose, he said. Addicts add cars which are fundamental parts of their sexual selves. The last piece to be added is the engine of serenity, which becomes an awesome moving force: "After some period of long sobriety, you finally reach the powerful engine that is serenity. I don't place the engine at the beginning point, since it works just the opposite way." Nor do addicts go from sobriety straight to serenity. They must first do a lot of work in connection with their sexuality. The message of the metaphor is that sobriety is the place to start, even if it does not feel peaceful right away.

Addicts agree that sobriety is a process that transforms their sexuality. Michelle said that her sexuality has gone "from unimaginable to abstract to concrete. What feels healthy now would have felt threatening and scary at an earlier time." Part of sobriety is cultivating your sexual self, a threatening thought for those in early recovery, when acting in may seem like the only alternative. "Part of growth," Michelle adds, "is accepting the timing, however long or short it takes, and staying with the present."

So two realities exist. Addicts have to start with sobriety, and they must accept that nurturing their sexuality will be part of their sobriety. To most addicts, this feels like an overwhelming job. It helps to break it down into three very discrete tasks: defining abstinence, setting boundaries, and focusing priorities.

DEFINE ABSTINENCE

Just as alcoholics abstain from mood-altering chemicals, sex addicts must abstain from behaviors that alter mood in destructive ways. For alcoholics, the chemicals are easily identified. The sex addict, however, has the more difficult job of identifying behaviors. The addict will have to write a list, which must be very concrete and specific as well as comprehensive. Abstinence is defined on the basis of these behaviors. In twelve step programs, many of the behaviors are specified as part of the first step, when the addicts admit the behaviors over which they are powerless.

In addition to first step data, addicts must explore all the patterns they know were part of their addiction. Underlying these patterns is a governing scenario; that is, certain fantasies or story lines provide a script for the addict's obsessive life. Rosalie showed wonderful self-knowledge about her addictive patterns. She connected them with the grandiosity and perfectionism that goes with a Masters of the Universe scenario:

> In my addiction I always thought I was better than anybody. They were better than me because I was a slut or a whore, but I was always better. I always deserved the best. In my head I always thought, Oh no, this person is working-class, no way. I need a man who's got money and wears a suit. Men in a suit, I mean I'm wild over men in a suit. If you have a three-piece suit and you have a car and you look professional, this is the ultimate. It's more of a turn-on than nudity. A man in a three-piece suit is my goal.

Rosalie's patterns included multiple relationships with successful, unavailable men. Working her way through college, she was a secretary in a building that held various companies. At one point she had simultaneous affairs with four company executives in that building alone—two of them presidents of their firms, all of them married. After a while, she said, "I was calling men by whatever name I was thinking of."

During the repair stage, which is discussed in the next chapter, part of relapse prevention is to figure out where governing scenarios like Rosalie's came from. To define abstinence, however, all that is necessary is to name the behaviors that cause the trouble. For Rosalie, for example, one such behavior was sex with unavailable men. So part of an abstinence definition for Rosalie might be: sex only within a committed relationship. A corollary might be: dating only men who are free to commit.

In fact, at the time of our interview, Rosalie had been in a successful relationship with a man for five months. From the point of view of abstinence, her comment about him was striking. "For the first time in my life, I'm with someone who's not more than ten years older than me, who's never had children, who isn't in a relationship, and who likes the same things I do."

The abstinence list itself has many uses. First, it clarifies what the abstinence goals are. It also serves as a tool for discussions with sponsors, group members, and therapists. By sharing the list, addicts receive feedback—whether it is about being too hard on themselves or about being in denial. The list becomes a means of contact with others in their program. Many recovering addicts carry their lists in their wallets to pull out when they experience cravings. For a sample abstinence worksheet see Exercise 7-2.

EXERCISE 7-2
ABSTINENCE WORKSHEET

Abstinence means concretely defining behaviors that you will abstain from as part of your recovery. To use one of these behaviors again means a slip; *to continue it over a period of time means a* relapse. *You identify these behaviors when you admit your powerlessness over them and you specify your unmanageability. List as many behaviors as you need to. Be very specific and concrete. Remember that addicts often amend, add to, or delete from their lists as circumstances and recovery warrant. No change should be made, however, without consulting with your group, sponsor, or therapist.*

Example:

No visits to strip joints, prostitution or outcall services, or pornography stores or theaters.

YOUR ABSTINENCE   As of (date): _____

1. _____

2. _____

3. _____

4. _____

5. _____

6. _____

YOUR ABSTINENCE   As of (date): _____

7. _____

8. _____

9. _____

10. _____

11. _____

12. _____

13. _____

14. _____

15. _____

16. _____

17. _____

18. _____

19. _____

20. _____

(Continue as required.)

Addicts must remember that this list will change as their understanding of their addiction expands. Michelle explained how this process worked for her:

The first two years my awareness grew as did my definition of abstinence: from no sexual contact to no flirting; no dressing in seductive, stimulating clothing; no pornography or erotica; limited masturbation; no abusive self-talk; no romance obsessions. Later I learned to judge my actions within a context and found that sexuality wasn't the curse. It was addiction. I could flirt if I was honest and there was an appropriate context. I could wear clothing which was flattering without hooking that obsessive seductive side of myself.

Knowing that the abstinence will change over time provides an important perspective for sobriety issues that are often confusing to addicts. One such issue is sexual preference. Some people reported that early in their recovery they tormented themselves with questions about whether their acting out behavior meant they were gay. This has partly to do with shame around addictive behavior and partly with a culture that has been oppressive to homosexuals. The best advice is for the addict to work on recovery first. Things will look very different after a period of sobriety. Then the addict can explore with a therapist, sponsor, and group which sexual expressions are congruent and comfortable.

Another tormenting issue for many is masturbation. Some addicts in our survey were able to use masturbation in healthy ways. Usually, they had set very specific limits and had dealt with the issue in their group and/or with their therapist. Other addicts, however, abstained from masturbation because it was too much part of their specific patterns of acting out. By far the majority were in this category. There is general agreement that early in recovery people should abstain from masturbation. Several factors argue for abstinence. First, masturbation involves fantasies, and the task of separating obsessive fantasies from healthy ones is too hard. Second, abstinence from masturbation helps the search for new forms of sexual expression. And, finally, for many masturbation is part of the problem and early in recovery their denial is too great for them to admit it.

Abstinence definitions will differ because the addictive patterns differ. There is no one catchall list. What is important is that abstinence be defined in consultation with others. Addicts are accustomed to making decisions alone and in secret. Part of surrender is to seek help from others. Whatever is agreed upon becomes the abstinence contract the addict lives with.

SET BOUNDARIES

More than anything else, boundaries help preserve abstinence. Boundaries become guidelines that help recovering people when situations are precarious or confusing. To set boundaries, addicts review their addictive patterns and rituals and then list those they will avoid because they could jeopardize abstinence—or simply wouldn't contribute to recovery or spiritual growth. Crossing over a boundary does not mean a slip or relapse. Rather, addicts use boundaries as a way to refocus on what they need to be doing for themselves.

Boundaries may involve situations, circumstances, people, and/or behaviors. For example, a man might decide to not respond to sexual jokes that are demeaning to women. He might choose to avoid personal conversations with his ex-wife because in such conversations in the past she would always somehow shame him, which led to his acting out. He thus limits himself to talking about arrangements concerning the children.

If this man is currently in a committed relationship, he does not share intimate feelings with women who are seductive or sending sexual signals. He focuses on business or avoids contact. Nor does he share information about his recovery with people that he works with. Boundaries become self-imposed limits that help the recovering addict live in balance and avoid crises and extremes.

Setting boundaries helps to reduce shame. Earlier we noted that shame-based persons have problems with permeable boundaries. Their need for approval is so high they have problems with setting limits and saying no to other people's demands. By, for example, setting boundaries around conversations, addicts learn that they do not owe explanations to everyone. Some information is personal and should be disclosed only to trusted persons. Boundaries help an addict regain control over whom to talk to and what to share.

The usefulness of boundary setting extends far beyond interpersonal interactions, to all areas of the addict's life. Exercise 7-3, a worksheet on boundaries, can serve as a starting point for the process.

EXERCISE 7-3
BOUNDARIES WORKSHEET

Boundaries are self-imposed limits that promote health or safety. They may involve situations, circumstances, people, and/or behavior that you avoid because they are dangerous, jeopardize your abstinence, or do not add to your recovery or your spirituality. Boundaries are guides to help you toward health. Crossing over a boundary does not signify a relapse but, rather, a need to focus again on priorities. List below boundaries that will help your recovery. Be as concrete as possible.

Example:
    I will avoid the southwest part of town because many of the places I used to act out are there.

YOUR BOUNDARIES: As of (date): _____

1. _____

2. _____

3. _____

4. _____

5. _____

6. _____

7. _____

8. _____

9. _____

10. _____

11. _____

12. _____

13. _____

YOUR BOUNDARIES: As of (date): _____

14. _____

15. _____

16. _____

17. _____

18. _____

19. _____

20. _____

21. _____

22. _____

23. _____

24. _____

25. _____

26. _____

27. _____

28. _____

29. _____

30. _____

The issue of how to integrate abstinence and boundaries with healthy sex is an important one. Again, our survey respondents were able to provide helpful advice. Their suggestions are listed on the next page.

ADDICTS' BEST ADVICE NUMBER 4:
Developing Sobriety and Healthy Sexuality

1. *Pick an extended period of celibacy.* The top priority for most addicts is to experience a period of celibacy. Celibacy helps the person to clear out unmanageability, to feel more alive again, and to reclaim repressed memories of childhood abuse experiences. (See Chapter Eight for celibacy strategies.)

2. *Be patient with yourself.* Gentleness, kindness, and self-care are watchwords. To change after years of compulsion is a huge task, and you will make mistakes. As one addict observed, "Don't make self-love contingent on abstinence."

3. *Accept yourself as a sexual person.* Sexuality and sobriety are, as another addict advised, "possible and not a contradiction in terms." Sex is not dirty and shameful. You must distinguish between your addiction and your sexuality. Sobriety is about addiction, not about sexuality. Your sexuality is to be embraced, not denied.

4. *Work on boundaries.* Boundaries give you clarity about your sexual self and help to reduce shame. As guidelines, they serve as a bulwark against denial, obsessive thinking, and relapse.

5. *Keep others current.* Always keep others in your program informed about happenings in your sexual life. When in doubt or when confronting something new, check it out. Have no secrets, and avoid becoming isolated.

6. *Understand that things will change.* Your vision of your sexuality will change dramatically with time in recovery. You will need to allow yourself that process.

7. *Accept the imperfect.* The search for perfection in relationships and sex caused many addicts to discard relationships before they knew their potential. The search was futile and the losses real.

FOCUS PRIORITIES

Sobriety is not about being on a diet. Diets lead to obsession. Sobriety leads to a new focus. A sobriety that only defined what *not* to do would miss what recovery is about—meeting human needs.

Addicts need to learn to nurture themselves, to reward themselves in healthy ways, and to find alternative highs. They need to capture the intimacy and acceptance that they had always sought through their addiction.

This concept of sobriety is the basis for the focus list. As part of sobriety, the addict makes a list that specifies new priorities on which to focus. Addicts need to understand that they are not giving up rewards but, rather, entering a new and unexplored territory that is rich in rewards.

In this process of shifting focus, two factors intimidate addicts. One is that addicts often do not feel entitled to a better life. Many addicts struggle with self-hatred and self-punishment. They ask, Do I really deserve good things? Am I worthwhile enough to have a decent life? They tend to deflect compliments and to find fault with expressions of support. So when others encourage them to shift their focus, they find it hard to imagine a future of successful recovery; instead, they cling to old shame-based scripts rooted in addictive patterns. Yet such imagining can actually "reprogram" addicts to alter their life course. So drawing up the focus list makes it easier to take the risk.

The other factor is that addicts often know of no alternatives. How can life be different? This inability to perceive other options is especially great when it comes to sex. What healthy sex is eludes addicts who are just beginning recovery. They may become obsessed with whether their lovemaking with their partner is addictive or healthy.

Addicts at this stage need to know that sobriety will transform their sexuality. Respondents gave us many examples of such transformations. One told us, "I used to think it was okay to play role-type sex games where someone pretended to be mean to me as long as we both consented. Now I seek intimacy. No more role-playing." Another described how sex had changed in his marriage: "My sexuality has softened and expanded. . . . Now it includes caressing her in the kitchen and letting her know I'm thinking about her when I'm away."

Two statements from our interviews capture especially well the spirit of healthy sexuality that evolves during recovery. The first is from a man in Texas:

Healthy sexuality has to do with being able to accept my sexual desires without shame and fear, and putting boundaries on my sexual behavior that help me to treat myself and others with care and respect. It is accepting the sexual dimension in my relationships while also recognizing the other aspects as well (not sexualizing every woman and every move). It is using sex as an expression of my need for nurture and intimacy and not using it for escape, conquest, control, or to fill up my needs for esteem.

The second is from a woman in Colorado:

Now I see my sexuality as my very own. It's precious to me, and I won't share it with anyone except my husband, who I love and loves me. I also am free to express my needs and desires to him for the first time, too, which is a wonderful, free feeling. Before I was always the giver but never would ask for anything for fear it would turn him off or something.

Addicts often describe healthy sex by contrasting it with the experience of their addiction. As discussed earlier, addictive behavior tends to be shame based, fearful, nonmutual, and exploitive. We can develop a model which offers a point-by-point contrast between addictive sexuality and healthy sexuality.

Addictive sex feels shameful. Often it is illicit, stolen, or exploitive. It compromises values and draws on fear to generate excitement. Addictive sex often reenacts childhood abuses, disconnecting one from oneself. A world of unreality is created, allowing self-destructive and dangerous behaviors. Based on conquest or power, it is seductive and dishonest. Serving to medicate and kill pain, addictive sex becomes routine, grim, and joyless. A tough taskmaster, the addiction requires a double life and demands perfection.

Healthy sex adds to self-esteem. It has no victims. It deepens life's meaning and uses vulnerability for excitement. Furthering one's sense of self, healthy sex helps the individual become an adult who assumes responsibility for needs. It expands on reality by relying on safety. It is mutual and intimate. Originating in integrity, healthy sex may include legitimate suffering; it dares to face pain. It presents challenges while integrating the most authentic parts of oneself. Healthy sex is fun and playful and allows for the imperfect.

Table 7-2 summarizes the differences between addictive and

healthy sexuality. This model of sexual health is general, of course.

TABLE 7-2
ADDICTIVE SEXUALITY VERSUS HEALTHY SEXUALITY

ADDICTIVE SEXUALITY	HEALTHY SEXUALITY
Feels shameful	Adds to self-esteem
Is illicit, stolen, or exploitive	Has no victims
Compromises values	Deepens meaning
Draws on fear for excitement	Uses vulnerability for excitement
Reenacts childhood abuses	Cultivates sense of being adult
Disconnects one from oneself	Furthers sense of self
Creates world of unreality	Expands reality
Is self-destructive and dangerous	Relies on safety
Uses conquest or power	Is mutual and intimate
Is seductive	Takes responsibility for needs
Serves to medicate and kill pain	May bring legitimate suffering
Is dishonest	Originates in integrity
Becomes routine	Presents challenges
Requires double life	Integrates most authentic parts of self
Is grim and joyless	Is fun and playful
Demands perfection	Accepts the imperfect

Each person must discover what healthy sexuality means for him or her. Addicts can begin by looking at their own abstinence list and thinking about what did *not* work for them. A focus list then becomes an addict's first effort to articulate sexual health. This list doesn't just address sexual health, however. Addicts need to include all the ways they are going to nurture themselves back to health. Exercise 7-4, a focus worksheet, shows how to start a focus list.

EXERCISE 7-4
FOCUS WORKSHEET

Recovering people prepare a list of what they will focus on. These are the rewards, the behaviors to embrace, or the situations to work for. Sobriety is not about depriving oneself, but about learning how to do things differently. To prepare this list, ask yourself questions like the following: What would feel good to me—personally, interpersonally, and sexually? What priorities do I need in my life? What do I deserve? How can I nurture myself in a way that is safe and life enhancing? Where do I need to take risks to grow? Be sure to include your vision of the ways sex can be healthy for you.

Example:

0. I will take the risk of sharing with my partner my feelings about our sexuality.

YOUR FOCUS PRIORITIES: As of (date): _____

1. _____

2. _____

3. _____

4. _____

5. _____

6. _____

7. _____

8. _____

9. _____

10. _____

11. _____

12. _____

YOUR FOCUS PRIORITIES: As of (date): _____

13. _____

14. _____

15. _____

16. _____

17. _____

18. _____

19. _____

20. _____

21. _____

22. _____

23. _____

24. _____

25. _____

26. _____

27. _____

28. _____

29. _____

30. _____

This section has emphasized that sobriety is the beginning of change. In remaining chapters we will explore other key aspects: celibacy, rebuilding relationships, and restoring family bonds. Yet the vitality, adventure, and joy of this rebuilding must not be lost amid all the tasks and issues. Few of our survey participants cap-tured this excitement better than Cliff, a retired executive, who, with his supportive and colorful manner, helped build a network of over fifty groups in his area. We enjoyed his observations about his emerging sexuality:

> What's happening now is that I'm going to let relationships be what they are and discover what they're going to be. It's been a recognition that throughout my life I had had an idea that I knew what the perfect relationship should be. The pioneering part is that I was sixty-eight last week and there's not much of a model for what you do when you're learning how to explore later-life relationships, so I'm will-ing to find out. About a year ago, George Abbott was out here. I admired him for a long time. He was producing a show on Broadway and he's one hundred. I just said I wonder what it'd be like to be happy, joyous, and free and be sexual in whatever way you are at one hundred. Then the question is, Do you want to be? I said the answer is yes, so I thought I'd go on one day at a time. As of today I have 11,674 days to go.

CHAPTER EIGHT

Years Two and Three: Rebuilding

If we are painstaking about this phase of our development, we will be amazed before we are half way through. We are going to know a new freedom and a new happiness. We will not regret the past nor wish to shut the door on it. We will comprehend the word serenity and we will know peace. No matter how far down the scale we have gone, we will see how our experience can benefit others. That feeling of uselessness and self-pity will disappear. We will lose interest in selfish things and gain interest in our fellows. Self-seeking will slip away. Our whole attitude and outlook on life will change. Fear of people and of economic insecurity will leave us. We will intuitively know how to handle situations which used to baffle us. We will suddenly realize that God is doing for us what we would not do for ourselves.

The Promises. Since they first appeared in the Big Book of Alcoholics Anonymous in 1939, these words have inspired millions. Their truth has been verified by countless stories in the lives of AA members. The Promises are an open-ended recipe for those struggling with addiction. If you take these twelve steps, you can have a predictable result. The Promises say, "we will be amazed before we are half way through."

For sex addicts in their second and third years of recovery, "half way through" was truly amazing. We were able to measure dramatic improvements in career status, financial stability, friendships, ability to cope with stress, spirituality, and self-image.

When we asked people in our survey what they considered the gifts of recovery, their responses read like the Promises. The following list ranks these gifts in order of significance to those surveyed:

1. *Empathy and compassion.* Love and acceptance of others and understanding of human suffering were universally recognized as the most important gift of recovery. The wrenching changes required of addicts deepened their existential sympathy for others.

2. *Introduction to spiritual life.* Addicts also universally acknowledged that recovery helped them cultivate a spiritual life. For many, this spiritual experience was new.

3. *Ability to care about self.* By confronting the shadows of self-hatred and shame, addicts increased their self-esteem and developed the ability to care for themselves. This also was new for many.

4. *Learning about family.* Recovery forced many to learn about their family of origin and family dysfunction. Relationship issues that had seemed mysterious became clarified through therapy, reading, and the recovery process.

5. *Friendships.* Connecting with others became a primary concern, as interpersonal skills grew and as recovering people learned the value of a healthy relationship.

6. *Realism about life.* Addicts used words like "problem solving," "perseverance," and "resourceful" in describing the changes in their lives.

7. *Reduced perfectionism.* Patience, kindness, and acceptance of oneself and others started to compete with the "do it right" messages of childhood in the shame-based family.

8. *Demythologized sexuality.* Many were grateful that their misperceptions around sex had been dispelled. The old myths had preserved addicts' sexual shame.

Some people's stories truly read like miracles. Helen, for example, regarded herself as having been "totally out of control" and "bouncing off the walls of the world." An incest victim at age ten, she was sent to a private boarding school for girls at age fifteen because of her sexual promiscuity. By her early twenties, she was having sex with hundreds of men a year. By her thirties, she had married, gotten divorced, and been physically and emotionally abusive to her three children. In addition to her sexual problem, she had a serious drug problem.

Help for Helen's sex addiction came through Overeaters Anonymous. She had started recovery for overeating and drug addiction but was still miserable. During an OA retreat, a fellow member shared his story about his sex addiction. She was stunned. She said, "I knew right there and then beyond a shadow of a doubt that that was why I was still in so much pain." Up until then, she added, "I had no idea that it had anything to do with my sexual behavior. I knew that I couldn't stop, that I was degrading myself, but I had no idea it was an addiction process."

Six years later her life was dramatically different. Helen described the differences:

> The biggest example in the material sense is that I did not think I was worthwhile to even clean houses. I come from a family of engineers. My brother is a nuclear physicist and somehow my life had gotten down to the point that I was not even worthwhile enough to clean houses. That's what I was doing for a living just six years ago. I went to school and got my LPN, and I came out to California and got my RN, and I wind up being the charge nurse of ICU. I have this sense of being able to be worth something, to accomplish something. I wanted to commit suicide in 1978 because I didn't think I was worth anything. If I'd have done that I wouldn't have found out that I could be an RN. Six years ago I lived in the low-income projects, cleaned houses for a living, was on Medicaid and food stamps. Now I own a house and have a car and I work as an RN every day.

Helen started her LPN in the second year of recovery. Much of her career change occurred during this repair stage. Helen told us that what helped her emerge from this stage was that "what I thought I would do was now different." How do recovering people achieve that sense of themselves "half way through"? As with the first year, the second and third years are associated with key tasks. These include experiencing a period of celibacy, developing a sense of self-affirmation, changing personal life-style, learning to prevent relapse, and developing a spiritual life. Fundamental to all these, however, is the challenge of building relationships.

BUILDING RELATIONSHIPS

When Helen was active in her addiction, she was isolated and filled with pain. In sharing her memories of that time, she observed, "I was constantly pushing down pain and saying, 'Oh God, don't let me feel. I'll do anything not to feel this.' " Helen relied on responses she learned as a kid to handle things "on her own." As an adult she learned to cover up things with bravado and humor but had "no connection with anything or anyone." The hardest part of starting recovery for Helen—as for many others—was the recognition that she had no support. In fact, "it was hell," she quipped, "to be forty and still trying to figure out what intimacy was."

The most important skill to be gained in recovery is the skill of developing support and intimacy. Viable, connected relationships reduce the pain, assist in problem solving, heal the deficits of childhood, and build a sense of self-worth. Yet, because of their early histories and the nature of addictive obsession, most addicts and coaddicts feel overwhelmed by the task of developing relationships.

The healing process eases them into it. As they feel the grief, they start to reach out. By the second year, they really have to confront the process of building relationships. Part of the success of twelve step support groups resides in their "learning by doing" process. The support group experience becomes a curriculum from which addicts learn or relearn intimacy. In other words, addicts learn to make intimacy simple. It may not be easy, but it can be simple. Some of the concrete advice addicts gave on building twelve step support was echoed as they talked about building relationships.

Almost everyone had to learn to use the phone effectively in order to reach out. Some objected that the phone was impersonal and hard to use, but in time everyone accepted its importance as a lifeline to supportive people.

Developing relationships with sponsors was seen as next most critical. Those who waited and put off working with a sponsor simply have a much harder time. In many ways the sponsor opens the door to learning how to ask for help. Relationship patterns developed with the sponsor can be generalized to others. Others beside the sponsor start to be important consultants. In fact, sponsors urge the development of a large network so the recovering person need never be isolated.

Finally, most of our respondents emphasized the importance of spending time with support group members outside of group. Helen observed that the group she met with on Friday nights had a ritual of going out to a restaurant to talk, eat, and relax. For her, these meals provided a safe, easy basis to develop friendships that now are important anchors in her life.

In many ways addiction serves as a dysfunctional form of intimacy. Addicts like Helen looked for a trusted source of comfort, care, and stress reduction. Recovering people find that what they always really wanted was closeness. Helen talked about how through her friendships she started accepting herself "more and more." What she looked for eluded her in her addiction, but she found it in her new, growing relationships.

If we break intimacy down into component parts, we can then compare what is healthy with what is dysfunctional and can better understand what a recovery program contributes. When teaching complex movements in athletics or the military, instructors break down difficult tasks into numbered movements. Addicts almost have to learn intimacy the same way—"by the numbers." Six capacities are needed for intimacy to exist: initiative, presence, completion, vulnerability, nurturing, and honesty. Each provides energy to the growth of a relationship.

Initiative. To be intimate, one has to risk being first. Calling, reaching out, expressing interest or care, inviting others to share activities or problems, revealing needs and wants—all characterize initiative. Initiative never stops. Intimacy can only be maintained by the constant renewal of initiative. Without it, mutuality cannot exist. Its opposite is the passive, isolated, victim stance often taken by those who believe in abandonment. Dysfunctional persons sometimes become seductive to avoid admitting that they have needs and wants. They rely on others to maintain their emotional connections and wait for things to happen. Recovery, however, requires connecting with others, encourages reaching out, and makes staying in touch a priority. Recovery groups encourage members to be clear about their needs and wants.

Presence. To say someone is emotionally present means that their feelings are available, that the whole person is totally engaged. People who are present listen and pay attention. They notice what happens and express their reactions. They are willing to spend time with no goal other than to be present. They seek and accept the presence of the other. When people are dysfunctional, their emotions are constricted. Shame creates distance and deflects others' efforts to connect, since any affirmation is felt to be undeserved. A person who fails to notice what happens in others is often distracted, inattentive, and self-preoccupied. Other people quickly perceive—to use a current metaphor—that the lights are on but nobody's home. In contrast, support groups practice availability to others. They ask members to accept the affirmation others offer, and they work to reduce shame. They encourage a "feeling" life where members listen to, respect, understand, and learn from one another's issues.

Completion. Trust builds when people finish things, including interpersonal transactions. A person who acknowledges care and outreach lets others know they have been heard so the message does not have to be sent again and again. Working for closure on problems, responding to others' needs and wants, and expressing appreciation for others' completed efforts all create a sense of safety and reliability.

Addicts tend to leave things unfinished, always working to keep their options open. Coaddicts, who usually set low levels of accountability, tend not to demand that things be finished. Overextension and loose ends add to the dysfunction, so issues and problems are put off and left unresolved. Closure is avoided. Needs and wants remain unheard. Efforts and contributions of others go unacknowledged so others doubt their impact. Addicts are perceived as evasive about responsibilities.

Twelve step programs urge closure and encourage accountability. The best specific example of this may be the "amends" process of the eighth and ninth steps, in which recovering persons do all that is possible to repair damage done. More generally, groups mark a person's progress because follow-through is necessary if the process is to work.

Vulnerability. When people are vulnerable, they share their thoughts and feelings. They talk to others about their dilemmas and involve them in their decisions. People who are vulnerable allow feedback. They reveal parts of themselves including fears and inadequacies. When people are dysfunctional, they keep everything secret and private. Their thoughts and feelings remain unshared. No one else knows how their decisions get made. By hiding their internal dialogues, addicts strive to appear fearless and invulnerable, disguising feelings of inadequacy. Working the twelve steps, however, opens one up to others, requires consultation, and invites feedback. Owning to one's powerlessness is a fundamental acknowledgment of dependency. The walls of secrecy break down. Trust builds.

Nurturing. Nurturing involves caring for other people. People who are nurturing express care for others, empathize with their pain, and affirm their value. They support, encourage, and offer suggestions. They do things to help others, taking care not to diminish them in any way. They touch and allow themselves to be touched. Dysfunctional people withdraw from others who have needs. They are critical and judgmental when others need help. They dismiss, or talk others out of, intense feelings. Removed and untouchable, they fail to come through. Support groups bring out compassion for others. Sponsorship models nurturing so that nurturing exchanges become the norm for recovering people.

Honesty. When people are honest, they are able to claim both positive and negative feelings. They are clear about their priorities and values. Honest people are specific about disagreements, provide feedback when asked, and admit their flaws and mistakes. Those with whom they are intimate know them fully. Honesty is impaired when significant feelings remain unshared or unacknowledged, when preferences are not expressed. People become dishonest when they are vague or manipulative about disagreements. They hide flaws and cover mistakes. No one knows the total truth. They rely on third parties to communicate. Those who use a twelve step program embrace a discipline of "rigorous honesty." The twelve steps contain inventories that require ownership of feelings and flaws. Determining and living priorities are the keys to "working the program." Honest participants see exposing their secret lives as vital to recovery.

Table 8-1 summarizes characteristics of healthy intimacy and dysfunctional intimacy and relates them to the twelve step recovery process. Addiction and intimacy dysfunction are functions of each other. Part of the reason the twelve steps succeed is that they heal the intimacy dysfunction of addicts and coaddicts.

TABLE 8-1
INTIMACY AND RECOVERY

SIGNS OF INTIMACY	HEALTHY INTIMACY	DYSFUNCTIONAL INTIMACY	TWELVE STEP RECOVERY PROCESS
Initiative	Calls; reaches out; risks expression of care; invites others to share activities or problems; expresses wants and needs; takes responsibility to maintain relationship.	Passive; seeks isolation; victim stance (it happens to me); belief in abandonment; seductive to avoid admitting needs or wants. Relies on others to maintain relationship.	Supports connecting with others; encourages outreach; priority on staying in touch; respects clarity around needs and wants.
Presence	Emotionally available to others; listens and attends to others; explicit about reactions; spends time with others; notices what happens with others; accepts attention of others.	Emotionally constricted; shame makes distant and removed; deflects attention as undeserved; fails to notice what happens to others; distracted and nonattentive; evasiveness leaves others wondering who person really is.	Practices availability to others; asks acceptance of personal affirmations; reduces shame; encourages a ''feeling'' life; involved with others' issues.
Completion	Builds trust by finishing things; finalizes arrangements with others; acknowledges care and out-	Overextension and loose ends provide sense of undependability; closure avoided; issues and prob-	Urges closure; encourages accountability; supports tasks being done; amends process requires

SIGNS OF INTIMACY	HEALTHY INTIMACY	DYSFUNCTIONAL INTIMACY	TWELVE STEP RECOVERY PROCESS
	reach so transactions are finished; works for closure on problems; responsive to others' needs and wants; expresses appreciation for completed efforts.	lems put off and unsolved; unresponsive to others' needs and wants so they end up feeling unheard; seldom acknowledges contribution or efforts of others, so they wonder if they had any impact; evasive about responsibilities.	that all that can be done, is; marks progress; followthrough necessary if process is to work.
Vulnerability	Shares process of thinking and feeling; talks about dilemmas; involves others in discussions; allows feedback; reveals self not shared with others; fears and sense of inadequacy available to others.	Thinks things through in private; feelings unshared so no one knows decision process; internal dialogues unshared, but relied upon; appears fearless and unshakable because feelings of inadequacy are disguised.	Step work opens addict up to others, requires consultation and invites feedback; owning powerlessness a fundamental acknowledgment of dependency; breaks down walls of secrecy; builds trust.
Nurturing	Cares for others; makes caring statements; empathizes with others' pain; supportive; encouraging; offers suggestions; affirms value of others; does things to help others when it does not	Withdraws from others when they are in need; criticizes their efforts and judges their motives; dismisses or talks others out of intense feelings; removed and untouchable; fails	Support groups bring out compassion for others; sponsorship models nurturing; nurturing exchanges are the norm; mutual help and assistance are key; acceptance and affirmation are

SIGNS OF INTIMACY	HEALTHY INTIMACY	DYSFUNCTIONAL INTIMACY	TWELVE STEP RECOVERY PROCESS
	diminish them in any way; touches others.	to help when needed.	recovery themes; healthy physical touch.
Honesty	Claims positive and negative feelings; clear about priorities and values; specific about disagreements; provides feedback when asked; admits flaws and mistakes; is fully known to intimates.	Significant feelings remain unshared or acknowledged; preferences not expressed; vague and manipulative about disagreements; hides flaws and covers mistakes; no one has total truth; relies on third parties to communicate.	"Rigorous honesty" is basis of program; step inventories require ownership of feelings; determining and living priorities are key to program; exposing secret life is vital to recovery.

One striking fact about the second and third years emerged from our survey: the most common mistake made by recovering people was to stop going to group. Some recovering addicts, on completing the grieving stage and stopping the behavior, felt so much better that they were convinced they could go it alone. Denial set in; rationales such as shortage of time emerged. At the least, these people experienced a slowdown in recovery; some met with total disaster.

In essence, these addicts had missed the next level of the program, in which bonds are deepened and relationship skills reintroduced. Over and over, respondents advised that new persons needed to stick with the process. Progress after the first year is more incremental but in many ways more substantial. When addicts were asked about creating a personal support network, they responded with phrases like "it takes time," "don't give up," and "take small steps, but keep taking them." No doubt exists in the minds of recovering people that the most important task of the second and third years is to build relationships. The support initiated during the hard times of the first year opens the gate to what addicts always were looking for. Once that gate is open, the task is to walk in.

EXPERIENCING CELIBACY

"It was not until I recommitted to a period of celibacy after a year and a half of recovery that my recovery took off—energy in work, relationships, and creativity." These words from Carl, a forty-seven-year-old engineer, echoed the sentiments of many others. A single man, he added an observation about couples: "I have heard married folk say similar things about their spousal relationship. A celibacy commitment after a couple of years was like being married for the first time."

What is it about celibacy that makes it such a source of renewal? Celibacy, as distinguished from abstinence, is the cessation of all sexual activity including masturbation. To many, celibacy appears strangely out of keeping with our times. How can celibacy help recovering people? Isn't it just going to the opposite extreme—sexually acting in? Mightn't it reinforce the old hangups, negative thinking, and shame that caused the problem in the first place? Paradoxically, celibacy seems to help recovering people access parts of their sexual selves that had never been available to them before.

Therapists have long recognized celibacy as a strategy for reclaiming sexual feelings. For decades it has been used with problems like inhibited sexual desire. With sex addiction, therapists quickly saw the advantages of celibacy. First, it stops the unmanageability and crises often involved early in recovery. For many, it simply makes clear how powerless they have become. Patients are more available for therapy because they start to feel emotions they have not felt for years. Finally, from a therapeutic point of view, child abuse memories which have long been repressed often surface during a period of celibacy.

There is some disagreement about when and for how long celibacy should occur. Many therapists and treatment programs ask recovering people to experience celibacy at an early point. The goal is to help the addict with first step issues like powerlessness and defining sobriety. Other addicts do not work on celibacy until the second or even third year. This was true of most of our survey respondents who used celibacy. Some cycled through a number of periods of celibacy during different stages of their recovery and found new perspectives in each experience. Joan, for example, told us, "I've had many periods of celibacy. In the first three months it cleared my mind so I could make choices for myself. Later I learned I was a lot of other things besides a sex addict!"

In all, 61 percent of our respondents used a period of celibacy. Current use of a celibacy period for recovering people is probably much greater.

The length of time of the celibacy period is usually established by a contract with the group or therapist. Celibacy periods of respondents varied from one month up to two years. The optimum appears to be three to four months. Sometimes contracts are open ended. One woman told us that her open-ended contract resulted in fifteen months of celibacy. She said she could never have made a fifteen-month commitment ahead of time. She simply agreed to stay celibate until she had renegotiated her contract with both her sponsor and her therapist. For her to accomplish what she had to it took that long. She said she knew that until enough healing took place, she could not have been sexually active and still kept a sense of self and boundaries (or chosen a healthy partner).

Healing is the issue. Celibacy is a time for healing. It represents a time-out in order to restore balance within. A man from California told us: "From resentment at not having a sexual outlet in early recovery, I am now grateful for the time to grow developmentally and complete my lost childhood—only without sex."

For some, the celibacy task was a measure of powerlessness. When they tried to be celibate, they found they could not and sought more support. One New Jersey man told us he attempted celibacy several times without success. He knew he needed more help. He went to a treatment facility, which helped him launch a successful experience; as a result, he told us, "I have been able to get in touch with feelings that I never had before."

Some entered celibacy to satisfy others. A good example is Rich, whose wife brought the idea home from a Co-SA (Co-Sex Addicts) meeting. He observed, "I resented it at first but love it now. We are more intimate than ever because of it. . . . I am better in touch with myself and we have never been happier."

Whatever it took to get them there, addicts were happier for having experienced celibacy. Their reasons vary. One man found that it took pressure off him to perform with his wife, so when they were sexual, it was successful. Another used celibacy to deepen the experience of doing the fourth step inventory. A third knew that celibacy was the only way to maintain sobriety until he got healthier. A woman learned that she could have decent relationships with men when they were not sexual; power and control issues that destroyed previous intimacy opportunities were absent. Following are some typical comments recovering people made about their celibacy experience.

CELIBACY AS PART OF RECOVERY

Being celibate enabled me to get clear about many of the triggers of my addiction. It enabled me to see how totally I mortgaged myself to sex and romance.

Celibacy deepened my appreciation of how much I care about my wife.

It's the heart of recovery for me.

I realized I would continue to live if I didn't have sex. For me that's a big realization.

It inspired me that others were able to do it successfully. It allowed me to get in touch with my feelings.

It helped me focus on my needs and made me aware that I wasn't a good receiver. I gave but never verbalized my needs. Celibacy helped me discover a wonderful area of intimacy I never knew before.

Tremendously helpful. Freed me—saw how it was without it, got closer to my wife.

Provided a time to regroup my forces apart from the "front line." Celibacy is not a solution in itself, but represents stepping back to reexamine the problem.

A chance to get perspective and distance from my sexual intoxication/ enslavement.

I realized that the only times I thought about masturbating were not for sexual release, but when I was lonely or hurt. This taught me that recovery was a lot more than having sex or not being sexual.

I finally got my feet on the ground and saw reality.

I was able to define the parameters of my addiction and decide what exactly my issues were without worrying about how all this affected my partner.

Gave me time to deal with childhood issues and addiction issues.

Allowed me time to take care of my needs.

I started to feel my feelings. My celibacy got me out of the forest so I could see the trees.

Helped my wife and me to really experience that there is life after addiction, that there is more to intimacy than genital intimacy.

I disconnected from the need to protect my supply.

Celibacy was great. I began to feel like I owned my body. No one else. More than anything else it was a great period in my life.

Allowed me to concentrate; released new energy.

I can't imagine recovery without it. It gave me a new level of presence to myself, my feelings, my delight in being alive and being in the presence of and present to others and nature.

Celibacy has risks. We interviewed a lesbian woman who had been celibate for four years in her recovery; she recognized that she had lapsed into sexual anorexia. For her, celibacy became a manifestation of acting in and not a choice designed to promote sexual growth. How does one prevent celibacy from being a catalyst to flip from one obsessional extreme to the other?

There are some clear-cut strategies to ensure that the celibacy period does what is intended. Above all, addicts need to be intentional about the goals of the celibacy period. They can best do that by drawing up a contract with someone else, for example, a sponsor or therapist. The contract, verbal or written, should be explicit about when the celibacy period is over. It should establish either a time limit or, if open-ended, times at which the decision will be reviewed by others.

Consider what Charlene told us when she was asked about how she perceived the difference between healthy celibacy and acting in:

Acting in is just the other side of the coin from acting out, and it can be as much a sign for me of addiction as the acting out, even though the consequences out in the world aren't noticeable. It means a certain kind of isolation. During my celibacy, I've been in touch with my program, my Higher Power, and my friends. Sex has very much to do with my life, and if I am not open to it, I'm not engaged with my life. When I'm afraid to be open to a sexual relationship, that for me is acting in. Fear then is the motivation. In my celibacy, rather than fear, it's been more a sense of choice that this was something I wanted and needed.

Note that Charlene relied upon two things. First, she did not become isolated but stayed in touch with those who mattered to her. Second, she was intentionally looking for what she needed, as opposed to reacting to fear. If there is planning at the outset and sharing, celibacy can be an extremely useful strategy. We asked addicts for advice about beginning a celibacy period. Their responses, in order of importance, are summarized below.

ADDICTS' BEST ADVICE NUMBER 5:
Beginning a Celibacy Period

1. *View it as a time-out, not an end.* A celibacy period will provide you space to refocus on other needs. It is not a sentence, not the end of your sexuality. On the contrary, celibacy will make you fully aware of your sexual self.

2. *Work through commitment issues with your partner.* The decision to be celibate will affect your partner. Respecting your partner means involving him or her in your thinking so you can commit together to the celibacy period.

3. *Get support from therapist, sponsor, and group.* You will need their guidance and help to maximize the experience. Being open with those in your support network will help you to implement your plan.

4. *Expect that it will raise issues.* For many this change is drastic and places life issues in sharp relief. Make this a goal and not a surprise.

5. *Understand that resistance is typical.* You may experience anger and resentment at first. This isn't surprising. We seldom embark gracefully on any ordeal that involves significant change and insight.

6. *Prepare yourself to experience new feelings.* The new feelings that emerge will be guides to parts of yourself you need to reclaim. As uncomfortable as these feelings may be, they will serve as significant allies in helping you become all you are.

7. *Plan active tasks to enhance the experience.* Select a specific step to work on, work on assignments from your therapist to help you accept nurturing and develop spiritual and sexual awareness, and keep a journal about the experience.

For many, celibacy becomes a gateway to a new sexuality. Despite sometimes astounding amounts of sexual behavior, many sex addicts have not really "experienced" their sexual selves. Celibacy is a beginning—a wiping clean of the sexual slate to prepare for a sexual rebirth. It is a time-out, a period for repair work at the most fundamental level, a time to make up for deficits stemming from a lost childhood. Nowhere is that repair work more necessary than in the area of self-affirmation—the next task of recovery.

SELF-AFFIRMATION

▪ John stands outside a colleague's office, collecting himself before going in. The colleague, an older man, has in the past been extremely judgmental about his work, in a way that reminds him of his father. Before walking in, John focuses on a recent session with his therapist in which they rehearsed for this meeting. He remembers his therapist saying to him, "This is not about you. It is about his shame and how threatened he is about the quality of your work. You have done well." John smiles and remembers the days when similar meetings with his colleague would be followed by visits to a massage parlor. Comforted, focused, and feeling strangely peaceful, he opens the door.

- Maria has hit some difficult times. A single parent, she is overwhelmed with the stresses of work and parenting. Worse, she recently had a cancerous tumor removed from her breast and is now undergoing chemotherapy. Though the prognosis is good, the chemotherapy takes its toll. She goes to her bedroom and pulls out a tape made for her while she was in treatment for her sexual addiction. Fellow patients, as well as staff, recorded affirming statements about her goodness, which they hoped she would remember. The tape has become one of her most precious belongings, connecting her to a watershed event in her life: going to treatment, facing her addiction, and discovering wonderful parts of herself. Now, at a moment when she feels extremely inadequate, the tape anchors her solidly. She calls her sponsor for more support. Her sponsor's love and warmth further calm her. As she hangs up, she remembers how during such moments in the past she would leave her children alone while she went in search of sexual affirmation.

- Carl stands up to speak at the conclusion of his twelve step support meeting. He has just received a medallion for eighteen months of sobriety. Tearfully, he describes how he had a massive slip after six months in the program and how he had to start all over again. His tears are tears of gratitude—he is profoundly grateful to the people who accepted him and supported him through that moment. The group custom on such occasions was for the medallion to be passed around so each member could hold it and comment on the person's progress. People speak of Carl's courage, which has been a model for everyone, of how easy he is to be with now, of his knowledge of the steps, and of his generosity in helping others. As he sits down, moved by their supportive words, a picture flashes through his mind of the day he stood before a judge in total shame and despair.

- Ed prepares his fourth step, an inventory of his life. The clergyman assisting him has insisted that Ed make a list of affirmations: positive statements about himself that are true. As he writes each statement, he thinks of reasons why it is not accurate. As he struggles, he realizes how deep the roots of his self-hatred are. He could not let his own statements stand, for fear people would find fault with them. Finally, he completes ten sentences that he can accept. He calls Joe, a program friend, and reads the list, half expecting to have to reduce it. Joe encourages him to expand the statements. As he listens, Ed recalls scenes when his parents strove to trim his ego.

Addiction starts with profound shame. Recovery starts in earnest with affirmation. Coming out of the shock and grief stages of recovery, the addict must let go of damaging and dysfunctional messages carried since childhood. In a real sense, this is a period of reparenting. By receiving affirming messages from others, addicts learn to construct a new, positive sense of themselves. They learn how to affirm themselves from within. New voices compete with and ultimately stifle the old voices. John, Maria, Carl, and Ed were learning to discard the imperatives from the past.

Affirmation begins with acknowledging an inner child. The recovering person pictures himself as a child of three or four, needy, vulnerable, and innocent. This child was dependent on others, noticed the world around him in detail, and loved to play. Care givers, however, were often exploitive, neglectful, and judgmental. They would make harsh demands of the child, condemn the child, restrict the child, and sometimes hurt the child. On the basis of this experience the child made essential conclusions about himself or herself and the world. These conclusions led to addiction. If left unchallenged, they would prevent recovery.

Part of the repair work at this stage of recovery is for the recovering person to nurture that inner child so that the vulnerability, playfulness, innocence, and other childlike qualities so essential to being a fully dimensional human being can be reclaimed. Obviously, childhood cannot be relived. But those qualities can be experienced in new ways. There are concrete strategies for this reclamation process:

1. *Seeking support.* Supportive people become cheerleaders for one another, giving encouragement and celebrating each increment of progress. They are the believers, confident of success. They help the recovering person rebound when disappointments occur. They keep coming back with enthusiasm for each new beginning.

2. *Finding validation.* When recovering people share their experiences, especially their childhood experiences, others validate their perceptions. As a child, the person may have felt uneasy or afraid although the family message was "accept the situation."

Now others, such as therapists and group members, confirm that the situation was crazy or dangerous, that there reason for feeling anxious. This validation helps recovering people learn that they can trust their own perceptions.

3. *Developing self-affirmations.* Creating your own affirmations is like programming yourself for recovery. The old dysfunctional programming is replaced by new beliefs and rules, so when it reappears, it is but an echo of the painful past. The statement "I trust myself" overrides the parental voice that says "I could never trust you." The old voice may come back, but now its power is reduced and it serves as a reminder of the value of recovery.

4. *Imaging change.* Part of self-affirmation is to see your future in strong, affirming ways. The capacity to imagine future change becomes a powerful factor in bringing that change into reality. Self-fulfilling prophecies have been shown to play a strong role in areas as diverse as education, management, sports medicine, and career development. It is no different in recovery from addiction. Sustaining a vision of a positive future becomes an extension of affirmation in the present.

There are a wealth of tools for implementing these strategies— books, tapes, and fellowships. Especially important are fellowships, for people raised in families disabled by addiction, for example, Adult Children of Alcoholics and Adult Children of Sex Addicts. Many addicts and coaddicts in our survey indicated that they supplement their regular meetings by attending an adult child group of some sort. Some said joining such a group was the turning point of their recovery. Below are some of the key resources for developing self-affirmation strategies.

RESOURCES FOR SELF-AFFIRMATION

Books

Melody Beattie, *Beyond Codependency and Getting Better All the Time.* San Francisco: Harper & Row, 1989.

Joy Miller and Marianne Ripper, *Following the Yellow Brick Road.* Deerfield Beach, Florida: Health Communications, 1988.

John Bradshaw, *Healing the Shame That Binds You.* Deerfield Beach, Florida: Health Communications, 1988.

Charles L. Whitfield, M.D., *Healing the Child Within.* Deerfield Beach, Florida: Health Communications, 1987.

John K. Pollard, III, *Self Parenting: The Complete Guide to Your Inner Conversations.* Malibu, California: Generic Human Studies Publishing, 1987.

Patrick J. Carnes, Ph.D., *A Gentle Path Through the Twelve Steps.* Minneapolis: CompCare Publications, 1989.

Dennis Wholey, *Becoming Your Own Parent.* New York: Doubleday, 1988.

Fellowships

Adult Children of Alcoholics
P.O. Box 25001
Minneapolis, MN 55458-6001
(612) 646-8730

Adult Children of Sex Addicts (ACSA)
P.O. Box 8084
Lake Street Station
110 E. 31st Street
Minneapolis, MN 55408
(Please enclose 50 cents for duplication and postage costs.)

Tapes

Timmen L. Cermak, M.D., *A Time to Heal,* New York: St. Martin's Press, 1989.

Louise L. Hay, *Self Healing,* Santa Monica: Hay House, 1986.

Louise L. Hay, *Loving Yourself,* Santa Monica: Hay House, 1984.

LIFE-STYLE CHANGE

"I never knew what having fun was," Sarah told us. Her addiction had dictated what fun was. "To me fun was going out, buying clothes, getting dressed, getting pretty, and going on a hunt.

Fun was shooting the prettiest bird I saw out there." Sarah was a thirty-four-year-old clinic administrator. The story she had to tell was a chilling one. From early in her life she had been sexually abused. Her addiction had transformed this abuse into a quest for power over men. From her treatment and subsequent three years of recovery, Sarah developed a very different picture of fun—fun without being driven or victimized. She said, "Today, fun is researching things I can do with my daughter and husband. Dancing, roller-skating, sitting down and playing with my daughter. Just being here now. In my addiction, I could not be here now."

Sarah admitted that her ability to play was mostly with friends and family. She still had trouble enjoying things by herself. Sarah, like many addicts, struggled with developing a balanced life-style. Without the addiction to structure their time, addicts are at a loss for how to live their lives. After living on the edge, what is there? Addicts like Sarah start to learn what they missed and how to live a gentler way.

Recovery requires this balance. Almost all relapse from any addiction starts with life-style imbalance. Living in the extremes—being frenetic, overextended, and depleted—leads to addictive feelings of entitlement (I deserve it) and denial (just a little will not matter). The rewards of relationship and the serenity of recovery will remain elusive under those circumstances. Put simply: addicts and coaddicts often do not know how to play or enjoy themselves. For many, stopping to smell the roses feels awkward, undeserved, and unproductive.

Addicts tend to bring old patterns with them. They resort to compulsive busyness or to workaholism. They do not have hobbies unless they are compulsive about them. They become embedded in a grim, solemn, life's-a-bitch stance. Their acting in precludes experimentation, humor, and celebration. No story in our whole survey better illustrates the transition necessary for recovery than that of Raymond.

Ray was a classic workaholic from the time he was a child. The messages he was given seemed designed to create a Master of the Universe. "I'd been told since the time I was a kid that as long as I worked hard I had a license to do almost anything else." When Ray's sexual addiction hit full tilt, work was the justification. In fact, Ray purchased sex with money. Besides spending an extraordinary amount of money on prostitutes, Ray used bonuses and salary increases to buy sex from his employees.

When Ray finally began treatment, his arrogance was still intact. He said, "I did things to appease them, still thinking I was smarter than anybody in this whole world." But as time passed, he saw that his standards were a prison for him. His therapists helped him to see that his compulsive working was intimately connected to his compulsive sexuality. He would deplete himself so completely that it justified sexuality, even when his addiction put his professional life at risk. He began to see that he allowed no fun or lightness in his arduous work schedule. He described his work values like this:

> We don't mix any pleasure with work because that might cut down the work. That might cut down the production. We're here to work, and when the work's done, then we'll play, but up until that point there's not going to be any fun connected with this. Don't go laughing and smiling and telling jokes on the job because that's not the attitude. Work is an attitude of seriousness. We just don't mix business with pleasure.

Learning about these two areas of compulsivity had a profound impact on Ray. He found that his workaholism was not helpful to him, although he had received lots of support and acceptance for it. But, Ray adds, "This sexual addiction was not socially accepted and it took me off my high horse. I was not accomplishing anything with either addiction." Despite these insights, Ray entered the repair stage with no clear sense of how to do things differently. He provided us with a very poignant description of how one of his sons became his teacher:

> My son is a hard worker, but he'll take off after he gets enough money. He'll go out of the country for maybe a week or take a trip for four, five days. I would've never done that. My God, that's sacrilegious. You may have vacation time, that's fine. But you don't just take off three, four times a year and goof off for four, five days at a time. He does this and he still takes care of his responsibilities. He's got a couple of guys working for him and he makes sure they get paid and so forth. But he has the ability to slow down on the job and go out or he'll take his little daughter and go someplace with her. Hell, I would never

take off to go to my kid's function during a school day. Take time off of work to go watch a school function, are you kidding? At night maybe, in fact I did at night, but not during the day. I could've done that and still be just as far as I am right now. Maybe further.

Learning to take time and enjoy oneself runs counter to the messages received by sex addicts who come from shame-based, rigid, disengaged families. As we have noted, the emphasis in these families was on "doing things right," creating human doings not human beings. With this in mind, consider the characteristics of play:

- Play is an act of trust based on feelings of safety with and confidence in others.

- Play allows coloring outside the lines, grants permission to make mistakes, and encourages experiments.

- Play establishes no "right" or "only" way, but rather relies on creativity and imagination.

- Play engages people in the here and now, rather than allowing them to obsess about the past or the future.

- Play makes sense with nonsense, providing a vital resource for creativity and problem-solving.

- Play reduces shame and provides a sense of fulfillment.

- Play reduces tension, altering both mood and outlook.

- Play keeps focus on the important things: family, friends, children, and the change of seasons.

Commenting on his newfound capacity to have fun, Ray concluded, "I really found out who the hell I really am. I'm a real human being. I had some really crazy attitudes that justified things damaging to me and other people."

Reexamining one's life-style pays extraordinary recovery dividends. As new patterns are woven into a less hurried, more balanced life-style, healing occurs in some of the most damaged areas of sex addicts' lives. Ray offered a significant illustration when he described how his sexuality was changing:

My wife and I, we make sex last maybe an hour and a half
or so where it used to be fifteen, twenty minutes. It's hard
to restrain but it's wonderful. It's wonderful because I can
have an hour and a half enjoyment where before it was
fifteen minutes and turn over and go to sleep. We have a
much better sexual relationship than we ever had before in
all of our years together.

Ray is sixty; remarkably, he is now discovering what he has
always wanted. Note that the sexual changes he is making parallel
the changes he is making in his total life-style: going slower, playing,
spending time, and enjoying the outcomes.
   A simple but wonderful exercise that helps recovering people to
discern what they do want is called the Serenity Focus exercise.
Take some time. Stop. And enjoy it.

EXERCISE 8-1
SERENITY FOCUS

*List ten moments in your life in which you felt truly peaceful and
serene. Describe them in detail. What made them so peaceful for you?*

1. _____

_____

_____

2. _____

_____

_____

3. _____

_____

_____

4. _____

_____

_____

5. _____

_____

_____

6. _____

_____

_____

7. _____

_____

_____

8. _____

_____

_____

9. _____

_____

_____

10. _____

_____

_____

Now review these ten moments and find five things that they have in common. For example, perhaps you were not thinking of the future or the past, but rather you were absorbed in the moment. Pick out five other commonalities.

1. _____

2. _____

3. _____

4. _____

5. _____

Name three ways in which you can integrate more serene moments into your life.

1. _____

2. _____

3. _____

RELAPSE PREVENTION

Shirley was nine months into her second year of recovery. She went out of town to a conference. She was angry with her husband because he had been preoccupied the night before and had not responded to her sexual advances. She told us, "I had felt it important to have a special sexual night before I left." Besides feeling angry and rejected, she said, "I was also cocky about my recovery and thought I could handle more than I could without slipping back." She started drinking at a cocktail party and ended up accompanying a man to his room to watch fireworks from his balcony. Confident she would not end up in bed, she did.

Feeling enormous shame and pain upon her return, she went to her twelve step group. The group encouraged her to use it as a learning experience and not let despair lead to a downward spiral of more acting out. They assured her that she was lovable, that she could love herself, and that she had not given up on her goal of sexual sobriety. They made her take credit for the twenty-one months of success she had achieved. They pointed out that the pain was a measure of her progress: she felt pain at betraying her husband because she was acutely aware of her love for him. "Before recovery, I tried to deny my feelings for him to excuse my behavior," she explained.

People in Shirley's support system were also very tough on her. They pointed out that by ignoring her feelings of anger and rejection she set herself up for a slip. Seducing men at conferences and cruising cocktail parties were old patterns of behavior for her. In many ways she had not taken the steps necessary to prevent a slip.

The Big Book of Alcoholics Anonymous addresses this problem at the very beginning of the twelve step program. The book describes the problem of addiction as "cunning and baffling." With the best of intentions, addicts still end up doing what they do not want to do. The solution, the founders of AA suggested, was to go to "any lengths" to avoid being seduced into the old patterns. In Shirley's case, her sponsors were saying this meant she needed to deal promptly with her feelings of anger and rejection. She needed to avoid the cocktail scene or to go with someone who knew about her recovery and would give her support. As part of the repair work of the second and third years, addicts like Shirley need to consolidate their learnings about recovery, fine-tune their ability to avoid self-destructive behavior, and further define their boundaries. This process is called relapse prevention.

Alcoholics had to learn that preventing relapse was much more complicated than simply choosing not to drink. Classic advice was the famous HALT formula: never let yourself stay hungry, angry, lonely, or tired. The illness required each recovering person to define the patterns that would erode the firmest of resolves.

For addictions like eating and sex, this becomes even more crucial. Food and human contact are everywhere. With alcohol, a slip is a drink—necessarily major and readily definable. But with food and sex there are also many minislips, which can open the door to major slips. For the sex addict, lapsing into voyeurism in fantasy or visiting an old lover may not cause an immediate relapse, but it will certainly grease the slide to get there. This is why so many sex addicts who also have chemical addictions say sex addiction is tougher to recover from. Sexual addiction creates many more shades of gray. Experienced recovering people like Shirley's sponsors know this, which is why they are ruthless about boundary issues and relapse prevention. From experience they know that sex addiction adds a special energy to the notion of "cunning and baffling." It requires being able to identify triggers, reduce stress, and build relapse strategies.

Identify Triggers

G. Allen Marlatt, a pioneer of relapse prevention, coined an important phrase when he talked of "apparently irrelevant decisions." Relapses begin with choices that seem irrelevant at the time. But in retrospect they look like the path of a heat-seeking missile. Marlatt makes the same point Shirley's group did. Addicts must take responsibility to identify those times of vulnerability that appear safe, unrelated, or irrelevant but can trigger the addictive process. We asked addicts who slipped what preceded the slip. They reported the following:

IDENTIFYING TRIGGERS

Overwork. I overdid it and depleted myself and got head over heels infatuated with someone to fill me up.

Prostitutes staring at me when I least expected it. I became totally helpless.

I had not been completely honest with the 'other woman' and got into a situation I could not handle.

I was pink-clouding in the early months of sobriety and set myself up.

An old lover invited me and I thought I could handle it.

I stayed in phone contact with one of my lovers.

Feeling depressed and isolated over financial matters, I received some pornographic material I was still on a mailing list for.

I started cruising supermarkets and bars.

I was at a conference at a resort and experiencing a lot of professional pressure.

I started eating too much, which is always a clue that I'm in trouble.

I went to a bookstore during idle time.

Feeling exploited, I was angry and then became seductive to others.

A major trigger has been being around my family of origin.

Triggers are behaviors, rituals, conditions, and people who in some way activate the addictive pattern. Some triggers are obvious, for example, calling or seeing old lovers even without being physically sexual. This is not unlike the drug addict who decides to keep a stash but not use it. Cruising old haunts is another obvious trigger.

Some triggers are more indirect. Being depleted or emotionally overwhelmed leads to feelings of entitlement, which in turn provoke the addictive response. Some triggers are difficult to acknowledge, for example, being around family members who are shaming or abusive. (Acting out, in fact, can be a reenactment of the old family abuse patterns.) Relapse prevention requires clarity about those triggers. The clarity helps addicts expand their boundary lists and more concretely define bottom lines.

Reduce Stress

Harvard psychologist Ray Flannery conducted a study of people who respond to demanding situations without losing their sense of well-being. Four characteristics emerged. First, stress-resistant people were active in seeking solutions to challenges in their life. They did not wait for things to happen. Second, stress-resistant people were committed to a goal which added to the meaning of life. Third, stress-resistant people made healthy life-style choices; for example, they exercised regularly, used little or no alcohol, nicotine, or caffeine, and used relaxation or meditation techniques. Fourth, stress-resistant people sought support from others and had supportive relationships. These characteristics precisely parallel what our survey respondents said worked to help reduce stress and prevent relapse.

Recovering persons work to become stress resistant, knowing it is unrealistic to think there will be no more stress in their lives. Below answers recovering addicts gave to the question "How did you learn to handle stress in your recovery?" Taken together, these statements provide an overview of the range of resources used as part of recovery. They amplify the four characteristics of the stress-resistant person.

REDUCING STRESS

Not living in my addiction has, of course, relieved a lot of my stress. Finding other addicts like me who want to recover has relieved a lot of stress. I can talk to them about everything—without fear of judgment or ridicule. Also, the relaxation techniques I learned in treatment have been very helpful. I wasn't sleeping well before treatment. Now I do. Also, self-affirmations have helped a lot. Low self-esteem intensifies every stressful situation. Playing the piano—just for me—is also very relaxing. It gives me a little time out from reality.

I've also found it very important during periods of high stress to keep in contact with my sponsor, therapist, and friends, and talk about what's going on. I refuse to try to handle anything alone again! Meditation helps, but I have to make sure I don't stay isolated too much. Swimming has become an important activity for me also. The exercise is a great stress reducer, and being in the water is so calming and soothing!

Making phone calls to process feelings; reading recovery books. My church is like a shot in the arm every Sunday; contact with God (prayer). Being committed to my meeting every week. I do not miss it for any reason.

Using the telephone and being honest about the situation I'm in. Visiting a fellow member at a time of distress late at night. Asking for help, or stating my needs in time of distress. Getting in my car and disciplining myself to go to a recovering friend instead of an acting out friend. Plan recovering activities for the evening with recovering friends. Attend a meeting of SAA, AA, NA, ACOA (whatever is available). Allow myself to feel like crying, getting angry, and talking about it.

I learned some valuable tools in therapy:

1. *Be honest with my motives.*

2. *Be honest about consequences.*

3. *Be aware of the reality; not allow myself my destructive fantasy.*

4. *Let the situation ride at least 500 hours before defining it as a crisis.*

5. *I understand today that this, too, will pass and that, either way I go in making a decision, it will be okay in the long run.*

Talking about it, feeling it, attempting to be gentle with myself and with the little person inside. Avoiding too much contact with stressful people like my parents or people in deep struggle. Avoiding my rescue routine of taking all the responsibility for problems. I pay attention to relationship/ intimacy problems and see (with help) how they relate to old family stuff. I feel the most freedom when I am direct with my feelings.

I put an invisible boundary around myself to screen out other people's energy. I am extremely sensitive and easily feel other people's feelings, so to reduce stress, I have to protect myself physically. I teach learning-disabled and emotionally disturbed kids, so this is important. I rarely take work home. I try to get enough sleep. I eat healthy food as much as possible. I make daily phone calls to people I trust. I don't drive myself, push myself, to do things. I let go of the outcomes, the whens, wheres, and hows and do things as the urge comes, and the things get done. I spend lots of money on health—vitamins and supplements. I saw a chiropractor weekly for over two years. I get massages. I do weekly voice and body work sessions. Therapy weekly. I have two cats. I try to cut down on my driving and appointments. Some exercise daily. Breathing exercises.

Knowing that almost all pain is memory of the past or worry about the future. There is no pain in the NOW. Live in it! I meditate and sometimes feel free and almost joyful. My shame is probably not as bad as I think.

Going to meetings, praying, practicing serenity prayer. Letting go and letting God handle what I can't. ACA literature and meetings help a lot. I've learned that my worrying makes stressful situations five times more stressful to me than they were to begin with.

Being less serious sometimes and having fun. Learning positive self-talk, affirmations. Looking at matters I have to deal with as goals, not problems, and listing my goals. Being patient with myself and others.

Build Relapse Strategies

Treatment centers and therapists have long worked with sex addicts on developing strategies to prevent relapse when slips occur. Often these are called dress rehearsals or fire drills. Some have criticized this approach as giving permission to slip by planning for it. Yet such strategies truly acknowledge the addict's powerlessness and the "cunning and baffling" nature of the illness. Planning for the inevitable moment of weakness is an important discipline for recovering people if they are to minimize risk and prevent further damage.

One standard strategy used by therapists involves three phases. First, the addict is asked to describe the perfect acting-out fantasy. This gives the addict and the therapist a chance to figure out the scenarios that govern the addiction. Every addict's acting out is based on some script, usually programmed by the family or an abuse experience or some powerful childhood sexual experience. When the addict details what would make it perfect, the seeds of the compulsivity and destruction become clear. These then can be resolved therapeutically.

In the second phase, the addict imagines and records what the consequences would be if the fantasy were to become reality. All possibilities must be specified. By doing this, the addict starts to contaminate or spoil the fantasy. Addicts do not link their fantasies to the consequences. Making the link reduces both the power of the fantasy and the addict's vulnerability to relapse.

In the third phase, the therapist has the addict think about what he or she will do if a slip does occur. What if the fantasy and its consequences become reality, wreaking havoc in the addict's life? What plan of action exists? Once the addict starts to slip, he or she will be tempted to say, "Well, I've gone this far, why not go all the way?" A slip can then become a binge or a return to the addictive life. An exit strategy is a way out of this downward spiral. It allows the recovering person to go into "automatic pilot" and focus on damage control. Usually, this exit strategy takes the form of a contract with a therapist or sponsor. The contract specifies what the addict agrees to do if a slip occurs.

Some relapse strategies simply reduce risk. For example, sometimes cravings are triggered by the media—by radio songs, magazine ads, television commercials, and so forth. The addict can consciously use the media to trigger cravings. Consider the addict who gets into "channel switching," constantly searching for sexually stimulating scenes. Often, though, these cravings are unconsciously triggered. Advertising agencies work hard to insert sexual sizzle into commercials. Addicts who watch a car or soda commercial may suddenly experience sexual cravings but not associate them with the commercial. In fact, they may feel shame, blaming themselves for the cravings. In our survey people who felt vulnerable to media stimulation took "media breaks," time-outs from magazines, newspapers, television—whatever was troublesome. The media breaks reduced risk. They allowed the recovery to stabilize to the point where exposure to such stimulation was no longer a risk.

Addicts who did slip commented on other strategies that helped restore them to their recovery process.

RELAPSE STRATEGIES

I took on a lot of SA tasks to do. I made a list of reasons not to act out and carried them in my wallet.

I clarified what my bottom line was.

After my relapse, I realized I had to be very specific and honest with myself about the exact nature of my addiction.

Sharing immediately with my group was absolutely critical.

Promptly admitted the relapse, kept going to meetings, and held on to the idea that my sobriety date was real and valuable.

I had my phone fixed so I could not make long-distance calls.

I learned I could react differently to the situation next time. Realizing this helped my recovery.

I had relapse two years ago which caused another arrest with severe negative publicity afterward in the media. I realized I needed more intensive treatment and was admitted to a sexual dependency unit.

I used my relapse as a red flag that something was not right in my life. With my group, I figured out needs I had not identified and worked on.

Note that support seeking, clarification of boundaries, and "going to any lengths" all played important roles. We asked recovering people for their advice on resisting addictive cravings. The advice they gave is summarized below.

ADDICTS' BEST ADVICE NUMBER 6:
Resisting Addictive Cravings

1. *Develop spiritual strategies.* Meditation, yoga, prayer—whatever strategies help you connect with yourself and the rhythm of the universe—need to be deepened, strengthened, and practiced. Number one on almost everyone's list is the development of a spiritual base—a calm center, which helps you resist turmoil on the periphery.

2. *Decode feelings.* Sex that is about addiction and not sexuality is usually accompanied by feelings of shame, loneliness, fear, pain, or anger. Always check for these feelings. Remember that to act out a feeling sexually does not resolve the feeling. If you cannot decode your feelings, consult with a sponsor, a therapist, or group members. Remember the old twelve step aphorism: Horniness equals loneliness.

3. *Avoid trigger situations.* Identify situations, persons, and circumstances that can trigger addictive responses. Respect your powerlessness, and avoid those triggers. Remember, when in doubt, don't.

4. *Forgive yourself for slips.* If a slip occurs, turn it into a learning experience. Be gentle with yourself. Your shame will cause you to beat up on yourself, which will make you even more vulnerable.

5. *Work on nurturing yourself.* Exercise. Walk. Eat well. Rest. Enjoy massage, baths, and safe indulgences. Seek out nature, music, art, humor, and the companionship of good friends. Find time to take care of yourself. Make your living space a cocoon for your transformation. Buy yourself a teddy bear. You deserve this treatment.

6. *Avoid keeping cravings secret.* Keeping your cravings secret will add to their power. When you feel like acting out, go to people you trust so you are not alone. In general, secrets are about shame and shame always makes you more vulnerable. Secrets will separate you from others in recovery.

7. *Find alternative passions.* Seek hobbies, sports, and activities you enjoy. Cultivate these parts of your life so compulsive patterns in working, obsessing, or acting out have to compete with activities and interests that are rewarding. Alternative passions become new arenas for growth.

8. *Acknowledge your choices.* Avoid the feeling that you are a victim. You are powerless about your addiction, but you are in charge of your program of recovery and your life-style. In most areas you have choices, which can help you achieve the balance needed in your life. Be proactive instead of reactive, by acknowledging to yourself and to others what your choices are.

ALTERNATIVE HIGHS
AND SPIRITUALITY

When Ray, our compulsive workaholic, began treatment, he essentially had no spiritual life. About a third of the way through treatment, he would go to his window and gaze down the valley at the small church there. One Sunday morning, knowing that his wife was there praying, he felt so moved that he started to pray as well. At first, it was uncomfortable. He said, "I apologized to God so many times for being awkward and phony." But Ray persisted. Years later, at the time of his interview, he was able to say, "Now, if I don't pray in the morning, I feel like I've missed brushing my teeth."

How does a tough, hard-driving, at times tyrannical business-man attain spiritual peace? In many ways, the path is well worn. It goes all the way back to Roland H., the man who inspired Bill Wilson to his recovery and the founding of Alcoholics Anonymous. In 1931, after exhausting all other forms of help for his compulsive drinking, Roland, in desperation, sought out psychologist Carl Jung in Switzer-land. During the year that he saw Jung, Roland was for the first time able to abstain. He felt secure in his progress. To his great surprise, however, he soon relapsed. Seeing Jung as his last hope, he re-turned to his care. The conversation between Jung and Roland H. at that point was what Bill Wilson was later to characterize as "the first link in the chain of events that led to the founding of Alcoholics Anonymous." Carl Jung later described that conversation as follows:

> His craving for alcohol was the equivalent, on a low level, of the spiritual thirst of our being for wholeness, ex-pressed in medieval language, the union with God.
>
> How could one formulate such an insight in a language that is not misunderstood in our days? The only right and legitimate way to such an experience is that it happens to you in reality, and it can only happen to you when you walk on a path which leads you to higher understanding. You might be led to that goal by an act of grace or through a personal and honest contact with friends, or through a higher education of the mind beyond the confines of mere rationalism.

Jung put his finger on the key ingredient that the pioneers of AA had been looking for. Roland H., Bill W., and Dr. Bob had exhausted all help that science at that time could give. By incorpo-rating a spiritual component, they were finally able to create a process that had success.

The field of addiction treatment has long emphasized spiritual healing. Other health care fields, including cardiology and oncology, are now making significant progress toward a more holistic medi-cine. Pastoral care professionals are also integrating the new find-ings of behavioral science into their work. Yet many professionals still tend to characterize the twelve steps in clinical terms. They speak of the twelve steps as providing ego development and conscience formation, a grieving process to cope with change, and an existential position. All of this is accurate, but at the real core of the twelve steps is the truth laid bare by Jung and Roland H. sixty years ago: to overcome the complex biological, family, and social factors in addiction requires a level of surrender so complete that the only means of achieving and sustaining it are spiritual.

For Ray and others in our survey, the repair years saw a tremendous spiritual growth. After the first year, spirituality still eludes many but it is emerging. People who have experienced spiritual growth state clearly that it is a gradual process. Liza, from Atlanta, described what it was like to watch recovering people move into this phase of their growth:

> You cannot tell an addict at first, but in the AA book it says twice that we have a daily reprieve contingent on the maintenance of a spiritual condition. And if the person does not do something about his spiritual condition every day, in my opinion he is in danger. Now you have to translate that to people you sponsor or in groups to something very simple— for example, to just saying "God helped me" and "thank you" at the end of the day. Get them in the habit of talking to a Higher Power, whether they believe in one or not and then see what happens as they make progress. You support them as they move on into meditations or whatever they feel fits in their spiritual realm, then their learning deepens.

Dave, from San Francisco, talked about how for him spiritual growth started with a daily walk. He called it "Dave time," a time alone that he could count on. Eventually it evolved into a time for a high level of meditation and spiritual awareness. Dave's experience illustrates the concepts of theologian Henri Nouwen, who talked about "the conversion of loneliness into solitude."

In high school Dave had been intensely religious as a way to control his acting out. He had ended up with a "negative attitude about religion," becoming almost fanatically antireligious. Yet what helped him in recovery was the notion of a Higher Power. Initially, he had to think of a Higher Power in very concrete terms; for a while his group was his Higher Power. But over two and a half years, he said, "I worked into a more defined sense of spirituality for myself. It's a regular part of my life now."

A number of our participants reported intense spiritual experiences connected with their recovery. Barb, an addict in the Midwest, described what was essentially a conversion experience:

> I walked over to a bridge across the river and the wind was really strong and it was blowing my hair back and the sun was shining and the water was sparkling with the sun and I started crying tears of joy. I knew my Higher Power was with me. I knew I was forgiven. It took probably most of my shame away.

Her experience parallels that of Bill W. who had an "illumination of enormous impact and dimension." He wrote, "My release from the alcohol obsession was immediate. At once, I knew I was a free man."

For most of our survey, however, progress was gradual, daily, and incremental. We asked recovering people for their advice on developing a spiritual life. The answers are summarized below.

ADDICTS' BEST ADVICE NUMBER 7:
Developing a Spiritual Life

---

1. *Use the steps.* They are a proven recipe for spiritual wholeness. Remember that the program started with the realization that without the spiritual component, recovery could not happen. Decide a spiritual life is essential, not an option.

2. *Find guides.* Listen to others share their spiritual experiences and ask how healing happened in their lives. Brokenness, failure, and tragedy have helped many find parts of themselves they had not known. Most also started with anger or fear, skepticism or detachment.

3. *Separate religion from spirituality.* Many come with "baggage" about religious institutions that damaged or constricted their growth. Resentment about these experiences can cast shadows over genuine spiritual development. Organizations and institutions are not ends but are designed to help you have a spiritual life and build a spiritual community. Use only those which help.

4. *Connect with nature.* Spirituality starts with a sense of marvel at our existence and at the wonders of creation—other living things, the oceans and mountains, forests, deserts, and weather. Go for a walk. Watch stars. Take care of a pet. Notice your body. Play with children. Then connect these miracles with what else you see around you.

5. *Make a daily effort.* Key to spiritual life is constancy. Daily rituals that anchor your sense of stability help you achieve incremental spiritual growth. Then when leaps of faith are required and stress overwhelms you, a reservoir of accumulated strength awaits.

6. *Find ways to promote reflection.* Spirituality is about what is meaningful to you, what gives your life value. Find strategies that help you to reflect on meaning and value. Inspirational writing, daily meditation books, liturgy, prayer, journals, yoga exercises, and letter writing are the kinds of things that need to be part of your daily rituals. These also help you make sense out of special spiritual events.

7. *Surrender.* All inner journeys start with an "emptying" of self—a fact reflected in religious traditions. Addicts begin recovery with an admission of powerlessness and live their lives according to the principle of "letting go." Serenity, according to the prayer, is doing all you can and accepting that that is enough.

8. *Heal the sexual/spiritual split.* Much damage has been done to sexuality in the name of religion. The result inhibits progress on both planes. To heal, start by acknowledging that sexuality is about meaning and that spirituality is about meaning. Search for areas of commonness between the two. Be gentle with yourself about old torturous conflicts. They are not about you. They never were.

One of the more remarkable aspects of this intensification of spiritual life is the release of creative energy. This theme was expressed by many recovering people, but perhaps most aptly by Charlene. She noted that during her addiction much of her energy had gone into obsession and relationships. After her first year of recovery, that energy became available to her again. She explained it this way:

What happened was a tremendous burst of creativity. I started writing poetry, and it was just pouring out of me.

And after the poetry came songs. I started writing songs. I mean I really started writing. It just felt like they were given to me by my Higher Power.

As she looked back at those early years, she stressed that they were painful but "tremendously rich." Further, they laid the foundation for the next stage, the growth years.

CHAPTER NINE

Three Years Plus: Working a Program and Healthy Sex

Nick had been in SAA ten years. He celebrated by gathering to-gether program friends with whom he was especially close. They had breakfast at a hotel restaurant, in a small dining room set up for family-style eating. People filed in, exchanging warm embraces and welcomes. Breakfast was punctuated by remembrances, stories, and laughter. As Nick looked around him, he had two almost simul-taneous thoughts. First, many of these people had been with him since the beginning. And, second, it was a measure of the progress he had made that he could call a party in his own honor without feeling shame or anxiety.

When Nick's group started, it was the only one in the city. Many of the members knew they needed more than one meeting a week, so they gathered at a neighborhood restaurant for Monday morning breakfast. It was not actually a regular meeting, but rather a time to check in with one another and talk. Later the meeting became a Tuesday lunch somewhere else. Over the years, it re-mained a standing invitation, always available to members of the group.

A year after the group began, its members decided to go on a retreat together. They went to a camp that rented large cabins to groups. They planned and cooked their meals. They decided on topics they needed to work on and organized a program. There were trails for hiking, a swimming pool, and volleyball nets. The cost was modest, and the group paid for those who could not afford it. An extraordinary success, the retreat became an annual event, always held on the same weekend. Each retreat bonded the group even closer.

The group grew until it no longer fit its meeting space in a neighborhood church. Painfully, the group split. And two years later those groups split. Yet, two things remained constant. Many of those early friendships continued, even though the friends were in different groups. And each group maintained the traditions of a weekly meal and an annual retreat.

So when Nick's friends gathered at the breakfast to give him his ten-year medallion, it was an occasion to remember all those times together and to contrast them with how bad things had been before. Nick received gifts—some humorous, some meaningful, but all rooted in their history together. Universally, these friends affirmed Nick for his steadfastness. He was a mainstay of group life, regular in his meeting attendance, reliable as a sponsor, and dependable when he took on responsibilities. They also underlined Nick's progress. Two and a half years into recovery Nick had married and he now had two children. They reflected on how amazing a decade of recovery was.

They also acknowledged the loss they all experienced with the death of Michael, a group member who died of AIDS three years earlier. Nick had been Michael's sponsor and had mobilized the group to help Michael, his wife, and children throughout Michael's hospital stays. It was Nick who stayed in constant touch with Michael's wife, who was herself now dying of AIDS. He kept the group posted on the children's activities. It was he who for a long time had resisted taking Michael's name off the phone list, he who struggled most with grieving. His constancy to Michael mirrored his steadfastness to the group—a far cry from his chaotic days of acting out. Nick told us that, as a result of his support network, "I now realize that I can live through any experience, that there's no pain that's going to kill me, and there's no loss too hard to handle. I didn't know that when I started."

Nick's story follows a predictable pattern. Early in recovery, the task was to break the isolation surrounding the addiction. The task during the second and third years was to build relationships. This building of community relies on retreats and rituals, on meals and celebrations, on witnessing marriages, births, and deaths.

The relationships that have been built become an ongoing support network.

Breaking isolation—first year (crisis, shock, and grief)

↓

Building relationships—second and third years (repair)

↓

Creating support network—three years plus (growth)

Although a support network takes time to build, Nick's story shows that some people in the network are there from the beginning. Nick hypothesized that a special closeness exists among sex addicts: "This illness attacked the most sensitive and delicate parts of us. Connections I made with people very early in recovery were exquisite. That's the only way I can describe it."

The support network becomes the grounding force during the growth stage of recovery. The knowledge that their human needs will be met enables addicts to fundamentally restructure their most significant relationships—relationships with parents, partners, and children. Some people do not succeed, however. Addicts put it this way: they failed "to work the program."

WORKING THE PROGRAM

Not everyone made it the way Nick did. Jim was like Nick in that he was one of the early participants in the first support group in his city. He, too, worked hard on his recovery program and made extraordinary progress. His wife, Ann, joined a support group for coaddicts and felt good about her progress. But then changes occurred which brought disaster.

Jim started a new business. Excited by the challenge and motivated by the financial opportunity, he poured all of his energy into his work. Working evenings and weekends, he assured his family that this was temporary—just part of starting up. But the pace did not slow; within a couple of years it was clear the schedule had become permanent. Jim was in a pattern of compulsive work. Worse, this was happening at a time when, as part of her recovery, Ann wanted to deal with major issues concerning their marriage, their families, and their kids. Recovery had brought them far, but there was still much to do. She felt abandoned and felt she was getting no support with the kids. The feelings added great strain to the relationship.

Jim's attendance at meetings became irregular, as did his use of meditation. When his sponsor moved, Jim did not replace him. He himself was still a sponsor to four people, but even those contacts were becoming more infrequent. Jim was experiencing what Alcoholics Anonymous had described as the "subtle insanity" of relapse.

Jim and Ann reached the point where they were about to divorce. Jim's company had run out of capital and teetered on bankruptcy. And Jim was starting to slip. He felt so dispirited while on a business trip that he stopped to watch a strip show. In Jim's addictive pattern, strip shows were but a step away from prostitution. He knew this but went anyway.

Jim finally admitted to himself he was in trouble when he went to a massage parlor. He went to his group and declared himself a "newcomer." He got a new sponsor and started attending two meetings a week. He returned to his meditation discipline. He approached Ann with such honesty that she agreed to work through a reconciliation. His greatest obstacle was his pride. To start all over again when he had been one of the first to recover and when his friends had been able to maintain sobriety was a source of immense shame. Yet one thing his program friends were expert about was helping with shame—shame and powerlessness.

Jim's story serves as an important counterpoint to Nick's. Having succeeded in the repair stage, Jim felt so confident that he fell into living in the extremes again. The seductive call of the Master of the Universe became too great. He relaxed his recovery effort precisely at the time when he was ready to accomplish fundamental growth work. What he failed to do was what twelve step people refer to as "work the program."

As the figure on the next page shows, recovery work does not stop with the tasks and gains of the first three years. Rather, all this effort brings the recovering person to the point of working the program.

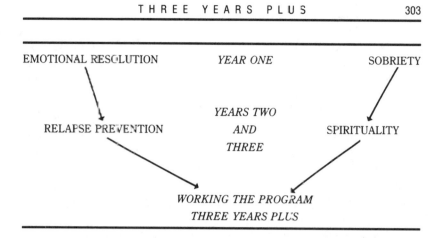

Working the program is not about just maintaining gains—it's not about just staying sober and being spiritual. The twelfth step of AA says it succinctly: "to practice these principles in all of our affairs." Working the program is about implementing program principles in core parts of personal and family life. It is a lifetime task.

With sex addiction, working the program means, above all, that individuals integrate recovery principles into their sexual life. The most important issue for all sex addicts is restoring healthy sexuality. The question most often asked by addicts in early recovery is, Is there healthy sex for sex addicts? A good analogy can be created by phrasing the question in terms of eating disorders: Can a compulsive overeater become a gourmet cook? The answer in both cases is yes. In fact, becoming more expert in sex or in food is a vital part of recovery.

HEALTHY SEXUALITY

Deanne and Jim went to a late Sunday matinee. The movie was not entertaining. Furthermore, it was filled with cultural stereotypes that left them both unsettled. When they got in their car afterward, it was early evening and sheets of rain poured down. A casual kiss led to some very intensive petting. Suddenly, though, Jim stopped and asked why they felt so sexual. They realized that the movie, vacuous as it was, had been really upsetting. They went to a restaurant, ate dinner, and talked for hours about the feelings generated by the show. In bed later that night, feeling peaceful and connected, they made love. Their gentle lovemaking kept pace with the rhythms of the rain. Contented, Deanne fell asleep thinking about how different their marriage was now.

Deanne and Jim had become more expert about their sexuality. They knew enough about their own interior worlds to sift through their emotional feelings and needs without sexualizing them. In the days when they had been active in their addiction, they would go through intense cycles of fights and sex. Usually, these occurred when they were avoiding some pain in their lives. These "fight and fuck" binges left them depleted and despairing. Whatever prompted the cycle remained unresolved or, worse, unacknowledged.

Even in professional circles, much of the information available on improving sexuality is largely confined to three areas. First and foremost there is a focus on techniques to enhance sexual pleasure. Second, people are helped to improve their sexuality by overcoming restrictive attitudes and beliefs learned in their families. Finally, there is a focus on relationship issues, especially by those who argue that if a couple is connected, sexual issues will take care of themselves. Physical techniques, attitudes and beliefs, and relationship issues are all important—but they are not enough.

Sex addicts are making a major contribution to our knowledge of sexuality. Sex addicts push us to deeper levels of understanding because of their sexual pain. They are caught by the reality of their illness. Jim, Deanne's husband, put it to us succinctly: "We have to recover from inside this addiction. My sexuality won't go away. I can stay out of a barroom, but I can't stay out of my body." Recovery means facing your sexual core and transforming the old destructive energy into something new. Jim emphasized that, far from becoming less interesting, sexuality gains a new intensity. "Instead of masquerading as something important that ends up being a horrible disappointment and source of despair, there comes a real richness that I thought I was looking for before."

A specialness about sex exists for addicts who work through those issues. They experience a depth of knowledge about themselves sexually that most people never attain. Forced by all their losses to face the abuse issues, the acting out, and the cultural and family dysfunction, addicts attach profound meaning to their sexuality. They tell us that once the wounds have healed over, the tissue is stronger than before—yet still very sensitive. Jim's words echoed the sentiments of many others:

I don't ever believe that sexuality means the same thing to me that it does to a normal person, so to speak. It will always mean more, and it will always be different. Recovery doesn't mean that I become like everybody else. Recovery means that I transcend the dead ends and the self-destructive stuff. Sexuality will always mean more in my relationship with my wife than it does for other people. It's not a matter of frequency or something like that. There's a fullness that I think it will always have.

Jim talked about a "gentle" sobriety. As we have already noted, sexual recovery is not a black-and-white choice, but a series of choices involving many shades of gray. For recovering people the most difficult question is how to know when they are being sexual in healthy ways and when their sexuality is addictive. A sexual choice may be well within the sobriety definition and personal boundaries and yet still be about self-medication. A more gentle sobriety allows for shades of gray. Jim stressed to us how important this was for him and Deanne:

It is important to be honest about times when you really know you're medicating. My wife and I are aware that as part of our addiction we have the tendency to medicate. So being aware of that, we are willing to say "No, I better not. I think I'd be medicating." Sometimes it's been a little in-between but talking about it, recognizing that there's maybe a fly in the ointment tonight, we decide to go ahead. Keeping it at that kind of conscious level between us makes it a relationship again. If I'm medicating myself one night by having sex and I don't say anything about it, then there's a real wall, a real barrier. But if I'm feeling "Gee, I'm not sure but I think I might be kind of medicating," but still one thing leads to another and maybe it comes out I sort of was, but it was something that we talked about, then we still have made that contact. Then the barrier isn't there. The pain might be there, but not as a barrier. So I think that's another way of enhancing it. It's talking about our recovery and our issues.

Sexual healing starts with a high level of awareness, a willingness to talk, and an ability to be emotionally present to yourself and to your partner. This is a hard challenge for all of us. Masters and Johnson noted their amazement at "how reticent most people are when it comes to talking about sex with their lovers." For addicts still in their addiction, the communication is difficult because of all the secrecy and shame. In recovery, because of the pain involved, addicts and their partners have to take even greater risks. Doing so, however, has rich rewards. Consider these comments by Sarah:

> I've been working with my husband on this right now. I think my sexuality has been enhanced by talking openly and yet gently about how it is for me. I have felt violated by penetration, and discussing this with my husband has opened up a whole new door for us. We have been able to come up with being able to talk with one another while we are making love. We are able to "be here now." In the past I used to go away, fade off, fantasize, or feel victimized. If I sit there, and it's hard to do, but if I can sit there and look at my husband, just be here now romantically, seductively, however the words come out, it seems to help us a lot.

Presence, communication, and awareness carry recovery into new realms of sexual healing. They are especially important because addicts and coaddicts are vulnerable to sexual traps, or as Jim termed them, "dead ends" that inhibit recovery. These traps often have their origin in shame-based, addicted families. They include:

- *Sexualized rage.* This is an anger beyond reason, usually directed at the opposite sex, whose members are blamed for all relationship failures (e.g., "Women always . . ."; "Men always . . .").

- *Sexualized conflicts.* Sex becomes a way to counter hurts and resentments or to reduce tension without resolving conflict, as in alternating cycles of sex and fighting.

- *Sexualized needs.* As a result of patterns developed in childhood, adults feel intensely sexual when they feel lonely, hurt, or depleted.

- *Sexual shame.* This means feeling profoundly ashamed for having sexual feelings and believing that a person is bad for having such feelings.

- *Sexual exploitation.* A person is deceptive, manipulative, or seductive because of the belief that sexual needs will not be met otherwise. Examples range from acting as if you have no sexual interest while working to turn others on, to picking partners who are vulnerable because of their pain, naïveté, or neediness.

- *Sexual double bind.* If you are good, you can't be sexual. If you feel sexual, you can't be good. So if sex makes you feel good, you wind up feeling bad about feeling good. Sex is dirty, so save it for someone you love!

- *Sexual self-destruction.* People may be caught in a pattern, usually learned in the family, of using sex to set themselves up for disaster— for example, continually setting up sexual situations that result in abuse or abandonment.

- *Gender shame.* This is a profound embarrassment and feeling of vulnerability about one's own sex, especially in relation to the opposite sex; for example, men may feel inadequate about expressing their feelings to women, who seem so much more skilled at this.

- *Sexual perfectionism.* Feeling compulsive about "doing it right" leads to immobilization and inability to do anything at all. A typical example of sexual perfectionism is needing to achieve the "right" orgasm.

- *Body shame.* This is a deep embarrassment about one's body or about certain aspects of one's body. People who feel body shame tend to continually compare themselves with others, who are slimmer, better developed, or more attractive.

Because they have been and still are vulnerable to these traps, addicts and coaddicts have all the more to work through. We asked recovering people what can be done, beyond therapy and twelve step work, to enhance sexuality. Their advice is summarized below.

ADDICTS' BEST ADVICE NUMBER 8:
Enhancing Sexuality

---

1. *Make a sexual leap of faith.* Sexual change is gradual, not sudden. You have to trust and believe that it will happen. (The most often

used phrase in this area of advice was "let go and let God.")
Attempts to do otherwise and control outcomes will destroy
sexual experience.

2. *Sustain sex with intimacy.* Sexual vitality comes from relationships. The challenges of closeness renew sexual interest and
deepen the meaning of sex.

3. *Talk before, during, and after.* Verbalizing passion, needs, and
fears is perhaps the best way of facilitating sexual intimacy.

4. *Overcome sexual shame through affirmation of each other.* Couples that did the best emphasized the strategy of mutual affirmation. Compliment your partner. Affirm all the positive things you
can see about his or her sexuality and about your sexuality
together. Don't stop.

5. *Respect boundaries and limits.* Building trust helps heal the sexual
wounds of the past. Both partners need permission to say no
without fear of reprisal or abandonment. Give profound respect
to the other's vulnerabilities and wishes—even when you don't
fully understand them, like them, or approve of them. Remember, trust is the goal. To seduce, manipulate, or test your
partner's boundaries is extremely destructive. Healing will shift
perspectives and boundaries. Breaking the trust again may lead
to irreparable damage.

6. *Pay attention to feelings.* Addicts and coaddicts learned to sexualize their needs and pain; yet their needs remained unfulfilled,
their pain went unattended to, and their sexuality was stifled.
Attend to your feelings. You might have to begin by just labeling
them. With time you will get better at sorting them out.

7. *See sex as legitimate joy.* Abandon the grim rules you learned that
kept you in addictive and coaddictive obsession. Have fun. Play.
Within your sobriety plan and your boundaries, allow for spontaneity and experimentation. Your recovery is about sexual growth,
which requires risk. Your recovery principles carve out an area
of safety so that you can risk yourself sexually in new, positive,
and rewarding ways.

8. *Take care of your body.* Physical health is basic to sexual health.
Exercise. Eat good food. Sleep well. Limit the use of drugs like

alcohol, nicotine, and caffeine. Do these things and you can trust that your body's responses will be limited only by your mind.

Beyond specific strategies, recovering people need a model of how healthy sexuality evolves. Like intimacy, sexuality can be broken down "by the numbers." By understanding each component, we can see how recovery principles can support a nurturing, flourishing sexuality.

EIGHT DIMENSIONS OF SEXUAL HEALTH

There are eight dimensions of human sexuality. They exist concurrently but can be examined separately. When they are fully developed, each reinforces the others. If a specific dimension is weak or impaired, the others are all affected. Taken together they become a map to one's sexual self.

1. Nurturing

Sex is a very nurturing act. It requires the capacity to nurture others, to nurture oneself, and to accept nurturing from others. Nurturing cannot be compartmentalized. A person who does not accept care from others very well will be unable to really accept sexual nurturing. Although a basic fact of sexual life is that a general comfort with nurturing is required, nurturing is something that addicts and coaddicts struggle with. They learned in their families to tolerate pain. They believe they do not deserve to be comforted. Learning how to care for themselves and to allow others to care for them is an essential recovery task.

The story of Roger illustrates this theme. Roger had studied for the ministry and his family had always emphasized sacrifice and service to others. Roger and his wife both brought in large salaries. Because of their backgrounds and the counterculture values of the early seventies, they started their marriage agreeing to give most of their income to worthy causes. They used the federal poverty level as a guideline for how much money they would keep for living expenses. Roger wore old clothes and pinched pennies. He put in many hours of volunteer service but did little or nothing for himself. And he was acting out all the time.

When Roger joined a twelve step fellowship, the people in his group noted his parsimonious ways. As he kept slipping in his sobriety, they started to press him on what he did to be kind to himself. The concept was clearly foreign to him. He struggled with the group and with his sobriety. Finally, one exasperated group member asked him what was something he had always wanted. Much to his own surprise, Roger blurted out "a Pendleton shirt." That very night the group went with him to a nearby shopping mall and stood by to support him as he picked out a shirt.

That shirt represented a watershed for Roger. His struggle to nurture himself early in recovery has evolved over time. He and his wife have since agreed to give away only 10 percent of their income. They live in a nice home on a lake, and Roger does many good things for himself. Now his program friends lovingly tease him about all the time he takes off. And he doesn't act out anymore.

Buying the shirt opened a door to extraordinary personal pain about the deficits and deprivation of his early life. Working through that pain taught him hard lessons about the importance of a softer, gentler way. He learned to nurture himself. Nowhere was this more clear than in his sexuality. Sometimes these days he and his wife curl up to cuddle in a pile of teddy bears—a far cry from where he began. You can change the circumstances, but the lesson of Roger's story is a common one for many in our survey.

2. Sensuality

Sex is a sensual experience. Yet, as with nurturing, sensual awareness during sex is possible only if a person is sensually aware in general. Temperature, texture, color, sounds, tastes, and smells fill our lives. However, because of our stress and preoccupations, the fact that we spend our time in buildings far from nature, and our tendency to live vicariously through the media, we do not attend much to our senses. So while our bodies are capable of gathering sense data, we often ignore the information our senses supply. And then we want to be sexual—an intensely sensual and personal experience—and we wonder why it is not what we expected.

The irony is that sensory awareness is the gateway to self-awareness. Many centering strategies like yoga and meditation, as well as many therapy strategies, start with basic sense awareness—awareness of one's own breathing, pulse, and muscle tension. Work on increasing spirituality or reducing stress develops sense awareness by encouraging the individual to stop to smell the roses. By tuning into our senses we learn much about ourselves. For example, massage therapists often find that clients become very emotional when certain muscle groups are worked on. Usually the clients don't know why. Massage can become a way of breaking through repression.

Sex is profoundly sensual and profoundly personal. It cannot be personal unless it is sensual. This means that sex requires slowing down and noticing the sensual. Slowing down does not preclude spontaneity. Rather, it means making oneself available to the sexual experience. In many ways, the principles involved in sensuality parallel the recovery principles that emphasize the "here and now" approach to life. Jim was very articulate about that:

> I think sensuality in sex has something to do with just the overall recovery experience. It isn't a matter of holding back. Somehow, it's actually more a matter of getting more into what we're doing together, whether it's kissing or stroking each other or whatever. We are not just rushing to the punch line. It's like a symphony instead of a three-minute song.

3. Sense of Self

Just as people can remain oblivious to their senses, they can also lose touch with themselves. Given the personal nature of sex, to be unconnected with oneself makes sex at best an empty gesture and at worst a high risk one. In contrast, when a person has a developed sense of self, sex becomes a matter of choice. One can be clear about whom to be sexual with, what feels good and what does not, and what expectations one has about a partner. When people are centered, their expressions of feelings drive passion and increase intimacy.

Efforts to help people enjoy their sexuality have sometimes focused on giving them permission to be as sexual as they want. Given our Puritan heritage and a sexually repressive culture, sexual liberation has been a healthy antidote to sexual shame. However, in a time when we are overthrowing traditional norms, we may overlook people's need to set parameters. Reluctance to do something, for example, may not be about hang-ups but about an experience of sexual abuse. We need also to support people in being able to say no, set boundaries, and acknowledge hurt. They do not have to tolerate pain in order to be sexual. Therapy helps people set limits so they feel safe. In that safety they can then risk new things. Each limit set becomes part of self-definition.

Similarly, being assertive strengthens the sense of self but to ask for what you want, you must know what you want. If you feel "little" or childlike inside, you may need to ask for nurturing and not sex. If you want something erotic from your partner, you may not get it unless you ask.

For addicts, self-knowledge and self-responsibility are vital to recovery. And yet their history blocks avenues for self-knowledge that are available to others. For example, many people learn much about what feels good through self-exploration and masturbation, and they crystallize what they want through fantasy. For many addicts, however, masturbation and fantasy are gateways to old self-destructive behaviors.

So how can sex addicts construct images that help them define themselves sexually? First, they cannot do it alone. Therapists, sponsors, and groups can provide addicts with support for positive new fantasies. Second, one of the surest routes is for addicts to explore their own history for positive sexual experiences. Exercise 9-1 provides an example of this approach. The person focuses on positive sexual experiences and searches for common threads. The images that emerge from this process can serve then as new guides to sexual self-expression. Third, since addicts start with sexual assumptions that are destructive, they must dispel old myths, get accurate information, and set new ground rules about sex.

EXERCISE 9-1
POSITIVE SEXUAL HISTORY WORKSHEET

To construct an internal sense of positive sexual health, review your own sexual history for times and events that made you feel good about yourself and your sexuality. If your sexual history includes lots of shame, pain, or abuse, this will at first seem difficult. Focus on those moments in which you felt truly yourself—those times when you felt peaceful, passionate, content, or happy. This worksheet will help you work through the implication of those moments for your sexual life.

Begin by describing at least eight events that were sexually positive for you. (Perhaps generate a long list on another sheet of paper and select the best eight.) After recording the events, determine what made each so special for you. Note the conditions, the process between your partner and you, and what you actually did that made the experience so good for you. Then look for what these events had in common, and list five commonalities. Finally, based on your learnings, list five practical steps you can take to enhance your lovemaking.

I. Describe the sexual event.
   *Example: Night on the beach
   with first lover*

II. Record what made it special.
   *Example: Ocean, stars, nature.
   Lots of time. No one knew
   where we were. Hours of
   touching.*

1._____

2._____

3._____

4._____

5._____

6._____

7._____

8._____

1._____

2._____

3._____

4._____

5._____

6._____

7._____

8._____

III. List five factors your special events had in common.

Example: Lots of physical contact, touching, and cuddling.

IV. List practical steps you will take to increase that factor in your lovemaking.
Example: Set up some "touch" sessions with my partner. Talk about the issue of touching. Make touching a daily goal.

1._____   1._____

2._____   2._____

3._____   3._____

4._____   4._____

5._____   5._____

4. Relationship Sexuality

Sexual identity starts at birth—"It's a boy" or "It's a girl"—and conditions our relationships with others. Each day, men and women relate to one another on the basis of their masculine and feminine selves. At this level, we are being sexual all the time. We acknowledge one another's differences, but we do not eroticize them. At this level, we can have nonerotic friendships or relationships with people of the same or opposite sex. Sexual roles, stereotypes, and expectations serve as filters to the intimacy possibilities.

Therapists listen carefully to how their clients characterize their relationships at this level. A man who says, "I get along well with guys but am real shy with women," or "I don't have any real friends who are men. It is easier for me to talk to women," reveals significant relationship patterns. Such patterns also tell therapists what to start looking for in family issues. Somewhere this person failed to learn how to relate to the opposite or same sex. Sexual health involves having and being comfortable with friends of both sexes. Not to have friends of both sexes limits our perceptions, our support base, and ultimately our sexuality.

Situations involving divorce serve as a good example. Consider the man who is devastated by divorce because he had no real male friends and his wife had been his only source of emotional support. Or consider the woman who lives with a domineering man and has given away pieces of herself for years. When she finds a support group of women, she begins to draw on them for strength and starts to insist on being heard. Her marriage, which had survived only because of her isolation, soon ends in divorce. Such scenarios fill our marital landscape. As we move to a new mutuality between the sexes, this dimension of our sexuality stands to gain the most.

Sex addicts have had few relationships that were not sexualized. Developing friendships without a sexual agenda feels foreign and, at first, pointless. Of the various addictions, sex addiction presents perhaps the greatest challenges of all. Sex addicts must do more than just develop support. They must learn to gain support without sexualizing it. We had a good example of this with Chris, a forty-one-year-old college professor.

Initially Chris went to two twelve step support groups that had only male members. Despite two years of recovery, Chris wound up separating from his wife. A while after the separation, Chris started going to a mixed SAA group. Chris regards going to that group as one of the best moves he ever made. He doubts that he would have been able to handle it earlier in recovery. Although he was apprehensive about being in a group with women, he soon found that like the other groups, this was a very safe place to be. Further, he found the feedback he received from women healing. As the actual legal process of the divorce proceeded, Chris's situation became particularly painful. Help from women in the group kept him from making serious mistakes. Chris learned that he could find reliable help and closeness and have fun with women in relationships that were not eroticized. Years later he counts two women from that group among his best friends.

That capacity for friendship is a basic building block for relationships that include sexual desire. For in such relationships the erotic component is added to friendship.

5. Partner Sexuality

Partner sexuality means that a special intimacy has evolved with someone, an intimacy that is clearly erotic. This closeness is not one-sided, but mutual and shared. For many who came into recovery with an existing sexual relationship, this dimension presents special challenges because of the damage to trust. For those who were single or who lost partners, sooner or later the specter of dating arises. The challenge for them becomes balancing their recovery needs with their shame and fears of abandonment.

For partners, specific challenges include the following: Can they be sexually intimate without being physical? Are they able to renew a sense of courtship and romance? Can they integrate nurturing, sensuality, and self-awareness into ongoing courtship behavior? There are some concrete strategies for meeting these challenges:

- Express clearly how attracted you are to your partner at moments you feel the attraction.

- Create signs, symbols, and gestures of specialness that express your desire.

- Affirm your partner's sexuality by making comments about him or her as a man or a woman. Compliment your partner's body or appearance.

- Take risks and talk to your partner about your sexual feelings.

- Acknowledge behaviors that create desire.

- Do things that you enjoy and that you know awaken desire in your partner.

- Accept the sexual affirmations and compliments your partner gives you.

Sex addicts are often surprised that profound sexual transactions can occur without touching. For those who spent years of their lives skipping over this level of intimacy, it is brand-new sexual terrain. For many couples in our survey, one of the gifts of a celibacy period was an opportunity to reclaim this sexual dimension.

For single people, dating was often terrifying. The old dating scenario equated dates with sex. As one woman told us, "If they were attracted to me, it meant I would be involved with them." Some even pointed out that they used to have sex with their dating partners because dating was so scary. Sex was a way to overcome the awkwardness. And if their partners did not have sex with them, it meant rejection.

Recovering people who are single have the problems that all who date have: uncertainty because of changing sex roles (who pays for dinner?), difficulty meeting people (where and how to meet them?), and problems deciding how much to tell about oneself (what if they ask about my divorce?). Addicts in recovery also face these issues: How do I tell them about my boundaries or my addiction? How will I know if what is happening is real and okay? Perhaps the toughest, however, is: After all the growth of my recovery, how do I find people who fit what I want?

Our survey respondents had much to say about what worked when dating. They provided down-to-earth dating tactics like:

- Be up-front about your feelings about dating.

- Don't be alone too much with new dating partners.

- Take phone numbers of group members with you.

- Go to safe places.

- Don't go out simply because you are asked.

- Be picky about whom you date.

- Make boundaries clear.

- Remember to work for friendship and companionship.

The most important learning recovering people shared about dating is to expect mistakes. Dating truly is a different experience from being married or paired. The guidelines for couples are simpler. Dating presents a lot of gray areas. Recovering people who are dating should bear in mind this imperative: Be gentle with yourself.

Recovery principles help. Sally, for example, in her addiction had been involved with many people at the same time. Given her history of multiple relationships, she found it frightening when she finally started to date and found herself attracted to two men at the same time. But working her recovery program made it different. First, she was honest with each of these men about her friendship with the other. Although it was difficult and at times painful, each one felt respected, for there were no secrets. In fact, Sally got kudos for her integrity and courage. Second, Sally was consistently checking with her support network. She was not alone in figuring out the steps she needed to take.

The key decision factor for Sally turned out to be her own sense of self. She told us, "It used to be that I was preoccupied with whether a man liked me or not. Now I asked myself, How do I feel in his presence?" Sally decided on one of the men and eventually married him. When interviewed two years after her marriage, she said about dating: "It sounds like a cliché, but for me it's true. The dating days were the hardest but in some ways the best of times." We asked recovering people for advice about dating. Their suggestions are summarized below.

ADDICTS' BEST ADVICE NUMBER 9:
Beginning to Date

---

1. *Heal first.* Wait for your program to stabilize. Take the time you need to work through celibacy, to develop support, and to understand your addiction. Most who took this time felt it was the "greatest gift" they could have given themselves.

2. *Take time to be known.* You have plenty of time. Aim for friendship. Avoid urgency. Enjoy yourself.

3. *Be selective.* Only date people in whose presence you feel most like yourself. If you find yourself slipping into shame—feeling the need to defend yourself or seek approval—consider it a warning.

4. *Share your plan.* When dating becomes steady, share how and under what terms you want to be sexual. Elicit from your partner his or her reactions to this as well as his or her intentions and values.

5. *Share your recovery.* Tell your partner about your history so you are not carrying a secret. There are two critical things to remember here: (1) If it is not safe enough to share this fact about yourself, it is not safe to be sexual, and (2) if you are sexual before your partner knows your history, it may be perceived as a betrayal when he or she does find out. If your partner accepts you as a recovering person, your fears of abandonment will dissipate. Seldom did we hear about addicts who were rejected for sharing their recovery if they did it up-front.

6. *Do pre-dates and post-dates with others.* Before and after dates, check it out with others, especially if you have any anxiety. No

one does it perfectly. Everyone makes mistakes. The real problems arise when you cease to share your process.

7. *Remember: this is a date, not an encounter group.* Acknowledge your feelings If you feel anxious or awkward, say so. Watch the intensity, however. You do not have to tell your life history or share childhood pain the first evening. Trust should be incremental, not instantaneous. Build up some history with your date; spend some time together first.

8. *Beware of cosmic relationships.* Intensity is not intimacy. Fast-forwarding the future—as when after a very brief courtship you are certain you have found "the one"—can be a fix for the emptiness of the present. Life mates are not determined in two days, even two dreamlike days. Many addicts spent one night that took years to untangle. There are magic evenings, however. Enjoy them. Listen to your intuitions. Trust history and recovery.

6. Nongenital Sexuality

"There was not anything I could do as far as touching went that did not lead to being sexual." With those words, Betty, a thirty-seven-year-old real estate agent from Philadelphia, launched into telling us about her recovery. Her pattern had included going to bars and picking up men, sometimes several men in one evening. She had been in many stormy, abusive relationships, with women as well as men. She stressed to us, "I had never learned there was healthy touch. So anytime a conversation started and then touching started, it was like right into the total sexual thing."

Betty learned about sexual addiction through ACOA and immediately knew it fit. Once she began a recovery program for her addiction, she also became clear about another issue in her life: her sexual preference was for women. She took an extended period of celibacy and then started dating. By the time we interviewed her, she was in a peaceful and nurturing lesbian relationship. Her account of how that happened goes like this:

> It's the first relationship I've entered where I've allowed myself to get to know this person by talking, by being with her, and by being intimate without sex. We'd sit and we'd

watch TV and we'd maybe hold each other or have our arms around each other or maybe hold hands. It was all little steps, but with both of us having our own reasons, we weren't sexual for probably two months. I can laugh about it today, but the first time we were, it got marked on the calendar.

Betty and others discovered that there are many ways to be sexual without being genital. The rich range of sexual expression includes holding, touching, caressing, fondling, and kissing. These areas of sexual comfort deepen and extend sexual satisfaction. To explore them requires both intimacy and time.

Our culture does not support this dimension of our sexuality. We tend to be fast paced and chronically short of time. We emphasize sizzle and look for immediate payoffs. Our movies and television shows often cut from first encounters to the bedroom. Sexual nurturing does not film well because it is slower and works on deeper, less obvious levels.

Twelve step recovery, with its emphasis on asking for what you want, in many ways supports nongenital sex. Betty commented on this issue by saying, "I'm taking care of myself so much more than I ever did. I'm really stating and recognizing that I have needs and that they have to be met." Many recovering addicts know they have real deprivation in terms of touching and holding, but seethe in resentment of themselves and others because they do not ask. And you do have to ask.

7. Genital Sexuality

Mark and Karen were committed to a period of celibacy and were working with a therapist. Up to this point their assignments had involved nurturing, touching, and exploring their senses. They had really enjoyed these assignments, and their celibacy had actually heightened their passion for each other. But now they received a very discomforting assignment. Their therapist asked them to explore masturbation. First, they were to masturbate in front of each other, with their partner's support. This support could be caressing, holding, or talking. Later, they were each to teach the other how to stimulate them to orgasm without intercourse.

Karen was terrified. She had never masturbated in front of anyone in her life. This was very private to her. She had to admit that her masturbation orgasms were "different" and in some ways better than those she had with Mark. She truly did not believe she could do it in front of him. Also, even though they had come so far in recovery over two and a half years, Karen still felt vulnerable at times with Mark.

Mark was shameful. His style of masturbation was very ritual-ized. When he had tried to show his past sexual partners, no one was able to do it the way that felt good. Worse, he feared that if he was not able to teach Karen, she would feel bad—and when she felt inadequate, she tended to attack him. And, he told himself with some dark humor, this would hardly be a circumstance under which he would want to be attacked.

Their therapist proceeded to set up individual sessions with each of them. In the private session, Karen listed all of her fears. The therapist pointed out that these issues were as much about trusting herself as trusting Mark. This rang true for Karen, since she had learned that lesson repeatedly in working through abuse and dysfunction in her family. Here was simply one more arena in which she had to take responsibility for herself. Sex was not something done to her, rather it extended from within.

Mark also had to look at himself. The therapist asked him how he felt about his masturbation ritual. Mark responded by noting that it clearly was part of his pattern of compulsivity. The therapist asked how badly he wanted a rewarding sexual life and what was he willing to risk to get it. When Mark brought up the matter of Karen's likely response, the therapist listed the issues at stake. In order to carry out the assignment Mark would have to allow himself to be nurtured by Karen, suspend judgment of both himself and her, and accept that it would be imperfect for a while. Mark recognized these as the same issues that had plagued him since the beginning of recovery.

In a joint follow-up session, the therapist underlined for Mark and Karen how their sexuality could flourish if they simply extended into their sexual relationship the recovery principles that had been so healing for them in other areas. Both of them had trouble because of their efforts to control. Successful sex meant "letting go." Pas-sion demands trust: trust of your body, trust of your sexuality, and trust of your partner. Orgasm is giving oneself over to elemental forces, with no conscious control or goal. Sex is the ultimate surrender.

Mark and Karen made crucial progress by completing their assignment. They did it imperfectly, learning much about themselves as well as about sex, and with the gentle support of their therapist, they even had fun. Their experience highlights several important facts about sexual recovery. First, despite the sometimes astounding amounts of sexual experience that they have, sex addicts often know very little about sex. With the support of their therapist, partner, and group, they need to learn more about their sexual responses, especially when it comes to genital sex. Not only do they have to add in other dimensions, like nurturing and sensuality, but they have to experiment with new forms of genital expression as well.

Second, issues are seldom isolated. What is a problem in the couple's relationship will manifest itself in their sexual relationship as well. Sexuality becomes a mirror to all the addictive issues of trust, shame, and intimacy. We believe that the reason we were not able to measure significant sexual progress until the growth stage of recovery was that sexuality could not thrive until the repair work was done.

One other factor serves to limit sexual progress until this point: the intimate connection between sexuality and spirituality.

8. Spiritual Sexuality

Scott Peck, well-known psychiatrist and author of *The Road Less Traveled*, makes the statement that the closest many people get to religious experience is orgasm. In fact, he observes that those lost in the "compulsive, driven" pursuit of sex are really searching for spirituality. Peck drives home the point that sexuality and spirituality are inextricably linked. He talks about both as a "yearning for wholeness." Sex is about meaning, and spirituality is about meaning. To involve one means to involve the other. He points to Abraham Maslow, who documented that one of the eighteen characteristics of self-actualized people was a sense of mysticism when sexual. Further, Peck insists that he distrusts religious conversions that are not accompanied by intensifying sexuality. Peck concludes that it is "hardly possible to arouse one without arousing the other."

Addicts talk of a "spiritual program of recovery." For sex

addicts, this presents a double challenge: to heal spiritually and to heal sexually. Many sex addicts suffered sexual damage from spiritual sources. Religious messages from their childhood equated sex with sin and evil. Lust was to be struggled against for the highest stakes of all: one's soul. The result was wounded, abused children who grew up hating their sexuality and possessing a cynical distrust of religion.

SPIRITUAL/SEXUAL WOUNDS

I became Catholic at the age of seventeen. I already had a tremendous sense of shame and guilt. Becoming Catholic didn't relieve me of my shame. I tried to be very pure. And then I'd fail. I'd go to confession and make a new resolution. But I'd always act out.

It started with the teaching that masturbation was a mortal sin.

My entire exploration of religious belief and theological training all indicated I was wrong and damned for what I had done.

When I was sixteen, my father insisted that I write a paper on the evil sin of masturbation.

At fifteen I was sexually abused by a priest.

The church's belief that it was sinful and shameful to talk about sex closed the door to knowledge. My minister believed that prayer and discipline would lead to control. The harder I tried the worse it got.

Feeling sexual feelings in my teens, I thought I was a sinful, awful person for having them, let alone for the relationship I had with the neighbor who exposed herself to me and teased me repeatedly. I remember being sexual with her daughter, touching and rubbing (no penetration) and then she and I praying in tears for forgiveness for our lust.

At eleven years of age, a friend began shoplifting Playboys and gave them to me. Not only were they sinful but I was damned to hell because they were stolen.

The fusion of sexual shame and religious condemnation in a child's mind leaves deep and lasting scars. One of the best metaphors for the damage was provided by Glenna, a forty-four-year-old graphic designer, who likened it to the movie *Village of the Damned.* As you read her words, remember that she speaks as an abuse victim whose compulsivity started early:

> I was raised Catholic. Catholics make a big deal about virginity, especially fifties and sixties Catholics. It was what it meant to be a Catholic girl, wear white Communion dresses and be a daughter of the Blessed Virgin Mary. I felt I had "orphaned myself" from this Blessed Mother by losing my virginity. Since I had lost it, it was my fault. In my child mind, there was no room for me in the Holy Family because of sex.
>
> By adolescence I faced a dilemma only my sex addiction could "resolve." Daily life was painful. There was a horror movie at the time called *Village of the Damned;* it featured a town taken over by space aliens who stole the souls of its captives. Zombie children walked around the streets going through empty rituals of play. I recognized myself as one of those "soul-less." My soul, if not murdered, was in critical condition and on a respirator. The only "relief" from my alienation was the occasional sexual contacts I had with adult men. I put up with degradation and shame for affection and attention. Sex, which I dreaded, was a ticket out of zombieland. And as an addict, I quickly ignored that it was also a ticket farther back into the pain.
>
> One of the worst things was that I had no clue as to why my life was bleak, why I wasn't like Hayley Mills in her movies. My guess was that I was hopelessly damned.

Spiritual and sexual wholeness prove elusive for those from the Village of the Damned. Part of recovery means decontaminating from the sexual negativity and abuse by parental and spiritual authorities. In the previous chapters, we have described the repair work necessary in order to bypass the old religious messages and move to a new spiritual path built on integrity and community. We have also detailed the fundamental reorientation toward sex that addicts must make. A fully dimensional sexuality requires one further step. Sex therapist Margo Anand defined this task as finding "a gentle and conscious way of 'bringing the spirit back to sex,' of honoring sexual union as a bridge between body and soul."

Our culture resists this task. Anand says that we have "lost the understanding that sexual energy is a physical expression of spiritual power." Despite centuries of literature testifying to the meaning and power of sex, we reduce it to a pastime. Yet we also surround couples with symbols of bonding. For sex addicts and their families, the significance of those bonds cuts the wounds deeper. If sex were in fact a meaningless gesture, much of the shame and obsession would not exist.

What are concrete ways for couples to explore the connection between the spiritual and the sexual? First, notice and comment when things happen. Return to Mark and Karen for a moment. When Karen got pregnant, they realized that conception had occurred on a special night when they were extremely connected and passionate. Standing in their kitchen, they acknowledged to each other how glad they were that the conception was on that special night and how awed they were by that fact. So part of it is maintaining awareness. Other steps include:

- Recalling sexual times together that have meaning for you.

- Expressing feelings during sexual moments when you are moved by wonder or spiritual presence.

- Using the suffering of the sexual past to give meaning to the sexual present.

- Searching your spiritual resources for support in your sexual life.

- With your partner, creating strategies for integrating spiritual and sexual intimacy.

- Identifying and removing remaining spiritual blocks to your sexuality.

- Sorting through your sexual history for experiences that have limited your spirituality.

- Talking about the importance of your partner as part of your sexual passion.

No doubt about it, this is one of intimacy's greatest challenges. To be spiritual with someone who knows you well is a great risk. To be sexually vulnerable also creates some of our greatest feelings of jeopardy. To combine the two presents a double-barreled challenge, perhaps unequaled in human intimacy.

SEXUAL RECOVERY

Recovery occurs on many different levels. Sexual recovery also is multidimensional. Note that many of the goals for sexual health are supported by the principles of recovery. Sometimes we interviewed people whose sobriety reflected more a tendency to acting in than a peaceful recovery. Characteristically their sexuality was restrained or nonexistent and their spirituality echoed the black-and-white rigidity of an earlier time. In many ways their recovery had not permitted enough healing for them to have sexual serenity.

TABLE 9-1
DIMENSIONS OF SEXUAL HEALTH AND TWELVE STEP SUPPORT

SEXUAL DIMENSION	CHARACTERISTICS REQUIRED	TWELVE STEP RECOVERY PRINCIPLES
1. **Nurturing**	Ability to nuture self and accept nurturing from others	Emphasis on self-care and self-affirmation
2. **Sensuality**	Awareness of senses—of temperature, texture, color, sound, taste, and smell	Here and now self-awareness; focus on the present, not future or past
3. **Sense of self**	Capacity to know and express desires, wants, and areas of discomfort	Development of self-knowledge and ability to take responsibility for oneself
4. **Relationship sexuality**	Ability to sustain warm and caring friendships that are not erotic with both the same and opposite sex	Basis of program is a fellowship of caring and friendship of men and women
5. **Partner sexuality**	A special intimacy with partner that is clearly erotic	Cultivation of capacity to be honest and intimate
6. **Nongenital sexuality**	The exploration of all the ways to be sexual without being genital	Priority is recovering addicts learning to ask for what they need

7. **Genital sexuality**	Ability to abandon self to passion in a temporary surrender of ego and control	Familiarity with the principles of powerlessness and letting go of control
8. **Spiritual sexuality**	Sexuality as an extension of the search for meaning and spirituality, a search shared with someone else	Emphasis on "conscious contact" with sources of meaning and one's Higher Power

Table 9-1 describes each of the eight sexual dimensions and the recovery principles that support them. We need to keep the perspective that recovery is a developmental process and takes time. Sexual health really did not start for our survey respondents until well into the third and fourth years of their recovery. Remember, recovery starts with withdrawal and addicts then typically do some work with celibacy to prepare a foundation for sexual renewal.

Withdrawal—Cessation of self-destructive sexual behavior

↓

Celibacy—Abstention from physical expressions of sexual life and a refocusing on the basics of sexuality, such as nurturing and sensuality

↓

Healthy Sexuality—Integration of lost, ignored, and new aspects of sexual life

Opportunities for sexual growth occur early in recovery, however. During celibacy, couples may focus on their nurturing and sensuality. Or a therapist may insist that a couple emerging from a celibacy period concentrate on nongenital sex for a period of time. Couples seem to do better when they see this concentrated work as an extension of their larger recovery effort. They are implementing the twelfth step of "practicing these principles" in their daily lives.

During this growth period, the addict takes on two other tasks, both of which have profound implications for a healthy sexuality. One is to face the family of origin; the other is to resolve issues relating to childhood abuse. The next chapter examines these two important tasks.

Three Years Plus: Family of Origin and Child Abuse

Cliff had put together recoveries from alcoholism and from sexual addiction. Over time he had shared with his three sisters and other family members the course of his progress. He had hopes of "bringing a halt to the addiction process in my generation by not keeping a secret." Indeed, through the ripple effect, his sharing his recovery had a profound impact on the family. He did not realize the scope of that impact until his eldest sister died. He described for us the family gathering after the funeral:

> A woman came over and chatted for a while, and she knew me but I had no idea who she was. So when she left I asked one of my other sisters who she was. She was one of my sister's best friends. Later she came back and said, "I really want to thank you." I said, "For what?" She said, "Well, about seven years ago I recognized I was having a problem with alcohol and your sister said, 'Well, Cliff has done very well. He's joined AA, so why don't you look at it.'" She also told my sister that she was having some problem with her husband. My sister said, "Well, Cliff joined a group that's concerned with sex and love addiction, you may want to find out about it." She said it changed their lives.

Two of my nieces came up and said they wanted to thank me as well. They said they were having trouble with drugs and "Mother told us you had a problem and what you'd done about it." So one of them went for therapy and the other went to the twelve steps.

Then a half brother came up and said, "You know, twenty-six years ago I turned to my wife and said, 'The surgeon general said you should stop smoking.' She said, 'Well, if you're going to stop smoking, stop drinking.' " So he said he stopped drinking and smoking.

My younger brother came down and said, "Don't fall over but I stopped drinking the first of the year and I found some guys in the shop who go to AA. I don't really like organizations but I meet with them in the shop."

A nephew said, "It's too bad Dad died before you got well. He was so worried about one of my sisters who had been married three times. Her second husband also had a sexual problem." I said, "Rob, just the fact that you sort of let us know what was going on helped." He's been sober thirteen years now.

The next generation throughout the family will have it easier because I haven't kept it a secret.

A single recovery can serve as a leaven for change in an entire family. One recovery can break rules about secrecy, can become a model for other addicts in the family, and can call attention to dysfunctional patterns. Sharing recovery with family members can have significant payoffs for the addict as well. In fact, facing family issues is one of the major tasks of this period of recovery.

A temptation exists to view childhood events as ancient history. Early in therapy families often question the use of "dredging up the past" or rousing the "sleeping dogs" that have been put to rest. The myth is that those events are over. Addicts have a different reality. Childhood scenes still have extraordinary power. For some, those events received new life because each acting out was a reenactment. Memories served as triggers for the addiction. Shame about the addiction reconnects to those memories. The rules and roles of the system that produced those childhood experiences continue, often essentially intact. Many told us that even though their behavior had stopped and they had made extraordinary changes in their lives, when they were around their families old feelings and behaviors returned as did urges to act out. Addicts must come to terms with their family of origin, the family they grew up in.

In *Facing Shame: Families in Recovery*, Merle Fossum and Marilyn Mason describe this process of change in the family as confronting an "invisible dragon." Addictions are "reservoirs of family shame" because they become "a central organizing principle" for the family as a system. Fossum and Mason indicate that "when we address addiction in a family, we open the door to the family shame. When families face their addiction crisis, they meet opportunities for fundamental growth and change. . . . When families break the rules by stopping compulsive behaviors, they find . . . the gift of intimacy."

How do addicts address this part of recovery? Breaking family of origin work down into specific tasks helps. Beyond actually sharing recovery with the family, five central tasks emerge.

1. *Add to the story.* A true appreciation of powerlessness comes with identifying the other addicts in the family. After the essential repair work is done, addicts start the detective work necessary to produce a genealogy of addiction. This task requires sufficient recovery and knowledge about addiction to break through family denial. One addict we talked to discovered his grandfather was an alcoholic by finding a collection of newspaper articles about his grandfather being drunk in public. He then found out that his aunt had been sent to a private girls' school because of her promiscuity and that her three marriages had been destroyed by compulsive affairs. Discoveries like this confirm the presence of addiction in the family, reduce the shame of the addict, and increase appreciation of addictive powerlessness.

2. *Understand the system.* Another aspect of powerlessness can unravel when recovering people comprehend the power of the family system. What roles did people play in the family? What were the rules? How did family members end up feeling shameful, especially about sex? All addicts and coaddicts have certain types of people who are problems for them. These are people who can easily push their buttons, who can make them feel angry, inadequate, or upset. These "archetype" personalities are learned in the family. The recovering person has to ask, who is like this in my family? Certain self-destructive situations repeat over and over again. The recovering person also needs to ask, how is this a re-creation of what went on in my family? Consider the addict who has always been extremely

aroused by women who are in pain and needy He learns that this arousal comes from his childhood, from his having been a surrogate spouse to his mother, who through years of loneliness and pain had turned to him for comfort. Now his inability to say no to hurting women makes sense and helps in his healing.

3. *Set boundaries.* Addicts come from families with poor boundaries. Parents and siblings are invasive, controlling, and judgmental. Recovery requires setting new boundaries, establishing what is okay and what is not okay. Recovering people will find themselves setting limits with family members like:

- Certain types of touches are not acceptable.

- Some aspects of personal life are not open to discussion.

- Judgmental and inflammatory comments will be ignored.

- Liquor will not be served to alcoholic parents in the home.

- Sexually exploitive jokes will not be tolerated.

- When visiting parents, the recovering person will stay at a hotel and not as guest in the parents' home.

- No money is loaned to relatives or friends.

- Some issues will only be discussed in the presence of a therapist.

Boundaries become the skeleton of a total restructuring of family relationships. They force new patterns of behavior and new rules about behavior. Boundaries ask for respect. The lack of them in the addict's childhood fostered shame and judgment.

4. *Finish transactions.* Addictive families avoid completing their conversations. Important feelings and facts are not communicated. Conflict is not resolved. Pain accumulates. Some things simply need to be said and finished:

- Truths about what happened in the family can be expressed.

- Wants and needs that have remained unaddressed can be described and even fulfilled.

- Amends can be made for harm that has been done.

- Pain about losses in the family can be shared.

- Secrets that cripple family functioning can be brought into the open.

- Realities about addiction can be described.

- Requirements of recovery that affect family life can be stated.

- Conflicts can be resolved so healing can begin.

- Feelings of love and care that once remained unsaid can be shared.

- Abuses can be aknowledged so that pretending stops.

Sometimes this work requires the assistance of a family therapist, who gathers all the family members together and over a period of time helps the family resolve their impasses. About 13 percent of the addicts in our study found their family too unsafe to be with. So they and others who could not work with their family members directly (as with parents who had died) found other means. Therapists can use techniques to help people work through issues with the family in absentia. The techniques often involve psychodrama and role play. Some therapists specialize in family reconstruction strategies, in which a group of people play the roles of family members. Whatever support is required, finishing with the family is a high priority.

5. *Be open to new relationships.* As more members of the family enter recovery programs and as the family changes because of therapy or the changes of its members, new relationship possibilities emerge. Fossum and Mason point out that the family must leave behind their great, overwhelming fear of intimacy. Often this starts with new coalitions and alliances among recovering family members. However, not all members of a family start recovery at the same time. Siblings, parents, and other relatives who need recovery will find their own path at their own time. Prodding will not help. Setting boundaries and completing transactions will. Change becomes an evolutionary process as new styles of relating become more common in the family.

Addicts must find stability in the roots of recovery and not look to their families of origin. Early recovery started with shame reduction, which evolved into the reparenting process we described as self-affirmation. By reducing the shame and building a primary sense of self-worth, the addict builds the foundation of family of origin work. The ripple effect can then begin.

Shame reduction—The addict diminishes the power that shame has given to the addictive cycle

↓

Affirmation—The addict integrates positive feelings of self-worth and learns to affirm from within

↓

Family of origin—The addict restructures relationships with the family by opening communication, setting boundaries, and completing transactions

Not all families experience transformation because of recovery. Most addicts, even those who made great progress, say they wished for more to happen. Some ran into such heavy denial that recovery issues tore the family apart. Even this worst possible outcome helps recovering people. For in their recovery, they no longer have to deny their own realities. They see and say their truth, for they have learned that their lives depend upon it. One of the better road maps to transforming family relationships is *The Road Less Traveled* by M. Scott Peck. He talks about how important this ruthless honesty is:

> We must always hold truth, as we can best determine it, to be more important, more vital to our self-interest than our comfort. Conversely, we must always consider our personal discomfort relatively unimportant, and indeed, even welcome it in the service of the search for truth. Mental health is an ongoing process of dedication to reality at all costs.

Peck adds an important caveat about family work. To take the position that "I am the way I am because of how my family was or because of how they abused me" is to miss the point. You are a participant. As with the addiction, you are powerless, but you have a responsibility to do something about it now. You are responsible for your behavior. Peck makes this point using the Greek story of Orestes.

Atreus, the grandfather of Orestes, challenged the gods—always a mistake for the Greeks—and as a result his whole family was cursed. His daughter Clytemnestra murdered her husband. Her son Orestes was then caught between the highest priority of the Greek code of honor, avenging his father's death, and the worst crime of the Greeks, killing his mother. In the end, he murdered his mother. His punishment was to be pursued by the Furies, frightening harpies who tormented him. Either way Orestes was bound to lose. He was powerless.

Even though the gods were willing to excuse his solution, Orestes did not duck responsibility. At his trial, he pointed out to all the gods assembled that it was he, no one else, who killed his mother. All he asked for was to be allowed to do something to get the curse lifted. The gods, moved by his integrity, gave him tasks to perform. When Orestes completed those tasks, the Furies were transformed into the Eumenides, the three sources of wisdom.

Peck comments on Orestes' nonvictim stance:

> Being an inevitable result of the original curse upon the House of Atreus, the Furies also symbolize the fact that mental illness is a family affair, created in one by one's parents and grandparents as the sins of the father are visited upon the children. But Orestes did not blame his family—his parents or his grandfather—as he well might have. Nor did he blame the gods or "fate." Instead he accepted his condition as one of his own making and undertook the effort to heal it. It was a lengthy process, just as most therapy tends to be lengthy. But as a result he was healed, and through this healing process of his own effort, the very things that had once caused him agony became the same things that brought him wisdom.

Recovering people face the same challenge. They are responsible for their addictive behavior. No one else can be held responsible. They, like Orestes, are the ones who actually did it. Having claimed that, they can confront the realities of their family of origin. They can say what is true about themselves and what is true about their families. Truly then, the demons who have pursued them can become the sources of grace and wisdom. In the family of origin, nowhere is this more true than in confronting issues of victimization.

VICTIMIZATION ISSUES

I always thought that seducing a woman ten years older was a fine first intercourse experience for a kid of thirteen. Now I understand the abuse and the cost to me in guilt and anxiety.

I see now that my parents were a team. My dad was a great enabler and should have said no to my mother. He should have stopped the abuse and gotten professional help.

When I had sex with my stepfather, I saw it as a way of taking control from my mother and I saw my stepfather as the victim. Today I believe he abused me because he was the parent.

Before recovery, all the secrets were locked up inside and I was afraid to let them out. I didn't realize all the pain I was holding inside.

Before recovery I could not remember abuse before the age of thirteen. Now I know there was physical, emotional, sexual, and verbal abuse at all ages at all times.

I just assumed I hadn't been abused. Now I know I was and that I had been passing it on.

I failed to see any abuse done to me and thought my sexual addiction was just about me. Now I know the damage—that older children as well as any adult can be abusive to a younger or less powerful person.

I thought at one time that neglect was simply a by-product of being in an eight-child family. I now know that neglect is abuse and that I lived with drug-dependent parents.

Awareness—recovery brings awareness of abuse. After the repair stage, addicts start to attack the victimization issues that have lingered as ghosts from the past. Therapists have learned that approaching childhood trauma needs to be a gradual process. They have also learned that victims need to have strong, human bonds so they can feel absolutely safe in talking about the abuse. So it is not surprising that many in our survey who were past the third year mark reported large gains in dealing with abuse. Their awareness of abuse had increased. Their support network had solidified. We often heard comments like "Three years out of treatment I became aware of the degree of abuse and the damage it caused. I finally accepted how severe the abuse was and how dysfunctional my behavior was."

In Chapter Four, we saw that sex addicts who were abused passed through a definite series of stages. We need to summarize and expand on these findings to understand the stages of development for *healing* the abuse experiences. There are five stages through which victims passed:

1. *Abuse.* Almost every addict experienced physical, sexual, and emotional abuse—both overt and covert. For many, remnants of those abusive patterns lingered well into adulthood.

2. *Early compulsive behavior.* Many addicts reported compulsive sexual behavior concurrent with or shortly after the abuse started. Reports of compulsive behavior at ages five and six were not uncommon.

3. *Repression.* The trauma of the abuse is covered over by increased tolerance, denial, disassociation, memory loss, and the medication of compulsivity. The victim loses touch with abuse events, sometimes even as they happen.

4. *Maladaptive responses.* Posttraumatic stress disorder creates maladaptive responses to stress, including dysfunction (self-destructive behavior, mental illness, abuse of others), addiction (compulsive reenactment, abuse as a trigger, medication of pain and shame), and superfunction (overachieving and compulsive working with no capacity for intimacy).

5. *Life crisis.* An event or series of events may create some sort of catastrophe or forced decision. Focus at this point is on the maladaptive behavior (in our study, the sexual addiction).

The legacy of the abuse behavior remains. Posttraumatic stress means stress reactions continue to occur long after the event. Research shows profound alterations in the neuropathways of the brain of trauma victims. These changes involve brain chemicals that are fundamental to the neurochemistry of addictions, as well as to the biochemistry of our sexuality. Taken together, a picture emerges of a series of neurochemical interactions that bring together genetic predisposition to addiction, posttraumatic stress following child abuse, and the chemistry of sexual functioning. The changes that occur are played out in the family and cultural systems, which have almost primordial power.

Victims of childhood abuse evidence many ongoing symptoms as adults, including the following behaviors:

- They tend toward all-or-nothing responses and have difficulty moderating the intensity of their responses. (We have called this acting in, acting out, and living in the extremes.)

- They reenact or relive abuse experiences. (This is seen in the acting out behaviors of sex addicts.)

- They have persistent overreactions to stress, resulting in escapist, avoidant, and numbing behaviors. (Sex addiction becomes a way to disconnect from stress.)

- They compulsively seek reexposure to circumstances connected with the trauma. (Trauma specialists call this "addiction to the trauma." We saw sex addicts repeatedly place themselves in jeopardy or in self-destructive circumstances.)

- They position themselves on one or the other end of the dependence-independence spectrum. They become dysfunctionally helpless or superfunctionally independent.

When the life crisis occurs, abuse victims are critically unprepared for that crisis. Obviously, what needs to stop first for sex addicts is the out-of-control behavior. Once recovery begins in earnest, addicts start learning new ways to cope with stress and develop the relationships necessary to do the work. This process continues through the repair stage. What then remains before total recovery can take place is fundamental healing with regard to the abuse experience itself.

The healing process, like the addiction process, has predictable stages. Each stage is associated with some emotional reaction, except for the first stage, in which the recovering person is still primarily in denial. As the recovering person learns about the role of abuse, the repression breaks, memories are reclaimed, and the recovering person feels fearful. When that fear is over-come, the secrets are shared, usually with anger. As the facts emerge, anger gives way to a period of mourning and sadness. During this time of grief, the victim develops a level of con-sciousness regarding the role abuse played in the larger story of the family. When this is acknowledged, the addict finally accepts the fact of the abuse as part of the addiction process, integrates the sadness and loss, and makes peace with it. The figure below sum-marizes this life cycle of abuse and recovery. Each stage, however, must be reviewed separately.

DENIAL

Why do victims not remember? Before age four, the hippocam-pus is not mature. The hippocampus is that part of the brain that records memories in terms of space and time. But the taxon system is functional. The taxon system is the part that registers memories

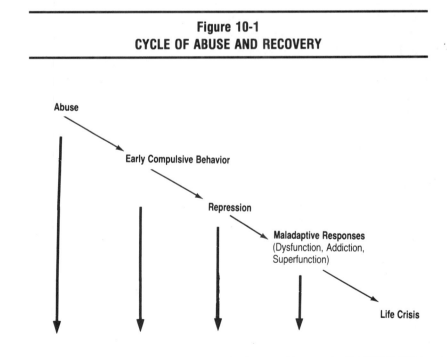

Figure 10-1
CYCLE OF ABUSE AND RECOVERY

of feelings and sounds. So victims of early abuse remember fragments but not the facts that would anchor them to time and place.
Victims therefore discount the fragments. With sobriety, however,
things become more clear. Consider this statement by Ken, a
forty-seven-year-old plant engineer from Chicago:

> I didn't consider myself an abused child until I got sober. I
> thought everyone was hit every day. I also had suppressed
> most of the memories. Since I experienced a period of
> complete sexual celibacy, I have had feeling memories of
> incest with my mother come back. I now know what
> happened with my mother is sexual abuse

Another factor is posttraumatic stress, which buries horrifying
memories. Joan, for example, put in over seventeen years in therapy before she found a therapist who diagnosed her sexual addiction
and abuse issues. Once they were diagnosed, she was flooded with
memories. She described it this way:

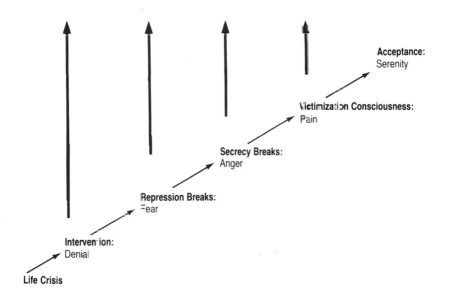

Acceptance:
Serenity

Victimization Consciousness:
Pain

Secrecy Breaks:
Anger

Repression Breaks:
Fear

Intervention:
Denial

Life Crisis

I was forty-five years old when I discovered the incest issues as part of therapy. My parents' abuse of me was so incredible—it's truly a miracle I'm alive. In recovery I can talk about it and more memories keep coming up. SLAA and my shrink saved my life.

The addiction, beyond having a numbing effect, adds its own level of denial. A major shift of perspective about childhood events occurs when addicts understand the addiction. Denny from Houston provided a good example when he told us, "I realize that what was happening with my female baby-sitter was not a form of manhood experience, but another example of sexual abuse."

Sometimes, it simply is the deceptive nature of child abuse. Consider this statement by another man from Houston, who was first abused by a female relative when he was six: "I realize now that I knew I shouldn't let her take my clothes off. Yet I liked the sexual play—she was warm, soft, and gentle. I thought she loved me and I was hungry for the physical closeness my mother was unable to give me."

Whatever the barrier, addicts must first struggle with their denial. This will be an ongoing battle. It was commonplace for addicts with many years of recovery to indicate they were still reclaiming abuse memories and putting pieces together.

FEAR

Nor does the fear go away. Fay told us, "I'm still wary of them. I'm afraid to be alone in the room with just one of them. I only became aware of that recently even though I avoided being alone with either of them for over twenty years." The fear persists as a nameless dread with many faces.

Terror stems from the fact that abuse can be horrifying. Experts on posttraumatic stress refer to this when they talk about "inescapable shock," which is at its very worst with people who were not prepared for what occurred—like children. Further, the victims fear that it can happen again.

There is also the fear about what happens if the victim names it for what it is. Will there be retaliation? Will there be disbelief? Many abused addicts remain intensely loyal to their parents because they fear hurting them or losing whatever relationship they do have.

Perhaps the worst fear that recovering people must face is this: What will it all mean if I admit this is true? The beliefs and myths that preserved a well-ordered world will crumble. What will replace it? Who will I be? What does that mean about my sexual behavior? Once the fear is confronted, though, all these changes will be perceived as a blessing. Fay told us, "I treasure the day the memories started to break through. It was the sign of an emotional healing and honesty, which was to serve me in continuing to face my sexual addiction."

ANGER

Anger helps recovering addicts to let go of the fear and break the silence. Anger gives power, commands respect, and provides dignity. The inner child can be vulnerable and open because the recovering adult protects that inner child. That child does not have to be abused. Anger must continue to be available should an attempt to abuse again occur. A reservoir of anger guarantees the integrity of new boundaries.

Yet, there is an important caveat. For all of its benefits, anger needs to be worked through like denial and fear. It should be available when you need it, but it should not be the dominating focus of recovery. Divorce provides a meaningful parallel. Following divorce, ex-partners typically feel anger at each other. Once the anger is felt and expressed, the grieving can begin. One cannot skip over the anger about the loss or about whatever damage has occurred. Each partner must then grieve and move on. Some partners fail to move on and stay stuck in the anger. Eight or nine years after divorce they are still angrily telling stories about the partner. Clinicians call this "negative intimacy." Staying in the anger keeps a connection with the old partner. Abuse victims who can only be angry also keep old abusive ghosts around. Addicts we interviewed noted this phenomenon. Fay, for example, observed:

> I have worked through the rage and resentment of the abuses I've suffered with the help of therapy. I feel sad when I see people stuck in the anger. I get upset with

therapists (often feminist therapists—and I, too, am a feminist) who encourage staying stuck in the anger. To me this is fostering "victim chauvinism."

In short, anger is the guide to a deeper pain and awareness. It is not the goal of the recovery process.

CONSCIOUSNESS AND PAIN

Robert Bly makes an astute observation about dealing with childhood abuse and neglect. "When you were young, you needed something you did not receive, and you will never receive it. And the proper attitude is mourning—not blame." Like our Greek hero Orestes, addicts at this stage learn to take responsibility for themselves. The facts of childhood cannot be changed. Further, addicts develop an awareness about how their parents and family care givers were also abused as children. What is harder for addicts to accept, however, is that they themselves also abused others. Childhood abuse experiences and their own abusive behavior together create a larger and painful picture, to which there is only one appropriate reaction: soul-felt sadness.

Following are four statements by recovering sex addicts which develop the themes of responsibility and consciousness. Note how the addicts have expanded their awareness to include their own behavior. They see an overall pattern of abuse, realizing that they lived in a system governed by abusive rules and that they themselves sometimes participated in this system.

ABUSE CONSCIOUSNESS

My understanding of the term abuse has become more subtle. At the same time that I would now label a wider range of behaviors as "abusive," I also see more clearly how I have contributed to the abusive situation. For example, since sarcastic put-downs were so integral a part of family fare, I would experience abusive comments as affectionate teasing and would elicit such abuse from boyfriends or male friends and then resent it. I've also become more attuned to my own abusive boundaries. I also see the ways I've become self-abusive. I'm less willing to tolerate abuse and at the same time I feel more understanding and empathy for the perpetrator as just another human being overwhelmed by life.

I have never seen myself as an abused person. I didn't realize I was an abuser. At least I never allowed myself to own it. At the age of fourteen, I had intercourse with my mother while she was drunk. I thought it was totally my fault that happened. I'm beginning to understand I was a victim and not a bad person. I am better able to recognize abuse today both to myself and others. For example, making a sexual joke about a woman is a form of abuse to her. Picking my nose until I bleed is abusing myself. Today I change these things with help.

I have seen that my identity as an abuser has decreased as I have become more aware of how I was abused. I have also become aware that I become abusive when I am in a situation that I don't want to be in and don't have the assertiveness or independence to (1) say so, (2) leave, or (3) change the situation. In other words, abuse is a reaction to feelings of powerlessness.

I had not considered the mutual oral sex with an older cousin to be abusive as I willingly participated. However, in retrospect, my older cousin had some responsibility for the event. It could be he was a sex addict, too. I am ashamed to say that I did the same type of things to boys six or seven years my junior when I was the age of my older cousin.

All the emotional reactions of the various stages can coexist in the addict. "Working through" does not mean that these reactions are finished. Rather they become integrated into the ongoing process of healing. Read the following statement from Bill, a sex addict from Indiana, and you will see denial, fear, anger, and consciousness as parallel reactions:

In recovery I see that physical and emotional abuse was much greater than I thought before—more incidents and much more severe. Touch and affirmative approval simply did not exist. The feeling of being unforgiven by my father was complete, as were my fear of him and fear of my anger lest I kill. In recovery I wondered if my memories were distorted and exaggerated by my secret shame and guilt from sexual aberrations. I do see more clearly that my parents suffered from abuse or neglect by their parents —perhaps worse than mine. But I also see how my rebellion made me a scapegoat and family lightning rod—getting much that I "deserved."

Notice also Bill's statement about having been the family lightning rod. Clarity about abuse further clarifies the events in the family of origin. The two are very interconnected. In fact, the same tasks necessary for family of origin work are in order for focusing on abuse issues:

- *Share the secret.* Tell people in the family who need to know what happened.

- *Add to the story.* Find out as much as possible about abuse in the family.

- *Understand the system.* Determine how the family functioned in connection with abuse events.

- *Set boundaries.* Establish limits regarding any invasive behavior that continues.

- *Finish transactions.* Resolve conflicts, make amends, and say what is necessary.

- *Be open to new relationships.* Explore new possibilities stemming from healing in the family.

- *Take responsibility.* Assess personal abusive behaviors.

The following worksheet was designed to help addicts work through the addiction and abuse issues in their family of origin. A list of books on family of origin and abuse issues is also provided.

EXERCISE 10-1
FAMILY OF ORIGIN
ADDICTION AND ABUSE WORKSHEET

This worksheet serves as an inventory to tasks you need to complete as you deal with addiction and abuse in your family. It will help you clarify and assign priorities to the work you need to do. Simply answer the questions by listing the tasks in each category. After completing the worksheet, you may feel overwhelmed. If so, go through the lists you have made and pick out five things that have high priorities. Then rank them in importance by selecting the most important of the five, the second most important, and so forth. Another strategy is to note if there are persons or issues that appear over and over again. Use them as your starting points. Be sure to share this list with your therapist and others in your support network.

	ADDICTION		ABUSE	
1. Share the secret	Do I need to share my addiction recovery with other family members? Who?	Persons: _____ _____ _____ _____	Do I need to share my abuse history with other family members? Who?	Persons: _____ _____ _____ _____
2. Add to the story	Do I need to ask about other addicts in the family? Whom shall I ask?	Persons: _____ _____ _____ _____	Do I need to ask about how I and others were abused? Whom shall I ask?	Persons: _____ _____ _____ _____
3. Understand the system	How can I learn more about how our family functioned?	Persons: _____ _____ _____	How can I learn more about the role abuse played in my family?	Persons: _____ _____ _____

4. **Set boundaries**	What boundaries on addictive behavior do I need to set?	Boundaries: ——— ——— ———	What boundaries on abusive behavior do I need to set with other family members	Boundaries: ——— ——— ———
5. **Finish transactions**	Do I still have things to say about addiction in our family? To whom? What?	Persons: ——— ——— ———	Do I still have things to say about abuse in our family? To whom? What?	Persons: ——— ——— ———
6. **Be open to new relationships**	Who can I possibly have a different relationship with?	Persons: ——— ——— ———	What patterns do I need to change in my relationships?	Patterns: ——— ——— ———
7. **Take responsibility**	What addictive behaviors of mine in the family do I need to take responsibility for?	Behaviors: ——— ——— ———	What abusive behaviors of mine in the family do I need to take responsibility for?	Behaviors: ——— ——— ———

RESOURCES FOR FAMILY OF ORIGIN AND VICTIMIZATION ISSUES

There are many resources that can help you with family of origin and abuse issues. Here are some of the best ones:

Merle A. Fossum and Marilyn J. Mason, *Facing Shame: Families in Recovery.* New York: W.W. Norton, 1986.

John Friel and Linda Friel, *Adult Children: The Secrets of Dysfunctional Families*. Pompano Beach, Florida: Health Communications, 1988.

Martha Baldwin, *Beyond Victim: You Can Overcome Childhood Abuse . . . Even Sexual Abuse!* Moore Haven, Florida: Rainbow Books, 1988.

Alice Miller, *For Your Own Good: Hidden Cruelty in Child-Rearing and the Roots of Violence*. New York: Farrar Straus Giroux, 1984.

M. Scott Peck, *The Road Less Traveled*. New York: Simon & Schuster, 1978.

John Bradshaw, *Bradshaw on: The Family*. Deerfield Beach, Florida: Health Communications, 1988.

Wendy Maltz and Beverly Holman, *Incest and Sexuality*. Lexington, Massachusetts: Lexington Books, 1987.

Pat Love, *The Emotional Incest Syndrome*. New York: Bantam, 1990.

Christine A. Courtois, *Healing the Incest Wound: Adult Survivors in Therapy* New York: W. W. Norton, 1988.

E. Sue Blume, *Secret Survivors*. New York: John Wiley, 1990.

To summarize the progression of tasks that addicts go through from the beginning of recovery, we must return to the starting point of addicts as abuse victims. As a result of posttraumatic stress and their maladaptive responses to stress, addicts are in a state of crisis. With crisis resolution in the first year of recovery, the denial cannot withstand the lessons the crisis teaches. The denial breaks.

During the repair stage, as addicts get stronger and participate in periods of celibacy, they work for balance in their life-style. They learn to moderate their all-or-nothing responses. Memories return as the repression breaks. They start to share the secrets during the growth stage. During the growth stage, as the secrets are shared, the gates to the pain are opened. Addicts' work on abuse issues happens interactively with their family of origin work. Figure 10-3 illustrates the typical sequence of events.

FIGURE 10-3
RECOVERY TASKS AND STAGES

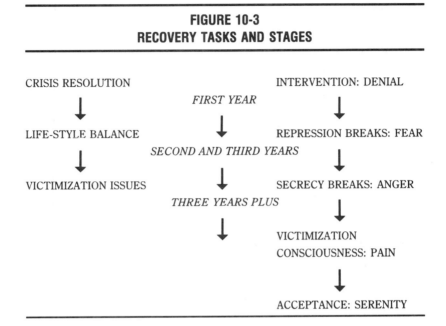

Once these tasks have been completed, the addict will have achieved the essence of the serenity prayer: "God grant me the serenity to accept the things I cannot change, the courage to change the things I can, and the wisdom to know the difference." Sex addicts cannot live their childhood over. But the legacy of fear, anger, and pain will add to their compassion as adults. It is now time to make peace with the past.

By connecting the tasks we have traced across the first five years of recovery, we can construct an image of the course of recovery. Figure 10-4 presents an additive model of recovery. It indicates the order in which sex addicts work through their tasks of recovery. The people we interviewed shared their recoveries with us, and in so doing, gave others a map of how it was done.

FIGURE 10-4
AN ADDITIVE MODEL OF RECOVERY

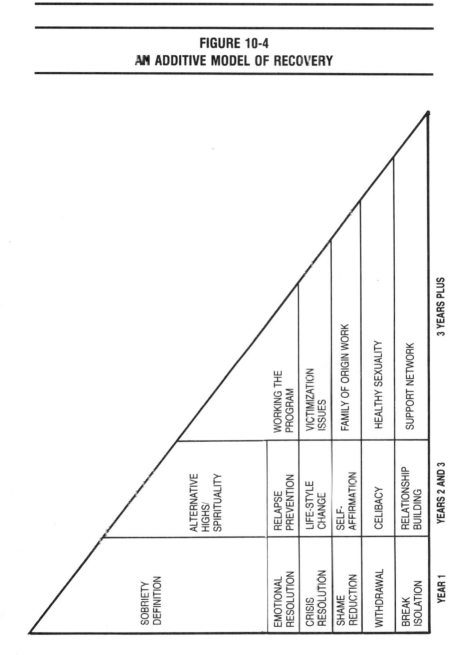

Family Renewal

The single most amazing accomplishment to me is that two people from incestuous backgrounds with chemical dependency history, both sexually dependent and codependent . . . were able to make a commitment not only to recovery but to recovery together. We are still here today and it's not codependence that's keeping this marriage together any longer. That doesn't mean it doesn't rear its ugly head, it's just not the glue anymore.

When Esther shared her accomplishment with us, we, too, were awed. How does a marriage between two people who are both alcoholics, sex addicts, and codependents repair itself while the couple raise six children in a blended family? Yet the story of Esther and Bill is not unique. We talked to many who had faced equally intimidating problems and were able to overcome them.

We also talked to codependents whose relationships did not survive. Their partners were not able to break into recovery or, in some cases, were in recovery but slipped back into old patterns. Sadly, they had to persist in their recoveries on their own, and for many it meant the loss of the relationship. The good news was the significant growth and happiness that recovery brought them.

Finally, we talked with recovering addicts whose partners refused to enter a recovery program or who could not maintain one. Again, recovery sometimes came at the cost of the relationship. Recovery is bittersweet when becoming healthy means losing a loved one.

This chapter reflects the input of the many who told us their stories. It is about those whose relationships were revitalized by recovery and those whose relationships did not survive.

The odds for a healthy relationship in our culture are not good. Note our divorce statistics. In 1920, one in seven marriages ended in divorce. In 1950, the rate was one in five, and by 1980, it jumped to one in two. Moreover, 80 percent of divorced people remarry and over 60 percent of those marriages are dissolved. Over half of our children will live in a single-parent home. Further testimony on relationship quality comes from the fact that over 30 percent of married women have been physically abused by their husbands at some point. One out of ten men will commit date rape. Thirteen percent of all homicides involve husbands killing their wives.

Such grim statistics batter our Norman Rockwell images of tranquil family life. This domestic turmoil reflects layers of addiction, abuse, and dysfunction, as well as massive social and cultural change. But these stories of recovery are a gift to us. Beyond representing models of recovery for addicts and their partners, they give hope to everyone by showing how healthy relationships can develop against all odds. Embedded in these stories are principles of healing for all relationships.

The course of recovery for coaddicts absolutely parallels that for addicts. To illustrate we have selected five coaddicts whose histories were as diverse as possible:

Macki—a twenty-nine-year-old gay man who had to give up his destructive relationship with his partner but who opened up whole new areas of growth for himself

Tony—a forty-three-year-old man whose recovery brought him to the point of divorcing his sex addict wife and back

Joanna—a coaddict in her early fifties whose recovery helped restore an impressive, trusting friendship with her husband

Maxine—a forty-year-old mother of four whose recovery meant divorce, as her husband was unable to maintain his recovery

Mary—a fifty-five-year-old woman whose marriage survived a horrendous history and moved into a powerful recovery

Although their histories varied dramatically, as coaddicts they experienced the same developmental stages of recovery we found for addicts. Table 11-1 summarizes some of their comments arranged by stage of recovery. By reviewing these comments, we can see the themes associated with each stage:

Developing stage. Despite growing awareness of the problem, denial persists, resulting at times in outrageous behavior.

Crisis/decision stage. Crisis or greater awareness leads to a commitment to change.

Shock stage. This is a period of emotional numbness, punctuated by conflict and relapse to old patterns.

Grief stage. Denial collapses and the full impact of the losses is grasped, resulting in intense pain.

Repair stage. This is an intense period of personal growth and renewal, which impacts on the relationship.

Growth. Relationship possibilities expand and learnings are integrated into daily intimacy.

The stages create a framework for how recovery works and allow individual progress to be measured.

TABLE 11-1
COADDICTS' COMMENTS ABOUT RECOVERY OVER TIME

DEVELOPMENTAL STAGE	CRISIS/DECISION STAGE	SHOCK STAGE
MACKI:		
In 1983, I knew he was in trouble. I tried to control him I felt homicidal toward him. Knowing there must be help, I called hotlines, AA, etc.	To fix him, I drove him to his SLAA meetings and waited outside. Efforts to control reached a crisis with raging arguments.	Felt numb first—and grateful for warmth and acceptance.
TONY:		
Counselor sent me to CoSA for six weeks—but I saw no need.	After six months of CoSA, I realized my extreme need to be needed, care-take, and control. I became aware of my role in our marital troubles, joined a men's group.	I fought a lot and would alternate fighting with compliance.
JOANNA:		
I was afraid the house of cards would fall apart if the truth came out. Awareness without recovery was the most awful stage.	I turned it over to God, assuming God would make me divorce him, make me grow up and stand on my own two feet.	I was relieved but confused. I still wanted to fix him.
MAXINE:		
My beliefs about divorce and holding family together kept me in there. I felt I couldn't do it alone with four kids.	In 1983, our business situation blew up and I made decision to join a twelve step group.	I felt real relief but numbness about what to do. My sponsor made me write a letter to God, turning my life over, which helped relieve the numbness.
MARY:		
I knew something was wrong, and I tried to "court" my husband back from affairs.	Reading a book on sex addiction provided the decision to change. Confronted my husband on his behavior.	My marriage was rocky. I still ignored reality.

GRIEF STAGE	REPAIR STAGE	GROWTH STAGE
MACKI:		
Uncontrollable crying, pounding my fists on the floor. Rage, dreams, my colitis went wild.	I learned to eat and sleep in healthy way and to have fun.	Now I can depend on others and relate to men nonsexually with caring. I can now share friendships with women also.
TONY:		
Pain, anger, and sadness over our separation. I actually filed for divorce.	We started talking with each other and reconciled.	I can recognize the opportunity to be codependent and can pass it up.
JOANNA:		
Pain and grief became all jumbled for me.	I said to him: "This is unacceptable." I realized I set a boundary for the first time.	I don't worry when he travels. Trust can go on now. This gives me a great sense of freedom.
MAXINE:		
I had to face that he might never change and I would have to leave. There was nothing else I could do but grieve.	I have grown so much, with positive things coming out of it.	Now I can be objective. I am able to recognize what's my problem and what is someone else's.
MARY:		
The worst hit me when I realized that he had constant multiple affairs throughout the twenty-eight years. I was angry and sad at the waste.	I began to write and to forge my own identity, and I went back to school.	These days when I feel hurt, I can identify it and work it out.

The sequence of improvements and changes differed somewhat from person to person. Generally, for coaddicts changes appear to start earlier than for addicts. The sequence of changes for coaddicts is summarized in Table 11-2. The findings must be regarded more tentatively than those for recovering addicts. Out of our total sample of addicts. 289 fit our requirements for advanced recovery—a respectable number. Because of the greater difficulty in finding coaddicts, only 99 coaddicts fit our requirements. So while consistent with our overall picture, coaddict recovery statistics will need to be validated by further research.

TABLE 11-2
COADDICTIVE RECOVERY OVER FIVE YEARS

FIRST SIX MONTHS	SECOND SIX MONTHS	SECOND AND THIRD YEARS
Other addiction relapse	*Career status	Coping with stress
Health problems	*Financial status	*Spirituality
	*Self-image	Friendship
	*Communication with partner	Healthy sexuality
	*Primary relationship	Life satisfaction

*Indicates continued improvement over measured period.

The first six months were times of intense emotional turmoil and pain, roughly paralleling what addicts experience in the second six months. It was at this point that coaddicts were most likely to have health problems. In addition, coaddicts who also had other addictions themselves were much more likely to experience relapse during this first six months.

In the second six months, coaddicts recorded gains that addicts did not see until the second year of recovery. Career, finances, and self-image improved dramatically and continued to improve over the course of the five years. Of extraordinary significance were improvements in communication with the partner and in the overall quality of the relationship. We believe that this major leap in intimacy with the addicted partners stems from the addicts finally acknowledging their own deep pain and the coaddicts starting to "let go" of control of the partner. When the addict emotionally acknowledges the problem, the coaddict is better able to relinquish the obsession and to focus on coaddictive recovery.

In the second and third years, coaddicts make gains in coping with stress, spirituality, and friendship. These gains continue and parallel the repair stage of the addict. In addition, coaddicts make progress in sexuality and overall life satisfaction. Most of the gains addicts report in the fourth and fifth years are in fact reported by coaddicts in their third.

Why do coaddicts report faster progress than addicts? There are probably several reasons. First, many coaddicts acknowledge the problem before the addict does. So they have progressed through stages of denial, crisis, and shock before the addict even starts. Second, in cases where coaddicts admit the problem after the addict, they seem to take less time to rebound. (Some, of course, never do rebound; they simply leave.) Third, once the addict commits to recovery, the coaddict's reactivity is greatly reduced.

The findings underline a major problem that the addict and coaddict must confront as a couple. The stages of progress they experience are often mismatched. The coaddict may become impatient with the addict, even though the addict is proceeding at a rate relatively similar to that of peers. Worse, some coaddicts may prematurely conclude that the relationship is not salvageable. To prevent premature or bad choices, coaddicts must first commmit to their own recovery.

COMMITTING TO RECOVERY

Most coaddicts starting recovery feel like they are running inches ahead of an avalanche of hope and despair. The possibility of a peaceful life and a nurturing relationship seems terribly remote. One coaddict told us, "I simply couldn't envision it at the start." Most cannot. The burning question for coaddicts as they face their relationship with an addict is, Should I leave? Although for some that question will have to be confronted in the course of recovery, it is usually best not confronted at the beginning. For openers, it is not in the coaddicts' interest. They need to work through their coaddictive issues so that they can recover. That happens best with their partner's support.

That addicts are supportive of their partners may run counter to stereotypes. A popular image is of the deluded sex addict being confronted by his or her distraught partner and thus coerced into getting help. Yet, as often the reverse is true. Addicts will get help but then meet resistance when they ask spouses or partners to get help for themselves—despite overwhelming evidence of need.

Esther, the mother of six whose statement started this chapter, was a classic example. Her husband went through treatment for his sex addiction and was convinced that they would never make it unless Esther went for treatment as well. He told her he was not coming home unless she went for an in-depth treatment for her coaddiction. Esther had already been through treatment for alcoholism and saw no need for further help. Yet, the ultimatum was there.

Esther was caught in a whirlwind: taking care of children, compulsive work and frenetic activities. She was absolutely committed to avoidance: "God damn it, no one's going to know what's really going on here." She was so committed to keeping up appearances and to her frenzied pace, she could not see how out of joint her life was. She noted with irony, "I mean the laundry would pile up for weeks and nobody could find anything, but there was Esther at the town hall at night looking beautiful."

When she arrived at treatment, she was "emotionless and scared at the same time." Having hit her crisis and shock stages, she became like "a machine." "That was my numbing mechanism—being like a machine, going through the motions. Underneath I was really a walking, collapsed woman. I thought that I was hopeless and that life was hopeless." Thinking about those days, she talked of how her life bounced from one extreme to another: "Everything was to excess. I really didn't know what I needed because I didn't have that fundamental frame of reference called 'I.' "

Esther had some wonderful advice for those who are just starting recovery and are experiencing shock and numbness:

> I think you have to have some appreciation and respect for how fragile your recovery is and how simultaneously critical it is to your ongoing survival—enough to accept for a while that your personal support network is going to be people in equivalent circumstances who are also working on recovery. It's too easy to get distracted by other things. A year later, a year and a half later, lots of things open up to you that aren't directly connected to recovery

work and I think if you work hard at setting that recovery framework, those are all possibilities.

As Esther suggests, the idea that things happen in stages helps provide perspective.

The question at this point is not, Should I divorce my spouse? Rather, it is, How do I start my recovery? Esther also stressed "acceptance that it might have taken years to get to the sick point before you started recovery, so things are not going to miraculously change overnight. But the best scenario is that both persons are in recovery."

Esther's sentiment was echoed by coaddicts around the country. Both persons need to enter recovery for themselves. Consider this statement by a coaddict from California: "We've had pretty good success with people putting their marriages back together or maybe starting for the first time at really having a marriage. The ones that do it are the ones where both are going to the meetings." A coaddict from Utah said the same thing in a different way: "I don't see how any marriage can make it if one person's trying to grow and get well and knows that they're sick and the other person doesn't." Addicts, too, added to the chorus, attesting to the difference recovery made in their partners:

She's learning how to get her needs met in other ways. I'm able to be more honest about my addiction.

It took the focus off me. She got support for herself.

My wife realizes she is responsible for her own recovery, peace, and happiness.

I cannot manipulate my wife anymore. She doesn't enable me as she once did. Even when we struggle, we can give each other support.

If my wife had not gotten in recovery, I would have outgrown her.

I don't believe our relationship would have survived if we weren't both in recovery. The shame, guilt, and sexual issues are just as strong with the codependent.

My partner is taking care of his own needs and asking for help, which is more than he ever did before. We can share feelings now; we talk things out instead of stuffing. He's been vulnerable with me.

My partner's recovery has made our own continued relationship possible. Without it, I would not have put myself through any more. The whole family needs education and help. They are just as sick as the addict.

He started a CoSA group and he feels supported and not alone. He knows and understands the problem. He sees how he can detach and not let his feelings be determined by mine.

Sharing twelve steps and spirituality make it easier to solve problems.

Because of recovery, we are finally really married.

Coaddicts have a right to help. A good analogy is to think of marriage as a "reincarnational" event. What you do not work out in one relationship you will have to work out in the next. Consider it sort of a marital karma. Without help the probability of ending up in another dysfunctional relationship is almost certain. The coaddict must stop running and must face the avalanche. Many will be there to help.

How do coaddicts start? They begin with the tasks of the detachment phase.

FAMILY DETACHMENT

> I hate myself for loving you
> Can't break free from the things that you do.
> I want to walk but I'll run back to you
> That's why I hate myself for loving you.

Rock artist Joan Jett's refrain to her hit song captures the fundamental shame that binds coaddicts: To repeatedly extend yourself when you know that the person will be unreliable, unfaithful, and disrespectful is self-hating. So the coaddict feels ashamed. Yet note

Jett's words: "Can't break free from the things that you do." Caught and unable to break free, the coaddict is driven by obsession and denial.

Our music is filled with such anthems. Barbara Mandrell's hit "If Loving You Is Wrong, I Don't Want to Be Right" depicts a woman pressured by family and friends to accept there is "no future with a married man." The woman acknowledges there's a problem "knowing you have a wife and two little children depending on you, too." There are also problems in how little she can get from a man with other commitments. Yet, to the end she persists in preferring to be wrong and "give my love to a married man." Equally revealing are the words from this hit by Reeba MacIntyre:

> When whoever's in New England is through with you
> And Boston finds better things to do,
> You know it's not too late because you'll always
> Have a place to come back to.

Many dismiss such lyrics as emotional dramatics about the course of true love never being smooth. Some more insightfully see them as expressions of the pain of women who "love too much." Coaddicts—men and women alike—find these lyrics painfully close to their own agony. For coaddicts are fused—emotionally enmeshed— with the addict. Their only choice is to detach.

The first phase of recovery for coaddicts concerns detachment. Coaddicts need to refocus their lives and recover themselves, the "person" who has been lost in the coaddiction. As mentioned, the temptation is to try to decide about the relationship. Co- addicts typically try to define themselves by their relationships. Their personal recovery needs to be the priority, and it is a dif- ficult and arduous journey. The formidable tasks of this stage include:

1. *Learn to love without interfering with consequences.* This means to care for another person without intervening in his or her life. Disaster at work, financial chaos, arrests—whatever happens because of the addict's behavior is the addict's problem. As part of recovery, addicts must feel the full brunt of their powerless- ness. Any efforts to protect the addict divert energy from recov- ery for the coaddict. Extend support, but not help.

2. *Acknowledging own powerlessness over obsession.* In a twelve step support group or therapy—or even better, both—coaddicts need to admit how powerless they are. They must survey all the ways they obsess about or attempt to control the addict. This includes all the ways they try to influence the addict's recovery. They must reach a point of surrender, which means committing to stop.

3. *Acknowledging consequences of coaddictive behavior.* Part of coaddicts' surrender is to fully comprehend the costs of their behavior. Accepting powerlessness is admitting what did not work. Acknowledging chaotic unmanageability due to consequences is admitting what did happen. Realizing the costs deepens the commitment to stop.

4. *Defining a coaddictive sobriety.* Clarity about personal coaddictive patterns tells the person what to stop. Addicts are not the only ones who have a sobriety. Coaddicts must also abstain from their obsessional and dysfunctional behaviors. They must be clear about what a 'slip" is for them.

These tasks actually help coaddicts concentrate and focus on their own recoveries as they work through the grief and pain of the first year.

Perhaps the hardest task of early recovery is relinquishing control. Warren's coaddictive background was filled with the typical pendulum swings of addictive relationships. His primary way of coping was control: "My most basic thing was to lock into very static definitions of the world." A career veteran of the air force, he commented, "That's why the military appealed to me for so many years." When he met Carrie, she was rapidly approaching the height of her sexual acting out. She had just had her fifth abortion. She was involved in a vicious triangle with her ex-husband and ex-pimp. She was desperate and out of control. When Warren realized what was happening, he recognized the pattern of "once again being in an impossible relationship with somebody who was vulnerable and addicted—and an opportunity to control." At that point he was himself in recovery, and he describes what it was like for him:

Walking away from that possibility of controlling, pointing Carrie to a possible source of help and leaving myself unable to control her recovery or the relationship—that was high anxiety. I think there's such a thing as a challenge offered and not taken or a challenge offered and taken. I think I took the challenge at that time to let go, to say I want to remain in the relationship but seek partnership instead of control.

Some of our participants had more struggles than Warren with letting go of their partners. Mary Lou from Indianapolis told us a story that lays out this letting-go process step by step. Mary Lou came from a background that taught her "people who had problems were bad." So she started from the assumption "that nice people didn't have problems, my family didn't have problems. My aunts and uncles had problems, but we were better than that." When she learned about her husband being sexual with their seventeen-year-old baby-sitter, she was stunned. And as more revelations came, she attempted to "pretend that it wasn't going on." She also blamed herself, partly because her husband told her it was her fault and partly because of her own shame.

When she could ignore things no longer, she became obsessed with getting him into recovery. Years later, in recovery herself, she was very clear that her obsession was a way to avoid her own issues and fears: "He was my problem. It was very obvious. If he could stop his behavior, then the problem would go away." Her inability to see it any other way affected how she treated him, how she ran her business, and how she was with friends. "I was obsessed with him. He became my obsession."

What complicated this matter further for Mary Lou was that she had been through treatment for alcohol and food addiction. Her words are extremely significant for those who are already in one recovery program but have yet to deal with their coaddiction.

In my mind I was sane and I was recovering. I was in better shape than I had ever been in my life. I had lost all this weight and I was in recovery. I didn't even realize this other level of emotional recovery. I didn't know what being obsessed with another person was all about. I functioned the way I thought was normal. I've always been crazy. I've always been ruled by what my husband said or what the neighbors said or what my parents said, so I didn't have a mind of my own or any thought of my own until I started really getting into recovery in this area. I didn't feel like anything was wrong.

The turning point came when Mary Lou started to trust her own perceptions. In her family her perceptions had always been denied. Her reality was not valid. Combine this with her total fear about what would happen to their lives if the truth came out, and it's clear there were formidable obstacles to her saying what she thought. When she finally did, the impact on Art was huge. He already knew he was in trouble, but his wife's forthrightness propelled him to treatment:

> The real crisis came when my wife said I was dishonest. That just hit me like a ton of bricks. I'd always thought of myself as honest. I didn't lie and cheat and steal. My code of conduct was so separate from sexuality that the crisis was when I realized I was dishonest. It could no longer be compartmentalized. The thing called "me" now included dishonesty. That realization made me seek help.

Although Art was now in recovery, Mary Lou was still unable to let go and detach. Art felt he was making progress by all indicators, yet his wife kept wanting more and criticizing him. Art said, "She was absolutely nuts. I wasn't making enough phone calls, I wasn't going to enough meetings. Nobody could have been perfect enough for her." Mary Lou's thinking was still rooted in seeing herself as responsible for changing him:

> I kept thinking if only I could get him to get the right sponsor or get the right meetings he would hear the recovery he needed and then he would change and then our life could be okay. Then I heard about the three truths from my counselor and my sponsor: my truth, his truth, and the truth. I just kept thinking that if I just stuck with it long enough the truth would come out and it would be mine. Everybody would say, "Mary Lou was right all along." I was like in a boat using toothpicks instead of paddles.

Mary Lou finally reached the point of giving up control. As so often occurs in life, the result was seemingly paradoxical: by letting go of the relationship she got to keep it. She told us: "Three years ago I finally surrendered and gave up trying to fix him and tell him what meetings to go to and how to get well. I just gave him up because it wasn't getting anywhere." Mary Lou's advice to newly recovering coaddicts was given in no uncertain terms: "Stop taking shit. Stop feeling guilty. You didn't cause it. You cannot cure it. The quicker you learn to care for yourself, the quicker you get well. Letting go does not mean losing."

Art said much the same from the addict's point of view: "You go through a period of blaming each other, but at some point that has to stop. Figuring out who was crazier or whose fault things are has to end. It's the beginning of getting better." A revolution occurs in the relationship when both partners acknowledge fundamentally their powerlessness. They have a new equality from which to build. In that sense of commonness, shame can be abandoned, old destructive family messages discarded, and a new bond forged. Art described what the new balance meant for him:

> It used to be if we put our grievances on the table hers would always seem so much worse that I didn't have much right to ask for what I needed. Then we reached a point where I could ask for my needs to be met. I could confront her about things that bothered me about her. I had the same power in the relationship. Early on she left me with the feeling that I was lucky she was still there. Then I started to feel respected and equal.

Mary Lou and Art experienced what professionals call differentiation. *Differentiation* was first used to describe typical stages of child development. A child learns to separate from the all-enveloping parent by going through developmental stages of being different, or apart from, until equal with that parent. All children go through that process from the terrible twos through adolescent defiance. Family and marriage researchers have long noticed that couples go through a similar developmental process. When falling in love, they are inseparable, totally focused on each other. Then each person works to separate his or her own identity from the identity as a couple. Healthy couples learn to be both paired and separate—and equal.

This is differentiation. Couples that either fail to be separate persons or fail to bond have problems. Almost all marital problems can be described in terms of some sort of imbalance between separateness and togetherness.

Shame-based couples who have experienced the boundary problems of abuse and the dysfunction of addiction have severe problems with this task of differentiation. The detachment phase of early recovery requires a heart-wrenching focus on being separate. This task is as important for individual growth as it is for relationship growth. To suggest that you must work first on your recovery is more than a helpful slogan. Without this work, nothing happens.

When all family members accept their common issues, real growth becomes possible. As noted earlier, in the second half of the first year, coaddicts already see a dramatic improvement in their relationship and their ability to communicate. Our belief is that reflects their ability to let go of control and start engaging their partner from the perspective of a common problem.

Once differentiation is firmly established, coaddicts and addicts are ready for the next phase of recovery: establishing boundaries. They face the question, After I learn how to be separate, how can I be with you and not lose myself again?

FAMILY BOUNDARIES

Preserving a hard-won sense of self is not an easy task. A coaddict named Juilee spoke of the difficulties of "having to stay focused on recovery when every fiber in my body wanted to say, 'Okay you win! I'll stop my meetings. I'll go back to who I was. I'll be me again. I'll be who you want me to be: a people-pleasing codependent.' " Juilee felt she was constantly struggling between easy choices and what she needed to do for herself. When she was separated from her husband for a period of time, Juilee met a real Mr. Right. She told us, "He promised me the moon, but I turned him down. I didn't want to mess up my recovery." Sometimes recovery demands hard choices.

Always, recovery requires taking care of yourself. And it starts with the basics. Esther talked about how she neglected the basics because of her compulsive working and her codependency. She was constantly overextended because, instead of insisting that people help her, she attempted to do it all herself. Yet the realities of a family of six children would not go away. "The laundry has to be done, the dishes have to be done, the house has to be picked up—all the fundamentals of daily existence we could never manage while we were in addiction." Essentially Esther was having to deal with the fear of setting boundaries. What would happen if she insisted other members of the family take on their share of the burden? Her description of her internal struggle underlines some important issues for coaddicts at this stage:

> I had to acknowledge that not only could I not do it all, but it was okay to not do it all. In fact, I had a right to sleep, a right to eat a meal on time, and a right to expect that other people will collectively meet the needs of the house. My recovery gave me the chance to recapture some very healthy and legitimate strengths of mine that had long been lost. I actually started to have days that were totally peaceful. I never had that before.

Esther accurately described one of the fundamental problems of coaddicts: the loss of self. She talked of herself being on "remote control," taking care of everybody else but herself. She commented, "I really was almost out of the picture except physically. There was no 'I.' Recovery meant reconnecting with myself, reclaiming my soul piece by piece." For coaddicts, as for addicts, this essential task requires repair work to gain life-style balance. Learning to affirm oneself and reduce shame helps minimize overextension and crisis. Esther did have a right to ask for the basics—and more.

Vital to the reclaiming process is a spiritual life. Conversely, vital to a spiritual life is a healthy sense of self. Coaddiction recovery brings people quickly to that reality. For Esther, developing spirituality was central to the recovery but not easy. For anyone who has struggled with a low sense of self-worth and with negative feelings about church, her words provide helpful counsel:

> Spirituality was a real hard one for me because I walked into this program something to the right of an atheist. The thing that made it possible for me to even see it as

something worth tackling was seeing what it did in other people. Developing spirituality doesn't mean clinging to a creed, belonging to a particular church, absorbing doctrine. Spirituality really is something very distinct from that and has to do with one's relationship with oneself and all around you. I realized that I was not just spiritually bankrupt, spirituality simply wasn't even in my vocabulary. It is essential to recovery, yet it is an issue for a lot of people because by the time we hit rock bottom, spiritual issues that in healthy people are nurtured have long since been abandoned whether because of fear or cynicism or the need to keep the coaddiction alive. So, ironically, it's probably the most distant thing from us and yet the most critical to recovery and health.

To accomplish this primary goal of reclaiming themselves, coaddicts must establish their essential limits, both with themselves and with family members. Boundary setting means that coaddicts must be willing to:

1. *Take responsibility for self.* Coaddicts can determine what their needs are and arrange that they be met. They can nurture themselves or ask for help from others.

2. *Have ongoing support independent of partner.* For most that means joining a fellowship such as Co-SA or S-Anon which is designed specifically for coaddicts to sex addicts. In this way they receive independent perspectives from other coaddicts who struggled with the same issues. Further, they'll have an emotional support network in place, no matter what happens to the addict.

3. *Preserve and respect differences.* Shame-based families lock into conflicts because of a need for agreement. Their belief is: If you do not agree, you are against me. Coaddicts need to abandon these power struggles. They must respect the differences of others and not sacrifice their own uniqueness.

4. *Be clear about their boundaries.* For limits to be successful, they need to be expressed and to be unambiguous. They cannot be tentative or speculative. Coaddicts must say what they want so others will not mistake what is meant.

Obviously, injecting new boundaries into a relationship will totally restructure that relationship. As the coaddict becomes more centered and the addict does necessary repair work, an opportunity to rebuild the partnership develops. If "paired and separate" is the goal for a healthy relationship, the individual partners can now start to focus on the "paired" part. Each partner comes from a position of greater strength because of their individual recoveries. They must now negotiate how they can be together—or if they can.

Again, the challenges are many. We asked recovering couples what were the biggest difficulties they as couples had to work through. Nine problems surfaced consistently. In the order of frequency of mention, these problems are:

1. Old grievances, resentments, and fights came back. Couples needed to resolve, forgive, and stop old patterns.

2. When the sexual addiction was finally arrested, other sexual issues emerged. Who initiated sex the most? What happened when desire for sex differed? What do we do about inhibited sexual desire or impotence?

3. When partners started dealing with abuse issues, some basic sexual premises in their relationship changed. Often it took a lot of time to explore new ways to be together without engaging old scripts about victimization.

4. Working out recovery commitments was hard. Couples had to learn to balance time between program involvements and relationship needs.

5. Each partner reached a moment of having to decide whether to recommit to the relationship. This moment was sometimes acknowledged, sometimes not.

6. Once sex addiction and coaddiction stopped, other compulsivities like working and spending became visible. Often these were shared by both partners.

7. Major shifts in friends occurred. A total realignment of friendships—individual and as a couple—forced major readjustments.

8. Relapses happened for some, plunging the couple back into old patterns of obsession and despair. Overcoming relapses was directly linked to how much support the couple had.

9. Building intimacy and trust was for many a "first time" experience, since deception had been present from the beginning. Therefore, being vulnerable to the other was an extraordinary risk.

Despite these problems, many couples were able to rebuild successfully. Rebuilding meant new rules and responsibilities. It required an openness to try and a willingness to bond again. Arizona physician Jennifer Schneider talks of the opportunities that exist in the challenges recovering couples have. In her book *Back from Betrayal,* she writes:

> [The recovery process] provides a wonderful opportunity for us to start over again with the same person in a relationship of increased intimacy, honesty, and communication. Working through problems together, sharing the experience of spiritual growth in a Twelve Step program, learning to communicate in the language of the recovery program, and making new friends who are also in recovery programs—all these shared experiences can create a new, powerful bond between us that might give us a better relationship than we ever had before. Moreover, we will both be in the marriage by choice and not because we need another person in order to feel whole.

How do couples do it? From our point of view, couples who succeeded were able to do four things at this stage. We'll look at each in turn.

First, they were able to *develop new rules for their relationship.* Of special importance were new rules about conflict. All couples experience conflict. Clinicians have long taught "fair fighting" as a way to stop dysfunctional arguments. Shame-based, addictive relationships are particularly vulnerable to ineffective ways of dealing with conflict, because of the blame, fault finding, and self-righteousness associated with deep shame. We observed that a veritable revolution occurred for couples who learned new, nonpunishing ways to deal with inevitable problems. We asked recovering people what they had learned about solving conflict; their responses are summarized below.

ADDICTS' BEST ADVICE NUMBER 10:
Solving Conflicts

1. *Work for win-win solutions.* Shame-based couples tend to look at all issues in terms of right and wrong and to see all conflicts as ending with a winner and a loser. Search for solutions that make each partner a winner. Seldom is there just one way to do things. Find the alternatives.

2. *Use the twelve steps.* Stop the fight and share with each other what step you need to use in connection with this problem. Use the tools your recovery gives you.

3. *Agree on times to work on problems.* Fighting when you are tired and depleted is counterproductive. Agree that it is all right to talk about the problem at another time, one acceptable to both. Have a rule about times of the day when intense issues need to be tabled.

4. *Avoid dramatic exits.* Threatening abandonment is great drama but also destructive to those whose history is filled with it. Remember, shame is about abandonment. If you need a time-out, ask for it.

5. *Focus on the issues, not on history.* Shame-based couples do not resolve things because they keep escalating the conflict by adding in other unresolved problems. Cut down on the backlog by concentrating on the current disagreement.

6. *Avoid cheap shots.* Partners know each other's vulnerabilities. Fighting is an act of trust and an invitation to intimacy. Do not sabotage it by demeaning, disrespectful, or exploitive comments. Support, do not exult, when your partner admits an error.

7. *Accept issues and feelings of others.* They are realities for the other person, even if they seem alien or unreal to you. Validating your partner's experiences will add dramatically to your ability to solve things together.

8. *When stuck, consult with others.* Therapists, trusted friends, sponsors, other couples—all can be resources. If as a couple you have no one to talk to, you do not have the resources you need. Find support for your relationship.

Second, couples who succeeded were able to *reclaim intimacy.* The majority had to come to an understanding of what intimacy was. The experience of recovery for couples shines through their definitions of intimacy. Here are selected examples:

Physically, emotionally, and spiritually sharing ourselves with each other. Maintaining comfort with ourselves, a healthy sense of ourselves as individuals.

Sharing thoughts and feelings without the other trying to "fit" into them; being supportive and listening instead. Admitting when I am afraid, and asking for love.

A nonjudging, trusting relationship between two people who accept each other for who they are, respect each other's boundaries, and love each other unconditionally.

Actively sharing my feeling reality with my wife. Being able to allow her her feelings and to offer support to her.

A feeling of connectedness where it is safe to be me; physical affection, laughing together.

Ability to share the child within me with my partner.

Open, honest communication; playing fair. Being aware of and avoiding old behaviors and manipulations. Owning my feelings and mistakes and showing respect. Allow the other person their process and give the outcome to God. Trusting that the other won't go away; being vulnerable and willing to feel without fear of being fixed or changed. Breaking no-talk rules. Being true to ourselves and each other.

Intimacy to me is shared experiences: it is holding hands, it is a kiss at certain partings and returns. It is discussing family—children and grandchildren—and problems. It is doing things for my wife that she likes and attempting to return to her some of the care and consideration she has shown for me and our daughters. It is the closeness one feels when it is possible to communicate without language—with just touches, glances, looks.

Being intimate twenty-four hours a day—not just at bedtime, like in the past. I feel close to my wife while I'm at work, traveling, or at home. I can think pleasant thoughts or just call her to hear her voice. Intimacy is caring, listening, and being there when needed. I don't have to touch my wife to feel intimate. I had no idea this was possible. Intimacy is touching her hair or a gentle hug. It is the freedom to enjoy one another without strings attached.

Couples attributed their renewed intimacy to a number of key factors. Celibacy periods were important for most and were mentioned the most often. Couples also emphasized the vital importance of each partner being strong in his or her own recovery. Reading, therapy, workshops, and conferences taught new skills—and even language to be intimate. There were many jokes about "psychobabble," "recovery talk," and "therapy speak." Yet there was no doubt about people's gratitude.

Third, couples who succeeded were able to *restore trust.* In sex addiction and coaddiction, the trust issues are extremely important. Both partners came from histories of abuse and abandonment. Infidelities and betrayals were legion. Invasive, hurtful, self-righteous, and vengeful behavior was common. Coming out of these experiences left people with a certain solemnity about our human ability to inflict our worst on those we love. Many talked about their gratitude for the special understanding of human nature and capacity for empathy they had gained through recovery. The empathy comes from having worked through such extraordinary pain and from a basic sense of integrity. Consequently, when we asked recovering people for their advice for restoring trust, their suggestions, summarized below, have a special credibility.

ADDICTS' BEST ADVICE NUMBER 11:
Restoring Trusting Relationships

---

1. *Give it a lot of time.* This was universally seen as the most important advice. Phrases like "patience," "go slow," and "a day at a time" were very common. This reflects the old Al-Anon wisdom: "nothing major the first year."

2. *Be willing to lose it in order to get it.* Both partners have to resolve not to give up parts of themselves in order to keep the other from leaving. If you can be fully who you are and your partner does not leave, you have something. Fidelity to self is the ultimate act of faithfulness to the other.

3. *Restore self first.* Do the repair work that you yourself need and your perceptions of the relationship will change dramatically. Most people's unhappiness in the relationship is about themselves and not their partner. You have to trust yourself before you can trust the other.

4. *Accept the illness in the other.* Start by acknowledging at the deepest level of yourself that you both are powerless and fully involved in the illness. It is as hard for your partner as it is for you.

5. *Admit mistakes promptly.* Avoid blame. Work for honesty and accuracy, not for proving what is right. Self-righteousness inevitably kills intimacy.

6. *Share spirituality.* Explore ways to be spiritual together that are simply for the two of you.

7. *Use the amends steps.* Reverse the blame dynamic by taking responsibility for pain you have inflicted on the other. Do what you can to make up for it. Use steps eight and nine as a model for daily living with your partner.

8. *Remember, it's never going to be perfect.* Just as the "ultimate partner" does not exist, neither does the "ultimate relationship." Accepting human limits in ourselves helps us in being generous with our loved ones.

9. *Be with other recovering couples.* Attend open meetings together. Join fellowships of couples. Go on couples' retreats. Socialize with couples. Support other couples. Have couple friends.

10. *Have fun together.* All work on recovery with no play makes for great intensity, not intimacy. Closeness comes from shared common experiences, including the fun ones. Remember, play is in its own way an act of trust.

Note that at this stage of recovery couples emphasize the importance of having other recovering couples for support. This reflects a growing realization that in all the twelve step programs, the emphasis on individual recovery can often place additional strains on relationships. One husband told us, "Besides personal support as a couple, you need couple support because the world out there is ready to tell you the price tag's out of your reach. Throw the marriage away. But if you want the marriage to work, you have to have support."

When each recovering person just goes to his or her own meetings, the result in some ways parallels what happens for people who are recently divorced. When you meet one ex-spouse and hear his or her "story" of how the divorce happened, you are outraged. Then you meet the other, and you begin to wonder if they ever lived together because the stories are so different. Their problem was, in fact, that there was no longer a common "story" or a common reality. Similarly, recovering people attend their respective fellowships—AA or Al-Anon, OA or O-Anon, GA or G-Anon, and so forth—and tell their stories. Each group is missing the perspective of the partners. Until recently there have been few places where couples could go to work the twelve steps together. Most of the people we contacted had developed such support from friends, from attending functions together, or in joint therapy.

A very promising start, however, has been made by a new fellowship called Recovering Couples Anonymous (RCA). This support group focuses exclusively on the needs of couples. A custom from this program illustrates how such an effort can foster trust and intimacy in a relationship. Early in their RCA experience, partners are asked to exchange pictures of each other taken when they were children. The goal of the exchange is to promote awareness of the vulnerable child within your partner. No more powerful metaphor exists in capturing the vulnerability necessary to restore trust.

Resources for coaddicts and couples have expanded significantly over the past few years. Some of the best of these resources are listed below.

RESOURCES FOR COADDICTION AND COUPLESHIP

Books

Jennifer P. Schneider, *Back From Betrayal*. Center City, Minnesota: Hazelden, 1987.

Jennifer P. Schneider and Burt Schneider, *Sex, Lies, and Forgiveness*. Center City, Minnesota: Hazelden, 1991.

Sherod Miller, Daniel Wackman, Elam Nunnally, and Phyllis Miller, *Connecting With Self and Others*. Littleton, Colorado: Interpersonal Communication Programs, 1988.

Mic Hunter, *The First Step*. Minneapolis, Minnesota: CompCare Publications, 1989.

David R. Mace, *Close Companions: The Marriage Enrichment Handbook.* New York: Continuum Publishing, 1982.

Fellowships

CoSA National Service Organization
P.O. Box 14537
Minneapolis, MN 55414
(612) 537-6904

Recovering Couples Anonymous (RCA)
P.O. Box 27317
Golden Valley, MN 55422
(612) 473-3752

S-ANON International Family Groups
P.O. Box 5117
Sherman Oaks, CA 91413
(818) 990-6910

Co-dependents of Sex and Love Addicts Anonymous (CO-SLAA)
P.O. Box 614
Brookline, MA 02146-9998

SCA-ANON
East:
P.O. Box 1585 Old Chelsea Station
New York NY 10011
West:
4391 Sunset Boulevard #520
Los Angeles, CA 90029

In many ways, this boundary setting period is a time to test the integrity of the system. Partners can determine if given all the changes, this relationship will make it. Much of that choice has to do with safety. Partners can ask, is it:

- safe to be honest and accurate?
- safe to have conflict?
- safe to be different?

- safe to be intimate?
- safe to commit?
- safe to be sexual?

Sometimes that safety is never achieved. In some cases the problem is slips or relapses on the part of the addict. In others, it's that one of the partners refuses to get into recovery or therapy. We also found cases where both partners entered into recovery and worked hard in therapy but ultimately determined that theirs was an ill-conceived relationship. Some relationships are simply not salvageable and should never have been. Those who could not continue with their partner nonetheless learned much that helped prepare them for a new relationship. They did not need to repeat their own history.

We also found couples who persisted in their relationship even though conditions were not improving. We heard a sad story from Stan, a forty-nine-year-old marketing director from Oregon. Through two and a half years of recovery, he has stayed committed to his relationship with his wife although she chose to do nothing about her own recovery. Here are his words:

> I went home and I told my wife that I was going into treatment. I said I had been diagnosed as a sex addict. I told her what that meant and her comment was, "Ah, that's the big family secret that everyone's been talking about." From that day forward she just has shut down. She thinks it's gross. She calls the people in the program "slime." She is having a very negative reaction to it. Until I had that label on my forehead I was okay. I had a lot of problems and I was oversexed and all of this kind of stuff but as soon as she could get a handle on a label it changed things. It just has not been a fun two years. I don't know if I will ever get that relationship back. As far as I know right now, we will live out the marriage as best we can. I don't know if she will have the ability for any kind of emotional relationship with me because she will never be able to trust me again.

While tragic and unhappy, Stan's situation supplies an important contrast with couples who were able to commit to a process of healing. They are significant pioneers in the renewal of human intimacy. Their experiences can offer hope about what is possible.

Couples who do go through the boundaries stage make a decision to stay in the relationship. They then enter the next phase—bonding—in which they recommit to each other.

FAMILY BONDING

It's strange that I am so happy and so grateful for this horrible problem because of where it has gotten us. I wouldn't wish it on anyone, but because of the work we were able to do, we are in a totally different place than we were before and I thought our marriage was good before.

This somewhat paradoxical statement comes from Joanie, a fifty-year-old principal of a junior high school. She, like all coaddicts, hit the predictable rough points, but in retrospect now sees them as gateways to her own growth. Her marriage had been filled with strife and shame. In fact, she laughed during the interview about how they used to go to restaurants to get away from the kids and talk. They would end up fighting and creating such a scene that they were too embarrassed to return. The problem was, they ran out of restaurants.

Real growth started for Joanie when her husband Larry went to an in-patient treatment facility. Joanie's therapist, Sally, who had been pushing her, increased the pressure. Joanie described one of her therapy sessions:

I would say to Sally, "This marriage is the most important thing," and she would say, "Joanie, more important than you, yourself?" I totally erased myself, and it was like I was a big zero. It was the marriage I was saving. She was real tough with me. She'd say "No, this marriage is not worth sacrificing your life." So I had to get in touch with a whole lot of things before I could begin trusting the marriage. She really forced that with me while Larry was away.

Joanie made the predictable discoveries of early recovery, including the importance of taking responsibility for herself. "Before I thought anything I'd done could not possibly compare to what he did. He was responsible for all my unhappiness. In recovery, I discovered that I contribute to my problems. I hated knowing that." The same principles learned in the detachment phase applied to the boundary phrase of recovery. Here is an example of what Joanie learned about conflict:

> In the past I always "knew" that Larry was wrong in his attitude about our son. I was the educator; I knew how it should be handled. I think I have found out that I don't know all the answers and that I need to listen to what he has to say. If it's going to work, we are together on the same side; the problem is out there and together we'll solve it. Rather than, he's going to convince me and I'm going to convince him; one of us will overpower the other. I think that in hearing what he has to say and taking it in, I realized that I need to know what he has to say. It was my pompous attitude that was the major problem.

Recovery had brought Joanie and Larry to an incredible point of integrity. Integrity, however, requires action. Now they had to face bonding.

In our study, we found the bonding phase measurably different from what preceded. Coaddicts rated the quality of their relationship meaningfully higher around the end of the third year of recovery. In fact, while all dimensions continued to improve, improvements in the relationship were remarkable: After taking a big jump in the second six months and improving steadily in the second and third years, quality of relationship increased dramatically at the end of the third year. We took that as a sign of the couple's moving to a deeper level where they could truly be both paired and separate. The testing time of the boundary period was over. The couples had sufficient integrity and safety to bond.

As researchers, we were struck by a significant sign of the recommitment process. Many of the couples went through a ceremony or ritual involving the renewal of marriage vows. There appeared to be a high need for a symbolic experience reflecting what was happening. One couple, for example, brought to a group of recovering couples flowers, gifts, and readings, shared them with their friends, and then exchanged promises of renewed fidelity.

Another sign of commitment was making the relationship a priority, especially to share more common experiences. Joanie and Larry had decided to take some time to pursue activities together. For Larry, this meant selling his business. For Joanie, this meant leaving her administrative position, which she enjoyed and where she was very loved by kids and teachers. She told us about the choice:

> Larry went through a change of career, selling his business, which was all-encompassing. I gave up my work, I left school. The idea was that we wanted to create a life where we had time to be with each other. The roller coaster we were on careerwise didn't allow for the kind of time we wanted to spend. Of course I had a total identity crisis, crying in my garden, thinking, "Who am I if I am not running a school?" But I knew I wanted to do some writing and I knew I wanted our relationship different. We wanted a more manageable life.

The deepening bond was also reflected in an improvement of the partners' sexual life. To some extent, sexual progress paralleled the deepening trust. Other factors were present as well. Couples successful in their search for sexual vitality tended to do the following things:

- They gave each other permission to be different sexually, especially about sex roles.
- They were willing to talk about differences such as levels of need or what feels good.
- They got away from the idea that intercourse is the goal of sex.
- They felt they could express sexual needs without creating obligation.
- They shared a sense of equality, especially about sexual initiative.
- They had clarity about sex as addiction/medicating versus sex as intimacy.
- They were willing to confront sexual problems and talk about them.
- They were open about desire and passion.

How did couples feel about their sexuality at this stage of recovery? Their words become a testimony to their hard work:

Both of us take care of each other's needs and our own in a trusting, loving way.

Sex with no motive, regret, or abuse.

It is a pleasure instead of a misunderstood duty.

It feels equal. It doesn't have to happen. It feels like a choice. It's an extension of our sharing. It doesn't numb, it expresses.

A sharing, nonpressured mutual respect which either can or cannot lead to sexual intercourse. That is the really changed part of the relationship. Before, everything had the hidden agenda of sex.

Gentleness, softness, caring—sex is no longer the most important part of our lovemaking. I find myself searching for adjectives to describe what goes on inside me. Sexuality is a mental, not physical, process. I am a different person. Possibly it's because I stay in balance with myself and with the relationship. When I'm in balance, my love flows without restrictions or conditions.

Note how recovery themes echo in their sexuality. Joanie had an apt way of expressing this integration of recovery into all aspects of life: "I see recovery as kind of an evolution. The more we learn and the more we apply, the more we grow." For her, sexuality was no exception. Joanie had had deep fears about her sexual attractiveness to Larry. Trust deepened to the point where she accepted the authenticity of his desire for her. But the next step was even bigger. She discovered "that I am responsible for my own sexuality, my own pleasure, and if I want to get pleasure out of this, I have to do something about it." While it is another recovery principle that works with sex, taking responsibility for yourself can have some unexpected turns. Consider this amusing anecdote about a sexual assignment from her therapist:

Sally would give us tasks to do to enhance our lovemaking and make it more erotic. I must say a lot of techniques were helpful but turned out funny. She used to say dress up or crazy or just get out of the routine. You know we've been married a really long time. So I decided I was going to dress up in a Halloween costume and I did. It was really ridiculous and it turned Larry off. He couldn't have gotten it up if he worked all day. What we learned from that is, let's just be real and let's be ourselves and that was a funny memory. We really have a wonderful sexual relationship. It's great. Trusting that and trusting the process of recovery has gotten us every place, but trying to play games and trying to push it was a disaster.

Joanie and Larry bring new depth to problems that many of us have. All of us want intimacy, sexual fulfillment, and spiritual peace. Yet they and the others in this book were gifted by having an addiction to overcome. If their journey is to be helpful to the rest of us, we need to clearly analyze and understand it.

Coaddicts experience the three phases of family recovery—detachment, boundaries, and bonding. The tasks of each phase are summarized in Figure 11-1 on the following page. In the same figure, we have shown the additive model of recovery. The figure shows us at a glance the total picture of recovery from sex addiction. We can see the interaction between personal and relationship recovery.

Many things contributed to Joanie and Larry's progress. Twelve step support certainly helped. Their hard work and trust that things would get better were indispensable. Joanie was insistent about how important their therapist was. In fact, she choked back tears when talking about Sally: "She really just has tremendous compassion. We felt really loved by her. And it really mattered."

That is what this book ultimately is about. We started with a group of people wounded by sexual addiction. We studied those who transformed that addiction into a new life. By collecting their stories, we see how even now their sexuality is part of their healing. By taking them seriously, we can be like Joanie's therapist Sally. Like her, we can be moved by compassion, and it will matter . . . if we can hear.

FIGURE 11-1
AN ADDITIVE MODEL OF RECOVERY

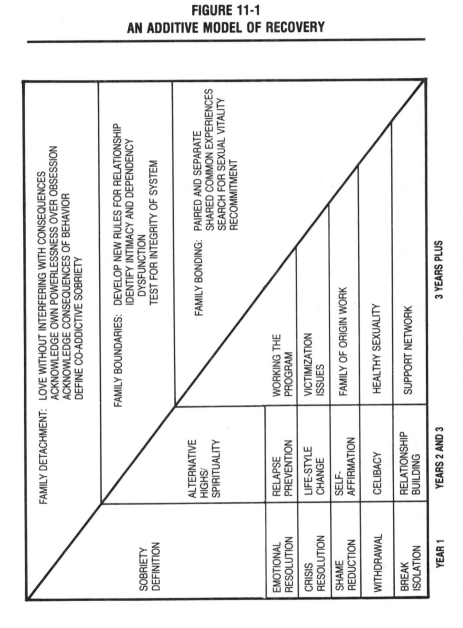

From Boundaries to Frontiers: Toward a New Culture

Whenever addicts or coaddicts set a new boundary, they are contributing to cultural change. They are literally creating for all of us a new frontier in our sexuality. They are exposing the shame of child abuse, rigid negative sexual attitudes, and sexism and sexual exploitation. Their search for a fulfilling and expressive sexual life serves to give each of us permission to be sexually more human. The old stereotypes and fears can subside. A new vision of our sexual selves can empower us all. In that sense, recovery from sex addiction is a gift to the culture.

Yet the culture continues to resist and at times is hostile to the whole concept of sexual addiction. One woman observed to us, "People admired me for my ability to have all these men. When I stopped, they thought there was something wrong with me." She added that it was a problem for them because now they "had to look at what they were doing." One man talked about recovery as culture shock: "It's a crazy paradox. When I was sick, I felt I was alone with my disease. Now that I feel great in my recovery, I feel judged by society as sick.' A common theme throughout the interviews was that our culture does not support recovery. Summarized below are typical comments addicts made about how the culture is part of the problem.

CULTURE AND SEX ADDICTION

Our culture is set up to produce addicts and then condemns them for being such.

Our culture enables and supports addiction.

There is a special and profound loneliness in an oppressive culture.

The culture does not support what it preaches about intimacy and commitment.

Our culture popularizes both addicts and coaddicts.

The culture supports the addiction. Buys it, sells it, stuffs it down your throat.

People don't see the pain; they see the glamour.

The whole culture is there to support sex and love addiction. Commercials, television, movies—all media support it. The media make promises nobody can fulfill, and the love addiction is basically the whole idea of the happy ending.

Sex addicts are misunderstood because the culture understands quantity of sex but not the fear and problems of intimacy.

In our culture, sex is used to substitute for love so much that pain of real addiction is not appreciated. It's hard to explain an addiction that's not based on a substance.

In our culture, sex addicts will help define normal because the culture is so confused about sexuality.

   People in recovery also recognize how the culture enables coaddiction. Joan, a coaddict with five years of recovery, described it as a problem of cultural stereotypes: "By traditional perceptions you look caring and loving—and that's the trap. You get support for the suffering and being a victim—not for recovery. It becomes hard to convince others that coaddicts also have a problem." Joan added that what made it worse was that "we bear the same stigma as the addict for being associated with something so 'horrible!' "
   A further irony is that prejudice exists even among those most likely to be sympathetic: people in recovery from other addictions.

Jake, a corporate attorney from the Midwest, was recovering from both alcoholism and sex addiction. He found that AA meetings were not always safe places to talk about sex addiction. On one occasion another man shared a very moving story about his sex addiction. Later people joked about the "sex fiend." Another time sex addiction came up and there was a round of jokes about sex addicts. Jake told us, 'I felt sick. I felt physically ill and I had to get out. I was deeply hurt. '

Cultural insensitivity creates three problems for sex addicts. First, it becomes harder for sex addicts to identify their own illness. In order to understand sex addiction people seize upon extreme examples so it winds up looking very different from norms in the culture. A very perceptive comment about this phenomenon came from a forty-year-old lesbian named Penny:

> It took me so long to get that I was a sex addict because my behavior seemed really minor compared to what I pictured a sex addict being. When I watched the Oprah Winfrey show it was really clear that the culture expects a sex addict to do out-of-the-ordinary things. Well, shame and devastation occurred in my life without a lot of visible stuff going on. It was big stuff for me, but on a scale of one to ten, it was a pretty low number. Yet it was like life or death. It reminds me of my arthritis. It took me years to get that I really was sick because I didn't look sick. I could pass for a normal person, just like I could pass for a "non–sex addict." I just feel grateful that I'm in recovery now.

The second problem cultural insensitivity creates is that it perpetuates stereotypes that add to the shame. Penny described, for example the difficulties confronted by lesbians. "My first concept of lesbians was very sexualized. In the culture heterosexual men promote that assumption, which appears as a common theme in pornography." The problem Penny points out is that lesbians grow up in our culture absorbing this assumption. To see lesbians as out of control not only is inaccurate but inhibits recovery. For Penny now, the important reality of recovery goes against the cultural assumptions: "It is possible to have a loving, healthy relationship between two women, and until recovery there were very few role models."

The third problem with cultural insensitivity is secrecy. Many in our survey shared the pain of leaving the secret life of an addict for another secret life, that of a recovering person. They found they could not share freely the joys and discovery of their recovery process. Shame and secrecy partly caused the problem; shame and secrecy obscure the solution. The following are some typical comments about this issue:

Society would have us be in a closet. It's worse for us than for alcoholics.

Secrecy before was to hide the behavior. Secrecy now is to survive and maintain anonymity. It still feels bad to be secretive.

Secrecy even in the organized program (SAA) creates a double bind: I need the safety of anonymity but the secrecy hurts.

It's a tightrope—I learned to talk about addiction openly in safe places like SAA but at the same time to conceal it from the larger society.

Trying to be perceived as normal is difficult, since culture judges us as permanently crazy.

Sex and love addicts are where alcoholics were fifty years ago.

Remember, "sex" and "addict" are two words very charged with shame.

I wish I could share openly with nonaddicted friends, but most people don't understand and don't know what sexual health is.

The hardest part is not being able to share this great story with anyone or give testimony to a spiritual awakening.

Some people's stories still came out despite efforts to preserve anonymity. One humorous incident, which did not have bad consequences, came to us from Tony, a fifty-nine-year-old business executive. Tony lived in a suburban neighborhood, and his daughter, who was supportive of his recovery, lived down the street. One Friday night, Tony's patio had been used for a party and his outside stereo speakers were left on. Tony described to us the events of the fateful Saturday morning that followed:

I would take tapes from therapy sessions and listen to them afterward so I could learn from them. I was behind in listening to them and so got up at 5:30 in the morning, put the tapes on my tape machine, and started listening. My daughter called me about 7:30 and said, "Dad, I don't know what you've got on the loudspeakers outside but the whole neighborhood is listening." I was broadcasting to the neighborhood my therapy tapes.

For Tony, the "broadcast" was actually quite helpful. He found the humor in the experience helped him take himself less seriously. More important, subsequent conversations with neighbors and friends had some very positive outcomes. He remarked, "I learned that sharing could be helpful."

The problem is, how do sex addicts share their stories and remain safe in a culture that fails to comprehend? The answer is to start with those who are the most safe: your family and friends.

CHANGE: FAMILY, FRIENDS, AND CULTURE

"If we see ourselves as the center of a group of family and friends, and if we are truthful, healing will ripple out and the culture will change.' This statement came from Cliff, the recovering man described in Chapter Ten whose life changes inspired so many in his family to enter recovery programs for themselves. Cliff, like many others, did not have to preach; those who were close could see the difference. Recovering addicts serve as models for change.

Our survey enabled us to see and even measure some ripple effects of recovery. We asked 277 addicts with advanced recovery to identify members of their family of origin who needed to be in recovery from addiction or coaddiction. Further, we asked them how many were in recovery already and how many had yet to start. Table 12-1 summarizes the data by categories of addictive behavior. These figures are based on perceptions and can't be objectively confirmed. But keep in mind that these are the perceptions of people with long-term recovery. The numbers raise significant questions.

TABLE 12-1
ADDICT'S PERCEPTIONS OF RECOVERY IN THEIR FAMILY OF ORIGIN

ADDICTIVE BEHAVIOR	% MEMBERS IN RECOVERY	MEMBERS IN RECOVERY	MEMBERS NOT IN RECOVERY
Anorexia	52%	9	17
Alcoholism	48%	78	164
Nicotine	43%	64	149
Bulimia	40%	8	20
Drug addiction	39%	32	82
Coaddiction	36%	72	199
Compulsive overeating	20%	23	115
Sexual addiction	16%	23	147
Compulsive gambling	13%	4	30

The table lists the addictive behaviors in order of percentage of family members in recovery. Note that some behaviors like anorexia and alcoholism show real progress, with close to half of those in need of help receiving it. Yet sex addiction lags far behind the others, along with compulsive gambling and compulsive overeating. Note, too, that other than codependency, the only behaviors to exceed sex addiction in terms of the numbers needing recovery are alcoholism (164) and nicotine (149). These differences probably reflect the reality that recovery from sex addiction is not nearly as prevalent as recovery from alcoholism. The encouraging part is that there is progress. Inroads are being made into our cultural denial. In the families of recovering sex addicts, progress is being made across *all* the addictive disorders. When people find recovery, it spreads in the family. As Cliff suggests, the ripple effect will impact the culture. One coaddict told us, "All of our close friends and relatives know about our recovery and respect it."

For the present there are strategies for surviving within an unresponsive culture. We asked recovering people for their coping strategies. Their responses included the following:

I moderate my attitude toward others while maintaining integrity.

I keep the outside shame (society's shame) from coming in. My own shame is enough.

I don't support the sex industry (porn, etc.) and am sensitive to sexually exploitative materials.

I educated my therapist and he started a group.

I am active in the women's movement to help change the culture.

Our own reflection and process becomes an antidote to popular culture.

I believe there is hope, that I can live my recovery, talk about it, and break the shame.

I search out the ways love exists in our culture.

I ignore inappropriate jokes, media, and songs which misportray sexual abuse and addiction.

I am able now to "live in the world" by taking good care of myself.

We can support sex addicts in their quest for change. We can reduce the stigma attached to sex addiction, encourage recovery programs, and educate others about its importance. Research, legislation, and treatment efforts can reflect the fact that multiple addictions are common both in families and in individuals. We can acknowledge the reality of coaddicted family members by developing further resources for them. We can support efforts to address these issues in minority and disadvantaged populations. We can confront sexual prejudice and oppression such as sexism, sexual harassment, sexual exploitation, and homophobia. We can expand our efforts to prevent sexual violence and to treat perpetrators humanely, firmly, and with safety.

Most important, we can teach our children about sex so that it is not secret or forbidden. We can assist parents in helping their offspring through the turmoil we call adolescence. We must confront the abuse of children and the exploitation of vulnerable adults. Above all, adults need to become sexually healthy so that they can model sexual health for their children.

Technological and other changes have brought us to a critical point. Communications, politics, and ecology teach us every day how events in one part of the world affect the other parts. We are developing a profound sense of how interconnected we all are. This awareness of our interdependence requires that we change how we relate to one another at our most basic level: our sexuality. The old willful, exploitative patterns based on power and force will destroy us. New patterns of mutuality, respect, and collaboration will preserve us.

As has happened before in our history, our most wounded people become our teachers. Sex addicts have much to teach us about the sexual challenges we face. They know the impact of force and exploitation, rigidity and prejudice, disconnection and abandonment. Therein lie the dignity and importance of the stories we have told. May our culture match in action the clarity of their message.

N O T E S

CHAPTER 1

page 23 Lawrence Sanders, *The Seduction of Peter S.* (New York: Putnam, 1983).

pages 30–31 Harvey B. Milkman and Stanley Sunderwirth, *Craving for Ecstasy: The Consciousness and Chemistry of Escape* (Lexington, MA: Lexington Books, 1986), p. 45.

page 31 Dorothy Tennov, *Love and Limerance: The Experience of Being in Love* (New York: Stein & Day, 1979).

page 31 Michael R. Liebowitz, *The Chemistry of Love* (Boston: Little, Brown, 1983). An excellent review article by Ron Rosenbaum, "The Chemistry of Love," appeared in *Esquire*, vol. 101, n. 6 (June 1984), pp. 100-110.

page 32 Marvin Zuckerman, *Sensation Seeking: Beyond the Optimal Level of Arousal* (Hillsdale, NJ: Lawrence Erlbaum, 1983).

pages 34–35 Nan Robertson, *Getting Better: Inside Alcoholics Anonymous* (New York: Morrow, 1988), p. 36.

pages 35–36 James T. Brous, "Sex and Love Addiction—Myth or Reality?" forthcoming article.

CHAPTER 2

page 52 Elizabeth B. Connell, "AIDS: The Pattern Is Changing," *Medical and Health Annual* (Chicago: Encyclopaedia Britannica, 1989), p. 52.

page 60 Patrick J. Carnes, *Contrary to Love: Helping the Sexual Addict* (Minneapolis: CompCare, 1989), p. 209.

page 66 Anne L. Horton et al. (eds.), *The Incest Perpetrator: A Family Member No One Wants to Treat* (Newbury Park, CA: Sage, 1990).

CHAPTER 3

page 95 John Bradshaw, *Healing the Shame That Binds You* (Deerfield Beach, FL: Health Communications, 1988), p. 12.

page 97 David H. Olson, Hamilton I. McBubbin, et al., *Families: What Makes Them Work* (Newbury Park, CA: Sage, 1983).

page 100 Gershen Kaufman, *Shame: The Power of Caring* (Cambridge, MA: Schenkman Books, 1980), p. 119.

page 104 Merle A. Fossum and Marilyn J. Mason, *Facing Shame: Families in Recovery* (New York: Norton, 1986), pp. 105–122.

CHAPTER 4

page 107 Brenda A. Miller et al. "The Role of Childhood Sexual Abuse in the Development of Alcoholism in Women," *Violence and Victims,* vol. 2, no. 3 (1987), pp. 157–171.

page 107 Damasis J. Rohsenhow, Richard Corbett, and Donald Devine, "Molested as Children: A Hidden Contribution to Substance Abuse?" *Journal of Substance Abuse Treatment* 5 (1988): 13–18.

page 107 Mark I. Singer, Marcia K. Petchers, and David Hussey, "The Relationship between Sexual Abuse and Substance Abuse among Psychiatrically Hospitalized Adolescents," *Child Abuse and Neglect* vol. 13, no. 3 (Fall 1989), pp. 319–325.

page 107 Marsha Runtz and John Briere, "Adolescent Acting Out and Childhood History of Sexual Abuse," *Journal of Interpersonal Violence* 1 (1986): 326–334.

page 108 Patrick J. Carnes, *Contrary to Love: Helping the Sexual Addict* (Minneapolis: CompCare, 1989), p. 125.

page 111 One of the best summaries of all of these definitional issues can be found in Jeffrey J. Haugaard and N. Dicken Reprecci, *The Sexual Abuse of Children* (San Francisco: Jossey-Bass, 1988).

page 112 A matrix was developed of twenty-six perpetrators and forty-eight behaviors. The richness and the significance of this data requires thorough reporting in the scholarly literature. Only highlights are underlined here, in keeping with the larger mission of this book.

page 113 For a summary of incidence data, see Haugaard and Reprecci, *The Sexual Abuse of Children.*

page 118 David Calof, "Adult Survivors of Incest and Child Abuse, Part One: The Family Inside the Adult Child," *Family Therapy Today* 3 (September 1988): 1–5.

page 122 James W. Prescott, "Body Pleasure and the Origins of Violence," *The Futurist,* vol. 9, no. 2 (April 1975), pp. 64–74.

page 125 See Patrick J. Carnes, "Sexual Addiction," in Anne L. Horton et al. (eds.), *The Incest Perpetrator: A Family Member No One Wants to Treat* (Newbury Park, CA: Sage, 1990), pp. 126–143.

page 129 Professionals will note the multiple regression analysis yielded significance values of $P < .0001$ for sexual abuse and $P < .0002$ for physical abuse.

CHAPTER 5

page 169 Michael F. Shaughnessy, "A Book Review of Three Contemporary Popular Psychology Books: *Men Who Hate Women and the Women Who Love Them; Men Who Can't Love;* and *Women Men Love, Women Men Leave.*" *Journal of Polymorphous Perversity,* vol. 5, no. 2 (1988), p. 23.

pages 169–170 Anne Wilson Schaef, *Escape from Intimacy* (San Francisco: Harper & Row, 1989), pp. 47, 107.

CHAPTER 6

pages 183–184 Tom Wolfe, *The Bonfire of the Vanities* (New York: Farrar, Straus, Giroux, 1987), pp. 12, 54.

CHAPTER 7

page 223 *Sex and Love Addicts Anonymous* (Boston: Augustine Fellowship, Sex and Love Addicts Anonymous, Fellowship Wide Services, 1986), pp. 103, 105.

page 224 See Arnold M. Washton, "Cocaine Abuse and Compulsive Sexuality," *Medical Aspects of Human Sexuality* 23 (December 1989): 32–39.

page 233 Key books for reducing shame are: John Bradshaw, *Healing the Shame That Binds You* (Deerfield Beach, FL: Health Communications, 1988); and Merle A. Fossum and Marilyn J. Mason, *Facing Shame: Families in Recovery* (New York: Norton, 1986). Both are excellent guides for recovering people. Gershen Kaufman's, *The Psychology of Shame* (New York: Springer, 1989) is excellent but written for the professional.

page 235 A process for sorting out feelings organized as a fifth step can be found in Patrick J. Carnes, *A Gentle Path Through the Twelve Steps* (Minneapolis: CompCare, 1989).

CHAPTER 8

page 259 *Alcoholics Anonymous* (New York: Alcoholics Anonymous World Services, 1976), p. 83.

page 287 G. Allen Marlatt, *Relapse Prevention* (New York: Guilford Press, 1985).

page 288 Raymond Flannery, "The Stress Resistant Person," *Harvard Medical School Health Letter,* vol. 14, no. 4 (February 1989), pp. 5–7.

pages 294–295 "The Bill W./Carl Jung Letters," *Grapevine* (January 1963).

CHAPTER 9

page 306 William A. Masters, Virginia E. Johnson, and Robert C. Kolodny, *Sex and Human Loving* (Boston: Little, Brown, 1982).

page 325 Margo Anand, *The Art of Sexual Ecstasy: The Path of Sacred Sexuality for Western Lovers* (Los Angeles: Jeremy P. Tarcher, 1989), p. 31.

CHAPTER 10

page 330 Merle A. Fossum and Marilyn J. Mason, *Facing Shame: Families in Recovery* (New York: Norton, 1986), p. 123.

pages 333, 334 M. Scott Peck, *The Road Less Traveled* (New York: Simon & Schuster, 1978), pp. 51, 295.

page 342 Robert Bly with Bill Moyers, *A Gathering of Men* (New York: Journal Graphics, 1990), p. 12.

page 342 For a study of characteristics of abusing versus nonabusing sex addicts, see Patrick J. Carnes, "Sexual Addiction," in Anne L. Horton et al. (eds.), *The Incest Perpetrator: A Family Member No One Wants to Treat* (Newbury Park, CA: Sage, 1990), pp. 126–143.

CHAPTER 11

page 369 Jennifer P. Schneider, *Back from Betrayal: Recovering from His Affairs* (San Francisco: Harper & Row, 1988).

Self-Assessment Surveys

1. AN INVENTORY OF PROBLEM SEXUAL BEHAVIORS, FEELINGS, AND THOUGHTS

We modified the original survey to allow you to reflect on your own sexual experiences and compare them with the experiences of sex addicts. The inventory is composed of a list of sexual behaviors, feelings, and thoughts. Please read each statement. Circle the number to indicate the frequency (how often) of that behavior, thought, or feeling. If you have no experience corresponding to the statement, simply leave blank. By completing the inventory, you will then have a profile of the sexual behavior in your life.

Frequency
1. one time
2. seldom
3. periodically
4. often
5. very often

BEHAVIOR, FEELING, OR THOUGHT

BEHAVIOR RELATED TO PREOCCUPATION, FANTASY, AND RITUALIZATION:

Behavior related to preoccupation, fantasy, and ritualization: *Circle one:*

1. Thinking or obsessing about sex   1 2 3 4 5
2. Fantasizing about past or future sexual experiences   1 2 3 4 5
3. Spending a large amount of time preparing for a
   sexual episode (e.g., making up yourself, listening
   to music that energizes "the addict")   1 2 3 4 5
4. Neglecting responsibilities and commitments (e.g.,
   work, family, health) in order to prepare for your
   next sexual episode   1 2 3 4 5
5. Thinking that sex is love   1 2 3 4 5
6. Thinking that your "special" sexual needs make you
   different from others   1 2 3 4 5
7. Thinking that next time things will be different (e.g.,
   "I'll find the right lover next time.")   1 2 3 4 5
8. Thinking that if you are sexual with someone, you
   will have them in your power   1 2 3 4 5
9. Feeling a need to be sexual in order to feel good
   about yourself   1 2 3 4 5
10. Denying or suppressing your sexuality and sexual
    feelings for periods of time   1 2 3 4 5
11. Dramatizing a particular role (e.g., the "virgin," the
    "hurt little boy," the "intellect") as part of your
    ritualizing behavior   1 2 3 4 5
12. Rationalizing or denying consequences of your sex-
    ual addiction (e.g., "Everyone is sexual," "I just
    need a little more than others need.")   1 2 3 4 5
13. Thinking deluded thoughts (e.g., "Women just need
    to be warmed up," "I only masturbate to fall asleep.")   1 2 3 4 5
14. Having sex even though you don't really want to or
    feel like it   1 2 3 4 5
15. Feeling that you have to follow through with sex,
    because you successfully hooked someone through
    your ritual (e.g., suggestive flirting, creating a sex-
    ualized atmosphere)   1 2 3 4 5
16. Feeling depressed, hopeless, or unworthy following
    a sexual encounter   1 2 3 4 5
17. Feeling desperate or anxious ("white knuckling")
    between periods of sexual acting out   1 2 3 4 5

18. Maintaining an open calendar and failing to make commitments because you fear missing an opportunity to be sexual   1 2 3 4 5
19. Using sex as a means to find love   1 2 3 4 5
20. Other behavior related to preoccupation, fantasy, or ritualization, specify_____   1 2 3 4 5

BEHAVIOR RELATED TO MASTURBATION:

21. Masturbating yourself   1 2 3 4 5
22. Masturbating a sexual partner   1 2 3 4 5
23. Masturbating with objects   1 2 3 4 5
24. Masturbating to the point of physical injury or infection   1 2 3 4 5
25. Masturbating in cars   1 2 3 4 5
26. Masturbating in public places such as movie theaters, tanning salons, or store dressing rooms   1 2 3 4 5
27. Masturbating with mechanical or electrical devices   1 2 3 4 5
28. Other behavior related to masturbation, specify___   1 2 3 4 5

BEHAVIOR RELATED TO PORNOGRAPHY (SEXUAL EXPLOITATION OR SEXUALIZATION OF PEOPLE):

29. Looking at sexually explicit magazines   1 2 3 4 5
30. Keeping sexually explicit material or magazines at home or work   1 2 3 4 5
31. Watching sexually explicit videotapes   1 2 3 4 5
32. Making sexually explicit videotapes   1 2 3 4 5
33. Taking sexually explicit photographs   1 2 3 4 5
34. Patronizing adult book stores   1 2 3 4 5
35. Watching or looking at child pornography   1 2 3 4 5
36. Watching strip or peep shows   1 2 3 4 5
37. Sexualizing people or materials (e.g., advertisements, catalogues) that are not sexually explicit   1 2 3 4 5
38. Looking for sexually suggestive moments on TV or in films   1 2 3 4 5
39. Maintaining a "collection" of pornographic materials   1 2 3 4 5
40. Other behavior related to pornography, specify___   1 2 3 4 5

BEHAVIOR RELATED TO BUYING OR SELLING SEX:

41. Patronizing saunas, massage parlors, or rap lounges   1 2 3 4 5
42. Paying someone for sexual activity   1 2 3 4 5
43. Participation in phone sexual activity   1 2 3 4 5

44. Receiving money in exchange for sexual activity   1 2 3 4 5
45. Receiving drugs in exchange for sexual activity   1 2 3 4 5
46. Pimping others for sexual activity   1 2 3 4 5
47. Using an escort or phone service   1 2 3 4 5
48. Spending money on someone in order to have sex   1 2 3 4 5
49. Being sexual because someone spent money on you   1 2 3 4 5
50. Other behavior related to buying or selling sex,
    specify_____   1 2 3 4 5

BEHAVIOR RELATED TO SEX PARTNERS:

51. Having many relationships at the same time   1 2 3 4 5
52. Having successive relationships one right after another 1 2 3 4 5
53. Having one-night stands   1 2 3 4 5
54. Having affairs outside your primary relationship   1 2 3 4 5
55. Engaging in sex with anonymous partners   1 2 3 4 5
56. Swapping partners   1 2 3 4 5
57. Urging your partner to have sex with persons out-
    side your relationship   1 2 3 4 5
58. Using sexual seduction to gain power over another
    person   1 2 3 4 5
59. Participating in group sex   1 2 3 4 5
60. Hustling in singles clubs, bars, or health clubs   1 2 3 4 5
61. Cruising beaches, parks, parking lots, or baths   1 2 3 4 5
62. Belonging to a nudist club to find sex partners   1 2 3 4 5
63. Using the personal columns to find sex partners   1 2 3 4 5
64. Engaging in sexual activity outside your sexual ori-
    entation in pursuit of a new sexual high   1 2 3 4 5
65. Placing and answering ads in swinger magazines   1 2 3 4 5
66. Other behavior related to sex partners, specify___   1 2 3 4 5

BEHAVIOR RELATED TO EXHIBITIONISM (EXPOSING BODY OR BODY PARTS IN PUBLIC FOR SEXUAL PURPOSES):

67. Exposing yourself from a car   1 2 3 4 5
68. Exposing yourself from stage or for hire   1 2 3 4 5
69. Exposing yourself in public places, such as parks,
    streets, school yards, etc.   1 2 3 4 5
70. Exposing yourself from your home   1 2 3 4 5
71. Exposing yourself for home videos or photographs   1 2 3 4 5
72. Exposing yourself through your choice of clothing   1 2 3 4 5
73. Exposing yourself by being sexual or dressing/
    undressing in public or semi-public places   1 2 3 4 5

74. Exposing yourself in showers, locker rooms, or public rest rooms   1 2 3 4 5
75. Other behavior related to exhibitionism, specify___   1 2 3 4 5

BEHAVIOR RELATED TO VOYEURISM (SECRETLY OBSERVING OTHERS FOR YOUR SEXUAL PURPOSES):

76. Watching people through windows of their houses or apartments   1 2 3 4 5
77. Using binoculars or telescopes to watch people   1 2 3 4 5
78. Hiding in secret places (e.g., closets, under beds) in order to watch or listen to people   1 2 3 4 5
79. Asking strangers or acquaintances inappropriate personal details about their sex lives   1 2 3 4 5
80. Sexualizing others that you observe in public places (e.g., shopping malls, restaurants, or office buildings)   1 2 3 4 5
81. Sexualizing others in health clubs, locker rooms, rest rooms, or showers   1 2 3 4 5
82. Other behavior related to voyeurism, specify___   1 2 3 4 5

BEHAVIOR RELATED TO INAPPROPRIATE LIBERTIES:

83. Touching or fondling other people inappropriately   1 2 3 4 5
84. Telling sexually explicit stories or using sexually explicit language at inappropriate times or places (e.g., at work, with children present)   1 2 3 4 5
85. Bringing sex or sexualized humor into your conversations   1 2 3 4 5
86. Using flirtatious or seductive behavior to gain attention of others   1 2 3 4 5
87. Making inappropriate sexual phone calls   1 2 3 4 5
88. Making inappropriate sexual advances or gestures toward other persons   1 2 3 4 5
89. Touching people but acting as if it were an accident   1 2 3 4 5
90. Other behavior related to inappropriate liberties specify___   1 2 3 4 5

BEHAVIOR RELATED TO VICTIMIZATION (USING FORCE OR THREATS):

91. Forcing sexual activity on a child outside your family   1 2 3 4 5
92. Forcing sexual activity on your spouse or partner   1 2 3 4 5

93. Forcing sexual activity on a member of your family (e.g., brother, sister, daughter, nephew) 1 2 3 4 5
94. Forcing sexual activity on a person whom you know (e.g., acqaintance, friend, or other unrelated adult) 1 2 3 4 5
95. Forcing sexual activity on a person whom you do **not** know 1 2 3 4 5
96. Engaging in sexual activity with a consenting minor 1 2 3 4 5
97. Exposing children to your sexual activities (e.g., engaging in sexual activity with open doors, inappropriate nudity) 1 2 3 4 5
98. Sharing inappropriate sexual information with children 1 2 3 4 5
99. Willingly giving up power or acting out the victim role in your sexual activity 1 2 3 4 5
100. Using a power position to exploit or be sexual with another person (e.g., clergy to parishioner, therapist to client, employer to employee) 1 2 3 4 5
101. Administering drugs to another person in order to force sexual activity 1 2 3 4 5
102. Using alcohol to take sexual advantage 1 2 3 4 5
103. Other behavior related to victimization, specify___ 1 2 3 4 5

OTHER SEXUAL BEHAVIOR:

104. Crossdressing (identifying with your gender, but dressing in the clothes of the other gender) 1 2 3 4 5
105. Dressing and behaving like the other gender with a psychological preference to be the other gender 1 2 3 4 5
106. Using sexual aids to enhance your sexual experience (e.g., vibrators, artificial vaginas) 1 2 3 4 5
107. Engaging in sexual activity with animals 1 2 3 4 5
108. Using drugs to enhance your sexual experience 1 2 3 4 5
109. Receiving physical harm or pain during your sexual activity to intensify your sexual pleasure 1 2 3 4 5
110. Causing physical harm or pain to your sex partner during sexual activity to intensify your sexual pleasure 1 2 3 4 5
111. Paying for sexually explicit phone calls (e.g., Dial-a-Porn) 1 2 3 4 5
112. Seeking humiliating or degrading experiences as part of sex 1 2 3 4 5
113. Other behavior, feeling, or thought, specify___ 1 2 3 4 5

2. ABUSE SURVEY

Many people who are in recovery for sexual addiction report that they have been victims of some form of abuse. In this survey you are asked to think about any time(s) in your life that you have been a victim of emotional, physical, or sexual abuse.

Read each form of abuse. For each form of abuse you have been a victim of, indicate your age(s) when the abuse occurred. Next indicate overall frequency of the abuse using the following scale: 1 = one time; 2 = seldom; 3 = periodically; 4 = often; and 5 = very often. Then, in the final column, indicate the relationship of the abuser(s) to you (e.g., father, sister, stepmother, spouse/partner, aunt, minister, therapist, stranger, adult neighbor).

FORM OF ABUSE	AGE	FREQUENCY	ABUSING PERSON(S)
Sexual Abuse:			
Example: Flirtatious and suggestive language	6, 12–17	4	stranger, adult neighbor
____ 1. Flirtatious and suggestive language	_____	___	_____
____ 2. Propositioning	_____	___	_____
____ 3. Inappropriate holding, kissing	_____	___	_____
____ 4. Sexual fondling	_____	___	_____
____ 5. Masturbation	_____	___	_____
____ 6. Oral sex	_____	___	_____
____ 7. Forced sexual activity	_____	___	_____
____ 8. Household voyeurism (inappropriate household nudity, etc.)	_____	___	_____

_____ 9. Sexual hugs   _____   ___   _____

_____10. Jokes about your body   _____   ___   _____

_____11. Use of sexualizing
language   _____   ___   _____

_____12. Penetration with objects _____   ___   _____

_____13. Bestiality (forced sex
with animals)   _____   ___   _____

_____14. Criticism of your physical
or sexual development _____   ___   _____

_____15. Other's preoccupation
with your sexual
development   _____   ___   _____

_____16. Other forms of sexual
abuse, specify   _____   ___   _____

_____

Physical Abuse:

Example: Shoving	8, 18–30	5	mother, stepfather, spouse

_____17. Shoving   _____   ___   _____

_____18. Slapping or hitting   _____   ___   _____

_____19. Scratches or bruises   _____   ___   _____

_____20. Burns   _____   ___   _____

_____21. Cuts or wounds   _____   ___   _____

_____22. Broken bones or
fractures   _____   ___   _____

_____ 23. Damage to internal
organs   _____ ___ _____

_____ 24. Permanent injury   _____ ___ _____

_____ 25. Beatings or whippings _____ ___ _____

_____ 26. Inadequate medical
attention   _____ ___ _____

_____ 27. Pulling and grabbing
hair, ears, etc.   _____ ___ _____

_____ 28. Inadequate food or
nutrition   _____ ___ _____

_____ 29. Other forms of physical
abuse, specify   _____ ___ _____

_____

Emotional Abuse:

Example: Neglect   2–6, 15   3   grandparent, father

_____30. Neglect (i.e., significant
persons are emotionally
unavailable; inadequate
emotional or physical
care)   _____ ___ _____

_____ 31. Harassment or malicious
tricks   _____ ___ _____

_____ 32. Being screamed or
shouted at   _____ ___ _____

_____ 33. Unfair punishments   _____ ___ _____

_____ 34. Cruel or degrading
tasks   _____ ___ _____

_____ 35. Cruel confinement
(e.g. locked in closet,
excessive long-term
grounding)   _____ ___ _____

_____ 36. Abandonment (e.g., lack
of supervision, lack of
security, being left or
deserted)   _____   ____   _____

_____ 37. Touch deprivation   _____   ____   _____

_____ 38. Overly strict dress
codes   _____   ____   _____

_____ 39. No privacy   _____   ____   _____

_____40. Having to hide injuries or
wounds from others   _____   ____   _____

_____ 41. Forced to keep secrets _____   ____   _____

_____ 42. Having to take on adult
responsibilities as a
child   _____   ____   _____

_____ 43. Having to watch beating
of other family members_____   ____   _____

_____ 44. Being caught in the
middle of parents' fights _____   ____   _____

_____ 45. Being blamed for family
problems   _____   ____   _____

_____ 46. Other forms of emotional
abuse, specify   _____   ____   _____

_____

POSTTRAUMATIC STRESS SYNDROME FROM CHILD ABUSE

Reflecting on your life, record any examples you can of posttraumatic stress you have experienced.

1. **Disassociation:** Disembodied, unmoved detachment; search for escape; susceptible to trance; multiple personality disorder

_____

_____

_____

2. **Flashback:** Distortion of past, present, future

_____

_____

_____

3. **Confusion:** Inability to respond to parallel situations

_____

_____

_____

4. **Displaced anxiety:** Insomnia, nervousness, unexplained irritability

_____

_____

_____

5. Exaggerated distrust: Feeling that love means being used

_____

_____

_____

6. Fusion of sex with associated emotions: Sex fused with nurturing, fear, loneliness, vulnerability

_____

_____

_____

7. Tolerance for pain: Ignoring needs, seeking pain

_____

_____

_____

8. Perfectionism: Need to be adult, grown-up, fully competent, never making mistakes

_____

_____

_____

9. Dependency avoidance: Don't ask for help, don't get involved or trust love, don't need anybody

_____

_____

_____

10. Shame: Feeling unworthy, unlovable, immoral, sinful

_____

_____

_____

3. COADDICTIVE INVENTORY

Forty statements that coaddicts said were true about themselves were selected from our survey to make the Coaddictive Inventory. You can compare your experience with their experience by reading through the list of statements and marking each item true or false. When you have finished, total the number you marked as true about yourself. Then turn to the assessment that follows.

	True	False
1. I was constantly thinking or obsessing about the sex addict's behaviors and motives.	___	___
2. I engaged in insane or strange behaviors.	___	___
3. I was preoccupied and forgetful.	___	___
4. I had emotional blackouts.	___	___
5. I engaged in self-destructive behaviors.	___	___
6. I was destructive to others.	___	___
7. I changed clothes out of the sight of the sex addict.	___	___
8. I checked the sex addict's personal mail, purse, briefcase, or other personal belongings for clues.	___	___
9. I blamed myself for all the problems related to the addiction.	___	___
10. I believed that if I changed, my partner would stop acting out.	___	___
11. I experienced free-floating shame and anxiety.	___	___
12. I used sex as a tool for manipulation or to patch disagreements.	___	___
13. I focused totally on the sex addict involved in the addiction, to avoid my own feelings.	___	___
14. I became numbed to my own sexual needs and wants.	___	___
15. I accepted the addict's sexual norms as my own.	___	___
16. I made excuses not to be sexual with the addict.	___	___
17. I became "hyper" sexual for the addict.	___	___
18. I felt sex was the most important sign of love.	___	___
19. I took responsibility for the addict's behaviors and for the consequences of these behaviors.	___	___
20. I kept secrets to protect the addict.	___	___
21. I kept overly busy and overextended.	___	___
22. I rarely felt intimate during sex.	___	___
23. I lied to cover up for the addict.	___	___
24. I went on emotional binges.	___	___
25. I became increasingly self-righteous and punitive.	___	___
26. I became overextended financially.	___	___
27. I totally denied the problems.	___	___
28. I tried to create dependency situations where I was indispensable.	___	___
29. I always had a crisis or problem upon which to focus.	___	___

30. I made threats to leave, but I never followed through. ____ ____
31. I gave up life goals, hobbies, and interests.   ____ ____
32. I changed my dress or appearance to accommodate the
    addict's wishes.   ____ ____
33. I believed I could eventually change the addict.   ____ ____
34. I played martyr, hero, or victim roles.   ____ ____
35. My life became increasingly unmanageable.   ____ ____
36. I acted against my own morals, values, and beliefs.   ____ ____
37. My emotions were out of control.   ____ ____
38. I denied my intuitions.   ____ ____
39. I joined with the addict to present a united front to the
    world.   ____ ____
40. I felt more and more unworthy as a person.   ____ ____

ASSESSING YOUR COADDICTIVE BEHAVIOR, THOUGHTS, AND FEELINGS

Coaddicts responded to similar items as follows, based on the number marked "true."

Score	%	
1–9	5	
10–19	27	95% scored 10 or more
20–29	30	63% scored 20 or more
30–40	38	33% scored 30 or more

If you scored over 10, you were like 95 percent of the coaddicts. If you scored over 20, you were like 63 percent of coaddicts. If you scored over 30, you were like 33 percent of coaddicts. The higher your score, the more coaddictive behaviors, thoughts, and feelings you identify with. The purpose of the inventory is to encourage you to think about your life. If you wish, you might also look again at Table 5-2 (on page 167), which groups coaddicts' responses into characteristics. Are there any particular characteristics your responses fit?

_____

_____

_____

4. COADDICT CONSEQUENCES SURVEY

Some consequences of coaddiction are listed below. Check each one you have experienced or are experiencing as a result of coaddiction.

EMOTIONAL CONSEQUENCES:

_____ 1. Attempted suicide

_____ 2. Suicidal thoughts or feelings

_____ 3. Homicidal thoughts or feelings

_____ 4. Feelings of extreme hopelessness or despair

_____ 5. Failed efforts to control sexual acting out of your partner

_____ 6. Feeling like two people (i.e., living a public and a secret life)

_____ 7. Emotional instability (depression, paranoia, fear of going insane)

_____ 8. Loss of touch with reality

_____ 9. Loss of self-esteem

_____10. Loss of life goals

_____11. Acting against your own values and beliefs

_____12. Strong feelings of guilt and shame

_____13. Strong feelings of isolation and loneliness

_____14. Strong fears about your future

_____15. Emotional exhaustion

_____16. Feeling out of touch with your own sexuality (asexual or sexual shame)

_____17. Other emotional consequences, specify:

_____

PHYSICAL CONSEQUENCES:

_____18. Venereal diseases

_____19. AIDS or AIDS Related Complex

_____ 20. Risking unwanted pregnancy because of lack of birth control or inadequate birth control (self or partner)

_____ 21. Unwanted pregnancy (self or partner)

_____ 22. Abortion (self or partner)

_____ 23. Physical injury to genitals, breasts, colon, etc.

_____ 24. Extreme weight loss or gain

____ 25. Physical problems (e.g., ulcers, high blood pressure)
____ 26. Sleep disturbances (e.g., not enough sleep, too much sleep)
____ 27. Victim of rape
____ 28. Self-abuse (e.g., cutting, burning, or bruising oneself)
____ 29. Victim of physical abuse by another person
____ 30. Involvement in potentially abusive or dangerous situations
____ 31. Vehicle accidents
____ 32. Physical exhaustion
____ 33. Other physical consequences, specify:

SPIRITUAL CONSEQUENCES:

____ 34. Strong feelings of spiritual emptiness
____ 35. Feeling disconnected from yourself and the world
____ 36. Feeling abandoned by God or higher power
____ 37. Anger at your higher power or God
____ 38. Loss of faith in anything spiritual
____ 39. Other spiritual consequences, specify:

FAMILY AND PARTNERSHIP CONSEQUENCES:

____ 40. Feeling alone or isolated in your family
____ 41. Loss of partner or spouse
____ 42. Increase in marital or relationship problems
____ 43. Jeopardizing the well-being of your family
____ 44. Loss of your family's respect
____ 45. Increase in problems with your children
____ 46. Loss of family of origin's support
____ 47. Loss of your family of origin
____ 48. Other family or partnership consequences, specify:

CAREER AND EDUCATIONAL CONSEQUENCES:

_____ 49. Decrease in productivity at work

_____ 50. Demotion at work

_____ 51. Loss of coworkers' respect

_____ 52. Loss of the opportunity to work in the career of your choice

_____ 53. Failing grades in school

_____ 54. Dropping out of school

_____ 55. Loss of educational opportunities

_____ 56. Other career or educational consequences, specify:

_____

OTHER CONSEQUENCES:

_____ 57. Loss of important friendships

_____ 58. Loss of interest in hobbies or activities

_____ 59. Court or legal involvement due to the addict's sexual behaviors

_____ 60. Financial problems

_____ 61. Engaging in illegal sexual activities, which could have led to arrest

_____ 62. Other consequences, specify:

_____

List ten examples of powerlessness (loss of control) over your coaddictive behaviors.

1. _____

_____

2. _____

_____

3. _____

_____

4. _____

_____

5. _____

_____

6. _____

_____

7. _____

_____

8. _____

_____

9. _____

_____

10. _____

_____

List ten examples of how your life became unmanageable because of your coaddiction.

1. _____

_____

2. _____

_____

3. _____

_____

4. _____

_____

5. _____

_____

6. _____

_____

7. _____

_____

8. _____

_____

9. _____

_____

10. _____

_____

Selected Data Sets

Our survey effort has generated significant amounts of data, which will take us years to analyze fully. We will elaborate our findings in the research literature over time. Selected aspects of our research have recently been presented in *The Incest Perpetrator: A Family Member No One Wants to Treat,* edited by Anne L. Horton et al. (Newbury Park, CA: Sage, 1990), and in special issues of the *American Journal of Preventive Psychiatry and Neurology,* as well as other scholarly collections. A constantly updated bibliography of this work can be obtained by writing the author at the Institute for Behavioral Medicine, Golden Valley Health Center, 4101 Golden Valley Road, Golden Valley, Minnesota, 55422.

Although there are limits on what can be included in a book intended for the general public, we do want to underscore some of our findings. We have selected, therefore, several key segments of our data to support descriptions appearing in the book.

One of the questions of general interest is what kind of behaviors sex addicts do and how often they do them. In Chapter Two we reported some data from a self-assessment tool used in our general survey which asked addicts to rate behavior in terms of both power and frequency. A modified version of the inventory is reprinted in Appendix A. A complete summary of the data from the survey, with percentages, means, and standard deviations, appears as item 1.

Clinicians may obtain an analysis of comparisons with nonaddicted adult samples from the Institute for Behavioral Medicine, as noted above.

Another important finding described in the book was that the addicts and coaddicts tend to come from families that are rigid and disengaged. We used an instrument developed by David Olson and colleagues at the Family Social Science Department of the University of Minnesota. Called FACES III, it assesses families using the circumplex model developed by Olson and his colleagues. (See *The Family* by Hamilton McCubbin and David Olson, Sage Publications, 1988.) Given the important implications of the data on family, we included summary charts of the family of origin assessment results which were too complex to go in the text. We excluded people in early recovery because we assumed more clarity of perception by those who had been in recovery for some time. Items 2 and 3 present the data for 204 addicts and 48 coaddicts.

We also made the similar assumption that those further along in recovery would have more awareness of their child abuse experiences. Item 4 summarizes reports of abuse by 277 of our sample in terms of percentages, means, and standard deviations. This item corresponds to the Abuse Survey included in Appendix A.

Item 5 summarizes nine areas of demographics which provide a context for the conclusions the book presents. Readers will note that survey respondents most often were white and highly educated. As discussed in the text, the same was true in studies from the early years of alcoholism recovery. Those alcoholics who first accessed help tended to be more educated and affluent.

1. PERCENTAGE INDICATING ACTIVITY, MEANS, AND S.D.'S FOR FREQUENCY OF SEXUAL ACTIVITIES BY MALE, FEMALE, AND TOTAL SAMPLE

ACTIVITY STATEMENT	MALE (N=752)			FEMALE (N=180)			TOTAL (N=932)		
	%	MEAN	S.D.	%	MEAN	S.D.	%	MEAN	S.D.
1. Thinking or obsessing about sex.	97	4.2	.78	92	4.0	.88	96	4.2	.80
2. Fantasizing about past or future sexual experiences.	93	3.8	.86	90	3.8	.86	92	3.8	.86
3. Spending a large amount of time preparing for a sexual episode (e.g., making up yourself, listening to music that energizes "the addict").	59	3.1	.95	74	3.7	.98	62	3.3	.98
4. Neglecting responsibilities and commitments (e.g., work, family, health) in order to prepare for your next sexual episode.	74	3.3	.92	74	3.5	1.03	74	3.4	.94
5. Thinking that sex is love.	63	3.7	1.11	77	4.0	1.09	65	3.8	1.12
6. Thinking that your "special" sexual needs make you different from others.	68	3.7	.99	65	3.8	1.10	67	3.7	1.01
7. Thinking that next time things will be different (e.g., "I'll find the right lover next time.").	64	3.5	1.05	73	4.0	1.04	66	3.6	1.06
8. Thinking that if you are sexual with someone, you will have them in your power.	51	3.4	1.10	74	3.8	1.07	55	3.5	1.11
9. Feeling a need to be sexual in order to feel good about yourself.	77	4.0	.90	81	3.9	1.02	78	4.0	.92

Item	%	M	SD	%	M	SD	%	M	SD
10. Denying or suppressing your sexuality and sexual feelings for periods of time.	67	3.3	1.01	73	3.6	1.02	68	3.3	1.02
11. Dramatizing a particular role (e.g., the "virgin," the "hurt little boy," the "intellect") as part of your ritualizing behavior.	45	3.5	1.06	59	3.6	1.07	48	3.5	1.06
12. Rationalizing or denying consequences of your sexual addiction (e.g., "everyone is sexual," "I just need a little more than others need").	77	3.8	.95	73	3.9	1.01	77	3.6	.96
13. Thinking deluded thoughts (e.g., "women just need to be warmed up," "I only masturbate to fall asleep").	71	3.7	.95	59	3.7	1.10	69	3.7	.98
14. Having sex even though you don't really want to or feel like it.	70	3.2	.97	84	3.6	.99	73	3.3	.99
15. Feeling that you have to follow through with sex, because you successfully hooked someone through your ritual (e.g., suggestive flirting, creating a sexualized atmosphere).	60	3.3	1.07	79	3.7	1.07	64	3.4	1.08
16. Feeling depressed, hopeless, or unworthy following a sexual encounter.	84	4.1	1.00	88	4.1	1.01	85	4.1	1.00
17. Feeling desperate or anxious ("white knuckling") between periods of sexual acting out.	73	3.8	.99	66	3.8	1.02	72	3.8	.99
18. Maintaining an open calendar and failing to make commitments because you fear missing an opportunity to be sexual.	51	3.4	1.10	57	3.5	1.12	52	3.4	1.11
19. Using sex as a means to find love.	63	3.7	1.07	79	4.3	.95	66	3.9	1.07
21. Masturbating yourself.	93	4.2	.94	83	3.7	1.00	91	4.1	.99
22. Masturbating a sexual partner.	61	3.1	1.07	64	3.2	1.03	62	3.2	1.06
23. Masturbating with objects.	44	2.7	1.03	58	3.0	1.09	47	2.8	1.05
24. Masturbating to the point of physical injury or infection.	40	2.5	.95	27	2.6	.93	38	2.5	.95
29. Looking at sexually explicit magazines.	87	3.5	1.08	64	2.8	.91	83	3.4	1.08
30. Keeping sexually explicit material or magazines at home or work.	67	3.7	1.18	38	3.1	1.21	61	3.6	1.20
31. Watching sexually explicit videotapes.	73	3.3	1.16	57	2.6	.95	70	3.2	1.16
32. Making sexually explicit videotapes.	7	2.0	1.22	6	1.6	.80	7	2.0	1.17
33. Taking sexually explicit photographs.	22	2.1	1.05	23	1.9	.77	22	2.1	1.00
34. Patronizing adult book stores.	64	3.2	1.18	25	2.2	.87	57	3.1	1.20
35. Watching or looking at child pornography.	10	2.4	1.11	2	1.5	.87	9	2.3	1.12

	N	M	SD	N	M	SD	N	M	SD
36. Watching strip or peep shows.	55	2.9	1.16	26	2.3	1.09	50	2.8	1.16
37. Sexualizing people or materials (e.g., advertisements, catalogues) that are not sexually explicit.	75	3.6	1.08	47	3.5	1.06	70	3.6	1.07
41. Patronizing saunas, massage parlors, or rap lounges.	31	2.9	1.21	8	2.5	1.20	27	2.9	1.21
42. Paying someone for sexual activity.	47	2.7	1.21	7	2.5	.93	39	2.7	1.20
43. Participation in phone sexual activity.	38	2.6	1.12	31	2.7	1.12	36	2.7	1.12
44. Receiving money in exchange for sexual activity.	11	2.2	1.18	23	3.3	1.42	11	2.7	1.36
45. Receiving drugs in exchange for sexual activity.	8	2.4	1.18	21	3.0	1.35	12	2.4	1.29
46. Pimping others for sexual activity.	4	2.4	1.33	4	3.0	1.07	4	2.5	1.31
47. Using an escort or phone service.	19	2.4	1.15	3	2.7	1.80	16	2.4	1.18
51. Having many relationships at the same time.	40	3.1	1.22	65	3.1	1.29	45	3.1	1.24
52. Having successive relationships one right after another.	42	3.5	1.14	66	4.0	1.05	47	3.6	1.14
53. Having one-night stands.	64	3.2	1.25	71	3.2	1.30	65	3.2	1.26
54. Having affairs outside your primary relationship.	57	3.1	1.29	73	3.3	1.25	60	3.2	1.28
55. Engaging in sex with anonymous partners.	49	3.6	1.29	44	3.1	1.29	48	3.5	1.30
56. Swapping partners.	10	2.2	1.02	20	2.2	1.10	12	2.2	1.05
57. Urging your partner to have sex with persons outside your relationship.	17	2.2	1.02	24	2.4	1.14	18	2.2	1.06
58. Using sexual seduction to gain power over another person.	37	3.3	1.11	63	4.0	1.01	42	3.5	1.12
59. Participating in group sex.	29	2.4	1.05	31	2.3	1.14	29	2.4	1.07
60. Hustling in singles clubs, bars, or health clubs.	27	3.2	1.07	38	3.3	1.18	29	3.2	1.10
61. Cruising beaches, parks, parking lots, or baths.	48	3.7	1.15	22	3.2	1.18	43	3.6	1.16
62. Belonging to a nudist club to find sex partners.	3	2.3	1.09	2	3.7	1.89	3	2.5	1.27
63. Using the personal columns to find sex partners.	17	2.4	1.13	12	3.1	1.34	16	2.5	1.18
64. Engaging in sexual activity outside your sexual orientation in pursuit of a new sexual high.	26	2.7	1.15	33	2.8	1.24	27	2.7	1.17
67. Exposing yourself from a car.	21	2.9	1.33	21	2.2	.97	21	2.8	1.30
68. Exposing yourself from stage or for hire.	3	2.3	1.26	11	2.6	1.39	5	2.4	1.33
69. Exposing yourself in public places, such as parks, streets, school yards, etc.	20	3.0	1.22	8	2.7	1.19	18	3.0	1.22
70. Exposing yourself from your home.	23	2.7	1.19	23	3.0	1.14	23	2.7	1.19
71. Exposing yourself for home videos or photographs.	14	2.1	.97	21	2.1	1.12	15	2.1	1.01

Item	N	M	SD	N	M	SD	N	M	SD
72. Exposing yourself through your choice of clothing.	27	2.9	1.13	47	3.5	1.10	31	3.1	1.15
73. Exposing yourself by being sexual or dressing/undressing in public or semi-public places.	23	3.0	1.09	23	2.7	1.22	23	2.9	1.13
76. Watching people through windows of their houses or apartments.	46	2.6	1.01	13	2.2	.94	40	2.5	1.01
77. Using binoculars or telescopes to watch people.	27	2.5	1.05	3	1.8	.40	22	2.5	1.05
78. Hiding in secret places (e.g., closets, under beds) in order to watch or listen to people.	17	2.4	1.04	5	2.0	.94	14	2.4	1.04
79. Asking strangers or acquaintances inappropriate personal details about their sex lives.	23	2.6	.88	16	3.2	1.09	22	2.7	.94
80. Sexualizing others that you observe in public places (e.g., shopping malls, restaurants, or office buildings).	76	4.1	.97	53	3.8	1.10	71	4.0	.99
83. Touching or fondling other people inappropriately	41	2.7	1.04	26	2.6	1.10	38	2.7	1.05
84. Telling sexually explicit stories or using sexually explicit language at inappropriate times or places (e.g., at work, with children present).	34	2.9	.94	41	3.4	1.13	35	3.0	1.00
85. Bring sex or sexualized humor into your conversations.	57	3.2	1.01	59	3.5	1.04	58	3.3	1.02
86. Using flirtatious or seductive behavior to gain attention of others.	53	3.5	1.02	76	3.8	.97	57	3.6	1.02
87. Making inappropriate sexual phone calls.	21	2.5	1.21	15	2.9	1.26	20	2.6	1.22
88. Making inappropriate sexual advances or gestures toward other persons.	38	2.9	.98	33	3.0	1.11	37	2.9	1.00
91. Forcing sexual activity on a child outside your family.	9	1.8	.98	3	1.5	.50	8	1.8	.95
92. Forcing sexual activity on your spouse or partner.	25	2.6	1.18	15	2.4	.87	23	2.6	1.15
93. Forcing sexual activity on a member of your family (e.g., brother, sister, daughter, nephew).	13	2.1	1.11	8	1.9	1.12	12	2.0	1.11
94. Forcing sexual activity on a person whom you know (e.g., acquaintance, friend, or other unrelated adult).	16	2.1	.96	11	2.4	1.22	15	2.1	1.01
95. Forcing sexual activity on a person whom you do not know.	10	2.2	1.09	4	2.4	1.18	8	2.2	1.10
96. Engaging in sexual activity with a consenting minor.	22	2.1	.94	11	2.3	1.24	20	2.1	.98
97. Exposing children to your sexual activities (e.g., engaging in sexual activity with open doors, inappropriate nudity).	10	2.4	1.04	16	2.3	1.01	11	2.4	1.04

No.	Item	%	M	SD	%	M	SD	%	M	SD
98.	Sharing inappropriate sexual information with children.	7	2.4	1.02	8	2.3	1.10	7	2.4	1.04
99.	Willingly giving up power or acting out the victim role in your sexual activity.	24	2.9	1.14	52	3.5	1.29	29	3.1	1.22
100.	Using a power position to exploit or be sexual with another person (e.g., clergy to parishioner, therapist to client, employer to employee).	20	2.5	1.18	11	2.5	1.27	18	2.5	1.19
101.	Administering drugs to another person in order to force sexual activity.	9	2.6	1.07	2	2.8	1.30	8	2.6	1.09
104.	Crossdressing (identifying with your gender, but dressing in the clothes of the other gender).	20	2.4	1.20	5	2.4	1.34	17	2.4	1.21
105.	Dressing and behaving like the other gender with a psychological preference to be the other gender (transvestism).	6	2.9	1.19	3	3.2	.98	5	2.9	1.17
106.	Using sexual aids to enhance your sexual experience (e.g., vibrators, artificial vaginas).	32	2.6	.96	48	3.1	1.07	35	2.8	1.01
107.	Engaging in sexual activity with animals.	27	1.8	.85	19	2.0	1.11	25	1.8	.90
108.	Using drugs to enhance your sexual experience.	33	3.4	1.20	47	3.5	1.20	36	3.4	1.20
109.	Receiving physical harm or pain during your sexual activity to intensify your sexual pleasure.	20	2.7	1.00	33	2.8	1.14	22	2.8	1.04
110.	Causing physical harm or pain to your sex partner during sexual activity to intensify your sexual pleasure.	14	2.6	1.05	12	2.4	1.00	14	2.6	1.04
111.	Paying for sexually explicit phone calls (e.g., DIAL-A-PORN).	22	2.6	1.20	5	2.2	1.03	18	2.6	1.20
25.	Masturbating in cars.	59	2.8	1.22	36	2.4	1.03	55	2.7	1.21
26.	Masturbating in public places such as movie theaters, tanning salons, or store dressing rooms.	41	2.9	1.25	23	2.0	.88	37	2.8	1.24
27.	Masturbating with mechanical or electrical devices.	19	2.5	1.00	39	3.0	.98	23	2.6	1.02
38.	Looking for sexually suggestive moments on tv or in films.	74	3.6	1.01	56	3.5	1.08	70	3.6	1.02
39.	Maomtaomomg a "collection" of pornographic materials.	42	3.5	1.24	17	3.4	1.53	37	3.5	1.27
48.	Spending money on someone in order to have sex.	42	2.8	1.06	25	2.8	1.12	39	2.8	1.07
49.	Being sexual because someone spent money on you.	17	2.6	1.04	53	3.5	1.20	24	3.0	1.19
65.	Placing and answering ads in swinger magazines.	10	2.0	.94	4	2.8	1.60	9	2.0	1.04
74.	Exposing yourself in showers, locker rooms, or public rest rooms.	20	3.2	1.26	8	2.5	.81	18	3.1	1.24

		Total			Females			Males	
	%	M	SD	%	M	SD	%	M	SD
81. Sexualizing others in health clubs, locker rooms, rest rooms, or showers.	43	3.6	1.13	36	3.4	1.00	42	3.6	1.11
89. Touching people but acting as if it were an accident.	33	2.5	.98	24	2.7	.93	31	2.5	.97
102. Using alcohol to take sexual advantage.	29	2.7	1.07	16	3.4	1.35	27	2.8	1.13
112. Seeking humiliating or degrading experiences as part of sex.	11	3.4	1.12	14	3.4	1.06	11	3.4	1.10

Note: Statistics for items 25, 26, 27, 38, 39, 48, 49, 65, 74, 81, 89, 102, and 112 based on sample sizes of 500, 118, and 618 for males, females, and total, respectively.

2. ADDICTS' FAMILY OF ORIGIN

COHESION

ADAPTABILITY		Disengaged	Separated	Connected	Enmeshed	Row Total
	Chaotic	5 2.5%	3 1.5%	1 .5%	0	9 4.5%
	Flexible	8 3.9%	2 1.0%	0	0	10 4.9%
	Structured	25 12.3%	3 1.5%	0	0	28 13.8%
	Rigid	139 68.1%	15 7.4%	3 1.5%	0	157 77.0%
	Column Total	177 86.8%	23 11.4%	4 2.0%	0 0%	204*

*Because percentages were rounded off to one decimal place, column and row percentage totals do not equal 100%.

3. COADDICTS' FAMILY OF ORIGIN

COHESION

		Disengaged	Separated	Connected	Enmeshed	Row Total
	Chaotic	5 4.2%	3 2.1%	0	0	3 6.3%
	Flexible	1 2.1%	0	0	0	1 2.1%
ADAPTABILITY	**Structured**	3 6.3%	1 2.1%	3 6.3	0	7 14.7%
	Rigid	30 62.5%	6 12.5%	1 2.1%	0	37 77.1%
	Column Total	36 75.1%	8 16.7%	4 8.3%	0 0	48*

*Because percentages were rounded off to one decimal place, column and row percentage totals do not equal 100%.

4. PERCENTAGE INDICATING ABUSE, MEANS, AND S.D.'S FOR FREQUENCY OF TYPES OF ABUSE BY MALE, FEMALE, AND TOTAL SAMPLE

ABUSE STATEMENT	MALE (N = 220)			FEMALE (N = 55)			TOTAL (N = 275)		
	%	MEAN	S.D.	%	MEAN	S.D.	%	MEAN	S.D.
1. Flirtatious and suggestive language	21	3.5	.94	60	3.8	1.10	23	3.7	1.02
2. Propositioning	22	2.7	1.15	51	3.4	1.08	22	3.0	1.18
3. Inappropriate holding, kissing	25	2.7	1.13	56	3.4	1.21	24	3.0	1.20
4. Sexual fondling	43	2.7	1.28	58	3.5	1.32	36	2.9	1.34
5. Masturbation	28	3.1	1.29	35	3.4	1.50	23	3.2	1.35
6. Oral sex	25	2.6	1.34	36	3.1	1.45	21	2.7	1.39
7. Forced sexual activity	15	2.5	1.22	58	2.7	1.43	19	2.6	1.33
8. Household voyeurism (inappropriate household nudity)	25	3.4	1.14	36	3.4	1.32	21	3.4	1.19
9. Sexual hugs	14	3.3	.94	33	3.3	1.11	14	3.3	1.01
10. Jokes about your body	29	3.5	1.17	58	3.7	.85	27	3.5	1.07
11. Use of sexualizing language	17	3.8	.96	44	3.8	1.03	18	3.8	.99
12. Penetration with objects	11	2.9	1.00	22	3.3	1.49	10	3.1	1.20
13. Bestiality (forced sex with animals)	3	1.8	.69	11	2.8	1.67	3	2.3	1.37
14. Criticism of your physical or sexual development	25	3.3	1.06	64	3.7	1.05	26	3.5	1.07
15. Other's preoccupation with your sexual development	13	3.6	.94	44	3.8	1.04	15	3.7	.99
17. Shoving	30	3.4	1.22	45	3.6	1.13	26	3.5	1.20
18. Slapping or hitting	45	3.4	1.09	62	3.4	1.33	38	3.4	1.16
19. Scratches or bruises	12	3.6	1.25	38	3.5	1.14	14	3.6	1.21
20. Burns	4	2.6	1.64	11	1.5	.76	4	2.1	1.45

21. Cuts or wounds	5	2.8	1.59	18	2.9	1.14	6	2.8	1.40
22. Broken bones or fractures	2	3.0	1.58	13	1.7	.70	3	2.2	1.27
23. Damage to internal organs	0	4.0	0	7	2.3	.83	1	2.6	1.02
24. Permanent injury	1	4.5	.50	11	3.0	2.00	2	3.4	1.87
25. Beatings or whippings	36	3.4	1.14	44	3.1	1.30	29	3.3	1.18
26. Inadequate medical attention	5	2.9	1.44	29	3.3	1.26	8	3.1	1.36
27. Pulling and grabbing hair, ears, etc.	19	3.5	1.10	36	3.7	1.00	10	3.5	1.07
28. Inadequate food or nutrition	7	4.1	.93	13	4.4	.73	6	4.2	.80
30. Neglect (i.e., significant person(s) are emotionally unavailable)	71	4.3	.78	71	4.5	.59	56	4.3	.75
31. Harassment or malicious tricks	29	3.7	1.07	47	3.7	1.06	26	3.7	1.07
32. Being screamed or shouted at	56	3.8	.95	69	4.1	.88	46	3.9	.94
33. Unfair punishments	36	3.5	1.09	44	3.7	1.14	30	3.5	.93
34. Cruel or degrading tasks	13	3.8	.91	24	3.8	.97	12	3.8	1.19
35. Cruel confinement (e.g., locked in closet, excessive long-term grounding)	20	3.0	1.28	25	3.6	1.04	16	3.2	1.26
36. Abandonment (e.g., lack of supervision, lack of security, being left or deserted)	44	3.8	1.19	47	3.8	1.17	35	3.8	1.19
37. Touch deprivation	45	4.5	.68	58	4.7	.67	38	4.5	.69
38. Overly strict dress codes	13	4.2	.87	20	4.2	1.03	11	4.2	.92
39. No privacy	28	4.1	.93	38	4.2	.87	24	4.1	.92
40. Having to hide injury or wounds from others	11	3.2	1.46	22	3.3	1.11	11	3.2	1.36
41. Forced to keep secrets	30	3.9	1.27	55	3.9	1.09	27	3.9	1.22
42. Having to take on adult responsibilities as a child	42	4.2	1.02	60	4.3	.72	36	4.2	.95
43. Having to watch beating of other family members	21	3.3	1.12	36	3.5	1.36	19	3.4	1.20
44. Being caught in the middle of parents' fights	43	3.7	1.04	36	4.0	.74	33	3.8	1.00
45. Being blamed for family problems	27	3.7	1.10	60	3.8	1.05	26	3.8	1.08

5. SAMPLE POPULATION CHARACTERISTICS

1. **Sample size:** 932 addicts completed at least portions of the survey. They resided in every state in the United States and some provinces of Canada.

2. **Age:** The average age of the respondents was forty, with the youngest being nineteen and the oldest being seventy.

3. **Gender:** 82 percent were men and 18 percent were women.

4. **Race:** 93 percent were white; 2 percent were Native American; 2 percent were black; and 2 percent listed themselves as "other."

5. **Family status:** 34 percent reported being single; 23 percent were divorced; 6 percent were separated; and 41 percent were married. 13 percent said they were in a primary relationship. 30 percent indicated living with a partner and children.

6. **Sexual orientation:** 11 percent were bisexual; 18 percent were homosexual; 63 percent were heterosexual; and 8 percent were unsure of their sexual preference.

7. **Level of education:** some high school or high school graduate—8 percent; some college—22 percent; vocational or trade school—7 percent; college graduate—25 percent; postgraduate education—38 percent.

8. **Religious affiliation:** Protestant—23 percent; Catholic—22 percent; Jewish—3 percent; higher power—36 percent; atheist or agnostic—1 percent; other—9 percent; unsure—6 percent.

9. **Fellowship membership:** 311 respondents who were in advanced recovery indicated active involvement in a twelve step program for sex addiction. Of those who named a fellowship, 6 percent came from Sexual Compulsives Anonymous, 15 percent from Sex and Love Addicts Anonymous, 26 percent from Sexaholics Anonymous, and 37 percent from Sex Addicts Anonymous. An additional 5 percent were members of small local or regional fellowships for sex addiction.

I N D E X

A

Abandonment
  of children, 122–23
  feelings of, 76
Abstinence, 244–48. *See also*
    Celibacy
  worksheet, 246–47
Accidents, 36
Accountability, 264
Acting in, 105–6, 243
  definition of, 235
  swing between acting out
    and, 235–38
Acting out, 22
  acting in distinguished from,
    235
  shame cycle and, 104–6
  swing between acting in and,
    235–38
Addiction(s). *See also* Sex
    addiction
  additive model of, 136–42
  basic types of, 69

child abuse and, 108
across generations, 70–72
genetic predisposition to, 71–72
model for a common pattern of
  acquisition of, 71–72
multiple, 225–26
of other family members,
  70–71
total number of addicts, 77
"Addict within," shame reduction and, 229–33
Adult Children of Alcoholics,
  238, 278
Adult Children of Sex Addicts
  (ACSA), 278
Affirmation
  and approval of children,
    98–99, 101
  self-, 274–78
AIDS, 15, 37, 84
  prostitution and, 52
Alcoholics Anonymous, 34–36,
  38, 215, 220
  twelve steps of, 179–80

ABOUT THE AUTHOR

PATRICK J. CARNES, Ph.D. is a nationally known speaker and pioneer in the field of sexual addiction. He is the author of *Out of the Shadows, A Gentle Path Through the Twelve Steps,* and *Contrary to Love.* Dr. Carnes is a senior fellow of the Golden Valley Institute for Behavioral Medicine. The Institute for Behavioral Medicine is dedicated to the treatment and study of behavioral medicine and provides ongoing professional training, educational materials, and research and development resources for the national behavioral medicine community. Dr. Carnes also designed the Sexual Dependency Unit at Golden Valley Health Center, the first in-patient program of its kind in the country.